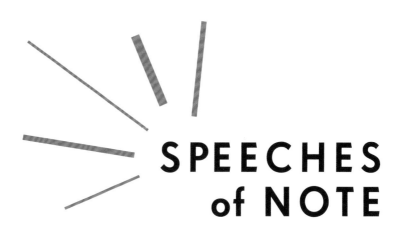

SPEECHES
of NOTE

# SPEECHES
## of NOTE

AN ECLECTIC
COLLECTION
OF ORATIONS
DESERVING OF A
WIDER AUDIENCE

COMPILED BY
## SHAUN
## USHER

TEN SPEED PRESS
California | New York

All rights reserved.
Published in the United States by Ten Speed Press, an imprint of the Crown Publishing Group,
a division of Penguin Random House LLC, New York.
www.crownpublishing.com
www.tenspeed.com

Ten Speed Press and the Ten Speed Press colophon are registered trademarks of Penguin
Random House LLC.

Originally published in hardcover in the United Kingdom by Hutchinson, a division of
Penguin Random House UK, London, in 2018.

Library of Congress Cataloging-in-Publication Data is on file with the publisher.

Hardcover ISBN: 978-0-399-58006-2
eBook ISBN: 978-0-399-58007-9

Printed in China

Cover Design by Lizzie Allen
Interior Design and Typesetting by Will Webb and Lindsay Nash

10 9 8 7 6 5 4 3 2 1

First U.S. Edition

For Karina

# CONTENTS

Speeches hold enormous power. They can start deadly wars or even bring them to a close. They can expose truths long hidden. They can impart advice so profound as to alter lives. They can celebrate the legacies of those departed. They can persuade a nation to change course. A perfectly pitched speech, delivered at the right time, can bring together people from the most disparate of backgrounds and, if only for the duration of the speech itself, unite them.

In this modern age, as hyper-connected as we are and with technology in our pockets that enables us to record and broadcast at the press of a button, speeches can find audiences reaching the millions when once they might have been heard only by a few. Footage of these speeches is being shared online at lightning pace, racing through vast, globe-spanning networks of like-minded people and achieving a potency and impact that not long ago would have been impossible.

This book is a celebration of all of this human emotion captured in oratory old and new. The speeches here are windows through which you are able to step into someone's shoes and imagine standing in front of an audience, as these people once did with hearts in their mouths, adrenaline coursing through their veins, countless eyes upon them, unsure whether the words they were soon to speak would be received as they hoped, whether the risk would pay off, whether their message would result in lives changed, affirmed, or even ended.

In compiling this collection I have resisted the urge to merely cover the speeches we all know so well, so while you will indeed find oratory by the greats in these pages, you will also be introduced to some lesser-known speeches previously ignored through no fault of their own: George Bernard Shaw's warm and rousing toast to Albert Einstein, a man "challenging the axioms of science"; the commencement address affectionately given to graduates at Long Island University by Kermit the Frog; Tilda Swinton's homage to friend and "fellow freak" David Bowie, intimately delivered despite his absence, three years before his death; Nick Cave's marvelous lecture on his relationship with the love song; and many more.

← Martin Luther King Jr. delivers a speech at the Gillfield Baptist Church, Petersburg, VA, May 1960, photographed by Howard Sochurek

Other speeches here are engrossing because they were never delivered and to this day remain unspoken, as with the chilling draft scripted for Queen Elizabeth II in 1983 by officials imagining the onset of World War III, and the powerful words that Native American Wamsutta Frank B. James was stopped from delivering at a U.S. state dinner in 1970. Some speeches became notable before their reader had even taken to the podium, as evidenced by the thick script in the jacket pocket of Theodore Roosevelt that slowed the course of a would-be assassin's bullet to such an extent that he was able to address the crowd, as planned, wearing a blood-stained shirt.

Where possible, to further immerse you and bring you closer to the historical moment, I have tracked down and included images of the speeches themselves – that is, the very document from which these people read as they made their voices heard. Some are typewritten, some composed by hand. Accompanying other addresses are photographs of the speeches being delivered; elsewhere, some gorgeous illustrations. In instances where recordings are available, they have been transcribed as accurately as possible. For those speeches where no such audio exists, I have referred to historical transcripts.

No doubt there are speeches you believe should have made it into this book – indeed, there are many I am yet to discover or have recommended and I'd love you to share your favorites with me on Twitter @SpeechesOfNote.

All told, you have in your hands a book quite unlike any other: a lusciously produced roller-coaster ride through seventy-five speeches of note, all of which are deserving of a wider audience.

Shaun Usher
Speeches of Note

# I KILLED A SOLITARY MAN

On August 14, 1738, in County Wicklow, Ireland, a man named George Manley was hanged for murder. Very little is known about his life, or indeed the crime for which he paid the ultimate price. What we do know, however, is that moments before his death at Wicklow's gallows, Manley gave a speech to all who had assembled to witness the spectacle.

My Friends,

You assemble to see what? A man take a leap into the abyss of death. Look and you shall see me go with as much courage as Curtius, when he leapt into the gulf to save his country from destruction. What then will you see of me? You say that no man without virtue can be courageous. You see, I am courageous. You'll say I have killed a man. Marlborough killed his thousands and Alexander his millions. Marlborough and Alexander,* and many others who have done the like, are famous in history for Great Men. But I killed one solitary man. Aye, that's the case. One solitary man. I'm a little murderer and must be hanged. Marlborough and Alexander plundered countries. They were Great Men. I ran in debt with the alewife,† I must be hanged.

Now, my friends, I have drawn a parallel between two of the greatest men that ever lived and myself. But these were men of former days. Now I'll speak a word of some of the present days. How many men were lost in Italy and upon the Rhine, during the last war, for settling a king in Poland?‡ Both sides could not be in the right. They are Great Men, but I killed a solitary man, I'm a little fellow. The King of Spain takes our ships, plunders our merchants, kills and tortures our men – but what of all that? What he does is good: he's a Great Man, he is clothed in purple, his instruments of murder are bright and shining; mine was but a rusty gun, and so much for comparison.

Now, I would fain know what authority there is in Scripture for a rich man to murder, to plunder, to torture and ravage whole countries; and what law it is that condemns a poor man to death for killing a solitary man or for stealing a solitary sheep to feed his family. But bring the matter closer to our own country: what is the difference between running in a poor man's debt, and by the power of gold or any other privilege preventing him from obtaining his right, and clapping a pistol to a man's breast and taking from him his purse? Yet the one shall thereby obtain a coach, and honours and titles etc. The other: what? A cart and a rope.

From what I have said, my brethren, you may, perhaps, imagine I am hardened. But believe me, I am fully convinced of my follies and acknowledge the just judgment of God has overtaken me. I have no hopes, but from the

* Alexander III of Macedon – otherwise known as Alexander the Great – created one of the largest empires of the ancient world. General John Churchill, 1st Duke of Marlborough, led the allied forces during the War of the Spanish Succession at the beginning of the eighteenth century.

† A woman who brewed and sold ale.

‡ The War of the Polish Succession (1733–35) was a major European conflict sparked by a Polish civil war over the succession to Augustus II.

merits of my Redeemer, who I hope will have mercy on me, as he knows that murder was far from my heart and what I did was through rage and passion, being provoked thereto by the deceased.

Take warning, my dear comrades: Think! Oh think! What I would now give, that I had lived another life.

# JE T'AIME, PAPA

On September 28, 2000, Canada's fifteenth prime minister, Pierre Trudeau, died of prostate cancer. Trudeau was a charismatic and popular man, who had served a total of fifteen years in office. During the state funeral, days later, thousands lined the streets of Montreal; inside the Notre-Dame Basilica itself could be found such people as Fidel Castro, Leonard Cohen and Jimmy Carter. But the ceremony was also notable for a moving speech ably delivered by Trudeau's eldest son, Justin, then a 28-year-old schoolteacher. Indeed, his eulogy was *so* well delivered that some commentators wondered aloud whether he could one day follow in the footsteps of his late father. Fifteen years later, Justin Trudeau would become the twenty-third prime minister of Canada.

→ Justin Trudeau at the casket of his father, former Canadian Prime Minister Pierre Trudeau, photographed by Paul Chiasson

Friends, Romans, countrymen.

I was about six years old when I went on my first official trip. I was going with my father and my grandpa Sinclair up to the North Pole.

It was a very glamorous destination. But the best thing about it was that I was going to be spending lots of time with my dad because in Ottawa he just worked so hard.

One day, we were in Alert, Canada's northernmost point, a scientific military installation that seemed to consist entirely of low, shed-like buildings and warehouses.

Let's be honest. I was six. There were no brothers around to play with and I was getting a little bored because Dad still somehow had a lot of work to do.

I remember a frozen, windswept Arctic afternoon when I was bundled up into a Jeep and hustled out on a special top-secret mission. I figured I was finally going to be let in on the reason of this high-security Arctic base.

I was exactly right.

We drove slowly through and past the buildings, all of them very grey and windy. We rounded a corner and came upon a red one. We stopped. I got out of the Jeep and started to crunch across towards the front door. I was told, no, to the window.

So I clambered over the snowbank, was boosted up to the window, rubbed my sleeve against the frosty glass to see inside and as my eyes adjusted to the gloom, I saw a figure, hunched over one of many worktables that seemed very cluttered. He was wearing a red suit with that furry white trim.

And that's when I understood just how powerful and wonderful my father was.

Pierre Elliott Trudeau. The very words convey so many things to so many people. Statesman, intellectual, professor, adversary, outdoorsman, lawyer, journalist, author, prime minister.

But more than anything, to me, he was Dad.

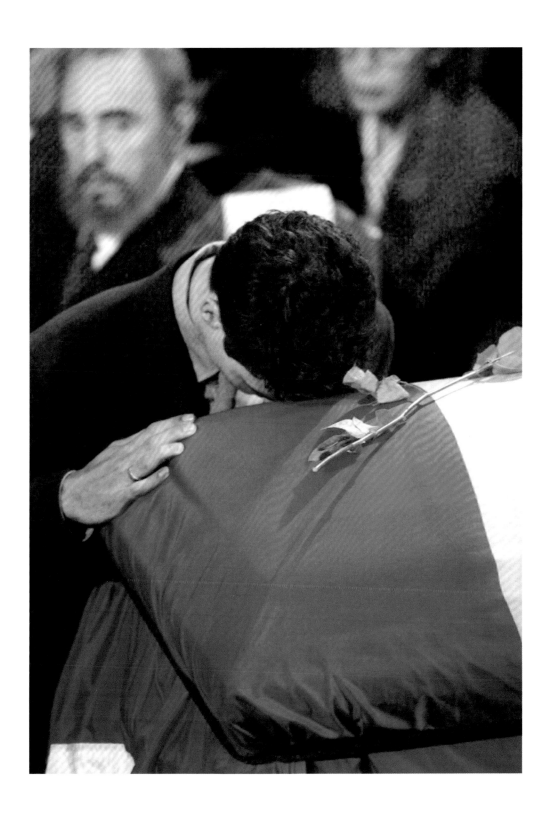

And what a dad. He loved us with the passion and the devotion that encompassed his life. He taught us to believe in ourselves, to stand up for ourselves, to know ourselves and to accept responsibility for ourselves.

We knew we were the luckiest kids in the world. And we had done nothing to actually deserve it. It was instead something that we would have to spend the rest of our lives working very hard to live up to.

He gave us a lot of tools. We were taught to take nothing for granted. He doted on us but didn't indulge.

Many people say he didn't suffer fools gladly, but I'll have you know he had infinite patience with us. He encouraged us to push ourselves, to test limits, to challenge anyone and anything. There were certain basic principles that could never be compromised.

As I guess it is for most kids, in Grade 3, it was always a real treat to visit my dad at work.

As on previous visits this particular occasion included a lunch at the parliamentary restaurant which always seemed to be terribly important and full of serious people that I didn't recognize.

But at eight, I was becoming politically aware. And I recognized one whom I knew to be one of my father's chief rivals.

Thinking of pleasing my father, I told a joke about him – a generic, silly little grade-school thing.

My father looked at me sternly with that look I would learn to know so well, and said: 'Justin, never attack the individual. One can be in total disagreement with someone without denigrating him as a consequence.'

Saying that, he stood up and took me by the hand and brought me over to introduce me to this man. He was a nice man who was eating with his daughter, a nice-looking blonde girl a little younger than I was.

My father's adversary spoke to me in a friendly manner and it was then that I understood that having different opinions from those of another person in no way precluded holding this person in the highest respect.

Because mere tolerance is not enough: we must have true and deep respect for every human being, regardless of his beliefs, his origins and his values. That is what my father demanded of his sons and that is what he demanded of our country. He demanded it out of love – love of his sons, love of his country. That is why we love him so. These letters, these flowers, the dignity of the crowds who came to say farewell – all of that is a way of thanking him for having loved us so much.

My father's fundamental belief never came from a textbook. It stemmed from his deep love for and faith in all Canadians and over the past few days, with every card, every rose, every tear, every wave and every pirouette, you returned his love.

It means the world to Sacha and me. Thank you.

We have gathered from coast to coast to coast, from one ocean to another, united in our grief, to say goodbye.

But this is not the end. He left politics in '84. But he came back for Meech. He came back for Charlottetown.* He came back to remind us of who we are and what we're all capable of.

But he won't be coming back anymore. It's all up to us, all of us, now.

The woods are lovely, dark and deep. He has kept his promises and earned his sleep.

Je t'aime, Papa.

* The Meech Lake Accord (1987) and the Charlottetown Accord (1992) were both series of proposed amendments to the Canadian consitution, which Trudeau opposed.

# OUR SPIRIT REFUSES TO DIE

In 1970, Wampanoag leader Wamsutta Frank B. James was invited, somewhat misguidedly, by the Commonwealth of Massachusetts to speak at a state dinner organized to commemorate the 350th Anniversary of the Pilgrims' arrival in Cape Cod on the east coast of North America. James accepted the invitation, and soon enough allowed the organizers to read the draft of a speech in which he spoke of his people's mistreatment at the hands of the English – a speech they would never allow him to make due to its "inflammatory" message. Rather than read an alternative provided by the planners, James refused to attend. Instead, he organized the first ever National Day of Mourning to commemorate the struggles faced by Native Americans. It continues annually to this day.

I speak to you as a man – a Wampanoag Man. I am a proud man, proud of my ancestry, my accomplishments won by a strict parental direction ("You must succeed – your face is a different color in this small Cape Cod community!"). I am a product of poverty and discrimination from these two social and economic diseases. I, and my brothers and sisters, have painfully overcome, and to some extent we have earned the respect of our community. We are Indians first – but we are termed "good citizens." Sometimes we are arrogant but only because society has pressured us to be so.

It is with mixed emotion that I stand here to share my thoughts. This is a time of celebration for you – celebrating an anniversary of a beginning for the white man in America. A time of looking back, of reflection. It is with a heavy heart that I look back upon what happened to my People. Even before the Pilgrims landed it was common practice for explorers to capture Indians, take them to Europe and sell them as slaves for 220 shillings apiece. The Pilgrims had hardly explored the shores of Cape Cod for four days before they had robbed the graves of my ancestors and stolen their corn and beans. *Mourt's Relation** describes a searching party of sixteen men. Mourt goes on to say that this party took as much of the Indians' winter provisions as they were able to carry. Massasoit, the great Sachem [chief] of the Wampanoag, knew these facts, yet he and his People welcomed and befriended the settlers of the Plymouth Plantation. Perhaps he did this because his Tribe had been depleted by an epidemic. Or his knowledge of the harsh oncoming winter was the reason for his peaceful acceptance of these acts. This action by Massasoit was perhaps our biggest mistake. We, the Wampanoag, welcomed you, the white man, with open arms, little knowing that it was the beginning of the end; that before fifty years were to pass, the Wampanoag would no longer be a free people.

What happened in those short fifty years? What has happened in the last 300 years?

History gives us facts and there were atrocities; there were broken promises – and most of these centered around land ownership. Among ourselves

* *Mourt's Relation* was a booklet written around 1620, which related the story of the *Mayflower* Pilgrims in Plymouth.

we understood that there were boundaries, but never before had we had to deal with fences and stone walls. But the white man had a need to prove his worth by the amount of land that he owned. Only ten years later, when the Puritans came, they treated the Wampanoag with even less kindness in converting the souls of the so-called savages. Although the Puritans were harsh to members of their own society, the Indian was pressed between stone slabs and hanged as quickly as any other "witch." And so down through the years there is record after record of Indian lands taken and, in token, reservations set up for him upon which to live. The Indian, having been stripped of his power, could only stand by and watch while the white man took his land and used it for his personal gain. This the Indian could not understand; for to him, land was survival, to farm, to hunt, to be enjoyed. It was not to be abused. We see incident after incident where the white man sought to tame the "savage" and convert him to the Christian ways of life. The early Pilgrim settlers led the Indian to believe that if he did not behave, they would dig up the ground and unleash the great epidemic again. The white man used the Indian's nautical skills and abilities. They let him be only a seaman – but never a captain. Time and time again, in the white man's society, we Indians have been termed "low man on the totem pole."

Has the Wampanoag really disappeared? There is still an aura of mystery. We know there was an epidemic that took many Indian lives – some Wampanoags moved west and joined the Cherokee and Cheyenne. They were forced to move. Some even went north to Canada! Many Wampanoag put aside their Indian heritage and accepted the white man's way for their own survival. There are some Wampanoag who do not wish it known they are Indian for social or economic reasons. What happened to those Wampanoags who chose to remain and live among the early settlers? What kind of existence did they live as "civilized" people? True, living was not as complex as life today, but they dealt with the confusion and the change. Honesty, trust, concern, pride, and politics wove themselves in and out of their daily living. Hence, he was termed crafty, cunning, rapacious, and dirty.

History wants us to believe that the Indian was a savage, illiterate, uncivilized animal. A history that was written by an organized, disciplined people, to expose us as an unorganized and undisciplined entity. Two distinctly different cultures met. One thought they must control life; the other believed life was to be enjoyed, because nature decreed it. Let us remember, the Indian is and was just as human as the white man. The Indian feels pain, gets hurt, and becomes defensive, has dreams, bears tragedy and failure, suffers from loneliness, needs to cry as well as laugh. He, too, is often misunderstood.

The white man in the presence of the Indian is still mystified by his uncanny ability to make him feel uncomfortable. This may be the image the white man has created of the Indian; his "savageness" has boomeranged and isn't a mystery; it is fear; fear of the Indian's temperament!

High on a hill, overlooking the famed Plymouth Rock, stands the statue of our great Sachem, Massasoit. Massasoit has stood there many years in silence. We, the descendants of this great Sachem, have been a silent people. The necessity of making a living in this materialistic society of the white man caused us to be silent. Today, I and many of my people are choosing to face the truth. We ARE Indians!

Although time has drained our culture, and our language is almost extinct, we, the Wampanoags, still walk the lands of Massachusetts. We may be fragmented, we may be confused. Many years have passed since we have been a people together. Our lands were invaded. We fought as hard to keep our land as you the whites did to take our land away from us. We were conquered, we became the American prisoners of war in many cases, and wards of the United States Government, until only recently.

Our spirit refuses to die. Yesterday we walked the woodland paths and sandy trails. Today we must walk the macadam highways and roads. We are uniting. We're standing not in our wigwams but in your concrete tent. We stand tall and proud, and before too many moons pass we'll right the wrongs we have allowed to happen to us. We forfeited our country. Our lands have fallen into the hands of the aggressor. We have allowed the white man to keep us on our knees. What has happened cannot be changed, but today we must work towards a more humane America, a more Indian America, where men and nature once again are important; where the Indian values of honor, truth, and brotherhood prevail. You the white man are celebrating an anniversary. We the Wampanoags will help you celebrate in the concept of a beginning. It was the beginning of a new life for the Pilgrims. Now, 350 years later it is a beginning of a new determination for the original American: the American Indian.

There are some factors concerning the Wampanoags and other Indians across this vast nation. We now have 350 years of experience living amongst the white man. We can now speak his language. We can now think as a white man thinks. We can now compete with him for the top jobs. We're being heard; we are now being listened to. The important point is that along with these necessities of everyday living, we still have the spirit, we still have the unique culture, we still have the will and, most important of all, the determination to remain as Indians. We are determined, and our presence here this evening is living testimony that this is only the beginning of the American Indian, particularly the Wampanoag, to regain the position in this country that is rightfully ours.

# LET US PICK UP OUR BOOKS AND OUR PENS

On October 9, 2012, a Taliban gunman boarded a school bus in Pakistan, identified fifteen-year-old Malala Yousafzai by name, and shot her in the head. From the tender age of eleven, Yousafzai had been campaigning about the importance of all children to be given an education and had written widely read blogs for the BBC about life, and lack of schooling, under Taliban rule – factors which led to her attempted murder. Yousafzai survived the attack following intensive surgery in Pakistan and the U.K., and nine months later, on her sixteenth birthday, she confidently addressed the Youth Assembly at the United Nations Headquarters in New York with an inspiring speech that was broadcast around the globe.

In the name of God, the most beneficent, the most merciful. Honourable UN Secretary General Mr Ban Ki-moon, respected president of the General Assembly Vuk Jeremić, honourable UN envoy for global education Mr Gordon Brown, respected elders and my dear brothers and sisters: assalamu alaikum.

Today it is an honour for me to be speaking again after a long time. Being here with such honourable people is a great moment in my life and it is an honour for me that today I am wearing a shawl of Benazir Bhutto Shaheed. I don't know where to begin my speech. I don't know what people would be expecting me to say, but first of all thank you to God for whom we all are equal and thank you to every person who has prayed for my fast recovery and a new life. I cannot believe how much love people have shown me. I have received thousands of good-wish cards and gifts from all over the world. Thank you to all of them. Thank you to the children whose innocent words encouraged me. Thank you to my elders whose prayers strengthened me. I would like to thank my nurses, doctors and the staff of the hospitals in Pakistan and the UK and the UAE government who have helped me to get better and recover my strength.

I fully support Mr Ban Ki-moon the UN Secretary General in his Global Education First Initiative and the work of UN special envoy Mr Gordon Brown and the respected president of the UN General Assembly Vuk Jeremić. I thank them for their leadership, which they continue to give. They continue to inspire all of us to action.

Dear brothers and sisters, do remember one thing: Malala Day is not my day. Today is the day of every woman, every boy and every girl who have raised their voice for their rights.

There are hundreds of human rights activists and social workers who are not only speaking for their rights, but who are struggling to achieve their goals of peace, education and equality. Thousands of people have been killed by the terrorists and millions have been injured. I am just one of them.

So here I stand. . . . So here I stand, one girl among many. I speak not for myself, but so those without a voice can be heard. Those who have fought for their rights. Their right to live in peace. Their right to be treated with dignity. Their right to equality of opportunity. Their right to be educated.

Dear friends, on the 9th of October 2012, the Taliban shot me on the left side of my forehead. They shot my friends, too. They thought that the bullets would silence us. But they failed. And out of that silence came thousands of voices. The terrorists thought they would change my aims and stop my ambitions. But nothing changed in my life except this: weakness, fear and hopelessness died. Strength, power and courage was born.

I am the same Malala. My ambitions are the same. My hopes are the same. And my dreams are the same.

Dear sisters and brothers, I am not against anyone. Neither am I here to speak in terms of personal revenge against the Taliban or any other terrorist group. I am here to speak up for the right of education for every child. I want education for the sons and daughters of the Taliban and all the terrorists and extremists.

I do not even hate the Talib who shot me. Even if there was a gun in my hand and he was standing in front of me, I would not shoot him. This is the compassion that I have learned from Muhammed, the Prophet of mercy, Jesus Christ and Lord Buddha. This the legacy of change I have inherited from Martin Luther King, Nelson Mandela and Muhammed Ali Jinnah. This is the philosophy of non-violence that I have learned from Gandhiji, Bacha Khan and Mother Teresa. And this is the forgiveness that I have learned from my father and from my mother. This is what my soul is telling me: be peaceful and love everyone.

Dear sisters and brothers, we realise the importance of light when we see darkness. We realise the importance of our voice when we are silenced. In the same way, when we were in Swat, the north of Pakistan, we realised the importance of pens and books when we saw the guns. The wise saying, 'The pen is mightier than the sword', was true. The extremists were and are afraid of books and pens. The power of education frightens them. They are afraid of women. The power of the voice of women frightens them. And that is why they killed fourteen innocent students in the recent attack in Quetta. And that is why they killed female teachers and polio workers in Khyber Pakhtunkhwa. That is why they are blasting schools every day, because they were and they are afraid of change, afraid of the equality that we will bring to our society.

And I remember that there was a boy in our school who was asked by a journalist: 'Why are the Taliban against education?' He answered very simply by pointing to his book, he said: 'A Talib doesn't know what is written inside this book.'

They think that God is a tiny, little conservative being who would send girls to the hell just because of going to school. The terrorists are misusing the name of Islam and Pashtun society for their own personal benefits. Pakistan is a

peace-loving, democratic country. Pashtuns want education for their daughters and sons. And Islam is a religion of peace, humanity and brotherhood. Islam says that it is not only each child's right to get education, rather it is their duty and responsibility.

Honourable Secretary General, peace is necessary for education. In many parts of the world, especially Pakistan and Afghanistan, terrorism, wars and conflicts stop children going to their schools. We are really tired of these wars.

Women and children are suffering in many ways in many parts of the world. In India, innocent and poor children are victims of child labour. Many schools have been destroyed in Nigeria. People in Afghanistan have been affected by the hurdles of extremism for decades. Young girls have to do domestic child labour and are forced to get married at early age. Poverty, ignorance, injustice, racism and the deprivation of basic rights are the main problems faced by both men and women.

Dear fellows, today I am focusing on women's rights and girls' education because they are suffering the most. There was a time when women social activists asked men to stand up for their rights. But, this time, we will do it by ourselves. I am not telling men to step away from speaking for women's rights, rather I am focusing on women to be independent, to fight for themselves. So dear sisters and brothers, now it is time to speak up. So today, we call upon the world leaders to change their strategic policies in favour of peace and prosperity.

We call upon the world leaders that all of these deals must protect women's and children's rights. A deal that goes against the rights of women is unacceptable.

We call upon all governments to ensure free, compulsory education all over the world for every child.

We call upon all the governments to fight against terrorism and violence. To protect children from brutality and harm.

We call upon the developed nations to support the expansion of educational opportunities for girls in the developing world.

We call upon all communities to be tolerant, to reject prejudice based on caste, creed, sect, colour, religion or gender. To ensure freedom and equality for women so they can flourish. We cannot all succeed when half of us are held back.

We call upon our sisters around the world to be brave, to embrace the strength within themselves and realise their full potential.

Dear brothers and sisters, we want schools and education for every child's bright future. We will continue our journey to our destination of peace and education. No one can stop us. We will speak up for our rights and we will bring change through our voice. We believe in the power and the strength of our words. Our words can change the whole world because we are all together, united for the cause of education. And if we want to achieve our goal, then let

SPEECHES OF NOTE

us empower ourselves with the weapon of knowledge and let us shield ourselves with unity and togetherness.

Dear brothers and sisters, we must not forget that millions of people are suffering from poverty, injustice and ignorance. We must not forget that millions of children are out of their schools. We must not forget that our sisters and brothers are waiting for a bright, peaceful future.

So let us wage a glorious struggle against illiteracy, poverty and terrorism, let us pick up our books and our pens. They are our most powerful weapons.

One child, one teacher, one book and one pen can change the world. Education is the only solution. Education first.

Thank you.

# I HAVE JUST BEEN SHOT

In 1912, four years after vacating the White House, Theodore Roosevelt found himself on the campaign trail once again, traveling around America to deliver up to twenty speeches each day in an ultimately unsuccessful bid to serve a third term as president. The fourteenth of October was like every other day, until, at approximately 8 p.m., as he left his hotel in Milwaukee to address a nearby crowd, one John Schrank aimed a revolver at Roosevelt and pulled the trigger. The bullet lodged in Roosevelt's chest wall, but not before passing through, and being slowed by, his thick coat and the speech sitting in the inside pocket. Luckily, that speech spanned fifty pages. The bullet remained in Roosevelt's body for the rest of his life, its extraction deemed too dangerous by doctors at a local hospital. Incredibly, those doctors didn't assess Roosevelt's injury until after he had delivered his speech.

Friends, I shall ask you to be as quiet as possible. I don't know whether you fully understand that I have just been shot; but it takes more than that to kill a bull moose. But fortunately I had my manuscript, so you see I was going to make a long speech, and there is a bullet – there is where the bullet went through – and it probably saved me from it going into my heart. The bullet is in me now, so that I cannot make a very long speech, but I will try my best.

And now, friends, I want to take advantage of this incident to say a word of solemn warning to my fellow countrymen. First of all, I want to say this about myself: I have altogether too important things to think of to feel any concern over my own death; and now I cannot speak to you insincerely within five minutes of being shot. I am telling you the literal truth when I say that my concern is for many other things. It is not in the least for my own life. I want you to understand that I am ahead of the game, anyway. No man has had a happier life than I have led; a happier life in every way. I have been able to do certain things that I greatly wished to do, and I am interested in doing other things. I can tell you with absolute truthfulness that I am very much uninterested in whether I am shot or not. It was just as when I was colonel of my regiment. I always felt that a private was to be excused for feeling at times some pangs of anxiety about his personal safety, but I cannot understand a man fit to be a colonel who can pay any heed to his personal safety when he is occupied as he ought to be with the absorbing desire to do his duty.

I am in this cause with my whole heart and soul. I believe that the Progressive movement is making life a little easier for all our people; a movement to try to take the burdens off the men and especially the women and children of this country. I am absorbed in the success of that movement.

Friends, I ask you now this evening to accept what I am saying as absolutely true, when I tell you I am not thinking of my own success. I am not thinking of my life or of anything connected with me personally. I am thinking of the movement. I say this by way of introduction, because I want to say something very serious to our people and especially to the newspapers. I don't know anything about who the man was who shot me tonight. He was seized at once by one of the stenographers in my party, Mr. Martin, and I suppose is now in the hands of the police. He shot to kill. He shot – the shot, the bullet went in here – I will show you.

I am going to ask you to be as quiet as possible for I am not able to give the challenge of the bull moose quite as loudly. Now, I do not know who he was or what he represented. He was a coward. He stood in the darkness in the crowd around the automobile and when they cheered me, and I got up to bow, he stepped forward and shot me in the darkness.

Now, friends, of course, I do not know, as I say, anything about him; but it is a very natural thing that weak and vicious minds should be inflamed to acts of violence by the kind of awful mendacity and abuse that have been heaped upon me for the last three months by the papers in the interest of not only Mr. Debs but of Mr. Wilson and Mr. Taft.*

* Roosevelt's opponents in the election: incumbent president William Howard Taft (Republican), Eugene V. Debs (Socialist) and eventual winner Woodrow Wilson (Democrat). Roosevelt himself, a former Republican, ran as a Progressive candidate and came in second.

Friends, I will disown and repudiate any man of my party who attacks with such foul slander and abuse any opponent of any other party; and now I wish to say seriously to all the daily newspapers, to the Republicans, the Democrat, and Socialist parties, that they cannot, month in month out and year in and year out, make the kind of untruthful, of bitter assault that they have made and not expect that brutal, violent natures, or brutal and violent characters, especially when the brutality is accompanied by a not very strong mind; they cannot expect that such natures will be unaffected by it.

Now, friends, I am not speaking for myself at all, I give you my word, I do not care a rap about being shot; not a rap.

I have had a good many experiences in my time and this is one of them. What I care for is my country. I wish I were able to impress upon my people – our people, the duty to feel strongly but to speak the truth of their opponents. I say now, I have never said one word on the stump against any opponent that I cannot defend. I have said nothing that I could not substantiate and nothing that I ought not to have said – nothing that I – nothing that, looking back at, I would not say again.

Now, friends, it ought not to be too much to ask that our opponents [speaking to someone on the stage] – I am not sick at all. I am all right. I cannot tell you of what infinitesimal importance I regard this incident as compared with the great issues at stake in this campaign, and I ask it not for my sake, not the least in the world, but for the sake of common country, that they make up their minds to speak only the truth, and not use that kind of slander and mendacity which if taken seriously must incite weak and violent natures to crimes of violence. Don't you make any mistake. Don't you pity me. I am all right. I am all right and you cannot escape listening to the speech either.

And now, friends, this incident that has just occurred – this effort to assassinate me – emphasizes to a peculiar degree the need of the Progressive movement. Friends, every good citizen ought to do everything in his or her power to prevent the coming of the day when we shall see in this country two recognized creeds fighting one another, when we shall see the creed of the "Havenots" arraigned against the creed of the "Haves." When that day comes then such incidents as this tonight will be commonplace in our history. When you make poor men – when you permit the conditions to grow such that the poor man as such will be swayed by his sense of injury against the men who try to hold what they improperly have won, when that day comes, the most awful passions will be let loose and it will be an ill day for our country.

Now, friends, what we who are in this movement are endeavoring to do is forestall any such movement for justice now – a movement in which we ask all just men of generous hearts to join with the men who feel in their souls that lift upward which bids them refuse to be satisfied themselves while their countrymen and countrywomen suffer from avoidable misery. Now, friends, what we Progressives are trying to do is to enroll rich or poor, whatever their social or industrial position, to stand together for the most elementary rights of good citizenship, those elementary rights which are the foundation of good citizenship in this great Republic of ours.

[Mr. Roosevelt's associates, fearing for his health, ask him to wrap up his speech.]

My friends are a little more nervous than I am. Don't you waste any sympathy on me. I have had an A-1 time in life and I am having it now.

I never in my life was in any movement in which I was able to serve with such whole-hearted devotion as in this; in which I was able to feel as I do in this that commonweal. I have fought for the good of our common country.

And now, friends, I shall have to cut short much of that speech that I meant to give you, but I want to touch on just two or three of the points.

In the first place, speaking to you here in Milwaukee, I wish to say that the Progressive party is making its appeals to all our fellow citizens without any regard to their creed or to their birthplace. We do not regard as essential the way in which a man worships his God or as being affected by where he was born. We regard it as a matter of spirit and purpose. In New York, while I was police commissioner, the two men from whom I got the most assistance were Jacob Riis, who was born in Denmark, and Arthur von Briesen, who was born in Germany – both of them as fine examples of the best and highest American citizenship as you could find in any part of this country.

I have just been introduced by one of your own men here – Henry Cochems. His grandfather, his father, and that father's seven brothers, all served in the United States army, and they entered it four years after they had come to this country from Germany. Two of them left their lives, spent their lives, on the field of battle. I am all right – I am a little sore. Anybody has a right to be sore with a bullet in him. You would find that if I was in battle now I would be leading my men just the same. Just the same way I am going to make this speech.

At one time I promoted five men for gallantry on the field of battle. Afterward in making some inquiries about them I found that two of them were Protestants, two Catholic, and one a Jew. One Protestant came from Germany and one was born in Ireland. I did not promote them because of their religion. It just happened that way. If all five of them had been Jews I would have promoted them, or if all five of them had been Protestants I would have promoted them; or if they had been Catholics. In that regiment I had a man born in Italy who distinguished himself by gallantry; there was another young fellow, a son of Polish parents, and another who came here when he was a child from Bohemia, who likewise distinguished themselves; and friends, I assure you, that I was incapable of considering any question whatever, but the worth of each individual as a fighting man. If he was a good fighting man, then I saw that Uncle Sam got the benefit of it. That is all.

I make the same appeal to our citizenship. I ask in our civic life that we in the same way pay heed only to the man's quality of citizenship, to repudiate as the worst enemy that we can have whoever tries to get us to discriminate for or against any man because of his creed or birthplace.

Now, friends, in the same way I want our people to stand by one another without regard to differences or class or occupation. I have always stood by labor-unions. I am going to make one omission tonight. I have prepared my speech because Mr. Wilson had seen fit to attack me by showing up his record in comparison with mine. But I am not going to do that tonight. I am going to simply speak of what I myself have done and what I think ought to be done in this country of ours.

It is essential that here should be organizations of labor. This is an era of organization. Capital organizes and therefore labor must organize. My appeal for organized labor is two-fold; to the outsider and the capitalist I make my appeal to treat the laborer fairly, to recognize the fact that he must organize, that there must be such organization, that the laboring man must organize for his own protection, and that it is the duty of the rest of us to help him and not hinder him in organizing. That is one half appeal that I make.

Now, the other half is to the labor man himself. My appeal to him is to remember that as he wants justice, so he must do justice. I want every labor man, every labor leader, every organized union man, to take the lead in denouncing disorder and in denouncing the inciting of riot; that in this country we shall proceed under the protection of our laws and with all respect to the laws, I want the labor men to feel in their turn that exactly as justice must be done them so they must do justice. They must bear their duty as citizens, their

into politics thirty-two years ago to the present time

been that the only safe course t       ue in this country

of ours is to treat each man on his w      neither discrimin-

ating in his favor not against him because of his creed or be-

cause of his birthplace.      Thirty-two years ago when I went

into the New York legislature, my close allies in that body

included men like O'Neill, Costello and Kelly, men like Kruse

and Miller, who had themselves been born or whose parents had

been born in Ireland or in Germany and neither they nor I were

capable of considering where the birthplace of any one of us

had been or what creed any one of us professed or what land

his parents came from.      All that any one of us demanded to

know about the others was whether t           quare and honest

men, good Americans, devoted to the        ests of our common

country.      During the time I was Police Commissioner of New

York, the two laymen from whom I got most assistance were

duty to this great country of ours, and that they must not rest content unless they do that duty to the fullest degree.

I know these doctors, when they get hold of me, will never let me go back, and there are just a few more things that I want to say to you.

And here I have got to make one comparison between Mr. Wilson and myself, simply because he has invited it and I cannot shrink from it. Mr. Wilson has seen fit to attack me, to say that I did not do much against the trusts when I was President. I have got two answers to make to that. In the first place what I did, and then I want to compare what I did when I was President with what Mr. Wilson did not do when he was governor.

When I took the office the antitrust law was practically a dead letter and the interstate commerce law in as poor a condition. I had to revive both laws. I did. I enforced both. It will be easy enough to do now what I did then, but the reason that it is easy now is because I did it when it was hard.

Nobody was doing anything. I found speedily that the interstate commerce law by being made perfect could be made a most useful instrument for helping solve some of our industrial problems. So with the antitrust law. I speedily found out that almost the only positive good achieved by such a successful lawsuit as the Northern Securities suit, for instance, was in establishing the principle that the government was supreme over the big corporation, but by itself that the law did not accomplish any of the things that we ought to have accomplished; and so I began to fight for the amendment of the law along the lines of the interstate commerce law, and now we propose, we Progressives, to establish an interstate commission having the same power over industrial concerns that the Interstate Commerce Commission has over railroads, so that whenever there is in the future a decision rendered in such important matters as the recent suits against the Standard Oil, the Sugar – no, not that – Tobacco – Tobacco Trust – we will have a commission which will see that the decree of the court is really made effective; that it is not made a merely nominal decree.

Our opponents have said that we intend to legalize monopoly. Nonsense. They have legalized monopoly. At this moment the Standard Oil and Tobacco Trust monopolies are legalized; they are being carried on under the decree of the Supreme Court. Our proposal is really to break up monopoly. Our proposal is to lay down certain requirements, and then to require the commerce commission – the industrial commission – to see that the trusts live up to those requirements. Our opponents have spoken as if we were going to let the commission declare what those requirements should be. Not at all. We are going to put the requirements in the law and then see that the commission requires them to obey that law.

← The glasses case and speech, which was folded in half and carried in the pocket of Theodore Roosevelt when he was shot on October 14, 1912

And now, friends, as Mr. Wilson has invited the comparison, I only want to say this: Mr. Wilson has said that the States are the proper authorities to deal with the trusts. Well, about 80 percent of the trusts are organized in New Jersey.

The Standard Oil, the Tobacco, the Sugar, the Beef, all those trusts are organized in the state of New Jersey and the laws of New Jersey say that their charters can at any time be amended or repealed if they misbehave themselves and give the government ample power to act about those laws, and Mr. Wilson has been governor a year and nine months and he has not opened his lips. The chapter describing what Mr. Wilson has done about trusts in New Jersey would read precisely like a chapter describing snakes in Ireland, which ran: "There are no snakes in Ireland." Mr. Wilson has done precisely and exactly nothing about the trusts.

I tell you, and I told you at the beginning, I do not say anything on the stump that I do not believe. I do not say anything I do not know. Let any of Mr. Wilson's friends on Tuesday point out one thing or let Mr. Wilson point out one thing that he has done about the trusts as governor of New Jersey.

And now, friends, there is one thing I want to say especially to you people here in Wisconsin. All that I have said so far is what I would say in any part of the Union. I have a peculiar right to ask that in this great contest you men and women of Wisconsin shall stand with us. You have taken the lead in progressive movements here in Wisconsin. You have taught the rest of us to look to you for inspiration and leadership. Now, friends, you have made that movement here locally. You will be doing a dreadful injustice to yourselves; you will be doing a dreadful injustice to the rest of us throughout the Union, if you fail to stand with us now that we are making this national movement. What I am about to say now I want you to understand. If I speak of Mr. Wilson I speak with no mind of bitterness. I merely want to discuss the difference of policy between the Progressive and the Democratic parties and to ask you to think for yourselves which party you will follow. I will say that, friends, because the Republican party is beaten. Nobody needs to have any idea that anything can be done with the Republican party.

When the Republican party – not the Republican party – when the bosses in control of the Republican party, the Barneses and Penroses, last June stole the nomination and wrecked the Republican party for good and all – I want to point out to you that nominally they stole that nomination from me, but it was really from you. They did not like me, and the longer they live the less cause they will have to like me. But while they don't like me, they dread you. You are the people that they dread. They dread the people themselves, and those bosses and the big special interests behind them made up their mind that they would rather see the Republican party wrecked than see it come under the control of the people themselves. So I am not dealing with the Republican party. There are only two ways you can vote this year. You can be progressive or reactionary. Whether you vote Republican or Democratic it does not make a difference, you are voting reactionary.

Now, the Democratic party in its platform and through the utterances of Mr. Wilson has distinctly committed itself to the old flintlock, muzzle-loaded doctrine of States' rights, and I have said distinctly we are for people's rights. We are for the rights of the people. If they can be obtained best through National Government, then we are for national rights. We are for people's rights however it is necessary to secure them.

Mr. Wilson has made a long essay against Senator Beveridge's bill to abolish child labor. It is the same kind of argument that would be made against our bill to prohibit women from working more than eight hours a day in industry. It is the same kind of argument that would have to be made; if it is true, it would apply equally against our proposal to insist that in continuous industries there shall be by law one day's rest in seven and a three-shift eight-hour day. You have labor laws here in Wisconsin, and the chamber of commerce will tell you that because of that fact there are industries that will not come to Wisconsin. They prefer to stay outside where they can work children of tender years, where they can work women fourteen and sixteen hours a day, where if it is a continuous industry, they can work men twelve hours a day and seven days a week.

Now, friends, I know that you of Wisconsin would never repeal those laws even if they are at your commercial hurt, just as I am trying to get New York to adopt such laws even though it will be to New York's commercial hurt. But if possible I want to arrange it so that we can have justice without commercial hurt, and you can only get that if you have justice enforced nationally. You won't be burdened in Wisconsin with industries not coming to the State if the same good laws are extended all over the other States. Do you see what I mean? The States all compete in a common market; and it is not justice to the employers of a State that has enforced just and proper laws to have them exposed to the competition of another State where no such laws are enforced. Now, the Democratic platform and their speakers declare we shall not have such laws. Mr. Wilson has distinctly declared that we shall not have a national law to prohibit the labor of children, to prohibit child labor. He has distinctly declared that we shall not have a law to establish a minimum wage for women.

I ask you to look at our declaration and hear and read our platform about social and industrial justice and then, friends, vote for the Progressive ticket without regard to me, without regard to my personality, for only by voting for that platform can you be true to the cause of progress throughout this Union.

# TAKE CARE OF YOUR ARTISTS

Shirin Neshat left her birth country of Iran as a young adult to study art in California, and after graduating from the University of California, Berkeley, unable to return to Iran due to the Islamic Revolution of 1979, she settled in New York and forged a successful career as an award-winning visual artist. In 2014, at the World Economic Forum, Neshat delivered a speech to numerous global leaders – including the president of Iran, Hassan Rouhani – and implored them to recognize the importance of art during periods of crisis.

→ Shirin Neshat, *Rebellious Silence*, 1994, photographed by Cynthia Preston

It's quite rare for a visual artist such as myself to address such an influential audience like you, and it must be rare for you to hear the voice of an artist whose world is the realm of fiction.

Yes, I am an artist, but as Picasso once said, "Art is the lie that enables us to realize the truth."

Yes, my work is fiction, but I believe that through fiction we can go deeper into the human psyche, deeper into reality, deeper into the universal plight of what it's like to be a human being on this planet today.

I tend to consider artists as a conduit, art and culture as a bridge between people and the people of power. I consider art as a form of communication, art as a way to have emotional and intellectual impact on people without having any specific political or ideological agenda.

Now if you have ever doubted the significance of culture in times of political crisis, I beg of you to look at the Iranian culture as an example.

Ever since the Islamic Revolution in 1979, when the Iranian image quickly declined from that rich, ancient culture of poets and mystics to now suddenly the barbaric land of fanatics and mullahs, violence and oppression, it was here, my friends, that Iranian artists and Iranian culture unquestionably became the saving grace of this nation, both in respect to their own people and the world at large.

When Iran was burning inside in the aftermath of the Islamic Revolution; when Iranians were kept hostage by their own government but isolated in the world; when we suddenly woke up to a country where religion ruled the state; when our people were massacred for the smallest gesture of protest; when families began to be separated for good; when the West decided to take revenge and its embargo hit us hard, collapsing our economy and our medical services; when our government deprived us of the basic human rights, the freedom of expression; when artists and intellectuals regularly became harassed, arrested and at times executed – our artists began to respond.

Musicians, writers, filmmakers, visual artists, intellectuals, all people of imagination worked very hard in light of censorship and all the given

boundaries and created the most powerful, imaginative, subversive artistic expressions, which quickly flourished into the world.

Now if I may take this opportunity and give a message to our newly elected President, Mr. Hassan Rouhani, a man whom I respect a great deal and whose initiatives have been much welcomed at home and abroad – I would ask of the President: if, for the past many decades, Iranian artists and intellectuals have protected and preserved our national dignity in the world, now we pass the torch on to you, Mr. President. It is now your turn to be that saving grace of our nation.

Mr. President, Iranians living inside and outside the country are badly broken, divided, separated, displaced. Show them unity. Show them democracy. Show them how we are all Iranians despite our class and religion – Muslims, Christianity, Jews.

Mr. President, let us erase the image of a country that fits the description of an "axis of evil." Let us build a new image of a country that could be a model for peace, democracy and justice.

And at last, Mr. President, this is from me: take care of your artists, your intellectuals, and accept that art is no crime, that it is every artist's responsibility to make art that is meaningful, that questions tyranny, that questions injustice. It is the artist's task to advocate change, peace and unity.

Let me leave you with a last quote from Picasso. He said, "Art washes away from the soul the dust of everyday life."

Good luck, Mr. President, and thank you all.

# DROP YOUR TAILS AND LEAVE THIS SWAMP

New York's environmentally focused Southampton College at Long Island University made national headlines in 1996 when its enterprising chancellor of three years, Robert F. X. Sillerman, chose to award the previously unheard-of "Honorary Doctorate of Amphibious Letters" to Kermit the Frog. Said Sillerman of the decision at the time: "This school is known for its world-class programs in marine and environmental sciences, and when you think of the 'green print,' you think of Kermit the Frog."

It is difficult to disagree; however, a handful of students made known their displeasure at such "debasement." Undeterred, Kermit showed his appreciation by giving a commencement speech to 245 of the college's students, most of whom responded with rapturous applause.

President Steinberg, Chancellor Sillerman, distinguished guests and my fellow amphibians, I stand here before you a happy and humble frog.

When I was a tadpole growing up back in the swamps, I never imagined that I would one day address such an outstanding group of scholars. And I am sure that when you were children growing up back in your own particular swamps or suburbs, you never imagined you would sit here on one of the most important days of your life listening to a short, green talking frog deliver your commencement address. All of us should feel very proud of ourselves, and just a little bit silly.

In any case, congratulations to all of you graduates. As we say in the wetlands, "Ribbit-ribbit-knee-deep-ribbit," which means: "May success and a smile always be yours, even when you're knee-deep in the sticky muck of life."

Now, I know that there are some people out there who wonder what brought me here today. Was it the incoming tide on Shinnecock Bay? Was it the all-you-can-eat midnight buffet aboard the *Paumanok*? Or was it the promise that I'd get to play basketball with Sidney Green and the Runnin' Colonials?* Don't let my spindly little arms fool you. I can slam-dunk one mean basketball. While those are all very good reasons for coming to this beautiful campus, today I am here for an even more important reason – to thank each and every one of you at Southampton College.

* Sidney Green was the head coach of the Runnin' Colonials college basketball team.

First, of course, I want to thank you for bestowing upon me this Honorary Doctorate of Amphibious Letters. To tell you the truth, I never even knew there was such a thing as "Amphibious" Letters. After all those years on *Sesame Street*, you'd think I'd know my alphabet. It just goes to show that you can teach an old frog new tricks.

It's great to have an honorary doctorate. I have spoken with my fellow honorees – Professor Merton, Ms. Meaker, Mr. Gambling – and as honorary doctors we promise to have regular office hours, put new magazines in our waiting room, and to make late-night house calls regardless of your health plan coverage. On behalf of all of us, thank you sincerely.

But I'm also here at Southampton to thank you for something even more important. I am here to thank you for the great work that you have done – and for the great work that you will be doing with your lives. You have dedicated yourselves to preserving the beauty that is all around us. While some might look out at this great ocean and just see a magnificent view, you and I know that this ocean – and every ecosystem – is home to an indefinable number of my fellow animals.

As you go out into the world, never lose sight of the fact that you are not just saving the environment, you are saving the homes and lives of so many of my relatives.

On behalf of frogs, fish, pigs, bears and all of the other species who are lower than you on the food chain, thank you for dedicating your lives to saving our world and our home. In the words of my cousin, Newt – no, not that Newt, this is another Newt – "We appreciate what you are doing more than you can even imagine."

And so I say to you, the 1996 graduates of Southampton College, you are no longer tadpoles. The time has come for you to drop your tails and leave this swamp. But I am sure that wherever I go as I travel around the world, I will find each and every one of you working your tails off to save other swamps and give those of us who live there a chance to survive. We love you for it.

Enjoy life, and thank you very much.

# I HAVE AIDS

In December 1984, thirteen-year-old Ryan White was given six months to live after contracting AIDS during a contaminated treatment for hemophilia, a blood condition with which he had lived since birth. By June 1985, keen to resume as normal a lifestyle as possible, Ryan attempted to return to school; however, due to ignorance and the intense stigma that surrounded the virus in its infancy, his wish was denied by school officials unable to ignore a petition signed by fearful parents and teachers. Ryan died in 1990, by which time he had returned to school, appeared regularly on television to tell his story and had become a beacon of hope for fellow AIDS sufferers the world over. In 1988, he even delivered a speech to the President's Commission on the HIV Epidemic.

Thank you, commissioners.

My name is Ryan White. I am sixteen years old. I have hemophilia, and I have AIDS.

When I was three days old, the doctors told my parents I was a severe hemophiliac, meaning my blood does not clot. Lucky for me, there was a product just approved by the Food and Drug Administration. It was called Factor VIII, which contains the clotting agent found in blood.

While I was growing up, I had many bleeds or hemorrhages in my joints which make it very painful. Twice a week I would receive injections or IVs of Factor VIII, which clotted the blood and then broke it down. A bleed occurs from a broken blood vessel or vein. The blood then had nowhere to go so it would swell up in a joint. You could compare it to trying to pour a quart of milk into a pint-sized container of milk.

The first five to six years of my life were spent in and out of the hospital. All in all I led a pretty normal life. Most recently my battle has been against AIDS and the discrimination surrounding it. On December 17, 1984, I had surgery to remove two inches of my left lung due to pneumonia. After two hours of surgery the doctors told my mother I had AIDS. I contracted AIDS through my Factor VIII, which is made from blood. When I came out of surgery, I was on a respirator and had a tube in my left lung. I spent Christmas and the next thirty days in the hospital. A lot of my time was spent searching, thinking and planning my life.

I came face to face with death at thirteen years old. I was diagnosed with AIDS: a killer. Doctors told me I'm not contagious. Given six months to live and being the fighter that I am, I set high goals for myself. It was my decision to live a normal life, go to school, be with my friends and enjoying day-to-day activities. It was not going to be easy.

→ Ryan White being interviewed in front of the Clinton County Courthouse in Frankfort, KY, *c*.1986

The school I was going to said they had no guidelines for a person with AIDS. The school board, my teachers and my principal voted to keep me out of

the classroom even after the guidelines were set by the ISBH [Indiana State Board of Health], for fear of someone getting AIDS from me by casual contact. Rumors of sneezing, kissing, tears, sweat and saliva spreading AIDS caused people to panic.

We began a series of court battles for nine months, while I was attending classes by telephone. Eventually, I won the right to attend school, but the prejudice was still there. Listening to medical facts was not enough. People wanted 100 percent guarantees. There are no 100 percent guarantees in life, but concessions were made by Mom and me to help ease the fear. We decided to meet them halfway: separate restrooms; no gym; separate drinking fountains; disposable eating utensils and trays – even though we knew AIDS was not spread through casual contact. Nevertheless, parents of twenty students started their own school. They were still not convinced. Because of the lack of education on AIDS, discrimination, fear, panic and lies surrounded me:

I became the target of Ryan White jokes.

Lies about me biting people.

Spitting on vegetables and cookies.

Urinating on bathroom walls.

Some restaurants threw away my dishes.

My school locker was vandalized inside and folders were marked "fag" and other obscenities.

I was labeled a troublemaker, my mom an unfit mother, and I was not welcome anywhere. People would get up and leave so they would not have to sit anywhere near me. Even at church, people would not shake my hand.

This brought on the news media, TV crews, interviews and numerous public appearances. I became known as the AIDS boy. I received thousands of letters of support from all around the world, all because I wanted to go to school. Mayor Koch, of New York, was the first public figure to give me support. Entertainers, athletes and stars started giving me support. I met some of the greatest like Elton John, Greg Louganis, Max Headroom, Alyssa Milano (my teen idol), Linden King (Los Angeles Raiders) and Charlie Sheen. All of these plus many more became my friends, but I had very few friends at school. How could these people in the public eye not be afraid of me, but my whole town was?

It was difficult, at times, to handle; but I tried to ignore the injustice, because I knew the people were wrong. My family and I held no hatred for those people because we realized they were victims of their own ignorance. We had great faith that with patience, understanding and education, that my family and I could be helpful in changing their minds and attitudes around. Financial hardships were rough on us, even though Mom had a good job at GM. The more I was sick, the more work she had to miss. Bills became impossible to pay. My sister, Andrea, was a championship roller skater who had to sacrifice too. There was no money for her lessons and travel. AIDS can destroy a family if you let it, but luckily for my sister and me, Mom taught us to keep going. Don't give up, be proud of who you are, and never feel sorry for yourself.

After two and a half years of declining health, two attacks of pneumocystis, shingles, a rare form of whooping cough and liver problems, I faced fighting chills, fevers, coughing, tiredness and vomiting. I was very ill and being tutored at home. The desire to move into a bigger house, to avoid living AIDS daily, and a dream to be accepted by a community and school, became possible and a reality with a movie about my life, *The Ryan White Story*.

My life is better now. At the end of the school year, my family and I decided to move to Cicero, Indiana. We did a lot of hoping and praying that the community would welcome us, and they did. For the first time in three years, we feel we have a home, a supportive school and lots of friends. The communities of Cicero, Atlanta, Arcadia and Noblesville, Indiana, are now what we call "home." I'm feeling great. I am a normal happy teenager again. I have a learner's permit. I attend sports functions and dances. My studies are important to me. I made the honor roll just recently, with two A's and two B's. I'm just one of the kids, and all because the students at Hamilton Heights High School listened to the facts, educated their parents and themselves, and believed in me.

I believe in myself as I look forward to graduating from Hamilton Heights High School in 1991.

Hamilton Heights High School is proof that AIDS education in schools works.

# EVERY ALIEN'S FAVOURITE COUSIN

From March to August 2013, more than 300,000 people headed for London's Victoria and Albert Museum to visit *David Bowie Is*, a record-breaking retrospective of a pioneering performer who needs little introduction, and who granted the institution unprecedented access to his archive for this celebration of a life and career. Days before the exhibition opened its doors to the public, a gala dinner was held in Bowie's honor – a gathering he was unable to attend. Instead, a speech was made by his good friend, the actor Tilda Swinton.

Dear Dave,

When I asked you if you wanted me to say anything here tonight, you said, 'Only three words; one of them testicular' – so I'll pass that on.

Here I am at the most eclectic of all the London branches of Bowie Anonymous. All the nicest possible freaks are here. We're in the Victoria and Albert Museum preparing to rifle through your drawers. It's truly an amazing thing.

This was my favourite playground as a child. Medieval armour, my fantasy space wear, and, alongside, when I was twelve – and a square sort of kid in a round pond sort of childhood, not far from here – I carried a copy of *Aladdin Sane* around with me, a full two years before I had the wherewithal to play it.

The image of that gingery bony pinky whitey person on the cover with the liquid mercury collarbone was – for one particular young moonage daydreamer* – the image of planetary kin, of a close imaginary cousin and companion of choice.

It's taken me a long time to admit, even to myself, let alone you, that it was the vision and not yet the sound that hooked me up – but if I can't confess that here and now, then when and where?

We all have our own roots, and routes, to this room. Some of us – the enviable – found the fellowship early in the funfests of Billy's Bowie Nights† or equivalent lodges from San Francisco to Auckland to Heidelberg and all points in between. For others, it was a more lonesome affair, paced out in a sort of private Morse code like following breadcrumbs through a forest.

I'm not saying that if you hadn't pitched up I would have worn a pie-crust collar and pearls like some of those I went to school with. I'm not saying that if you hadn't weighed in, [DJ and 'Blitz Kid'] Princess Julia would have been less inventive with the pink blusher.

Simply that, you provided the sideways like us with such rare and out-there company. Such fellowship. You pulled us in and left your arm dangling over our necks. And kept us warm – as you have for – isn't it? – centuries now.

You were. You are. One of us. And you have remained the reliable mortal in amongst all the immortal shapes you have thrown.

* 'Moonage Daydream' featured on Bowie's album *The Rise and Fall of Ziggy Stardust and the Spiders from Mars*.

† A late-seventies club night inspired by Bowie at Billy's nightclub in Soho, London.

Nothing more certain than changes.

Always with a weather eye out.

Always awake and clocking the fallout.

Those Mayans must have known something when they set their calendar down before January 2013. Because, of course, now all bets are off.

I know, because you told me, how tickled you were to knock Elvis – for once! – out of the headlines on your shared birthday this year. There's so much for all of us to be happy about since then. Yet, I think the thing I'm loving the most about the last few weeks is how clear it now is – how undeniable – that the freak becomes the great unifier. The alien is the best company after all. For so many more than the few.

They wanted a Bowie fan to speak tonight. They could have thrown a paper napkin and hit a hundred. I'm the lucky one, standing up to speak for all my fellow freaks anxious to win the pub quiz and claim their number one most super-fan T-shirt.

I want to give thanks to the Victoria and Albert Museum for indulging us so. For laying on our dream show. For showing us, as is written along the bottom of this month's Q magazine, 'why we all live in David's world now'.

To Gucci and Sennheiser for putting up the cash, laying on the sound and vision. To Geoffrey and Victoria for curating an entire universe so beautifully, on behalf of us all.

When I think of what it used to feel like once to be a freak who liked you, to feel like a freak like you – a freak who even looked a little like you – and then I think of the countless people of every size and feather who are going to walk through this trace of your journey here and pick up the breadcrumbs in the great hub of this mothership over these spring and summer months, and how familiar and stamped you are into *all* of our collective DNA. . . .

I'm just plain proud. So. Where are we now? Well, I know you aren't here tonight, but somehow, no matter. We are. And you brought us out of the wainscotting like so many freaky old bastards. Like so many fan boys and girls. Like so many loners and pretty things and dandies and dudes and dukes and duckies and testicular types. And pulled us together.

Together. By you. Dave Jones. Our not-so-absent, not-so-invisible, friend. Every alien's favourite cousin. Certainly mine.

We have a nice life.

Yours aye, Tilly

# IT FEELS OPPRESSIVE

In January 2014, during a televised interview on the subject of homophobia, Irish drag performer and activist Rory O'Neill accused two high-profile journalists, both of whom had publicly opposed same-sex marriage, of being homophobic. An immediate threat of legal action resulted in the broadcaster swiftly removing the episode from the airwaves, issuing an apology and paying a settlement, much to the chagrin of O'Neill. So much so that days later, dressed as his alter ego, Panti, he took to the stage after a performance of James Plunkett's play about the Dublin poor, *The Risen People*, and made his feelings known.

Hello. My name is Panti and for the benefit of the visually impaired or the incredibly naïve, I am a drag queen. I am also, I guess I would say, a performer of sorts and an accidental and occasional gay rights activist.

As you may have already gathered, I am also painfully middle class. My father was a country vet; I went to a nice school, and afterwards to that most middle class of institutions: art college. And although this may surprise some of you, I have always found gainful employment in my chosen field: gender discombobulation.

So the kind of grinding, abject poverty that we saw so powerfully on stage tonight is something I can thankfully say I have no experience of.

But I do know something about oppression, or at least oppression is something I can relate to. Now I am not for a minute going to compare my situation to Dublin workers of 1913, but I do know what it feels like to be put in your place.

Have any of you ever been standing at a pedestrian crossing when a car goes by and in it are a bunch of lads, and they lean out the window as they go by and they shout 'Fag!' and throw a milk carton at you?

Now it doesn't really hurt. I mean, after all, it's just a wet carton and anyway they're right – I am a fag. So it doesn't hurt. But it feels oppressive.

And when it really does hurt is afterwards, because it's afterwards I wonder and worry and obsess over what was it about me, what did they see in me? What was it that gave me away? And I hate myself for wondering that. It feels oppressive and the next time that I'm standing at a pedestrian crossing I hate myself for it but I check myself to see what is it about me that 'gives the gay away' and I check myself to make sure I'm not doing it this time.

Have any of you ever come home in the evening and turned on the television and there is a panel of people – nice people, respectable people, smart people – the kind of people who probably make good neighbourly neighbours, the kind of people who write for newspapers. And they are all sitting around and having a reasoned debate on the television, a reasoned debate about you. About what kind of a person you are, about whether or not you are capable of being a good parent, about whether you want to destroy marriage, about whether or not you are safe around children, about whether God herself thinks you are an abomination, about whether in fact maybe you are 'intrinsically disordered'. And even the nice TV presenter lady, who you feel is almost a friend because you see her being nice on TV all the time, even she thinks it's perfectly OK that they are all having this reasoned debate about who you are and what rights you 'deserved' or don't deserve.

And that feels oppressive.

Have you ever been on a crowded train with one of your best gay friends and a tiny part of you is cringing because he is being so gay and you find yourself trying to compensate for his gayness by butching up or by trying to steer the conversation onto safer, 'straighter' territory? And this is you who have spent the last thirty-five years of your life trying to be the best gay possible and yet there is still this small part of you that is embarrassed by his gayness.

And I hate myself for that. And that feels oppressive. And when I'm standing at the pedestrian bloody light I am checking myself.

Have you ever gone into your favourite neighbourhood café with the paper that you buy every day, and you open it up and inside is a 500-word opinion written by a nice middle-class woman, the kind of woman who probably gives to charity, the kind of woman who you would be totally happy to leave your children with. And she is arguing over 500 words so reasonably about whether or not you should be treated less than everybody else, arguing that you should be given fewer rights than everybody else. And when you read that, and the woman at the next table gets up and excuses herself to squeeze by you and smiles at you and you smile back and nod and say, 'no problem', and inside you wonder to yourself, 'Does she think that about me too?'

And that feels oppressive. And you go outside and you stand at the pedestrian crossing and you check yourself and I hate myself for that.

Have you ever turned on the computer and you see videos of people just like you in countries that are far away, and countries not far away at all, and they are being imprisoned and beaten and tortured and murdered and executed because they are just like you?

And that feels oppressive.

Three weeks ago I was on the television and I said that I believed that people who actively campaign for gay people to be treated less or treated differently are, in my gay opinion, homophobic. Some people, people who actively campaign for gay people to be treated less under the law, took great exception to that characterisation and they threatened legal action against me and RTÉ. RTÉ, in its wisdom, decided incredibly quickly to hand over a huge sum of money to make it all go away. I haven't been quite so lucky.

→ Panti Bliss, 2016, photographed by Sally Jubb

And for the last three weeks I have been lectured to by heterosexual people about what homophobia is and about who is allowed to identify it. Straight people have lined up – ministers, senators, barristers, journalists – have lined up to tell me what homophobia is and to tell me what I am allowed to feel oppressed by. People who have never experienced homophobia in their lives, people who have never checked themselves at a pedestrian crossing, have told me that unless I am being thrown into prison or herded onto a cattle train, then it is not homophobia.

And that feels oppressive.

So now Irish gay people, we find ourselves in this ludicrous situation where we are not only not allowed to say publicly what we feel oppressed by, we are not even allowed to think it because the very definition, our definition, has been disallowed by our betters.

And for the last three weeks I have been denounced from the floor of the Oireachtas* to newspaper columns to the seething morass of internet commentary, denounced for using 'hate speech' because I dared to use the word 'homophobia'. And a jumped-up queer like me should know that the word 'homophobia' is no longer available to gay people. Which is a spectacular and neat Orwellian trick because now it turns out that gay people are not the victims of homophobia – homophobes are the victims of homophobia.

But let me just say that it is not true. Because I don't hate you.

I do, it is true, believe that almost all of you are probably homophobes. But I'm a homophobe. I mean, it would be incredible if we weren't. I mean, to grow up in a society that is overwhelmingly and stiflingly homophobic and to somehow escape unscathed would be miraculous. So I don't hate you because you are a homophobe. I actually admire you. I admire you because most of you are only a bit homophobic. And to be honest, considering the circumstances, that is pretty good going.

But I do sometimes hate myself. I hate myself because I fucking check myself when standing at pedestrian crossings. And sometimes I hate you for doing that to me.

But not right now. Right now, I like you all very much for giving me a few moments of your time. And for that I thank you.

* The Oireachtas, or parliament, in Ireland is made up of the Dáil, its lower house; the Seanad, its upper house; and the president.

# I AM ALWAYS OFFENDED BY SEXISM

When, in 2012, it was revealed that the Speaker of the Australian House of Representatives, Peter Slipper, had sent sexually offensive text messages to an aide, Australian Prime Minister Julia Gillard found herself under attack in Parliament from the Leader of the Opposition, Tony Abbott. He told all assembled that each day Gillard continued to support the Speaker was "another day of shame for a government which should already have died of shame." Gillard responded with a fifteen-minute speech that was fueled by fury – an eloquent takedown in which she methodically accused Abbott of hypocrisy, and which will forever be remembered as her defining moment.

Thank you very much, Deputy Speaker, and I rise to oppose the motion moved by the Leader of the Opposition. And in so doing I say to the Leader of the Opposition I will not be lectured about sexism and misogyny by this man. I will not. And the Government will not be lectured about sexism and misogyny by this man. Not now, not ever.

The Leader of the Opposition says that people who hold sexist views and who are misogynists are not appropriate for high office. Well, I hope the Leader of the Opposition has got a piece of paper and he is writing out his resignation. Because if he wants to know what misogyny looks like in modern Australia, he doesn't need a motion in the House of Representatives, he needs a mirror. That's what he needs.

Let's go through the opposition leader's repulsive double standards, repulsive double standards when it comes to misogyny and sexism. We are now supposed to take seriously that the leader of the opposition is offended by Mr Slipper's text messages, when this is the Leader of the Opposition who has said, and this was when he was a minister under the last government – not when he was a student, not when he was in high school – when he was a minister under the last government.

He has said, and I quote, in a discussion about women being under-represented in institutions of power in Australia – the interviewer was a man called Stavros – the Leader of the Opposition says, 'If it's true, Stavros, that men have more power generally speaking than women, is that a bad thing?'

And then a discussion ensues, and another person says, 'I want my daughter to have as much opportunity as my son.' To which the Leader of the Opposition says, 'Yeah, I completely agree, but what if men are, by physiology or temperament, more adapted to exercise authority or to issue command?'

Then ensues another discussion about women's role in modern society, and the other person participating in the discussion says, 'I think it's very hard to deny that there is an underrepresentation of women,' to which the Leader of the Opposition says, 'But now, there's an assumption that this is a bad thing.'

This is the man from whom we're supposed to take lectures about sexism. And then of course it goes on. I was very offended personally when the Leader of the Opposition, as Minister of Health, said, and I quote, 'Abortion is the easy way out.' I was very personally offended by those comments. You said that in March 2004, I suggest you check the records.

I was also very offended on behalf of the women of Australia when in the course of this carbon pricing campaign, the Leader of the Opposition said, 'What the housewives of Australia need to understand as they do the ironing. . . .' Thank you for that painting of women's roles in modern Australia.

And then of course, I was offended too by the sexism, by the misogyny of the Leader of the Opposition catcalling across this table at me as I sit here as Prime Minister, 'If the Prime Minister wants to, politically speaking, make an honest woman of herself . . .', something that would never have been said to any man sitting in this chair. I was offended when the Leader of the Opposition went outside in the front of Parliament and stood next to a sign that said 'Ditch the witch'.

I was offended when the Leader of the Opposition stood next to a sign that described me as a man's bitch. I was offended by those things. Misogyny, sexism, every day from this Leader of the Opposition. Every day in every way, across the time the Leader of the Opposition has sat in that chair and I've sat in this chair, that is all we have heard from him.

And now, the Leader of the Opposition wants to be taken seriously; apparently he's woken up after this track record and all of these statements, he's woken up and he's gone, 'Oh dear, there's this thing called sexism, oh my lord, there's this thing called misogyny. Now who's one of them? Oh, the Speaker must be because that suits my political purpose.'

Doesn't turn a hair about any of his past statements, doesn't walk into this Parliament and apologise to the women of Australia. Doesn't walk into this Parliament and apologise to me for the things that have come out of his mouth. But now seeks to use this as a battering ram against someone else.

Well, this kind of hypocrisy should not be tolerated, which is why this motion from the Leader of the Opposition should not be taken seriously.

And then second, the Leader of the Opposition is always wonderful about walking into this Parliament and giving me and others a lecture about what they should take responsibility for.

Always wonderful about that – everything that I should take responsibility for, now apparently including the text messages of the Member for Fisher [Peter Slipper]. Always keen to say others should assume responsibility, particularly me.

Well, can anybody remind me if the Leader of the Opposition has taken any responsibility for the conduct of the Sydney Young Liberals and the attendance at this event of members of his frontbench?

→ Prime Minister Julia Gillard speaks at Parliament House in Canberra, October 9, 2012, photographed by Lukas Coch

Has he taken any responsibility for the conduct of members of his political party and members of his frontbench who apparently, when the most vile things were being said about my family, raised no voice of objection? No one walked out of the room; no one walked up to Mr Jones and said that this was not acceptable.*

Instead of course, it was all viewed as good fun until it was run in a Sunday newspaper and then the Leader of the Opposition and others started ducking for cover.

Big on lectures of responsibility, very light on accepting responsibility himself for the vile conduct of members of his political party.

Third, Deputy Speaker, why the Leader of the Opposition should not be taken seriously on this motion.

The Leader of the Opposition and the Deputy Leader of the Opposition have come into this place and have talked about the Member for Fisher. Well, let me remind the Opposition and the Leader of the Opposition particularly about their track record and association with the Member for Fisher.

I remind them that the National Party preselected the Member for Fisher for the 1984 election, that the National Party preselected the Member for Fisher for the 1987 election, that the Liberal party preselected Mr Slipper for the 1993 election, then for the 1996 election, then for the 1998 election, then for the 2001 election, then for the 2004 election, then for the 2007 election and then for the 2010 election.

And across many of those preselections, Mr Slipper enjoyed the personal support of the Leader of the Opposition. I remind the Leader of the Opposition that on 28 September 2010, following the last election campaign, when Mr Slipper was elected as Deputy Speaker, the Leader of the Opposition at that stage said this, and I quote.

He referred to the Member for Maranoa, who was also elected to a position at the same time, and then went on as follows: 'And the Member for Fisher will serve as a fine complement to the Member for Scullin in the chair. I believe that the Parliament will be well served by the team which will occupy the chair in this chamber. I congratulate the Member for Fisher, who has been a friend of mine for a very long time, who has served this Parliament in many capacities with distinction.'

The words of the Leader of the Opposition on record, about his personal friendship with Mr Slipper, and on record about his view about Mr Slipper's qualities and attributes to be the Speaker.

No walking away from those words, they were the statement of the Leader of the Opposition then. I remind the Leader of the Opposition, who now comes in here and speaks about Mr Slipper and apparently his inability to work with or talk to Mr Slipper, I remind the Leader of the Opposition he attended Mr Slipper's wedding. Did he walk up to Mr Slipper in the middle of the service

* In September 2012, at a Sydney University Liberal club dinner, conservative broadcaster Alan Jones was recorded saying that Julia Gillard's recently deceased father had "died of shame."

and say he was disgusted to be there? Was that the attitude he took? No, he attended that wedding as a friend.

The Leader of the Opposition is keen to lecture others about what they ought to know or did know about Mr Slipper. Well, with respect, I'd say to the Leader of the Opposition that after a long personal association including attending Mr Slipper's wedding, it would be interesting to know whether the Leader of the Opposition was surprised by these text messages. He's certainly in a position to speak more intimately about Mr Slipper than I am, and many other people in this Parliament, given this long personal association.

Then of course the Leader of the Opposition comes into this place and says, and I quote, 'Every day the Prime Minister stands in this Parliament to defend this Speaker will be another day of shame for this Parliament, another day of shame for a government which should already have died of shame.'

Well, can I indicate to the Leader of the Opposition the Government is not dying of shame, my father did not die of shame, what the Leader of the Opposition should be ashamed of is his performance in this Parliament and the sexism he brings with it.

Now about the text messages that are on the public record or reported in the . . . That's a direct quote from the Leader of the Opposition so I suggest those groaning have a word with him.

On the conduct of Mr Slipper, and on the text messages that are in the public domain, I have seen the press reports of those text messages. I am offended by their content. I am offended by their content because I am always offended by sexism. I am offended by their content because I am always offended by statements that are anti-women.

I am offended by those things in the same way that I have been offended by things that the Leader of the Opposition has said, and no doubt will continue to say in the future. Because if this today was an exhibition of his new feminine side, well, I don't think we've got much to look forward to in terms of changed conduct.

I am offended by those text messages. But I also believe, in terms of this Parliament making a decision about the speakership, that this Parliament should recognise that there is a court case in progress. That the judge has reserved his decision, that having waited for a number of months for the legal matters surrounding Mr Slipper to come to a conclusion, that this Parliament should see that conclusion.

I believe that is the appropriate path forward, and that people will then have an opportunity to make up their minds with the fullest information available to them.

But whenever people make up their minds about those questions, what I won't stand for, what I will never stand for is the Leader of the Opposition coming into this place and peddling a double standard. Peddling a standard for

Mr Slipper he would not set for himself. Peddling a standard for Mr Slipper he has not set for other members of his frontbench.

Peddling a standard for Mr Slipper that has not been acquitted by the people who have been sent out to say the vilest and most revolting things like his former Shadow Parliamentary Secretary Senator Bernardi.

I will not ever see the Leader of the Opposition seek to impose his double standard on this Parliament. Sexism should always be unacceptable. We should conduct ourselves as it should always be unacceptable. The Leader of the Opposition says do something; well, he could do something himself if he wants to deal with sexism in this Parliament.

He could change his behaviour, he could apologise for all his past statements, he could apologise for standing next to signs describing me as a witch and a bitch, terminology that is now objected to by the frontbench of the Opposition.

He could change a standard himself if he sought to do so. But we will see none of that from the Leader of the Opposition because on these questions he is incapable of change. Capable of double standards, but incapable of change. His double standards should not rule this Parliament.

Good sense, common sense, proper process is what should rule this Parliament. That's what I believe is the path forward for this Parliament, not the kind of double standards and political game-playing imposed by the Leader of the Opposition now looking at his watch because apparently a woman's spoken too long.

I've had him yell at me to shut up in the past, but I will take the remaining seconds of my speaking time to say to the Leader of the Opposition I think the best course for him is to reflect on the standards he's exhibited in public life; on the responsibility he should take for his public statements; on his close personal connection with Peter Slipper; on the hypocrisy he has displayed in this House today.

And on that basis, because of the Leader of the Opposition's motivations, this Parliament today should reject this motion and the Leader of the Opposition should think seriously about the role of women in public life and in Australian society because we are entitled to a better standard than this.

# THE SECRET LIFE OF THE LOVE SONG

In 1998, Australian musician Nick Cave was invited by the Vienna Poetry Academy to host a series of song-writing classes with a group of aspiring lyricists, which would be preceded by a lecture of his choosing. He accepted, and began by delivering a long, rich and invaluable talk about the love song that drew on both his award-winning, decades-long career as a singer-songwriter and the notable love songs of others to explore their everlasting appeal. A year later he revived the speech, in slightly revised form, at London's Royal Festival Hall.

With a crooked smile and a heart-shaped face
Comes from the West Country where the birds sing bass
She's got a house-big heart where we all live
And plead and counsel and forgive
Her widow's peak, her lips I've kissed
Her glove of bones at her wrist
That I have held in my hand
Her Spanish fly and her monkey gland
Her Godly body and its fourteen stations
That I have embraced, her palpitations
Her unborn baby crying, 'Mummy'
Amongst the rubble of her body
Her lovely lidded eyes I've sipped
Her fingernails, all pink and chipped
Her accent which I'm told is 'broad'
That I have heard and has been poured
Into my human heart and filled me
With love, up to the brim, and killed me
And rebuilt me back anew
With something to look forward to
Well, who could ask much more than that?
A West Country girl with a big fat cat
That looks into her eyes of green
And meows, 'He loves you,' then meows again

That was a song called 'West Country Girl'. It is a Love Song.

It began, in its innocence, as a poem, written about two years ago in Australia, where the sun shines. I wrote it with my heart in my mouth, detailing in list form the physical details which drew me toward a particular person . . . the West Country Girl. It set forth my own personal criteria of beauty, my own particular truth about beauty, as angular, cruel and impoverished as it probably was. It was a list of things I loved, and, in truth, a wretched exercise in flattery, designed to win the girl. And it worked and it didn't work. But the peculiar magic of the Love Song, if it has the heart to do it, is that it endures where the object of the song does not. It attaches itself to you and together you move through time. But it does more than that, for just as it is our task to move forward, to cast off our past, to change and to grow, in short, to forgive ourselves and each other, the Love Song holds within it an eerie intelligence all of its own – to reinvent the past and to lay it at the feet of the present.

'West Country Girl' began in innocence and in sunshine, as a simple poem about a girl. But it has done what all true Love Songs must do in order to survive, it has demanded the right to its own identity, its own life, its own truth. I've seen it grow and mutate with time. It presents itself now as a cautionary tale, as a list of ingredients in a witches' brew, it reads as a coroner's report or a message on a sandwich-board worn by a wild-eyed man who states, 'The End of the World is at Hand'. It is a hoarse voice in the dark that croaks, 'Beware . . . beware . . . beware.'

Anyway, I'm getting ahead of myself. My name is Nick Cave, and I've got a few things to tell you.

> People just ain't no good
> I think that's well understood
> You can see it everywhere you look
> People just ain't no good
>
> We were married under cherry trees
> Under blossom we made our vows
> All the blossoms come sailing down
> Through the streets and through the playgrounds
>
> The sun would stream on the sheets
> Awoken by the morning bird
> We'd buy the Sunday newspapers
> And never read a single word
>
> People they ain't no good
> People they ain't no good
> People they ain't no good
>
> Seasons came, seasons went
> The winter stripped the blossoms bare
> A different tree now lines the streets
> Shaking its fists in the air

The winter slammed us like a fist
The windows rattling in the gales
To which she drew the curtains
Made out of her wedding veils

People they ain't no good
People they ain't no good
People they ain't no good

To our love send a dozen white lilies
To our love send a coffin of wood
To our love let all the pink-eyed pigeons coo
That people they just ain't no good
To our love send back all the letters
To our love a valentine of blood
To our love let all the jilted lovers cry
That people they just ain't no good

It ain't that in their hearts they're bad
They can comfort you, some even try
They nurse you when you're ill of health
They bury you when you go and die
It ain't that in their hearts they're bad
They'd stick by you if they could
But that's just bullshit, baby
People just ain't no good

People they ain't no good
People they ain't no good
People they ain't no good
People they ain't no good

I performed an earlier, more conservative, lo-tech version of this lecture at the Poetry Academy in Vienna last year. I was invited to go there and actually teach a group of adult students about songwriting. But first they wanted me to give a public lecture. The subject I chose was the Love Song, and in doing it – I mean, standing up in front of a crowd of people and teaching, lecturing – I was filled with a host of conflicting feelings. The strongest, most insistent of these feelings was one of abject horror. Horror, because my late father was an English literature teacher at the high school I attended back in Australia – you know, where the sun shines. I have very clear memories of being about twelve years old and sitting, as you are now, in a classroom or hall, watching my father, who would be standing, up here, where I am standing, and thinking to myself, gloomily and miserably – for, in the main, I was a gloomy and miserable child – 'It doesn't really matter what I do with my life as long as I don't end up like my father.' Now, at forty-one years old, it would appear that there is virtually no action I can take that does not draw me closer to him, that does not make me more like him. At forty-one years of age I have become my father, and here I am, ladies and gentlemen, teaching.

Looking back over the last twenty years, a certain clarity prevails. Amidst the madness and the mayhem, it would seem I have been banging on one particular drum. I see that my artistic life has centred around an attempt to articulate an almost palpable sense of loss which laid claim to my life. A great gaping hole was blasted out of my world by the unexpected death of my father when I was nineteen years old. The way I learned to fill this hole, this void, was to write. My father taught me this as if to prepare me for his own passing. Writing allowed me direct access to my imagination, to inspiration and, ultimately, to God. I found that through the use of language I was writing God into existence. Language became the blanket that I threw over the invisible man, which gave him shape and form. The actualizing of God through the medium of the Love Song remains my prime motivation as an artist. I found that language became a poultice to the wounds incurred by the death of my father. Language became a salve to longing.

The loss of my father created in my life a vacuum, a space in which my words began to float and collect and find their purpose. The great W. H. Auden said, 'the so-called traumatic experience is not an accident, but the opportunity for which the child has been patiently waiting – had it not occurred, it would have found another – in order that its life become a serious matter.' The death of my father was the 'traumatic experience' Auden talks about which left the hole for God to fill. How beautiful the notion that we create our own personal catastrophes and that it is the creative forces within us that are instrumental in doing this. Here our creative impulses lie in ambush at the side of our lives, ready to leap forth and kick holes in it – holes through which inspiration can rise. We each have our need to create, and sorrow itself is a creative act.

Though the Love Song comes in many guises – songs of exaltation and praise, songs of rage and of despair, erotic songs, songs of abandonment and loss – they all address God, for it is the haunted premise of longing that the true Love Song inhabits. It is a howl in the void for love and for comfort, and it lives on the lips of the child crying for his mother. It is the song of the lover in need of their loved one, the raving of the lunatic supplicant petitioning his god. It is the cry of one chained to the earth and craving flight, a flight into inspiration and imagination and divinity.

The Love Song is the sound of our endeavours to become God-like, to rise up and above the earth-bound and the mediocre. I believe the Love Song to be a sad song. It is the noise of sorrow itself.

We all experience within us what the Portuguese call 'saudade', which translates as an inexplicable longing, an unnamed and enigmatic yearning of the soul, and it is this feeling that lives in the realms of imagination and inspiration and is the breeding ground for the sad song, for the Love Song. 'Saudade' is the desire to be transported from darkness into light, to be touched by the hand of that which is not of this world. The Love Song is the light of God, deep down, blasting up through our wounds.

In his brilliant lecture entitled 'The Theory and Function of Duende', Federico García Lorca attempts to shed some light on the eerie and inexplicable sadness that lives at the heart of certain works of art. 'All that has dark sounds has "duende"', he says, 'that mysterious power that everyone feels but no philosopher can explain.' In contemporary rock music, the area in which I operate, music seems less inclined to have at its soul, restless and quivering, the sadness that Lorca talks about. Excitement, often; anger, sometimes – but true sadness, rarely. Bob Dylan has always had it. Leonard Cohen deals specifically with it. It pursues Van Morrison like a black dog and, though he tries to, he cannot escape it. Tom Waits and Neil Young can summon it. My friends The Dirty Three have it by the bucket-load but, all in all, it would appear that 'duende' is too fragile to survive the compulsive modernity of the music industry. In the hysterical technocracy of modern music, sorrow is sent to the back of the class, where it sits, pissing its pants in mortal terror. Sadness or 'duende' needs space to breathe. Melancholy hates haste and floats in silence. I feel sorry for sadness, as we jump all over it, denying it its voice, and muscling it into the outer reaches. No wonder sorrow doesn't smile much. No wonder sadness is so sad.

All Love Songs must contain 'duende' because the Love Song is never simply happy. It must first embrace the potential for pain. Those songs that speak of love, without having within their lines an ache or a sigh, are not Love Songs at all, but rather Hate Songs disguised as Love Songs and are not to be trusted. These songs deny us our human-ness and our God-given right to be sad, and the airwaves are littered with them. The Love Song must resonate with the whispers of sorrow and the echoes of grief. The writer who refuses to explore the darker regions of the heart will never be able to write convincingly about the wonder, the magic and the joy of love, for just as goodness cannot be trusted unless it has breathed the same air as evil – the enduring metaphor of Christ crucified between two criminals comes to mind here – so within the fabric of the Love Song, within its melody, its lyric, one must sense an acknowledgement of its capacity for suffering.

> Down the road I look and there runs Mary
> Hair of gold and lips like cherries
> We go down to the river where the willows weep

Take a naked root for a lovers' seat
That rose out of the bitten soil
But bound to the ground by creeping ivy coils
O Mary you have seduced my soul
Forever a hostage of your child's world

And then I ran my tin-cup heart along
The prison of her ribs
And with a toss of her curls
That little girl goes wading in
Rolling her dress up past her knee
Turning these waters into wine
Then she plaited all the willow vines
Mary in the shallows laughing
Over where the carp dart
Spooked by the new shadows that she cast
Across these sad waters and across my heart

Around the age of twenty, I started reading the Bible, and I found in the brutal prose of the Old Testament, in the feel of its words and its imagery, an endless source of inspiration, especially in the remarkable series of Love Songs/poems known as the Psalms. I found the Psalms, which deal directly with the relationship between man and God, teeming with all the clamorous desperation, longing, exhaltation, erotic violence and brutality that I could hope for. The Psalms are soaked in 'saudade', drenched in 'duende' and bathed in bloody-minded violence. In a lot of ways these songs became the blueprint for many of my more sadistic Love Songs. Psalm 137, a particular favourite of mine, which was turned into a chart hit by the fab little band Boney M., is a perfect example of this.

By the rivers of Babylon, there we sat down, yea,
We wept, when we remembered Zion
We hanged our harps upon the willows in the midst thereof
For there they that carried us away captive required
Of us a song; and they that wasted us required of us
Mirth saying, Sing us one of the songs of Zion.
How shall we sing the Lord's song in a strange land?
If I forget thee, O Jerusalem. Let my right hand
Forget her cunning.
If I do not remember thee, let my tongue cleave to
The roof of my mouth: If I prefer not Jerusalem above my chief joy
Remember, O Lord, the children of Edom in the

Day of Jerusalem; who said Rase it, rase it, even to
The foundation thereof.
Daughter of Babylon, who art to be destroyed;
Happy shall he be, that rewardeth thee as thou hast
Served us.
Happy shall he be, that taketh and dasheth thy little
Ones against the stones.

Here, the poet finds himself captive in 'a strange land' and is forced to sing a song of Zion. He declares his love to his homeland and dreams of revenge. The psalm is ghastly in its violent sentiments, as he sings to his God for deliverance, and that he may be made happy by murdering the children of his enemies. What I found, time and time again in the Bible, especially in the Old Testament, was that verses of rapture, of ecstasy and love could hold within them apparently opposite sentiments – hate, revenge, bloody-mindedness, etc. – these sentiments were not mutually exclusive. This idea has left an enduring impression upon my song-writing.

The Love Song must be borne into the realm of the irrational, the absurd, the distracted, the melancholic, the obsessive and the insane, for the Love Song is the clamour of love itself, and love is, of course, a form of madness. Whether it is the love of God, or romantic erotic love – these are manifestations of our need to be torn away from the rational, to take leave of our senses, so to speak. Love Songs come in many forms and are written for a host of reasons, as declarations of love or revenge, to praise or to wound or to flatter – I have written songs for all these reasons – but ultimately the Love Song exists to fill, with language, the silence between ourselves and God, to decrease the distance between the temporal and the divine.

But, within the world of modern pop music, a world that deals ostensibly with the Love Song, true sorrow is just not welcome. Of course, there are exceptions, and occasionally a song comes along that hides behind its disposable plastic beat, a love lyric of truly devastating proportions. 'Better the Devil You Know', written by the hit-makers Stock, Aitken & Waterman and sung by the Australian pop sensation Kylie Minogue, is such a song. The disguising of the terror of love in a piece of mindless, innocuous pop music is an intriguing concept. 'Better the Devil You Know' contains one of pop music's most violent and distressing love lyrics.

Say you won't leave me no more
I'll take you back again
No more excuses, no, no
'Cos I heard them all before
A hundred times or more

I'll forgive and forget
If you say you'll never go
'Cos it's true what they say
It's better the devil you know

Our love wasn't perfect I know
I think I know the score
If you say you love me, Oh boy
I can't ask for more
I'll come if you should call

I'll be here every day
Waiting for your love to show
Yes it's true what they say
Better the devil you know

I'll take you back
I'll take you back again

When Kylie Minogue sings these words there is an innocence to her voice that makes the horror of this chilling lyric all the more compelling. The idea presented within this song – dark and sinister and sad – that love relationships are by nature abusive, and this abuse, be it physical or psychological, is welcomed and encouraged, shows how even the most seemingly harmless of Love Songs has the potential to hide terrible human truths. Like Prometheus chained to his rock, the eagle eating his liver night after night, Kylie becomes Love's sacrificial lamb, bleating an earnest invitation to the drooling, ravenous wolf, to devour her time and time again, all to a groovy techno beat. 'I'll take you back. I'll take you back again.' Indeed. Here the Love Song becomes a vehicle for a harrowing portrait of humanity, not dissimilar to the Old Testament Psalms. Both are messages to God that cry out into the yawning void, in anguish and self-loathing, for deliverance.

　　As I said earlier, my artistic life has centred around the desire or, more accurately, the need, to articulate the various feelings of loss and longing that have whistled through my bones and hummed in my blood throughout my life. In the process I have written about 200 songs, the bulk of which I would say were Love Songs. Love Songs, and therefore, by my definition, sad songs. Out of this considerable mass of material, a handful of them rise above the others as true examples of all I have talked about. 'Sad Waters', 'Black Hair', 'I Let Love In', 'Deanna', 'From Her To Eternity', 'Nobody's Baby Now', 'Into My Arms', 'Lime Tree Arbour', 'Lucy', 'Straight To You'. I am proud of these songs. They are my gloomy, violent, dark-eyed children. They sit grimly on their own and do not

→ Nick Cave, 1999,
photographed by
Polly Borland

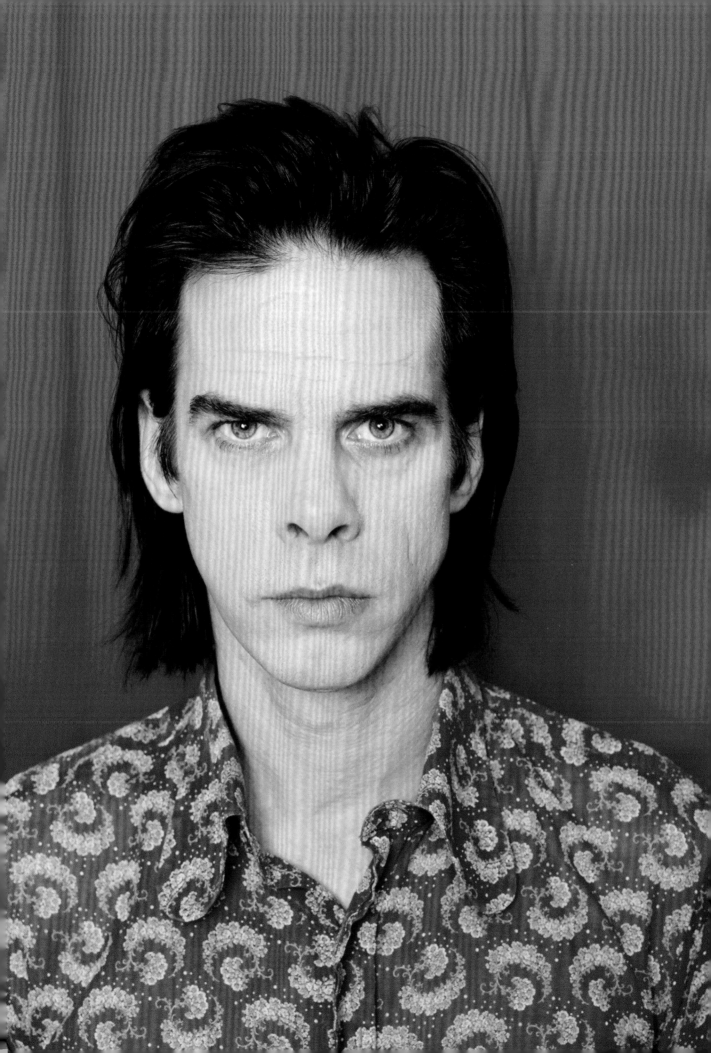

play with the other songs. Mostly they were the offspring of complicated pregnancies and difficult and painful births. Most of them are rooted in direct personal experience and were conceived for a variety of reasons, but this rag-tag group of Love Songs are, at the death, all the same thing – lifelines thrown into the galaxies by a drowning man.

Here, ladies and gentlemen, is a new one.

I hold this letter in my hand
A plea, a petition, a kind of prayer
I hope it does as I have planned
Losing her again is more than I can bear
I kiss the cold, white envelope
I press my lips against her name
Two hundred words. We live in hope
The sky hangs heavy with rain

Love Letter Love Letter
Go get her Go get her
Love Letter Love Letter
Go tell her Go tell her

A wicked wind whips up the hill
A handful of hopeful words
I love her and I always will
The sky is ready to burst
Said something I did not mean to say
Said something I did not mean to say
Said something I did not mean to say
It all came out the wrong way

Love Letter Love Letter
Go get her Go get her
Love Letter Love Letter
Go tell her Go tell her

Rain your kisses down upon me
Rain your kisses down in storms
And for all who'll come before me
In your slowly fading forms
I'm going out of my mind
Will leave me standing in
The rain with a letter and a prayer

Whispered on the wind
Come back to me
Come back to me
O baby please come back to me

The reasons I feel compelled to write Love Songs are legion. Some of these became clearer to me when I sat down with a friend of mine who, for the sake of his anonymity, I will refer to as 'G'. 'G' and I admitted to each other that we both suffered from the psychological disorder that the medical profession terms 'Erotigraphomania'. Erotigraphomania is the obsessive desire to write Love Letters. 'G' shared with me the fact that he had written and sent, over the last five years, more than 7,000 Love Letters to his wife. My friend looked exhausted, and his shame was almost palpable. We discussed the power of the Love Letter and found that it was, not surprisingly, very similar to that of the Love Song. Both serve as extended meditations on one's beloved. Both serve to shorten the distance between the writer and the recipient. Both hold within them a permanence and power that the spoken word does not. Both are erotic exercises in themselves. Both have the potential to reinvent, through words, like Pygmalion with his self-created lover of stone, one's beloved. But more than that, both have the insidious power to imprison one's beloved, to bind their hands with love-lines, gag them, blind them, for words become the defining parameter that keeps the image of the loved one, imprisoned in a bondage of poetry. 'I have taken possession of you,' the Love Letter, the Love Song, whispers, 'for ever.' These stolen souls we set adrift like lost astronauts floating for eternity through the stratospheres of the divine. Me, I never trust a woman who writes letters, because I know that I myself cannot be trusted. Words endure, flesh does not. The poet will always have the upper hand. Me, I'm a soul-catcher for God. Here I come with my butterfly-net of words. Here I catch the chrysalis. Here I blow life into bodies and hurl them fluttering to the stars and the care of God.

I'd like to look finally at a song I wrote for the *Boatman's Call* album. It is called 'Far From Me', and I have a few things to tell you about it.

For you, dear, I was born
For you I was raised up
For you I've lived and for you I will die
For you I am dying now
You were my mad little lover
In a world where everybody fucks everybody else over
You who are so
Far from me
So far from me

Way across some cold neurotic sea
Far from me
I would talk to you of all manner of things
With a smile you would reply
Then the sun would leave your pretty face
And you'd retreat from the front of your eyes
I keep hearing that you're doing your best
I hope your heart beats happy in your infant breast
You are so far from me
Far from me
Far from me

There is no knowledge but I know it
There's nothing to learn from that vacant voice
That sails to me across the line
From the ridiculous to the sublime
It's good to hear you're doing so well
But really, can't you find somebody else that you can ring and tell?
Did you ever care for me?
Were you ever there for me?
So far from me

You told me you'd stick by me
Through the thick and through the thin
Those were your very words
My fair-weather friend
You were my brave-hearted lover
At the first taste of trouble went running back to mother
So far from me
Far from me
Suspended in your bleak and fishless sea
Far from me
Far from me

'Far From Me' took four months to write, which was the duration of the relationship it describes.

    The first verse was written in the first week of the affair and is full of all the heroic drama of new love, describing the totality of feeling whilst acknowledging its parallel pain – 'for you I'm dying now.' It sets the two lover-heroes against an uncaring world – 'a world that fucks everybody over' – and brings in the notion of the physical distance suggested in the title. Verse one, and all is well in the garden. But the thing is, 'Far From Me' had its own agenda and was not about to allow itself to be told what to do. The song, as if awaiting the inevitable 'traumatic experience', simply refused to let itself be completed until the catastrophe had occurred. Some songs are tricky like that, and it is wise to keep your wits about you when dealing with them. I find more often than not that the songs I write seem to know more about what's going on in my life than I do. I have pages and pages of final verses for this song, written while the relationship was still sailing happily along. One such verse went:

> The Camellia, the Magnolia
> Have such a pretty flower
> And the bell from St Mary's
> Informs us of the hour

Pretty words, innocent words, unaware that any day the bottom was about to drop out of the whole thing. As I wrote the final verse of 'Far From Me' it became clear that my life was being dictated by the largely destructive ordinance of the song itself, that it had its own inbuilt destiny, over which I had no control. In fact, I was an afterthought, a bit-part player in its sly, mischievous and finally malicious vision of how the world should be.

Love Songs that attach themselves to actual experience, which are a poeticizing of real events, have a beauty unto themselves. They stay alive in the same way that memories do and, being alive, they grow up and undergo changes and develop. If a song is too weak to do that, if it is lacking in sufficient stamina and the will to endure, sadly, it will not survive. You'll come home one day and find it dead in the bottom of its cage. Its soul will have been reclaimed and all that will remain is a pile of useless words. A Love Song such as 'Far From Me' demanded a personality beyond the one I originally gave it, with the power to influence my own feelings and thoughts around the actual event itself. The songs that I have written that deal with past relationships have become the relationships themselves, heroically mutating with time and mythologising the ordinary events of my life, lifting them from the temporal plane and blasting them way into the stars. As the relationship itself collapses, whimpering with exhaustion, the song breaks free of it and beats its wings heavenward. Such is the singular beauty of song-writing.

Twenty years of song-writing have now passed, and still the void gapes wide. Still the inexplicable sadness, the 'duende', the 'saudade', the divine discontent, persists, and perhaps it will continue until I see the face of God himself. But when Moses desired to see the face of God, he was answered that he may not endure it, that no man could see the face of God and live. Well, me, I don't mind. I'm happy to be sad. For the residue, cast off in this search, the songs themselves, my crooked brood of sad-eyed children, rally round and, in their way, protect me, comfort me and keep me alive. They are the companions of the soul that lead it into exile, that sate the overpowering yearning for that which is not of this world. The imagination demands an alternate world and through the writing of the Love Song one sits and dines with loss and longing, madness and melancholy, ecstasy, magic and joy with equal measure of respect and gratitude.

# WRITING FOR THEATRE

By the time of his death in 2008, Harold Pinter had written twenty-nine plays, twenty-one screenplays, numerous works of fiction and poetry, and had directed twenty-seven theatre productions. His long career influenced and baffled in equal measure, and countless awards, including the Nobel Prize for Literature in 2005, met him en route. When he gave this insightful and rare speech to lucky attendees of the National Student Drama Festival in 1962, four years after the world premiere of perhaps his most famous work, *The Birthday Party*, 31-year-old Harold Pinter's career was still relatively young.

I'm not a theorist. I'm not an authoritative or reliable commentator on the dramatic scene, the social scene, any scene. I write plays, when I can manage it, and that's all. That's the sum of it.

I've had two full-length plays produced in London. The first ran a week, and the second ran a year. Of course, there are differences between the two plays. In *The Birthday Party* I employed a certain amount of dashes in the text, between phrases. In *The Caretaker* I cut out the dashes and used dots instead. So that instead of, say, 'Look, dash, who, dash, I, dash, dash, dash,' the text would read, 'Look, dot, dot, dot, who, dot, dot, dot, I, dot, dot, dot, dot.' So it's possible to deduce from this that dots are more popular than dashes, and that's why *The Caretaker* had a longer run than *The Birthday Party*. The fact that in neither case could you hear the dots and dashes in performance is beside the point. You can't fool the critics for long. They can tell a dot from a dash a mile off, even if they can hear neither.

It took me quite a while to grow used to the fact that critical and public response in the theatre follows a very erratic temperature chart. And the danger for a writer is where he becomes easy prey for the old bugs of apprehension and expectation in this connection. But I think Dusseldorf cleared the air for me. In Dusseldorf about two years ago I took, as is the continental custom, a bow with a German cast of *The Caretaker* at the end of the play on the first night. I was at once booed violently by what must have been the finest collection of booers in the world. I thought they were using megaphones, but it was pure mouth. The cast was as dogged as the audience, however, and we took thirty-four curtain calls, all to boos. By the thirty-fourth there were only two people left in the house, still booing. I was strangely warmed by all this, and now, whenever I sense a tremor of the old apprehension or expectation, I remember Dusseldorf, and am cured.

The theatre is a large, energetic, public activity. Writing is, for me, a completely private activity; a poem or a play, no difference. These facts are not easy to reconcile. The professional theatre, whatever the virtues it undoubtedly possesses, is a world of false climaxes, calculated tensions, some hysteria and a good deal of inefficiency. And the alarms of this world which I suppose I work in become steadily more widespread and intrusive. But basically my obligation has remained the same. What I write has no obligation to anything other than to itself. My responsibility is not to audiences, critics, producers, directors, actors or to my fellow men in general, but to the play in hand, simply.

I have usually begun a play in quite a simple manner; found a couple of characters in a particular context, thrown them together and listened to what they said, keeping my nose to the ground. The context has always been, for me, concrete and particular, and the characters concrete also. I've never started a play with any kind of abstract idea or theory. Apart from any other consideration, we are faced with the immense difficulty, if not the impossibility, of verifying the past. I don't mean merely years ago, but yesterday, this morning. What took place, what was the nature of what took place, what happened?

There is a considerable body of people just now who are asking for some kind of clear and sensible engagement to be evidently disclosed in contemporary plays. They want the playwright to be a prophet. There is certainly a good deal of prophecy indulged in by playwrights these days, in their plays and out of them. Warnings, sermons, admonitions, ideological exhortations, moral judgments, defined problems with built-in solutions; all can camp under the banner of prophecy. The attitude behind this sort of thing might be summed up in one phrase: 'I'm telling you!'

If I were to state any moral precept it might be: beware of the writer who puts forward his concern for you to embrace, who leaves you in no doubt of his worthiness, his usefulness, his altruism, who declares that his heart is in the right place, and ensures that it can be seen in full view, a pulsating mass where his characters ought to be. What is presented, so much of the time, as a body of active and positive thought is in fact a body lost in a prison of empty definition and cliché.

This kind of writer clearly trusts words absolutely. I have mixed feelings about words myself. Moving among them, sorting them out, watching them appear on the page, from this I derive a considerable pleasure. But at the same time I have another strong feeling about words which amounts to nothing less than nausea. Such a weight of words confronts us day in, day out, words spoken in a context such as this, words written by me and by others, the bulk of it a stale, dead terminology. Given this nausea, it's very easy to be overcome by it and step back into paralysis. I imagine most writers know something of this kind of paralysis. But if it is possible to confront this nausea, to follow it to its hilt, to move through it and out of it, then it is possible to say that something has occurred, that something has even been achieved.

Language, under these conditions, is a highly ambiguous business. So often, below the word spoken, is the thing known and unspoken. My characters tell me so much and no more, with reference to their experience, their

→ English playwright
Harold Pinter, 1960

aspirations, their motives, their history. Between my lack of biographical data about them and the ambiguity of what they say lies a territory which is not only worthy of exploration, but which it is compulsory to explore. You and I, the characters which grow on a page, most of the time we're inexpressive, giving little away, unreliable, elusive, obstructive, unwilling. But it's out of these attributes that a language arises. A language, I repeat, where under what is said, another thing is being said.

Given characters who possess a momentum of their own, my job is not to impose upon them, not to subject them to a false articulation. The relationship between author and characters should be a highly respectful one, both ways. And if it's possible to talk of gaining a kind of freedom from writing, it doesn't come by leading one's characters into fixed and calculated postures, but by allowing them to carry their own can, by giving them legitimate elbow-room. This can be extremely painful. It's much easier not to let them live.

I'd like to make quite clear at the same time that I don't regard my own characters as uncontrolled or anarchic. They're not. The function of selection and arrangement is mine. I do all the donkey-work, in fact, and I think I can say I pay meticulous attention to the shape of things, from the shape of a sentence to the overall structure of the play. This shaping is of the first importance. But I think a double thing happens. You arrange and you listen, following the clues you leave for yourself, through the characters. And sometimes a balance is found, where image can freely engender image and where at the same time you are able to keep your sights on the place where the characters are silent and in hiding. It is in the silence that they are most evident to me.

There are two silences. One when no word is spoken. The other when perhaps a torrent of language is being employed. The speech we hear is an indication of that which we don't hear. It is a necessary avoidance, a violent, sly, anguished or mocking smokescreen. When true silence falls, we are still left with echo but are nearer nakedness. One way of looking at speech is to say that it is a constant stratagem to cover nakedness.

We have heard many times that tired, grimy phrase, 'failure of communication', and this phrase has been fixed to my work quite consistently. I believe the contrary. I think that we communicate only too well, in our silence, in what is unsaid, and that what takes place is a continual evasion, desperate rearguard attempts to keep ourselves to ourselves. Communication is too alarming. To enter into someone else's life is too frightening. To disclose to others the poverty within us is too fearsome a possibility.

I am not suggesting that no character in a play can ever say what he in fact means. Not at all. I have found that there invariably does come a moment when this happens, when he says something, perhaps, which he has never said before. And where this happens, what he says is irrevocable, and can never be taken back.

A blank page is both an exciting and a frightening thing. It's what you start from. There follow two further periods in the progress of a play: the rehearsal period and the performance. A dramatist will absorb a great many things of value from an active and intense experience in the theatre, throughout these two periods. But finally, he is again left looking at the blank page. In that page is something or nothing. You don't know until you've covered it. And there's no guarantee that you will know then. But it always remains a chance worth taking.

# THE HEART AND STOMACH OF A KING

In August 1588, fully expectant that the Spanish Armada would soon invade the country and attempt to overthrow her on behalf of the Duke of Parma, the Queen of England, Elizabeth I, traveled to the village of Tilbury in Essex. She came to boost the morale of her army, many of whom were encamped on the Thames, ready to defend their country. This rousing speech was her rallying cry. The invasion was unsuccessful; Britain's win cemented Elizabeth's reputation as a force to be reckoned with. She remained in power until her death fifteen years later.

→ A transcript of the Queen's speech in the hand of Dr. Leonel Sharp, Chaplain to the Earl of Leicester, who was present at Tilbury

My loving people, We have been persuaded by some that are careful of our safety, to take heed how we commit ourselves to armed multitudes, for fear of treachery; but I assure you I do not desire to live to distrust my faithful and loving people. Let tyrants fear. I have always so behaved myself that, under God, I have placed my chiefest strength and safeguard in the loyal hearts and goodwill of my subjects; and therefore I am come amongst you, as you see, at this time, not for my recreation and disport, but being resolved, in the midst and heat of the battle, to live and die amongst you all; to lay down for my God, and for my kingdom, and my people, my honour and my blood, even in the dust.

I know I have the body but of a weak and feeble woman; but I have the heart and stomach of a king, and of a king of England too, and think foul scorn that Parma or Spain, or any prince of Europe, should dare to invade the borders of my realm: to which rather than any dishonour shall grow by me, I myself will take up arms, I myself will be your general, judge, and rewarder of every one of your virtues in the field.

I know already, for your forwardness you have deserved rewards and crowns; and We do assure you in the word of a prince, they shall be duly paid you. In the meantime, my lieutenant general shall be in my stead, than whom never prince commanded a more noble or worthy subject; not doubting but by your obedience to my general, by your concord in the camp, and your valour in the field, we shall shortly have a famous victory over those enemies of my God, of my kingdom, and of my people.

My louinge people, I haue bin perswaded by
som, yt are carefull of my saffty, to take heed
how I committed my selfe to armed multitudes for feare of treachery: Butt I tell you,
that I would not desyre to liue to distrust
my faythfull and louing people: lett tyrants feare: I haue so behaued my
selfe, yt vnder god I haue placed my
chiefest strength and safegard in ye loyall
harts and goodwill of my subiects: wher-
for I am com amoungst you all this tyme, for
my recreation and pleasure, being resolued
in ye middst and heate of yt battle to
liue and dye amoungst you all, to lay
down for my god, and for my kyng=
dom and for my people, myn honor
and my blood euen in ye dust: I know
I haue ye body butt of a weake and feble
woman, butt I haue yo harte and sto=
mark of a kinge, and of a kynge of
england too: and take foule scorn yt par=
ma or any prince of Europe should dare
to inuade ye borders of my realm:

# I STAND FOR PEACE AGAINST WAR

It was in France on January 9, 1949, that Spanish artist Pablo Picasso produced *La Colombe* – a delicately rendered dove that was soon used to illustrate the poster advertising the Paris Peace Congress that same year, and which led to Picasso's various doves becoming the organization's official emblem. A year after he created his lithograph, with the rapidly escalating Korean War at the forefront of many minds, Picasso accepted an invitation to the Peace Congress in Sheffield, England, and, despite his hatred of public speaking, gave a brief speech. It was met with a standing ovation.

← *La Colombe* by Pablo Picasso, 1949, lithograph on paper

Dear friends, I hope you will allow me to recall a personal memory.

My father, who lived in Barcelona, was a painter of animals. He was very fond of painting birds and, in particular, of painting doves. When his sight began to fail he handed his paintbrushes over to me and asked me to paint the delicate legs of the doves – a work he could no longer manage. When he found I was succeeding fairly well he gave up his paintbrushes and I took his place in the family of painters. How it would please him if he were alive today and could see how my modest doves have circled the world. I have contributed to the utmost of my ability, and with the same ardor that I have given to my art, to fight for the greatest and most just of all causes. I stand for life against death. I stand for peace against war.

I SELL THE SHADOW TO SUPPORT THE SUBSTANCE.

SOJOURNER TRUTH.

# THE WOMEN ARE COMING UP

Born into slavery circa 1797, it would be thirty long years until Sojourner Truth could escape and begin life as a free woman. By the time of her emancipation, as was the case with many former slaves, Truth could neither read nor write; what she did have, however, was a burning desire to fight for abolition and women's rights, to bring to an end the very conditions in which she began her life. Over the coming years and decades, Sojourner Truth did exactly that, giving impassioned speeches across the land and becoming one of the most recognized activists of the era. This was her most famous speech, delivered in May 1851 extemporaneously, with no script. It was published on June 21, 1851, in the Salem *Anti-Slavery Bugle*, just a few weeks later. As such, the accuracy of its wording will forever be debated to some extent – but not its heart.

May I say a few words? I want to say a few words about this matter.

I am a woman's rights.

I have as much muscle as any man, and can do as much work as any man. I have plowed and reaped and husked and chopped and mowed, and can any man do more than that?

I have heard much about the sexes being equal; I can carry as much as any man and can eat as much too, if I can get it. I am as strong as any man that is now.

As for intellect, all I can say is, *if women have a pint and man a quart – why can't she have her little pint full?* You need not be afraid to give us our rights for fear we will take too much, for we can't take more than our pint'll hold.

The poor men seem to be all in confusion, and don't know what to do. Why children, if you have woman's rights, give it to her and you will feel better. You will have your own rights, and they won't be so much trouble.

I can't read, but I can hear. I have heard the bible and have learned that Eve caused man to sin. Well if woman upset the world, do give her a chance to set it right side up again.

The Lady has spoken about Jesus, how he never spurned woman from him, and she was right. When Lazarus died, Mary and Martha came to him with faith and love and besought him to raise their brother. And Jesus wept – and Lazarus came forth.

And how came Jesus into the world? Through God who created him and woman who bore him. Man, where is your part?

But the women are coming up, blessed be God, and a few of the men are coming up with them. But man is in a tight place, the poor slave is on him, woman is coming on him, and he is surely between a hawk and a buzzard.

← One of the many *carte de visite* portraits of Sojourner Truth, which she sold to finance her speaking tours

# NO ONE WINS TONIGHT

On the evening of April 19, 1994, 63-year-old oil businessman John Luttig was shot twice in the head on the driveway of his home in Tyler, West Virginia. The shooter was Napoleon Beazley, a young man who, along with two friends, had decided to steal Luttig's Mercedes. Eight years later, despite having been just seventeen years of age at the time of the murder, Beazley was killed by lethal injection for his crime, much to the dismay of human rights campaigners who believed that juveniles should be spared execution. Indeed, this is now the case in the United States following a landmark Supreme Court decision in 2005. In his last moments, as he awaited his lethal injection, Napoleon Beazley was granted the opportunity to deliver some final words.

The act I committed to put me here was not just heinous, it was senseless. But the person that committed that act is no longer here – I am. I'm not going to struggle physically against any restraints. I'm not going to shout, use profanity or make idle threats. Understand though that I'm not only upset, but I'm saddened by what is happening here tonight. I'm not only saddened, but disappointed that a system that is supposed to protect and uphold what is just and right can be so much like me when I made the same shameful mistake.

If someone tried to dispose of everyone here for participating in this killing, I'd scream a resounding, "No." I'd tell them to give them all the gift that they would not give me, and that's to give them all a second chance. I'm sorry that I'm here. I'm sorry that you're all here. I'm sorry that John Luttig died. And I'm sorry that it was something in me that caused all of this to happen to begin with.

Tonight, we tell the world that there are no second chances in the eyes of justice. Tonight, we tell our children that in some instances, in some cases, killing is right. This conflict hurts us all. There are no sides. The people who support this proceeding think this is justice. The people that think that I should live think that is justice. As difficult as it may seem, this is a clash of ideals, with both parties committed to what they feel is right. But who's wrong if in the end we're all victims?

In my heart, I have to believe that there is a peaceful compromise to our ideals. I don't mind if there are none for me, as long as there are for those who are yet to come. There are a lot of men like me on death row – good men – who fell to the same misguided emotions, but may not have recovered as I have. Give those men a chance to do what's right. Give them a chance to undo their wrongs. A lot of them want to fix the mess they started, but don't know how. The problem is not in that people aren't willing to help them find out, but in the system telling them it won't matter anyway.

No one wins tonight. No one gets closure. No one walks away victorious.

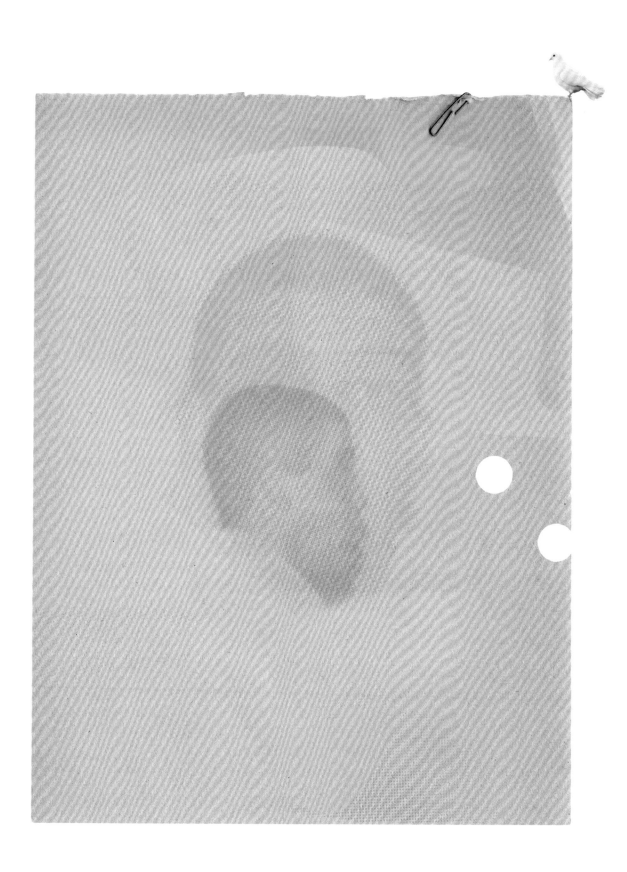

# THE ROOM IS YOUR OWN, BUT IT IS STILL BARE

In 1931, English novelist Virginia Woolf was invited by the London and National Society for Women's Service to give a talk about her profession, to shine a light on her successful career as a writer in such a male-dominated arena. Woolf agreed, and spoke of exactly that, but also of her battle with the "Angel in the House," the Victorian ideal of a docile, domesticated and pure woman – a term taken from Coventry Patmore's poem of the same name. The speech seen here is abbreviated, as reprinted posthumously in 1942's *The Death of the Moth and Other Essays* and titled "Professions for Women."

When your secretary invited me to come here, she told me that your Society is concerned with the employment of women and she suggested that I might tell you something about my own professional experiences. It is true I am a woman; it is true I am employed; but what professional experiences have I had? It is difficult to say. My profession is literature; and in that profession there are fewer experiences for women than in any other, with the exception of the stage – fewer, I mean, that are peculiar to women. For the road was cut many years ago – by Fanny Burney, by Aphra Behn, by Harriet Martineau, by Jane Austen, by George Eliot – many famous women, and many more unknown and forgotten, have been before me, making the path smooth, and regulating my steps. Thus, when I came to write, there were very few material obstacles in my way. Writing was a reputable and harmless occupation. The family peace was not broken by the scratching of a pen. No demand was made upon the family purse. For ten and sixpence one can buy paper enough to write all the plays of Shakespeare – if one has a mind that way. Pianos and models, Paris, Vienna and Berlin, masters and mistresses, are not needed by a writer. The cheapness of writing paper is, of course, the reason why women have succeeded as writers before they have succeeded in the other professions.

But to tell you my story – it is a simple one. You have only got to figure to yourselves a girl in a bedroom with a pen in her hand. She had only to move that pen from left to right – from ten o'clock to one. Then it occurred to her to do what is simple and cheap enough after all – to slip a few of those pages into an envelope, fix a penny stamp in the corner, and drop the envelope into the red box at the corner. It was thus that I became a journalist; and my effort was rewarded on the first day of the following month – a very glorious day it was for me – by a letter from an editor containing a cheque for one pound ten shillings and sixpence. But to show you how little I deserve to be called a professional woman, how little I know of the struggles and difficulties of such lives, I have to admit that instead of spending that sum upon bread and butter, rent, shoes and stockings, or butcher's bills, I went out and bought a cat – a beautiful cat, a Persian cat, which very soon involved me in bitter disputes with my neighbours.

What could be easier than to write articles and to buy Persian cats with the profits? But wait a moment. Articles have to be about something. Mine, I seem to remember, was about a novel by a famous man. And while I was writing this review, I discovered that if I were going to review books I should need to do battle with a certain phantom. And the phantom was a woman, and when I came to know her better I called her after the heroine of a famous poem, the Angel in the House. It was she who used to come between me and my paper when I was writing reviews. It was she who bothered me and wasted my time and so tormented me that at last I killed her. You who come of a younger and happier generation may not have heard of her – you may not know what I mean by the Angel in the House. I will describe her as shortly as I can. She was intensely sympathetic. She was immensely charming. She was utterly unselfish. She excelled in the difficult arts of family life. She sacrificed herself daily. If there was chicken, she took the leg; if there was a draught, she sat in it – in short she was so constituted that she never had a mind or a wish of her own, but preferred to sympathise always with the minds and wishes of others. Above all – I need not say it – she was pure. Her purity was supposed to be her chief beauty – her blushes, her great grace. In those days – the last of Queen Victoria – every house had its Angel. And when I came to write I encountered her with the very first words. The shadow of her wings fell on my page; I heard the rustling of her skirts in the room. Directly, that is to say, I took my pen in my hand to review that novel by a famous man, she slipped behind me and whispered: 'My dear, you are a young woman. You are writing about a book that has been written by a man. Be sympathetic; be tender; flatter; deceive; use all the arts and wiles of our sex. Never let anybody guess that you have a mind of your own. Above all, be pure.' And she made as if to guide my pen. I now record the one act for which I take some credit to myself, though the credit rightly belongs to some excellent ancestors of mine who left me a certain sum of money – shall we say five hundred pounds a year? – so that it was not necessary for me to depend solely on charm for my living. I turned upon her and caught her by the throat. I did my best to kill her. My excuse, if I were to be had up in a court of law, would be that I acted in self-defence. Had I not killed her she would have killed me. She would have plucked the heart out of my writing. For, as I found, directly I put pen to paper, you cannot review even a novel without having a mind of your own, without expressing what you think to be the truth about human relations, morality, sex. And all these questions, according to the Angel of the House, cannot be dealt with freely and openly by women; they must charm, they must conciliate, they must – to put it bluntly – tell lies if they are to succeed. Thus, whenever I felt the shadow of her wing or the radiance of her halo upon my page, I took up the inkpot and flung it at her. She died hard. Her fictitious

nature was of great assistance to her. It is far harder to kill a phantom than a reality. She was always creeping back when I thought I had despatched her. Though I flatter myself that I killed her in the end, the struggle was severe; it took much time that had better have been spent upon learning Greek grammar; or in roaming the world in search of adventures. But it was a real experience; it was an experience that was bound to befall all women writers at that time. Killing the Angel in the House was part of the occupation of a woman writer.

But to continue my story. The Angel was dead; what then remained? You may say that what remained was a simple and common object – a young woman in a bedroom with an inkpot. In other words, now that she had rid herself of falsehood, that young woman had only to be herself. Ah, but what is 'herself'? I mean, what is a woman? I assure you, I do not know. I do not believe that you know. I do not believe that anybody can know until she has expressed herself in all the arts and professions open to human skill. That indeed is one of the reasons why I have come here out of respect for you, who are in process of showing us by your experiments what a woman is, who are in process of providing us, by your failures and successes, with that extremely important piece of information.

But to continue the story of my professional experiences. I made one pound ten and six by my first review; and I bought a Persian cat with the proceeds. Then I grew ambitious. A Persian cat is all very well, I said; but a Persian cat is not enough. I must have a motor car. And it was thus that I became a novelist – for it is a very strange thing that people will give you a motor car if you will tell them a story. It is a still stranger thing that there is nothing so delightful in the world as telling stories. It is far pleasanter than writing reviews of famous novels. And yet, if I am to obey your secretary and tell you my professional experiences as a novelist, I must tell you about a very strange experience that befell me as a novelist. And to understand it you must try first to imagine a novelist's state of mind. I hope I am not giving away professional secrets if I say that a novelist's chief desire is to be as unconscious as possible. He has to induce in himself a state of perpetual lethargy. He wants life to proceed with the utmost quiet and regularity. He wants to see the same faces, to read the same books, to do the same things day after day, month after month, while he is writing, so that nothing may break the illusion in which he is living – so that nothing may disturb or disquiet the mysterious nosings about, feelings round, darts, dashes and sudden discoveries of that very shy and elusive spirit, the imagination. I suspect that this state is the same both for men and women. Be that as it may, I want you to imagine me writing a novel in a state of trance. I want you to figure to yourselves a girl sitting with a pen in her hand, which for minutes, and indeed for hours, she never dips into the inkpot. The image that comes to my mind when I think of this girl is the image of a fisherman lying sunk in dreams on the verge of a deep lake with a rod held out over the water.

← Virginia Woolf, 1927, photographer unknown

She was letting her imagination sweep unchecked round every rock and cranny of the world that lies submerged in the depths of our unconscious being. Now came the experience, the experience that I believe to be far commoner with women writers than with men. The line raced through the girl's fingers. Her imagination had rushed away. It had sought the pools, the depths, the dark places where the largest fish slumber. And then there was a smash. There was an explosion. There was foam and confusion. The imagination had dashed itself against something hard. The girl was roused from her dream. She was indeed in a state of the most acute and difficult distress. To speak without figure she had thought of something, something about the body, about the passions which it was unfitting for her as a woman to say. Men, her reason told her, would be shocked. The consciousness of what men will say of a woman who speaks the truth about her passions had roused her from her artist's state of unconsciousness. She could write no more. The trance was over. Her imagination could work no longer. This I believe to be a very common experience with women writers – they are impeded by the extreme conventionality of the other sex. For though men sensibly allow themselves great freedom in these respects, I doubt that they realise or can control the extreme severity with which they condemn such freedom in women.

These then were two very genuine experiences of my own. These were two of the adventures of my professional life. The first – killing the Angel in the House – I think I solved. She died. But the second, telling the truth about my own experiences as a body, I do not think I solved. I doubt that any woman has solved it yet. The obstacles against her are still immensely powerful – and yet they are very difficult to define. Outwardly, what is simpler than to write books? Outwardly, what obstacles are there for a woman rather than for a man? Inwardly, I think, the case is very different; she has still many ghosts to fight, many prejudices to overcome. Indeed it will be a long time still, I think, before a woman can sit down to write a book without finding a phantom to be slain, a rock to be dashed against. And if this is so in literature, the freest of all professions for women, how is it in the new professions which you are now for the first time entering?

Those are the questions that I should like, had I time, to ask you. And indeed, if I have laid stress upon these professional experiences of mine, it is because I believe that they are, though in different forms, yours also. Even when the path is nominally open – when there is nothing to prevent a woman from being a doctor, a lawyer, a civil servant – there are many phantoms and obstacles, as I believe, looming in her way. To discuss and define them is I think of great value and importance; for thus only can the labour be shared, the difficulties be solved. But besides this, it is necessary also to discuss the ends and the aims for which we are fighting, for which we are doing battle with these formidable obstacles. Those aims cannot be taken for granted; they must be perpetually questioned and examined. The whole position, as I see it – here in this hall surrounded by women practising for the first time in history I know not how many different professions – is one of extraordinary interest and importance. You have won rooms of your own in the house hitherto exclusively owned by men. You are able, though not without great labour and effort, to pay the rent. You are earning your five hundred pounds a year. But this freedom is only a beginning – the room is your own, but it is still bare. It has to be furnished; it has to be decorated; it has to be shared. How are you going to furnish it, how are you going to decorate it? With whom are you going to share it, and upon what terms? These, I think, are questions of the utmost importance and interest. For the first time in history you are able to ask them; for the first time you are able to decide for yourselves what the answers should be. Willingly would I stay and discuss those questions and answers – but not tonight. My time is up; and I must cease.

# PARTY OF LIFE

New York artist and activist Keith Haring found worldwide fame in the 1980s as his vibrant and distinctive public art spread from the subway stations of New York to the streets of places as far afield as Melbourne and Rio, cleverly managing to comment on a range of political and social issues by way of seemingly simplistic graffiti. Sadly,

Haring's life was cut short when in February 1990, at just thirty-one years of age, he died of AIDS. At a memorial service a few months after his death, on what would have been his thirty-second birthday, Keith's sister Kay gave a speech.

Keith was my big brother.

While I cannot tell you what it is like to lose a brother, I can tell you what it was like to have a brother like Keith.

Over the years, people have often questioned me: what was it like, growing up with Keith? – what is it like to have a brother that is famous? – was he always like this?

Well, I think that my memories of growing up with Keith are very much like remembering what he was just yesterday.

I remember, when we were kids, every summer we'd have penny-fairs in our backyard. We'd invite the whole neighborhood, charge admission, and run carnival games and contests. At the end of the day, we'd divide our profits and while my sisters and I were thinking of saving our money for future goals, Keith was inviting all the neighborhood kids to come downtown with us, and he'd treat everyone at the local ice cream shop.

I remember that Keith was always the leader in our latest exclusive "club," where we'd make up secret coded messages, have meetings and plan ways to upset our parents.

I remember that on Tuesday nights our church youth group would drive to a nearby city and spend the evening at a drop-in center for city kids; just hanging out with them, playing games and helping with art projects.

I remember that Keith was always drawing . . . it was his hobby, his pastime, his vehicle of expression, his very being.

So you see, it has always seemed to me that the brother who I grew up with is the same brother who all of you know.

← *Best Buddies* by Keith Haring, 1990

Only the neighborhood get-togethers became the Manhattan club scene, the art projects with kids grew to include thousands and thousands of youth, his generous nature reached to touch virtually millions, and the canvas on which he drew became the whole world.

I learned a lot from my big brother:

• that a wall was meant to be drawn on,

• a Saturday night was meant for partying,

• and that life is meant for celebrating!

Keith introduced me to designer clothes, New York City, the art world, sushi, and as a young teenager I learned that the only way to listen to the Grateful Dead and the Beatles was with the volume turned all the way up!

Keith showed me that it is possible to live what you believe. He covered hundreds of walls with his art, he made friends and partied around the world, and every year he had the most elaborate birthday celebrations to what he so appropriately named his "Party of Life."

Keith taught me strength in the face of death – and humor.

He had an IV hooked up to him constantly during the last few weeks and he nicknamed the milky-white fluid flowing into his arms his "slime." And I can't tell you how many times I caught him making faces at the nurses behind their backs.

Keith's battle with AIDS taught me that every day is worth living. When he tested HIV-positive, instead of complaining about the burden of the disease and in answer to a comment on how hard it must be to live with that knowledge, he replied, "No, it just makes everything that happens now so much better. 'Cause you never know when you're doing something for the last time, so you live each day like it is the last."

My life changed after that.

And Keith continued to draw, filling every space before him, leaving his mark; like there was no tomorrow.

Two days before he died, Keith was lying on the edge of his bed, and the window was open so you could see the city rooftops all the way out to the Empire State Building. Keith couldn't hold a marker anymore, so he took my hand, and with those smooth graceful strokes we all know so well, we painted in the sky with all of New York City as our backdrop.

And all that I can think now is that wherever Keith is, he's leaving those wonderful graffiti-chalk drawings all around him, and today, on the thirty-second birthday of our brother Keith, I'm sure there is the biggest "Party of Life" happening up in heaven right now!

# THEIR FIRST GREAT MARTYR CHIEF

As Abraham Lincoln and his wife sat in the presidential box at Ford's Theatre on the evening of April 14, 1865, a single bullet ended the life of the president, shot from a small Philadelphia Deringer handgun by actor and Confederate sympathizer John Wilkes Booth. Although Lincoln was not yet as widely revered as he would eventually become, the shock of his assassination was instant and far-reaching. For celebrated poet Walt Whitman, who for some time had felt a strong connection to the president despite their never having met, it was particularly difficult to comprehend. Exactly fifteen years later, Whitman reflected on Lincoln's life and death in a speech he would deliver on numerous anniversaries of the date throughout the next decade.

How often since that dark and dripping Saturday – that chilly April day, now fifteen years bygone – my heart has entertain'd the dream, the wish, to give of Abraham Lincoln's death its own special thought and memorial. Yet now the sought-for opportunity offers, I find my notes incompetent (why, for truly profound themes, is statement so idle? why does the right phrase never offer?) and the fit tribute I dream'd of, waits unprepared as ever. My talk here indeed is less because of itself or anything in it, and nearly altogether because I feel a desire, apart from any talk, to specify the day, the martyrdom. It is for this, my friends, I have call'd you together. Oft as the rolling years bring back this hour, let it again, however briefly, be dwelt upon. For my own part, I hope and desire, till my own dying day, whenever the 14th or 15th of April comes, to annually gather a few friends, and hold its tragic reminiscence. No narrow or sectional reminiscence. It belongs to these States in their entirety – not the North only, but the South – perhaps belongs most tenderly and devoutly to the South, of all; for there, really, this man's birth-stock. There and thence his antecedent stamp. Why should I not say that thence his manliest traits – his universality – his canny, easy ways and words upon the surface – his inflexible determination and courage at heart? Have you never realized it, my friends, that Lincoln, though grafted on the West, is essentially, in personnel and character, a Southern contribution?

And though by no means proposing to resume the Secession war tonight, I would briefly remind you of the public conditions preceding that contest. For twenty years, and especially during the four or five before the war actually began, the aspect of affairs in the United States, though without the flash of military excitement, presents more than the survey of a battle, or any extended campaign, or series, even of Nature's convulsions. The hot passions of the South – the strange mixture at the North of inertia, incredulity, and conscious power – the incendiarism of the abolitionists – the rascality and grip of the politicians, unparall'd in any land, any age. To these I must not omit adding the honesty of the essential bulk of the people everywhere – yet with all the seething fury and contradiction of their natures more arous'd than the Atlantic's waves in wildest equinox. In politics, what can be more ominous (though generally unappreciated then) – what more significant than the Presidentiads of Fillmore and Buchanan? Proving conclusively that the weakness and wickedness of elected rulers are just as likely to afflict us here, as in the countries of the Old World, under their monarchies, emperors and aristocracies. In that Old World were everywhere heard underground rumblings, that died out, only to again surely return. While in America the volcano, though civic yet, continued to grow more and more convulsive – more and more stormy and threatening.

In the height of all this excitement and chaos, hovering on the edge at first, and then merged in its very midst, and destined to play a leading part, appears a strange and awkward figure. I shall not easily forget the first time I ever saw Abraham Lincoln. It must have been about the 18th or 19th of February, 1861. It was rather a pleasant afternoon, in New York City, as he arrived there from the West, to remain a few hours, and then pass on to Washington, to prepare for his inauguration. I saw him in Broadway, near the site of the present Post Office. He came down, I think from Canal Street, to stop at the Astor House. The broad spaces, sidewalks and streets in the neighborhood, and for some distance, were crowded with solid masses of people, many thousands. The omnibuses and other vehicles had all been turn'd off, leaving an unusual hush in that busy part of the city. Presently two or three shabby hack barouches made their way with some difficulty through the crowd, and drew up at the Astor House entrance. A tall figure step'd out of the center of these barouches, paus'd leisurely on the sidewalk, look'd up at the granite walls and looming architecture of the grand old hotel – then, after a relieving stretch of arms and legs, turn'd round for over a minute to slowly and good-humoredly scan the appearance of the vast and silent crowds. There were no speeches – no compliments – no welcome – as far as I could hear, not a word said. Still much anxiety was conceal'd in that quiet. Cautious persons had fear'd some mark'd insult or indignity to the President-elect – for he possess'd no personal popularity at all in New York City, and very little political. But it was evidently tacitly agreed that if the few political supporters of Mr. Lincoln present would entirely abstain from any demonstration on their side, the immense majority, who were anything but supporters, would abstain on their side also. The result was a sulky, unbroken silence, such as certainly never before characterized so great a New York crowd.

Almost in the same neighborhood I distinctly remember'd seeing Lafayette on his visit to America in 1825. I had also personally seen and heard, various years afterward, how Andrew Jackson, Clay, Webster, Hungarian Kossuth, Filibuster Walker,* the Prince of Wales on his visit, and other *célèbres*, native and foreign, had been welcom'd there – all that indescribable human roar and magnetism, unlike any other sound in the universe – the glad exulting thunder-shouts of countless unloos'd throats of men! But on this occasion, not a

* Former U.S. President Andrew Jackson, Henry Clay, Daniel Webster and the Hungarian Lajos Kossuth were all politicians. William Walker was an American mercenary who carried out several private military expeditions in South America in order to seize control of territory (known as "filibustering").

voice – not a sound. From the top of an omnibus (driven up one side, close by, and block'd by the curbstone and the crowds), I had, I say, a capital view of it all, and especially of Mr. Lincoln, his look and gait – his perfect composure and coolness – his unusual and uncouth height, his dress of complete black, stovepipe hat push'd back on the head, dark-brown complexion, seam'd and wrinkled yet canny-looking face, black, bushy head of hair, disproportionately long neck, and his hands held behind as he stood observing the people. He look'd with curiosity upon that immense sea of faces, and the sea of faces return'd the look with similar curiosity. In both there was a dash of comedy, almost farce, such as Shakespeare puts in his blackest tragedies. The crowd that hemm'd around consisted I should think of thirty to forty thousand men, not a single one his personal friend – while I have no doubt (so frenzied were the ferments of the time), many an assassin's knife and pistol lurk'd in hip or breast-pocket there, ready, soon as break and riot came.

But no break or riot came. The tall figure gave another relieving stretch or two of arms and legs; then with moderate pace, and accompanied by a few unknown-looking persons, ascended the portico-steps of the Astor House, disappear'd through its broad entrance – and the dumb-show ended.

I saw Abraham Lincoln often the four years following that date. He changed rapidly and much during his Presidency – but this scene, and him in it, are indelibly stamped upon my recollection. As I sat on the top of my omnibus, and had a good view of him, the thought, dim and inchoate then, has since come out clear enough, that four sorts of genius, four mighty and primal hands, will be needed to the complete limning of this man's future portrait – the eyes and brains and finger-touch of Plutarch and Aeschylus and Michelangelo, assisted by Rabelais.

And now (Mr. Lincoln passing on from this scene to Washington, where he was inaugurated, amid armed cavalry, and sharpshooters at every point – the first instance of the kind in our history – and I hope it will be the last) – now the rapid succession of well-known events (too well known – I believe, these days, we almost hate to hear them mention'd) – the national flag fired on at Sumter – the uprising of the North, in paroxysms of astonishment and rage – the chaos of divided councils – the call for troops – the first Bull Run – the stunning cast-down, shock and dismay of the North – and so in full flood the Secession war. Four years of lurid, bleeding, murky, murderous war. Who paints those years, with all their scenes? – the hard-fought engagements – the defeats, plans, failures – the gloomy hours, days, when our nationality seem'd hung in pall of doubt, perhaps death – the Mephistophelean sneers of foreign lands and attachés – the dreaded Scylla of European interference, and the Charybdis of the tremendously dangerous latent strata of secession sympathizers throughout the free States (far more numerous than is supposed) – the long marches in summer – the hot sweat, and many a sunstroke, as on the rush to Gettysburg

How often since that dark and chilly Saturday — that dripping April day, now fifteen years bygone — my heart has X entertain'd the dream, the wish, to give of Abraham Lincoln's death its own special thought ~~~~~~ and memorial. Yet now the sought-for opportunity offers, I find my notes incompetent (why, for truly profound themes, is statement so idle? why does the right phrase never offer?) and the fit, suitable tribute I dreamed of, waits unprepared as ever. My speech talk here, indeed less because of itself or any thing in it and nearly altogether because I feel a desire, apart from any talk, to mark the day, the martyrdom. It is for this, my friends, I have cull'd you together. Oft as the rolling years bring back again, however this hour, let it again be dwelt upon. For my own part I hope and intend, till my own dying day, whenever the 14th or 15th of April comes, to annually gather a few friends around me, and hold its tragic reminiscence. No narrow or sectional reminiscence. It belongs to These States in their entirety — not the North only but the South — perhaps most tenderly and devoutly to the South, of all, for there really this man Lincoln's birth-stock. There and thence his antecedent stamp. Why should I not say that thence his manliest traits, his universality — his canny, easy ways and words, upon the surface, his inflexible determination and courage at heart. Have you never realised it, my friends, that Lincoln, though grafted on the West, is essentially, in personnel and character, a Southern contribution?

in '63 – the night battles in the woods, as under Hooker at Chancellorsville – the camps in winter – the military prisons – the hospitals (alas! alas! the hospitals).

The Secession war? Nay, let me call it the Union war. Though whatever call'd, it is even yet too near us – too vast and too closely overshadowing – its branches unform'd yet (but certain), shooting too far into the future – and the most indicative and mightiest of them yet ungrown. A great literature will yet arise out of the era of those four years, those scenes – an era compressing centuries of native passion, first-class pictures, tempests of life and death – an inexhaustible mine for the histories, drama, romance, and even philosophy, of peoples to come · indeed the vertebra of poetry and art (of personal character too), for all future America – far more grand, in my opinion, to the hands capable of it, than Homer's siege of Troy, or the French wars to Shakespeare.

But I must leave these speculations, and come to the theme I have assign'd and limited myself to. Of the actual murder of President Lincoln, though so much has been written, probably the facts are yet very indefinite in most persons' minds. I read from my memoranda, written at the time, and revised frequently and finally since.

The day, April 14, 1865, seems to have been a pleasant one throughout the whole land – the moral atmosphere pleasant too – the long storm, so dark, so fratricidal, full of blood and doubt and gloom, over and ended at last by the sun-rise of such an absolute National victory, and utter break-down of Secessionism – we almost doubted our own senses! [Confederate General Robert E.] Lee had capitulated beneath the apple-tree of Appomattox. The other armies, the flanges of the revolt, swiftly follow'd. And could it really be, then? Out of all the affairs of this world of woe and failure and disorder, was there really come the confirm'd, unerring sign of plan, like a shaft of pure light – of rightful rule – of God? So the day, as I say, was propitious. Early herbage, early flowers, were out. (I remember where I was stopping at the time, the season being advanced, there were many lilacs in full bloom. By one of those caprices that enter and give tinge to events without being at all a part of them, I find myself always reminded of the great tragedy of that day by the sight and odor of these blossoms. It never fails.)

But I must not dwell on accessories. The deed hastens. The popular afternoon paper of Washington, the little *Evening Star*, had spatter'd all over its third page, divided among the advertisements in a sensational manner, in a hundred different places, The President and his Lady will be at the Theatre this evening. . . . (Lincoln was fond of the theatre. I have myself seen him there several times. I remember thinking how funny it was that he, in some respects the leading actor in the stormiest drama known to real history's stage through centuries, should sit there and be so completely interested and absorb'd in those human jack-straws, moving about with their silly little gestures, foreign spirit, and flatulent text.)

← A draft of Walt Whitman's speech from 1880, first delivered in 1879

On this occasion the theatre was crowded, many ladies in rich and gay costumes, officers in their uniforms, many well-known citizens, young folks, the usual clusters of gas-lights, the usual magnetism of so many people, cheerful, with perfumes, music of violins and flutes (and over all, and saturating all, that vast, vague wonder, Victory, the nation's victory, the triumph of the Union, filling the air, the thought, the sense, with exhilaration more than all music and perfumes).

The President came betimes, and, with his wife, witness'd the play from the large stage-boxes of the second tier, two thrown into one, and profusely draped with the national flag. The acts and scenes of the pieces – one of those singularly written compositions which have at least the merit of giving entire relief to an audience engaged in mental action or business excitements and cares during the day, as it makes not the slightest call on either the moral, emotional, aesthetic, or spiritual nature – a piece ("Our American Cousin"), in which, among other characters, so call'd, a Yankee, certainly such a one as was never seen, or the least like it ever seen, in North America, is introduced in England, with a varied fol-de-rol of talk, plot, scenery, and such phantasmagoria as goes to make up a modern popular drama – had progress'd through perhaps a couple of its acts, when in the midst of this comedy, or non-such, or whatever it is to be call'd, and to offset it, or finish it out, as if in Nature's and the great Muse's mockery of those poor mimes, came interpolated that scene, not really or exactly to be described at all (for on the many hundreds who were there it seems to this hour to have left a passing blur, a dream, a blotch) – and yet partially to be described as I now proceed to give it.

There is a scene in the play representing a modern parlor, in which two unprecedented English ladies are inform'd by the impossible Yankee that he is not a man of fortune, and therefore undesirable for marriage-catching purposes; after which, the comments being finish'd, the dramatic trio make exit, leaving the stage clear for a moment. At this period came the murder of Abraham Lincoln. Great as all its manifold train, circling round it, and stretching into the future for many a century, in the politics, history, art, etc., of the New World, in point of fact the main thing, the actual murder, transpired with the quiet and simplicity of any commonest occurrence – the bursting of a bud or pod in the growth of vegetation, for instance. Through the general hum following the stage pause, with the change of positions, came the muffled sound of a pistol-shot, which not one-hundredth part of the audience heard at the time – and yet a moment's hush – somehow, surely, a vague startled thrill – and then, through the ornamented, draperied, starr'd and striped space-way of the President's box, a sudden figure, a man, raises himself with hands and feet, stands a moment on the railing, leaps below to the stage (a distance of perhaps fourteen or fifteen feet), falls out of position, catching his boot-heel in the copious drapery (the American flag), falls on one knee, quickly recovers himself, rises as if nothing had happen'd (he really sprains his ankle, but unfelt then) – and so the figure, Booth, the murderer, dress'd in plain black broadcloth, bare-headed, with full, glossy, raven hair, and his eyes like some mad animal's flashing with light and resolution, yet with a certain strange calmness, holds aloft in one hand a large knife – walks along not much back from the footlights – turns fully toward the audience his face of statuesque beauty, lit by those basilisk eyes, flashing with desperation, perhaps insanity – launches out in a firm and steady voice the words "Sic semper tyrannis" – and then walks with neither slow nor very rapid pace diagonally across to the back of the stage, and disappears. (Had not all this terrible scene – making the mimic ones preposterous – had it not all been rehears'd, in blank, by Booth, beforehand?)

A moment's hush – a scream – the cry of murder – Mrs. Lincoln leaning out of the box, with ashy cheeks and lips, with involuntary cry, pointing to the retreating figure, "He has kill'd the President." And still a moment's strange, incredulous suspense – and then the deluge! – then that mixture of horror, noises, uncertainty (the sound, somewhere back, of a horse's hoofs clattering with speed) – the people burst through chairs and railings, and break them up – there is inextricable confusion and terror – women faint – quite feeble persons fall, and are trampled on – many cries of agony are heard – the broad stage suddenly fills to suffocation with a dense and motley crowd, like some horrible carnival – the audience rush generally upon it, at least the strong men do – the actors and actresses are all there in their play-costumes and painted faces, with mortal fright showing through the rouge – the screams and calls, confused talk – redoubled, trebled – two or three manage to pass up water from the stage to the President's box – others try to clamber up – etc., etc.

In the midst of all this, the soldiers of the President's guard, with others, suddenly drawn to the scene, burst in (some 200 altogether) – they storm the house, through all the tiers, especially the upper ones, inflamed with fury, literally charging the audience with fix'd bayonets, muskets and pistols, shouting, "Clear out! Clear out! You sons of ——" . . . Such the wild scene, or a suggestion of it rather, inside the play-house that night.

Outside, too, in the atmosphere of shock and craze, crowds of people, fill'd with frenzy, ready to seize any outlet for it, come near committing murder several times on innocent individuals. One such case was especially exciting. The infuriated crowd, through some chance, got started against one man, either for words he utter'd, or perhaps without any cause at all, and were proceeding at once to actually hang him on a neighboring lamppost, when he was rescued by a few heroic policemen, who placed him in their midst, and fought their way slowly and amid great peril toward the station house. It was a fitting episode of the whole affair. The crowd rushing and eddying to and fro – the night, the yells, the pale faces, many frighten'd people trying in vain to extricate themselves – the attack'd man, not yet freed from the jaws of death, looking like a corpse – the silent, resolute, half-dozen policemen, with no weapons but their little clubs, yet stern and steady through all those eddying swarms – made a fitting side-scene to the grand tragedy of the murder. They gain'd the station house with the protected man, whom they placed in security for the night, and discharged him in the morning.

And in the midst of that pandemonium, infuriated soldiers, the audience and the crowd, the stage, and all its actors and actresses, its paint-pots, spangles, and gas-lights – the life blood from those veins, the best and sweetest of the land, drips slowly down, and death's ooze already begins its little bubbles on the lips.

Thus the visible incidents and surroundings of Abraham Lincoln's murder, as they really occur'd. Thus ended the attempted secession of these States; thus the four years' war. But the main things come subtly and invisibly afterward, perhaps long afterward – neither military, political, nor (great as those are) historical. I say, certain secondary and indirect results, out of the tragedy of this death, are, in my opinion, greatest. Not the event of the murder itself. Not that Mr. Lincoln strings the principal points and personages of the period, like beads, upon the single string of his career. Not that his idiosyncrasy, in its sudden appearance and disappearance, stamps this Republic with a stamp more mark'd and enduring than any yet given by any one man (more even than Washington's) – but, join'd with these, the immeasurable value and meaning of that whole tragedy lies, to me, in senses finally dearest to a nation (and here all our own) – the imaginative and artistic senses – the literary and dramatic ones. Not in any common or low meaning of those terms, but a meaning precious to the race, and to every age. A long and varied series of contradictory events arrives at last at its highest poetic, single, central, pictorial denouement. The whole involved, baffling, multiform whirl of the secession period comes to a head, and is gather'd in one brief flash of lightning-illumination – one simple, fierce deed. Its sharp culmination, and as it were solution, of so many bloody and angry problems, illustrates those climax-moments on the stage of universal Time, where the historic Muse at one entrance, and the tragic Muse at the other, suddenly bringing down the curtain, close an immense act in the long drama of creative thought, and give it radiation, tableau, stranger than fiction. Fit radiation – fit close! How the imagination – how the student loves these things! America, too, is to have them. For not in all great deaths, nor far or near – not Caesar in the Roman senate-house, or Napoleon passing away in the wild night-storm at St. Helena – not Paleologus, falling, desperately fighting, piled over dozens deep with Grecian corpses – not calm old Socrates, drinking the hemlock – outvies that terminus of the Secession war, in one man's life, here in our midst, in our own time – that seal of the emancipation of three million slaves – that parturition and delivery of our at last really free Republic, born again, henceforth to commence its career of genuine homogeneous Union, compact, consistent with itself.

Nor will ever future American Patriots and Unionists, indifferently over the whole land, or North or South, find a better moral to their lesson. The final use of the greatest men of a nation is, after all, not with reference to their deeds in themselves, or their direct bearing on their times or lands. The final use of a heroic-eminent life – especially of a heroic-eminent death – is its indirect filtering into the nation and the race, and to give, often at many removes, but unerringly, age after age, color and fiber to the personalism of the youth and maturity of that age, and of mankind. Then there is a cement to the whole people, subtler, more underlying, than any thing in written constitution, or courts or armies – namely, the cement of a death identified thoroughly with that people, at its head, and for its sake. Strange (is it not?) that battles, martyrs, agonies, blood, even assassination, should so condense – perhaps only really, lasting condense – a nationality.

I repeat it – the grand deaths of the race – the dramatic deaths of every nationality – are its most important inheritance-value – in some respects beyond its literature and art (as the hero is beyond his finest portrait, and the battle itself beyond its choicest song or epic). Is not here indeed the point underlying all tragedy? The famous pieces of the Grecian masters – and all masters? Why, if the old Greeks had had this man, what trilogies of plays – what epics – would have been made out of him! How the rhapsodes [ancient Greek performers of poetry] would have recited him! How quickly that quaint tall form would have enter'd into the region where men vitalize gods, and gods divinify men! But Lincoln, his times, his death – great as any, any age – belong altogether to our own, and are autochthonic [native]. (Sometimes indeed I think our American days, our own stage – the actors we know and have shaken hands or talk'd with – more fateful than anything in Aeschylus – more heroic than the fighters around Troy – afford kings of men for our Democracy prouder than Agamemnon – models of character cute and hardy as Ulysses – deaths more pitiful than Priam's.)

When, centuries hence (as it must, in my opinion, be centuries hence before the life of these States, or of Democracy, can be really written and illustrated), the leading historians and dramatists seek for some personage, some special event, incisive enough to mark with deepest cut, and mnemonize, this turbulent nineteenth century of ours (not only these States, but all over the political and social world) – something, perhaps, to close that gorgeous procession of European feudalism, with all its pomp and caste-prejudices (of whose long train we in America are yet so inextricably the heirs) – something to identify with terrible identification, by far the greatest revolutionary step in the history of the United States (perhaps the greatest of the world, our century) – the absolute extirpation and erasure of slavery from the States – those historians will seek in vain for any point to serve more thoroughly their purpose, than Abraham Lincoln's death.

Dear to the Muse – thrice dear to Nationality – to the whole human race – precious to this Union – precious to Democracy – unspeakably and forever precious – their first great Martyr Chief.

# THEY SHALL NOT PASS!

Dolores Ibárruri was born into poverty in Bilbao, northern Spain, as one of eleven children in a mining family. Before she had reached the age of thirty she had given birth to six children, only two of whom survived. Her entry into the world of politics was early, and Ibárruri was instantly a force to be reckoned with in the Spanish Communist Party. She gave this intense speech from the Ministry of the Interior a day after the Spanish Civil War had erupted, urging the Spanish population to reject fascism, after which Ibárruri became known to many as "La Pasionaria" (the Passion Flower). It is easy to see why.

Workers, anti-fascists and laboring people!

Rise as one man. Prepare to defend the Republic, our national freedom and the democratic liberties won by the people.

Following the communications of the government and of the People's Front, we are all aware of how serious the situation is. Our workers, together with the troops that have remained loyal to the Republic, are manfully and enthusiastically carrying on the struggle in Morocco and the Canary Islands.

Under the slogan "Fascism shall not pass, the butchers of October shall not pass!," communists, socialists, anarchists, republicans, soldiers and all forces loyal to the will of the people are destroying the traitorous rebels who have trampled us in the mud and betrayed their vaunted military honor.

The whole country is appalled by the actions of these villains. With fire and brimstone they wish to turn democratic Spain – the Spain of the people – into a hell of terrorism and torture. But they shall not pass!

All Spain has risen to the struggle. In Madrid the people have come out onto the streets, lending strength to the government through their determination and fighting spirit, so that we may, together, exterminate the reactionary fascist rebels.

Young men and women, sound the alarm. Rise and join the battle!

Heroic women of the people – remember the heroism of the Asturian women.[*] You, too, must fight alongside your menfolk and together with them defend the bread and security of your children, whose lives are in danger. Soldiers, sons of the people! Stand steadfastly as one man on the side of this government, on the side of the working people, on the side of the People's Front, on the side of your fathers, brothers and comrades. March with them to victory! Fight for the Spain of February 16.[†]

Working people of all political persuasions. The government has placed valuable means of defense into our hands in order that we may perform our duty with honor; in order that we may save Spain from the disgrace that would be brought upon her by the victory of these bloodthirsty October butchers. You

[*] Refers to an anti-fascist miners' strike in northern Spain, which developed into a revolutionary uprising before being crushed by Franco.

[†] The date of the 1936 Spanish general election, which was won by a left-wing coalition.

must not hesitate for a single moment. Tomorrow we shall be able to celebrate our victory. Be prepared for action. Every worker and every anti-fascist must regard himself as a mobilized soldier.

People of Catalonia, the Basque country, Galicia and all Spaniards! Rise in the defense of the democratic republic; rise to consolidate the victory won by the people on February 16. The Communist Party calls upon all of you to join our struggle. It calls upon all working people to take their place in the struggle, to completely eradicate the enemies of the Republic and of the freedom of the people.

Long live the People's Front.

Long live the alliance of all anti-fascists.

Long live the People's Republic!

SPEECHES OF NOTE

# THIS SACRED CAUSE

Born in Cambridgeshire, England, in 1760, Thomas Clarkson's tireless campaigning and research trips contributed to the passing of the Slave Trade Act 1807 in Parliament. This statute abolished the trading of slaves in British colonies and made it illegal to transport enslaved people on British ships, though trafficking between Caribbean islands and bondage within British colonies continued. Clarkson went on to co-found the Anti-Slavery Society with William Wilberforce and other abolitionists in 1823, pushing for full emancipation. By September 1840, Clarkson was in his advanced years, and delivered this speech in Ipswich to mark the development of a new society, formed to work alongside London's own.

My Friends!

I was invited to take the Chair on this Occasion, though I am utterly unfit for it on account of old age and Infirmities, and I am sorry to say, that I cannot remain in it long for the same Reason: and yet I did not see how I could refuse the Invitation, when I considered, that the great Question of the Abolition of Slavery and the Slave Trade, to which Subjects your attention is called this night, originated wholly with myself. Yes, I have worked in this sacred Cause from the Beginning, now fifty-six years; and though I have been broken down and disabled in the Pursuit of it, I am neither weary of it, nor dismayed; but I mean by the Blessing of God to continue my assistance to it, feeble as it must now be, as long as I am able.

Perhaps many of you here are not acquainted with the Subject of Slavery. I will therefore explain to you what it is. First, let us imagine a child to have been born of Slave-Parents. Poor unfortunate child! From that very Day his Birthday he is considered and classed as a Brute. From that very Day he becomes Property, the Property of a Master, who may sell him, and do with him what he pleases.

Let us now look at him as a grown up Man at his Labour in the Field. He works there, but he is not paid for his Labour. He works there, but not freely and willingly, as our Labourers do, but he is followed by a Driver, whose whip leaves the marks of its severity on his Back during the Remainder of his Life, but if he is found to be what is brutally called sulky or obstinate, there is yet in Store for him – the Chain – the Iron Neck – Collar with its frightful spikes – the Dungeon – and other modes of punishment.

But let us now look at him in another Situation. Weary of his Life he flies from Oppression and he runs away from the Estate; but he is almost sure of being brought back and returned to an enraged master; and have who can imagine, but they, who live in Slave Countries, what further Punishment awaits him. Perhaps he dies in consequence of the Cruelties then inflicted upon him; But the Murderer escapes. The Matter is hushed up. Who on the Estate dares to reveal it? But suppose the Fact, by some accident, to become known and a Jury to sit on the Body; still the murderer may escape for who are the Jury? They are all of them Slave-Owners; all interested in favouring one another in support of arbitrary Power. A Friend of mine was lately in one of the Carolinas, and near the spot, where a Jury had been assembled on account of the murder of a Slave. The poor man had been flogged to Death. In his agonies he called for a little Water, which was brought him. The Jury availed themselves of this circumstance, and though they saw before them his Body mangled and cut into pieces by the Whip, they returned a Verdict, that the administration of cold water in the then excited State of his Body occasioned his Death.

But there are other Evils belonging to Slavery and to Slavery alone. Perhaps a Slave has a Wife and Family. So much the worse; for He may be sold at any moment to go to a Plantation perhaps a hundred Miles off, never to see them more. The Wife may be severed from her Husband and Children in like Manner, and the Children may be severed from their Parents, one after another, or all together, as it suits the Purchaser. This is not an ideal Case, but a case of every Days' Occurrence.

These are some of the Evils which you are called upon this Night to try to put an End to. I do not doubt your Humanity. I do not doubt your Willingness to pity and befriend the oppressed at home, and can you overlook this monstrous oppression, these monstrous Outrages upon human Nature, which have been brought before you, because they take place in a foreign Land. Christianity, true Christianity, does not confine her Sympathy to Country or Colour, but feels for all who are persecuted wherever they may live. May I hope then that the Society, which is to be formed after this Meeting may meet with your Encouragement and Support.

My Friends!

I was invited to take the chair on this Occasion, though I am utterly unfit for it on account of old age and Infirmities, and I am sorry to say, that I cannot remain in it long for the same Reason: and yet I did not see how I could refuse the Invitation, when I considered, that the great Question of the Abolition of Slavery and the Slave Trade, to which Subjects your attention is called this night, originated wholly with myself. yes, I have worked in this sacred Cause from the beginning, now fifty six years; and though I have been broken down and disabled in the Pursuit of it, I am neither weary of it, nor dismayed; but I mean by the Blessing of God to continue my assistance to it, feeble as it must be now, as long as I am able.

Perhaps many of you here are not acquainted with the Subject of Slavery. I will therefore explain to you what it is. First, let us imagine a child to have been born of Slave-Parents. poor unfortunate child! From that very Day he is considered and classed as a Brute. From that very Day he becomes property, the Property of a master, who may sell him, and do with him what he pleases.

Let us now look at him as a grown up Man at his Labour in the Field. He works there, but he is not paid for his Labour. He works there, but not freely and willingly, as our Labourers do, but he is followed by a Driver, whose Whip leaves the marks of its severity on his Back during the Remainder of his Life; and if what is brutally called Obstinacy should require it, there is yet in Store for him — the Chain — the Iron Neck-Collar with its frightful Spikes — the Dungeon — and other Modes of Punishment.

But let us now look at him in another Situation. Weary of his Life he flees from Oppression and he runs away from the Estate; but he is almost sure of being brought back and returned to an enraged master; and here who can imagine, but they, who live in Slave Countries, what farther Punishment awaits him. Perhaps he dies in consequence of the Cruelties then inflicted upon him; But the Murderer escapes. The matter is hushed up. Who on the Estate dares to reveal it? But suppose the fact, by some accident to become known and a Jury to sit on the Body; still the murderer may escape, for who are the Jury? They are all of them Slave-owners; all interested in favouring one another in support of arbitrary Power. A friend of mine was lately in one of the Carolinas, and near the Spot, where a Jury had been assembled on account of the murder of a Slave. The poor man had been flogged to Death, & in his agonies he called for a little Water, which was brought him. The Jury availed themselves of this circumstance, and though they saw before them his Body mangled and cut into Pieces, by the Whip, they returned a Verdict, that the administration of cold Water in the then excited State of his Body occasioned his Death.

But there are other Evils belonging to Slavery, and to Slavery alone. Perhaps a Slave has a Wife and Family. So much the worse; for He may be sold at any moment to go to a Plantation perhaps a hundred miles off, never to see them more. The Wife may be severed from her Husband and Children in like manner, and the Children may be severed from their Parents, one after another, or all together, as it suits the Purchaser. This is not an odd case, but a Case of every days Occurrence.

These are some of the Evils which you are called upon this Night to try to put an end to. I do not doubt your Humanity. I do not doubt your willingness to pity and believe the oppressed at home, and can you overlook this monstrous Oppression, these monstrous Outrages upon human Nature, which have been brought before you, because they take place in a foreign Land. Christianity, true Christianity, does not confine her Sympathy to Country or Colour; but feels for all who are persecuted wherever they may live. May I hope then that the Society, which is to be formed after this meeting may meet with your Encouragement and Support.

# THE HOUR OF DEPARTURE HAS ARRIVED

In 399 BC, the seventy-year-old Greek philosopher Socrates stood in front of a 500-strong jury of his fellow Athenian citizens. Following six hours of arguments from the prosecution and defense, he was sentenced to death for the crime of "refusing to recognize the gods recognized by the state," and "corrupting the youth," both of which were brought on by teaching methods deemed inappropriate by his accusers. Of the 500 jurors present at Stoa Basileios that day, 360 voted for his execution: Socrates had no option but to drink a cup of poison hemlock. However, before he took his life, he gave this final speech to the hundreds of Athenians in attendance. Hours later, he died.

Not much time will be gained, O Athenians, in return for the evil name which you will get from the detractors of the city, who will say that you killed Socrates, a wise man; for they will call me wise even though I am not wise when they want to reproach you. If you had waited a little while, your desire would have been fulfilled in the course of nature. For I am far advanced in years, as you may perceive, and not far from death. I am speaking now only to those of you who have condemned me to death. And I have another thing to say to them: you think that I was convicted through deficiency of words – I mean, that if I had thought fit to leave nothing undone, nothing unsaid, I might have gained an acquittal. Not so; the deficiency which led to my conviction was not of words – certainly not. But I had not the boldness or impudence or inclination to address you as you would have liked me to address you, weeping and wailing and lamenting, and saying and doing many things which you have been accustomed to hear from others, and which, as I say, are unworthy of me. But I thought that I ought not to do anything common or mean in the hour of danger: nor do I now repent of the manner of my defense, and I would rather die having spoken after my manner, than speak in your manner and live. For neither in war nor yet at law ought any man to use every way of escaping death. For often in battle there is no doubt that if a man will throw away his arms, and fall on his knees before his pursuers, he may escape death; and in other dangers there are other ways of escaping death, if a man is willing to say and do anything. The difficulty, my friends, is not in avoiding death, but in avoiding unrighteousness; for that runs faster than death. I am old and move slowly, and the slower runner has overtaken me, and my accusers are keen and quick, and the faster runner, who is unrighteousness, has overtaken them. And now I depart hence condemned by you to suffer the penalty of death, and they, too, go their ways condemned by the truth to suffer the penalty of villainy and wrong; and I must abide by my award – let them abide by theirs. I suppose that these things may be regarded as fated – and I think that they are well.

And now, O men who have condemned me, I would fain prophesy to you; for I am about to die, and that is the hour in which men are gifted with prophetic power. And I prophesy to you who are my murderers, that immediately after my death punishment far heavier than you have inflicted on me will surely await you. Me you have killed because you wanted to escape the accuser, and not to give an account of your lives. But that will not be as you suppose: far otherwise. For I say that there will be more accusers of you than there are now; accusers whom hitherto I have restrained: and as they are younger they will be more severe with you, and you will be more offended at them. For if you think that by killing men you can avoid the accuser censuring your lives, you are mistaken; that is not a way of escape which is either possible or honorable; the easiest and noblest way is not to be crushing others, but to be improving yourselves. This is the prophecy which I utter before my departure, to the judges who have condemned me.

Friends, who would have acquitted me, I would like also to talk with you about this thing which has happened, while the magistrates are busy, and before I go to the place at which I must die. Stay then awhile, for we may as well talk with one another while there is time. You are my friends, and I should like to show you the meaning of this event which has happened to me. O my judges – for you I may truly call judges – I should like to tell you of a wonderful circumstance. Hitherto the familiar oracle within me has constantly been in the habit of opposing me even about trifles, if I was going to make a slip or error about anything; and now as you see there has come upon me that which may be thought, and is generally believed to be, the last and worst evil. But the oracle made no sign of opposition, either as I was leaving my house and going out in the morning, or when I was going up into this court, or while I was speaking, at anything which I was going to say; and yet I have often been stopped in the middle of a speech; but now in nothing I either said or did touching this matter has the oracle opposed me. What do I take to be the explanation of this? I will tell you. I regard this as a proof that what has happened to me is a good, and that those of us who think that death is an evil are in error. This is a great proof to me of what I am saying, for the customary sign would surely have opposed me had I been going to evil and not to good.

Let us reflect in another way, and we shall see that there is great reason to hope that death is a good, for one of two things: either death is a state of nothingness and utter unconsciousness, or, as men say, there is a change and migration of the soul from this world to another. Now if you suppose that there is no consciousness, but a sleep like the sleep of him who is undisturbed even by the sight of dreams, death will be an unspeakable gain. For if a person were to select the night in which his sleep was undisturbed even by dreams, and were to compare with this the other days and nights of his life, and then were to tell us how many days and nights he had passed in the course of his life better and

more pleasantly than this one, I think that any man, I will not say a private man, but even the great king, will not find many such days or nights, when compared with the others. Now if death is like this, I say that to die is gain; for eternity is then only a single night. But if death is the journey to another place, and there, as men say, all the dead are, what good, O my friends and judges, can be greater than this? If indeed when the pilgrim arrives in the world below, he is delivered from the professors of justice in this world, and finds the true judges who are said to give judgment there, Minos and Rhadamanthus and Aeacus and Triptolemus,* and other sons of God who were righteous in their own life, that pilgrimage will be worth making. What would not a man give if he might converse with Orpheus and Musaeus and Hesiod and Homer? Nay, if this be true, let me die again and again. I, too, shall have a wonderful interest in a place where I can converse with Palamedes, and Ajax the son of Telamon, and other heroes of old, who have suffered death through an unjust judgment; and there will be no small pleasure, as I think, in comparing my own sufferings with theirs. Above all, I shall be able to continue my search into true and false knowledge; as in this world, so also in that; I shall find out who is wise, and who pretends to be wise, and is not. What would not a man give, O judges, to be able to examine the leader of the great Trojan expedition; or Odysseus or Sisyphus, or numberless others, men and women too! What infinite delight would there be in conversing with them and asking them questions! For in that world they do not put a man to death for this; certainly not. For besides being happier in that world than in this, they will be immortal, if what is said is true.

* In Greek mythology, the demigods Minos, Rhadamanthus, Aeacus and – in some sources – Triptolemus were the judges of the dead in the underworld.

Wherefore, O judges, be of good cheer about death, and know this of a truth – that no evil can happen to a good man, either in life or after death. He and his are not neglected by the gods; nor has my own approaching end happened by mere chance. But I see clearly that to die and be released was better for me; and therefore the oracle gave no sign. For which reason also, I am not angry with my accusers, or my condemners; they have done me no harm, although neither of them meant to do me any good; and for this I may gently blame them.

Still I have a favor to ask of them. When my sons are grown up, I would ask you, O my friends, to punish them; and I would have you trouble them, as I have troubled you, if they seem to care about riches, or anything, more than about virtue; or if they pretend to be something when they are really nothing – then reprove them, as I have reproved you, for not caring about that for which they ought to care, and thinking that they are something when they are really nothing. And if you do this, I and my sons will have received justice at your hands.

The hour of departure has arrived, and we go our ways – I to die, and you to live. Which is better God only knows.

← *The Death of Socrates* by Jacques-Louis David, 1787, oil on canvas

# NORWAY IS YOU. NORWAY IS US.

In 2016, with the country's tensions frayed due to an anti-immigration, center-right government and a recent influx of asylum seekers to the region, the 79-year-old King of Norway applied an unexpectedly soothing balm in the form of a remarkable speech. Addressing a crowd of 1,500 guests in the gardens of the Royal Palace in Oslo, he spoke of nothing but inclusion and acceptance. Such was its power that footage of the speech had reached all corners of the globe within hours, its transcript translated into dozens of languages.

Dear all,

After traveling throughout the country over the course of many years, it is a great pleasure for us to host representatives from all over Norway.

A warm welcome to every one of you!

Those of you who are gathered here represent Norway as it is today.

So what is Norway?

Norway is high mountains and deep fjords. It is wide open spaces and rocky coastlines. It is islands and archipelagos. It is lush farmland and rolling moors.

The sea laps Norway's shores in the north, west and south.

Norway is midnight sun and polar night. It is harsh winters and mild winters. It is hot summers and cold summers.

Norway is a long and sparsely populated country.

But above all, Norway is its people.

Norwegians come from North Norway, Central Norway, Southern Norway – and all of the other regions. Norwegians have immigrated from Afghanistan, Pakistan and Poland, from Sweden, Somalia and Syria. My grandparents came here from Denmark and England 110 years ago.

It is not always easy to say where we are from, what nationality we are. Home is where our heart is – and that cannot always be confined within national borders.

Norwegians are young and old, tall and short, able-bodied and wheelchair users. More and more people are over 100 years old. Norwegians are rich, poor and in-between. Norwegians like football and handball, mountain climbing and sailing – while others prefer lounging on the sofa.

Some are self-confident, while others struggle to believe they are good enough as they are.

Norwegians work in shops, in hospitals, on offshore platforms. Norwegians work to keep us safe and secure, to keep our country free of pollution and to find new solutions for a green future. Norwegians farm the land and catch fish. Norwegians do research and teach.

13.00

2012

KONG HARALD V 75 år

NORGE

1806.

POSTEN

Norwegians are enthusiastic young people – and wise old people.

Norwegians are single, divorced, families with children, and old married couples. Norwegians are girls who love girls, boys who love boys, and girls and boys who love each other.

Norwegians believe in God, Allah, the Universe and nothing.

Norwegians like Grieg and Kygo, the Hellbillies and Kari Bremnes.

In other words: Norway is you.

Norway is us.

When we sing "Ja, vi elsker dette landet,"* we should remember that we are also singing about each other. Because we are this country. Thus, our national anthem is also a declaration of love for the Norwegian people.

My greatest hope for Norway is that we will be able to take care of one another.

That we will continue to build this country – on a foundation of trust, fellowship and generosity of spirit.

That we will feel that we are – despite our differences – one people.

That Norway is one.

Once again, a warm welcome to you all! I hope we will have an enjoyable time together.

* "Yes, we love this country"

# BREATHE AND PUSH

At Washington's Metropolitan AME Church on New Year's Eve 2016, at the end of a politically fraught year that bore witness to a widening of social divisions and a frightening rise in hate crimes, Sikh activist Valarie Kaur gave a powerful speech. Standing tall alongside a number of religious leaders, she spoke about her hopes and fears during a time of such turmoil.

* "The beloved community belongs to divine Oneness, and so does all that it achieves."

Waheguru Ji Ka Khalsa, Waheguru Ji Ki Fateh.*

On Christmas Eve 103 years ago, my grandfather waited in a dark and dank cell. He sailed by steamship across the Pacific Ocean from India to America leaving behind colonial rule, but when he landed on American shores immigration officials saw his dark skin, his tall turban worn as a part of his Sikh faith, and saw him not as a brother but as foreign, as suspect, and they threw him behind bars where he languished for months until a single man, a white man, a lawyer named Henry Marshall, filed a writ of habeas corpus that released him on Christmas Eve 1913.

My grandfather Kehar Singh became a farmer, free to practice the heart of his Sikh faith – love and oneness. So when his Japanese American neighbors were rounded up and taken to their own detention camps in the deserts of America he went out to see them when no one else would. He looked after their farms until they returned home. He refused to stand down.

In the aftermath of September 11th when hate violence exploded in these United States, a man that I called uncle was murdered. I tried to stand up. I became a lawyer like the man who freed my grandfather and I joined a generation of activists fighting detentions and deportation, surveillance and special registration, hate crimes and racial profiling. And after fifteen years, with every film, with every lawsuit, with every campaign, I thought we were making the nation safer for the next generation.

And then my son was born. On Christmas Eve, I watched him ceremoniously put the milk and cookies by the fire for Santa Claus. And after he went to sleep, I then drank the milk and ate the cookies. I wanted him to wake up and see them gone in the morning. I wanted him to believe in a world that was magical. But I am leaving my son a world that is more dangerous than the one that I was given. I am raising – we are raising – a brown boy in America, a brown boy who may someday wear a turban as part of his faith.

And in America today, as we enter an era of enormous rage, as white nationalists hail this moment as their great awakening, as hate acts against Sikhs and our Muslim brothers and sisters are at an all-time high, I know that there will be moments whether on the streets or in the school yards where my

son will be seen as foreign, as suspect, as a terrorist. Just as black bodies are still seen as criminal, brown bodies are still seen as illegal, trans bodies are still seen as immoral, indigenous bodies are still seen as savage, the bodies of women and girls seen as someone else's property. And when we see these bodies not as brothers and sisters then it becomes easier to bully them, to rape them, to allow policies that neglect them, that incarcerate them, that kill them.

Yes, rabbi, the future is dark. On this New Year's Eve, this watch night, I close my eyes and I see the darkness of my grandfather's cell. And I can feel the spirit of ever-rising optimism in the Sikh tradition Chardi Kala* within him.

So the mother in me asks "what if?" What if this darkness is not the darkness of the tomb, but the darkness of the womb? What if our America is not dead but a country that is waiting to be born? What if the story of America is one long labor? What if all of our grandfathers and grandmothers are standing behind us now, those who survived occupation and genocide, slavery and Jim Crow, detentions and political assault? What if they are whispering in our ears today, tonight, "You are brave"? What if this is our nation's great transition?

What does the midwife tell us to do? Breathe. And then? Push. Because if we don't push we will die. If we don't push our nation will die. Tonight we will breathe. Tomorrow we will labor in love through love, and your revolutionary love is the magic we will show our children.

Waheguru Ji Ka Khalsa, Waheguru Ji Ki Fateh.

* This is a state of mind loosely described as "ever-rising high spirits," which Sikhs aspire to attain.

← Valarie Kaur, photographed by Sharat Raju

# A GLORY HAS DEPARTED

Few people in human history have made an impression as lasting and as positive as Mahatma Mohandas K. Gandhi. Born in 1869, he made it his life's mission to spread a message of non-violence across the globe and to promote peace to all who would listen, no matter the price. Sadly, in 1948, aged seventy-eight, he met his end in the cruelest of ways when he was assassinated by a young Hindu extremist. At Parliament House in New Delhi, three days after Gandhi was killed and as millions of people around the world came to terms with his tragic death, a eulogy was delivered by the first prime minister of India and friend to Gandhi, Jawaharlal Nehru.

It is customary in this House to pay some tribute to the eminent departed, to say some words of praise and condolence. I am not quite sure in my own mind if it is exactly fitting for me or for any others of this House to say much on this occasion for I have a sense of utter shame both as an individual and as head of the government of India that we should have failed to protect the greatest treasure we possessed.

It is our failure in the past many months, to give protection to many an innocent man, woman and child. It may be that that burden and task was too great for us or for any government; nevertheless, it is a failure, and today the fact that this mighty person, whom we honoured and loved beyond measure, has gone because we could not give him adequate protection is shame for all of us. It is shame to me as an Indian that an Indian should have raised his hand against him; it is shame to me as a Hindu that a Hindu should have done this deed and done it to the greatest Indian of the day and the greatest Hindu of the age.

We praise people in well-chosen words and we have some kind of measure for greatness. How shall we praise him and how shall we measure him, because he was not of the common clay that all of us are made of? He came, lived a fairly long span of life and has passed away. No words of praise of ours in this House are needed, for he has had greater praise in his life than any living man in history and during these two or three days since his death he has had the homage of the world. What can we add to that? How can we praise him? How can we who have been children of his, and perhaps more intimately children of his than the children of his body, for we have all been in some greater or smaller measure the children of his spirit, unworthy as we were?

A glory has departed and the sun that warmed and brightened our lives has set, and we shiver in the cold and dark. Yet he would not have us feel this way. After all, that glory that we saw for all these years, that man with divine fire, changed us also – and such as we are, we have been moulded by him during these years; and out of that divine fire many of us also took a small spark which strengthened and made us work to some extent on the lines that he fashioned. And so if we praise him, our words seem rather small, and if we praise him, to some extent we also praise ourselves. Great men and eminent men have monuments in bronze and marble set up for them, but this man of divine fire managed in his lifetime to become enshrined in millions and millions of hearts so that all of us became somewhat of the stuff that he was made of, though to an infinitely lesser degree. He spread out in this way all over India, not just in palaces, or in select places or in assemblies, but in every hamlet and hut of the lowly and those who suffer. He lives in the hearts of millions and he will live for immemorial ages.

What, then, can we say about him except to feel humble on this occasion? To praise him we are not worthy – to praise him whom we could not follow adequately and sufficiently. It is almost doing him an injustice just to pass him by with words when he demanded work and labour and sacrifice from us; in a large measure he made this country, during the last thirty years or more, attain to heights of sacrifice which in that particular domain have never been equaled elsewhere. He succeeded in that. Yet ultimately things happened which no doubt made him suffer tremendously, though his tender face never lost its smile and he never spoke a harsh word to anyone. Yet, he must have suffered – suffered for the failing of this generation whom he had trained, suffered because we went away from the path that he had shown us. And ultimately the hand of a child of his – for he, after all, is as much a child of his as any other Indian – the hand of a child of his struck him down.

Long ages afterwards history will judge of this period that we have passed through. It will judge of the successes and the failures – we are too near it to be proper judges and to understand what has happened and what has not happened. All we know is that there was a glory and that it is no more; all we know is that for the moment there is darkness, not so dark certainly, because when we look into our hearts we still find the living flame which he lighted there. And if those living flames exist, there will not be darkness in this land, and we shall be able, with our effort, remembering him and following his path, to illumine this land again, small as we are, but still with the fire that he instilled into us.

He was perhaps the greatest symbol of the India of the past, and may I say, of the India of the future, that we could have had. We stand on this perilous edge of the present, between that past and the future to be, and we face all manner of perils. And the greatest peril is sometimes the lack of faith which comes to us, the sense of frustration that comes to us, the sinking of the heart and of the spirit that comes to us when we see ideals go overboard, when we see the great things that we talked about somehow pass into empty words, and life taking a different course. Yet, I do believe that perhaps this period will pass soon enough.

Great as this man of God was in his life, he has been greater in his death, and I have no shadow of a doubt that by his death he has served the great cause as he served it throughout his life. We mourn him, we shall always mourn him, because we are human and cannot forget our valued master, but I know that he would not like us to mourn him. No tears came to his eyes when his dearest and closest went away, only the firm resolve to persevere, to serve the great cause that he had chosen. So he would chide us if we merely mourn. That is a poor way of doing homage to him.

The only way is to express our determination, to pledge ourselves anew, to conduct ourselves so and to dedicate ourselves to the great task which he undertook and which he accomplished to such a large extent. So we have to work, we have to labour, we have to sacrifice and thus prove to some extent at least worthy followers of his.

This happening, this tragedy, is not merely the isolated act of a madman. It comes out of a certain atmosphere of violence and hatred that has prevailed in this country for many months and years, and more especially in the past few months. That atmosphere envelops us and surrounds us, and if we are to serve the cause he put before us we have to face this atmosphere, to combat it, struggle against it and root out the evil of hatred and violence.

So far as this government is concerned I trust they will spare no means, spare no effort to tackle it, because if we do not do that, if we in our weakness or for any other reason that we may consider adequate do not take effective means to stop this violence, to stop this spreading of hatred by word of mouth or writing or act, then, indeed, we are not worthy of being in this government, we are not certainly worthy of being his followers and we are not worthy of even saying words of praise for this great soul who has departed.

So that on this occasion or any other when we think of this master who has gone, let us always think of him in terms of work and labour and sacrifice, in terms of fighting evil wherever we see it, in terms of holding to the truth, as he put it before us, and if we do so, however unworthy we may be, we shall at least have done our duty and paid the proper homage to his spirit.

He has gone, and all over India there is a feeling of having been left desolate and forlorn. All of us sense that feeling, and I do not know when we shall be able to get rid of it. And yet together with that feeling there is also a feeling of proud thankfulness that it has been given to us of this generation to be associated with this mighty person.

In ages to come, centuries and maybe millennia after us, people will think of this generation when this man of God trod on earth, and will think of us who, however small, could also follow his path and tread the holy ground where his feet had been.

Let us be worthy of him.

← Pandit Jawaharlal Nehru, later prime minister of India, with Mohandas K. Gandhi

# THIS IS YOUR EVEREST

In 1997, the British and Irish Lions rugby squad spent six weeks playing a selection of teams in South Africa, including three Test matches against the most formidable of opponents: the country's national team, the Springboks. As luck would have it, a small documentary film crew were glued to the British team throughout the tour – and in the changing-room, moments before the first Test, they captured on film a speech given to the team by assistant coach Jim Telfer that has since gone down in sporting history as one of the greats. His words made an impact too. The Lions won that particular game, and returned home as winners of the Test series.

The easy bit has passed. Selection for the Test team is the easy bit. You have an awesome responsibility on the eight individual forwards' shoulders. Awesome responsibility. This is your fucking Everest, boys. Very few ever get a chance in rugby terms to get to the top of Everest. You have the chance today.

Being picked is the easy bit. To win for the Lions in a Test match is the ultimate, but you'll not do it unless you put your bodies on the line. Every one Jack of you for eighty minutes.

Defeat doesn't worry me. I've had it often and so have you. It's performance that matters. If you put in the performance, you'll get what you deserve. No luck attached to it. If you don't put it in, if you're not honest, then we're second-raters.

They don't rate us. They don't respect us. They don't respect you. They don't rate you. The only way to be rated is to stick one on them, to get right up in their faces and turn them back, knock them back. Outdo what they can do. Out-jump them, out-scrum them, out-ruck them, out-drive them, out-tackle them, until they're fucking sick of you.

Remember the pledges you made. Remember how you depend on each other – you depend on each other at every phase – teams within teams, scrums, line-outs, ruck balls, tackles. They are better than you've played against so far. They are better individually or they wouldn't be there. So it's an awesome task you have and it will only be done, as I say, if everybody commits themself now.

[Pointing to a whiteboard] That was written yesterday about us. Read it silently, take note of it, and then make a pledge.

You are privileged. You are the chosen few. Many are considered but few are chosen. They don't think fuck all of us. Nothing. We're here just to make up the fucking numbers.

[Reading from the whiteboard] 'Their weak point is the scrum. The Boks must exploit this weakness. The Boks must concentrate on the eight-man shove every scrum. Scrummaging will be the key. Their weakness is the scrum.'

Nobody's going to do it for you. You have to find your own solace, your own drive, your own ambition, your own inner strength, because the moment's arriving for the greatest game of your fucking lives.

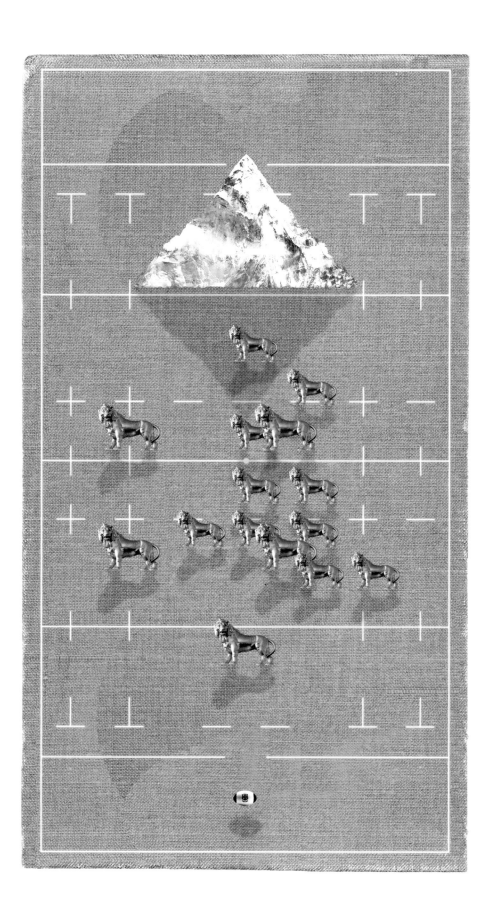

# GIRLS WITH DREAMS BECOME WOMEN WITH VISION

Formed in 2010, UN Women is a United Nations entity dedicated to championing gender equality and the empowerment of women throughout its member states. On International Women's Day in 2015, at a UN Women conference in New York, a speech was given by a young Hollywood actor that described her entry into the world of activism at the tender age of eleven. On May 19, 2018, almost three years after this address, Meghan Markle married Prince Henry of Wales, more commonly known as Prince Harry, becoming Her Royal Highness The Duchess of Sussex.

→ Meghan Markle at the UN Women conference, March 2015

Well, good evening. That doesn't feel like enough, does it? Great evening? Maybe that's better.

UN Secretary-General, Executive Director Phumzile, thank you. Distinguished ladies and gentlemen, I am tremendously honored to be UN Women's advocate for political participation and leadership. I am proud to be a woman and a feminist, and this evening I am extremely proud to stand before you on this significant day, which serves as a reminder to all of us of how far we've come, but also, amid celebration, a reminder of the road ahead.

I want to tell you a story that'll sort of give context to my being here and my work with UN Women. When I was just eleven years old, I unknowingly and somehow accidentally became a female advocate. It was around the same time as the Beijing conference, so a little over twenty years ago, where in my hometown of Los Angeles a pivotal moment reshaped my notion of what is possible. See, I had been in school watching a TV show in elementary school, and this commercial came on with the tagline for this dishwashing liquid and the tagline said, "Women all over America are fighting greasy pots and pans." Two boys from my class said, "Yeah, that's where women belong, in the kitchen." I remember feeling shocked and angry and also just feeling so hurt; it just wasn't right, and something needed to be done. So I went home and told my dad what had happened, and he encouraged me to write letters, so I did, to the most powerful people I could think of.

Now my eleven-year-old self worked out that if I really wanted someone to hear me, well then I should write a letter to the first lady. So off I went, scribbling away to our first lady at the time, Hillary Clinton. I also put pen to paper and I wrote a letter to my news source at the time, Linda Ellerbee, who hosted a kids news program, and then to powerhouse attorney Gloria Allred, because even at eleven I wanted to cover all my bases. Finally I wrote to the soap manufacturer. And a few weeks went by and to my surprise I received letters of encouragement from Hillary Clinton, from Linda Ellerbee, and from Gloria

Allred. It was amazing. The kids news show, they sent a camera crew to my home to cover the story, and it was roughly a month later when the soap manufacturer, Procter & Gamble, changed the commercial for their Ivory Clear dishwashing liquid. They changed it from "Women all over America are fighting greasy pots and pans" to "People all over America." It was at that moment that I realized the magnitude of my actions. At the age of eleven I had created my small level of impact by standing up for equality.

Now, equality means that President Paul Kagame of Rwanda, whose country I recently visited as part of my learning mission with UN Women, it means that he is equal to the little girl in the Gihembe refugee camp who is dreaming about being president one day. Equality means that UN Secretary General Ban Ki-moon is equal to the young intern at the UN who is dreaming about shaking his hand. It means that a wife, it means that a wife is equal to her husband; a sister to her brother. Not better, not worse – they are equal.

UN Women, as you guys know, has defined the year 2030 as the expiration date for gender inequality. And here's what's staggering: the studies show that at the current rate, the elimination of gender inequality won't be possible until 2095. That's another eighty years from now. And when it comes to women's political participation and leadership the percentage of female parliamentarians globally has only increased by 11 percent since 1995. Eleven percent in twenty years? Come on. This has to change. Women make up more than half of the world's population and potential, so it is neither just nor practical for their voices, for our voices, to go unheard at the highest levels of decision-making.

The way that we change that, in my opinion, is to mobilize girls and women to see their value as leaders, and to support them in these efforts. To have leaders such as President Kagame of Rwanda continue to be a role model of a country which has a parliamentary system comprised of 64 percent female leaders. I mean, it's the highest of any government in the world and it's unbelievable. We need more men like that, just as we need more men like my father who championed my eleven-year-old self to stand up for what is right. In doing this, we remind girls that their small voices are, in fact, not small at all, and that they can effect change. In doing this, we remind women that their involvement matters. That they need to become active in their communities, in their local governments, as well as in the highest parliamentary positions. It is just imperative: women need a seat at the table, they need an invitation to be seated there, and in some cases, where this is not available, well then, you know what, they need to create their own table. We need a global understanding that we cannot implement change effectively without women's political participation.

It is said that girls with dreams become women with vision. May we empower each other to carry out such vision – because it isn't enough to simply talk about equality. One must believe in it. And it isn't enough to simply believe in it. One must work at it. Let us work at it. Together. Starting now.

# LIFT OFF

In 2016, a Master of Education graduate named Donovan Livingston made ripples around the world when he gave a rousing spoken-word address at the Harvard Graduate School of Education's commencement ceremony. Footage of his lyrical speech, in which he poetically ruminates on the obstacles faced by students of color and calls for his fellow educators to help lift them to their true potential, was viewed by many millions in the space of hours and resulted in widespread international acclaim.

Good afternoon. Good afternoon. How is everyone doing today? Good. Good.

So greetings friends, family, faculty, staff, alumni and the illustrious Class of 2016, make some noise!

So my name is Donovan Livingston and I came to address you in the best way I know how. But you have to forgive me, I have to take this moment in for a little while.

When I spoke in my high school graduation several years ago, my high school English teacher threatened to replace me on the program or cut my microphone when she found out that I was interested in doing a poem as a part of my remarks. So I am eternally grateful for being able to share this piece of myself in my most authentic voice with you this afternoon.

So, spoken-word poetry, it insists on participation, so if you feel so compelled, snap, clap, throw up your hands, rejoice, celebrate. Class of 2016, this is your address and this is your day . . .

"Education then, beyond all other devices of human origin,
Is a great equalizer of the conditions of men."
Horace Mann, 1848

At the time of his remarks I couldn't read – I couldn't write.
Any attempt to do so, punishable by death.
For generations we have known of knowledge's infinite power.
Yet somehow, we have never questioned the keeper of the keys –
The guardians of information.

Unfortunately, I've seen more dividing and conquering
In this order of operations – a heinous miscalculation of reality.
For some, the only difference between a classroom and a plantation is time.
How many times must we be made to feel like quotas –
Like tokens in coined phrases? –
"Diversity. Inclusion."

There are days I feel like one, like only –
A lonely blossom in a briar patch of broken promises.
But hey, I've always been a thorn in the side of injustice.

Disruptive. Talkative. A distraction.
With a passion that transcends the confines of my own consciousness –
Beyond your curriculum, beyond your standards.
I stand here, a manifestation of love and pain,
With veins pumping revolution.
I am the strange fruit that grew too ripe for the poplar tree.
I am a DREAM Act,* Dream Deferred incarnate.
I am a movement – an amalgam of memories America would care to forget
My past alone won't allow me to sit still.
So my body, like my mind
Cannot be contained.

As educators, rather than raising your voices
Over the rustling of our chains,
Take them off. Un-cuff us.
Unencumbered by the lumbering weight
Of poverty and privilege,
Policy and ignorance.

I was in the seventh grade, when Ms. Parker told me,
"Donovan, we can put all of your excess energy to good use!"
And she introduced me to the sound of my own voice.
She gave me a stage. A platform.
She told me that our stories are the ladders
That make it easier for us to touch the stars.
So climb and grab them.
Keep climbing. Grab them.
Spill your emotions in the big dipper and pour out your soul.
Light up the world with your luminous allure.

To educate requires Galileo-like patience.
Today, when I look my students in the eyes, all I see are constellations.
If you take the time to connect the dots,
You can plot the true shape of their genius –
Shining in their darkest hour.

I look each of my students in the eyes,
And see the same light that aligned Orion's Belt

* The DREAM Act was a U.S. bill that aimed to provide young immigrants with a pathway to legal status. It failed to get through Congress, leaving many undocumented students in a legal limbo that remains to this day.

← Donovan Livingston, age 25, May 2016, photographed by Jill Anderson

And the pyramids of Giza.

† Harriet Tubman was an
African American slave
who escaped to freedom
via the Underground
Railroad. She went on to
guide a further 300 slaves
to freedom herself.

And the pyramids of Giza.
I see the same twinkle
That guided Harriet to freedom.[†]
I see them. Beneath their masks and their mischief,
Exists an authentic frustration;
An enslavement to your standardized assessments.

At the core, none of us were meant to be common.
We were born to be comets,
Darting across space and time –
Leaving our mark as we crash into everything.
A crater is a reminder that something amazing happened right here –
An indelible impact that shook up the world.
Are we not astronomers – searching for the next shooting star?
I teach in hopes of turning content into rocket ships –
Tribulations into telescopes,
So a child can see their true potential from right where they stand.
An injustice is telling them they are stars
Without acknowledging the night that surrounds them.
Injustice is telling them that education is the key
While you continue to change the locks.

Education is no equalizer –
Rather, it is the sleep that precedes the American Dream.
So wake up – wake up! Lift your voices
Until you've patched every hole in a child's broken sky.
Wake up every child so they know of their celestial potential.
I've been the black hole in a classroom for far too long;
Absorbing everything, without allowing my light to escape.
But those days are done. I belong among the stars.
And so do you. And so do they.
Together, we can inspire galaxies of greatness
For generations to come.
So no, no, sky is not the limit. It is only the beginning.
Lift off.

# IT WAS OUR PREJUDICE

On December 10, 1992, to mark the beginning of the International Year of the World's Indigenous People, Australian Prime Minister Paul Keating took to the podium in Redfern Park and gave a blunt and forceful speech. In front of an audience consisting partly of Indigenous Australians, he finally acknowledged their centuries-long mistreatment at the hands of British settlers and the results of such prolonged injustice on the Aboriginal community. To this day, Keating's speech is seen by many as a turning point in an incredibly complex relationship, and for this reason is often described as one of the greats.

Ladies and gentlemen,

I am very pleased to be here today at the launch of Australia's celebration of the 1993 International Year of the World's Indigenous People. It will be a year of great significance for Australia.

It comes at a time when we have committed ourselves to succeeding in the test which so far we have always failed.

Because, in truth, we cannot confidently say that we have succeeded if we have not managed to extend opportunity and care, dignity and hope to the Indigenous people of Australia – the Aboriginal and Torres Strait Islander people.

This is a fundamental test of our social goals and our national will: our ability to say to ourselves and to the rest of the world that Australia is a first-rate social democracy, that we are what we should be – truly the land of the fair go and the better chance.

There is no more basic test, I think, of how seriously we mean these things. It is a test of our self-knowledge. Of how well we know the land we live in. How well we know our history. How well we recognise the fact that, complex as our contemporary identity is, it cannot be separated from Aboriginal Australia. How well we know what Aboriginal Australians know about Australia.

Redfern is a good place to contemplate these things. . . . Just a mile or two from the place where the first European settlers landed, in too many ways it tells us that the failure to bring much more than devastation and demoralisation to Aboriginal Australia continues to be our failure.

More I think than most Australians recognise, the plight of Aboriginal Australians affects us all. In Redfern it might be tempting to think that the reality Aboriginal Australians face is somehow contained here, and that the rest of us are insulated from it. But of course, while all the dilemmas may exist here, as we all know, they are far from contained. We know the same dilemmas and more are faced all over Australia.

That is perhaps the point of this Year of the World's Indigenous People: to bring the dispossessed out of the shadows, to recognise that they are part of us, that we cannot give Indigenous Australians up without giving up many of our own deeply held values, much of our identity – and indeed our own humanity. Nowhere in the world, I would venture, is the message more stark than Australia.

We cannot simply sweep injustice aside. Even if our own conscience allowed us to, I am sure that in due course the world and the people of our region would not. There should be no mistake about this – our success in resolving these issues will have a significant bearing on our standing in the world. . . .

But however intractable the problems seem, we can't resign ourselves to failure – any more than we can hide behind our political opponents' contemporary version of Social Darwinism which says that to reach back for the poor and dispossessed is to risk being dragged down. That seems to me not only morally indefensible, but bad history.

We non-Aboriginal Australians should perhaps remind ourselves that Australia once reached out for us. Didn't Australia provide opportunity and care for the dispossessed Irish? Did it not for the poor of Britain? The refugees from war and famine and persecution in the countries of Europe and Asia?

Isn't it reasonable to say that if we can build a prosperous and remarkably harmonious multicultural society in Australia, surely we can find just solutions to the problems which beset the first Australians – the people to whom the most injustice has been done?

And, as I say, the starting point might be to recognise that the problem starts with us, the non-Aboriginal Australians. It begins, I think, with an act of recognition. Recognition that it was we who did the dispossessing. We took the traditional lands and smashed the traditional way of life. We brought the diseases and the alcohol. We committed the murders. We took the children from their mothers. We practised discrimination and exclusion. It was our ignorance and our prejudice. And our failure to imagine that these things could be done to us.

With some noble exceptions, we failed to make the most basic human response and enter into their hearts and minds. We failed to ask – how would I feel if this were done to me? As a consequence, we failed to see that what we were doing degraded us all.

If we needed a reminder of this, we received it in this year with the report of the Royal Commission into Aboriginal Deaths in Custody, which showed with devastating clarity that the past lives on in inequality, racism and injustice; in the prejudice and ignorance of non-Aboriginal Australians; and in the demoralisation and desperation, the fractured identity, of so many Aborigines and Torres Strait Islanders.

For all this, I do not believe that the report should fill us with guilt. Down the years, there has been no shortage of guilt, but it has not produced the response we need. Guilt, I think we have learned, is not a very constructive

→ Australian Prime Minister Paul Keating addressing the crowd at the launch of the 1993 International Year of the World's Indigenous People

Because, in truth, we cannot confidently say that we have succeeded ~~as we would like to have succeeded~~ if we have not managed to extend opportunity and care, dignity and hope to the indigenous people of Australia – the Aboriginal and Torres Strait Island people.

This is a **fundamental** test of our social goals and our national will: our ability to say to ourselves and the rest of the world that Australia **is** a first rate social democracy, that we **are** what we should be – **truly** the land of the fair go and the better chance.

There is no more basic test of how seriously we mean these things.

It is a test of our self-knowledge.

Of how well we know the land we live in. How well we know our history.

How well we recognise the fact that, complex as our contemporary identity is, it cannot be separated from Aboriginal Australia.

How well we know what Aboriginal Australians know about Australia.

Redfern is a good place to contemplate these things.

Just a mile or two from the place where the first European settlers landed, in too many ways it tells us that their failure to bring much more than devastation and demoralisation to Aboriginal Australia continues to be **our** failure.

More I think than most Australians recognise, the plight of Aboriginal Australians affects us all.

In Redfern it might be tempting to think that the reality Aboriginal Australians face is somehow contained here, and that the rest of us are insulated from it.

But of course, while all the dilemmas may exist here, they are far from contained.

We know the same dilemmas and more are faced all over Australia.

That is perhaps the point of this Year of the World's Indigenous People: to bring the dispossessed out of the shadows, to recognise that they are part of us, and that we cannot give indigenous Australians up without giving up many of our own most deeply held values, much of our own identity – and our own humanity.

Nowhere in the world, I would venture, is the message more stark than it is in Australia.

We simply cannot sweep injustice aside. Even if our own conscience allowed us to, I am sure, that in due course, the world and the people of our region would not.

There should be no mistake about this – our success in resolving these issues will have a significant bearing on our standing in the world.

However intractable the problems seem, we cannot resign ourselves to failure – any more than we can hide behind the/contemporary version of Social Darwinism which says that to reach back for the poor and dispossessed is to risk being dragged down.

That seems to me not only morally indefensible, but bad history.

We non–Aboriginal Australians should perhaps remind ourselves that Australia once reached out for us.

Didn't Australia provide opportunity and care for the dispossessed Irish?  The poor of Britain?  The refugees from war and famine and persecution in the countries of Europe and Asia?

Isn't it reasonable to say that if we can build a prosperous and remarkably harmonious multicultural society in Australia, surely we can find just solutions to the problems which beset the first Australians – the people to whom the most injustice has been done.

And, as I say, the starting point might be to recognise that the problem starts with us non–Aboriginal Australians.

It begins, I think, with that act of recognition.

## 8

Recognition that it was we who did the dispossessing.

**We** took the traditional lands and smashed the traditional way of life.

**We** brought the diseases. The alcohol.

**We** committed the murders.

**We** took the children from the mothers.

**We** practised discrimination and exclusion.

It was **our** ignorance and **our** prejudice.

And **our** failure to imagine these things being done to us.

## 9

With some noble exceptions, we failed to make the most basic human response and enter into their hearts and minds.

We failed to ask – how would I feel if this were done to me?

As a consequence, we failed to see that what we were doing degraded all of us all.

If we needed a reminder of this, we received it this year.

The Report of the Royal Commission into Aboriginal Deaths in Custody showed with devastating clarity that the past "lives on" in inequality, racism and injustice.

emotion. I think what we need to do is open our hearts a bit. All of us. Perhaps when we recognise what we have in common, we will see the things which must be done – the practical things.

There is something of this in the creation of the Council for Aboriginal Reconciliation. The Council's mission is to forge a new partnership built on justice and equity and an appreciation of the heritage of Australia's Indigenous people.

In the abstract those terms are meaningless. We have to give meaning to 'justice' and 'equity' – and, as I have said several times this year, we will only give them meaning when we commit ourselves to achieving concrete results.

If we improve the living conditions in one town, they will improve in another. And another. If we raise the standard of health by 20 per cent one year, it will be raised more the next. If we open one door, others will follow. When we see improvement, we will see more dignity, more confidence, more happiness – we will know we are going to win. We will need these practical building blocks of change. . . .

The Mabo Judgment* should be seen as one of these. By doing away with the bizarre concept that this continent had no owners prior to the settlement of Europeans, Mabo establishes a fundamental truth and lays the basis for justice. It will be much easier to work from that basis than has ever been the case in the past. For that reason alone we should ignore the isolated outbreaks of hysteria and hostility to Mabo, which we've heard in the past few months.

Mabo is an historic decision – we can make it an historic turning point, the basis of a new relationship between Indigenous and non-Aboriginal Australians. The message should be that there is nothing to fear or to lose in the recognition of historical truth, or the extension of social justice, or the deepening of Australian social democracy to include Indigenous Australians. In fact, as all of us, I think, here know, there is everything to gain. Even the unhappy past speaks for this.

Where Aboriginal Australians have been included in the life of Australia they have made remarkable contributions. Economic contributions, particularly in the pastoral and agricultural industry. They are there in the frontier and exploration history of Australia. They were there in the wars. In sport to an extraordinary degree. In literature and art and in music. In all these things they have shaped our knowledge of this continent and of ourselves.

They have shaped our identity. They are there in the Australian legend. And we should never forget – they have helped build this nation. And if we have a sense of justice, as well as common sense, we will forge a new partnership.

As I said, it might help if we non-Aboriginal Australians imagined ourselves dispossessed of land we had lived on for 50,000 years – and then imagined ourselves told that it had never been ours.

* The Mabo decision (1992) was named after Eddie Mabo, a Torres Strait Islander who challenged the Australian laws on land ownership. After ten years of legal wrangling, the high court ruled that native Australians had rights to the land that existed before the British arrived and those rights can still exist today.

Imagine if ours was the oldest culture in the world and we were told that it was worthless.

Imagine if we had resisted this settlement, suffered and died in the defence of our land, and then were told in history books that we had given up without a fight.

Imagine if non-Aboriginal Australians had served their country in peace and war and were then ignored in history books.

Imagine if our feats on the sporting fields had inspired admiration and patriotism and yet did nothing to diminish prejudice.

Imagine if our spiritual life was denied and ridiculed.

Imagine if we had suffered the injustice and then were blamed for it.

It seems to me that if we can imagine the injustice we can imagine the opposite. And we can have justice. I say we can have justice for two reasons. I say it because I believe that the great things about Australian social democracy reflect a fundamental belief in justice. And I say it because in so many other areas we have proved our capacity over the years to go on extending the realms of participation, opportunity and care.

Just as Australians living in the relatively narrow and insular Australia of the 1960s imagined a culturally diverse, worldly and open Australia, and in a generation turned this into reality, so we can turn the goals of reconciliation into reality.

There are very good signs that the process has begun. The creation of the Reconciliation Council is evidence of this. The establishment of the ATSIC – the Aboriginal and Torres Strait Islander Commission – is also evidence.

The Council indeed is the product of imagination and good will. ATSIC emerges from the vision of Indigenous self-determination and self-management. The vision has already become the reality of almost 800 elected Aboriginal Regional Councillors and Commissioners determining priorities and developing their own programs.

All over Australia, Aboriginal and Torres Strait Islander communities are taking charge of their own lives. And assistance with the problems which chronically beset them is at last being made available in ways developed by the communities themselves.

If these things offer hope, so does the fact that this generation of Australians is better informed about Aboriginal culture and Aboriginal achievement, and about the injustice that has been done, than any generation before it has been aware. So we are beginning to more generally appreciate the depth and the diversity of Aboriginal and Torres Strait Islander cultures. From their music and art and dance, we are beginning to recognise how much richer our national life and identity will be for the participation of Aboriginal and Torres Strait Islander people. We are beginning to learn what the Indigenous people have known for many thousands of years – how to live with our physical environment. Ever so gradually we are learning to see Australia through Aboriginal eyes, beginning to recognise the wisdom contained in their epic story. I think we are beginning to see how much we owe the Indigenous Australians and how much we have lost by living so apart.

I said we non-Indigenous Australians should try to imagine the Aboriginal view. It can't be too hard. Someone imagined this event today, and it is now a reality and a great reason for hope.

But there is one thing today we cannot imagine. We cannot imagine that the descendants of people whose genius and resilience maintained a culture here through 50,000 years or more, through cataclysmic changes to the climate and the environment, and who then survived two centuries of dispossession and abuse, will be denied their place in the modern Australian nation.

We cannot imagine that. We cannot imagine that we will fail.

And with the spirit that is here today I am confident that we won't fail.

I am confident we will succeed in this decade.

Thank you very much for listening to me.

# WE, THE PEOPLE

Barbara Jordan achieved more than most during her political career. In 1966, she became the first African American woman elected to the Texas Senate; in 1972, she became the only African American woman to become Governor of Texas, albeit for just one day when the Governor and Lt. Governor left town on governmental business; in 1994, she was awarded the Presidential Medal of Freedom. The list goes on. However, for many, Jordan is best remembered for the masterful opening speech she gave at the beginning of the impeachment hearings against Richard Nixon for the Watergate scandal in 1974 – thirteen minutes of measured eloquence that attracted nationwide praise and recognition.

Mr. Chairman, I join my colleague Mr. Rangel in thanking you for giving the junior members of this committee the glorious opportunity of sharing the pain of this inquiry.

Mr. Chairman, you are a strong man, and it has not been easy but we have tried as best we can to give you as much assistance as possible.

Earlier today, we heard the beginning of the Preamble to the Constitution of the United States, "We, the people." It is a very eloquent beginning. But when that document was completed, on the seventeenth of September in 1787, I was not included in that "We, the people." I felt somehow for many years that George Washington and Alexander Hamilton just left me out by mistake. But through the process of amendment, interpretation and court decision I have finally been included in "We, the people."

Today I am an inquisitor. An hyperbole would not be fictional and would not overstate the solemnness that I feel right now. My faith in the Constitution is whole, it is complete, it is total. I am not going to sit here and be an idle spectator to the diminution, the subversion, the destruction of the Constitution.

"Who can so properly be the inquisitors for the nation as the representatives of the nation themselves?" The subject of its jurisdiction are those offenses which proceed from the misconduct of public men. That is what we are talking about. In other words, the jurisdiction comes from the abuse or violation of some public trust. It is wrong, I suggest, it is a misreading of the Constitution for any member here to assert that for a member to vote for an article of impeachment means that that member must be convinced that the President should be removed from office. The Constitution doesn't say that.

The powers relating to impeachment are an essential check in the hands of the body, the legislature, against and upon the encroachments of the executive. The division between the two branches of the legislature, the House and the Senate, assigning to the one the right to accuse and to the other the right to judge, the framers of this Constitution were very astute. They did not make the accusers and the judges the same person.

We know the nature of impeachment. We have been talking about it a while now. It is chiefly designed for the President and his high ministers to somehow be called into account. It is designed to "bridle" the executive if he engages in excesses. It is designed as a method of national inquest into the conduct of public men. The framers confined in the Congress the power if need be, to remove the President in order to strike a delicate balance between a president swollen with power and grown tyrannical, and preservation of the independence of the executive.

The nature of impeachment is: "a narrowly channeled exception to the separation-of-powers maxim"; the federal convention of 1787 said that. It limited impeachment to high crimes and misdemeanors and discounted and opposed the term "maladministration." "It is to be used only for great misdemeanors," so it was said in the North Carolina ratification convention. And in the Virginia ratification convention: "We do not trust our liberty to a particular branch. We need one branch to check the others."

"No one need be afraid" – the North Carolina ratification convention – "No one need be afraid that officers who commit oppression will pass with immunity."

"Prosecutions of impeachments will seldom fail to agitate the passions of the whole community," said Hamilton in the Federalist Papers, no. 65. "We divide into parties more or less friendly or inimical to the accused." I do not mean political parties in that sense.

The drawing of political lines goes to the motivation behind impeachment; but impeachment must proceed within the confines of the constitutional term "high crime[s] and misdemeanors." Of the impeachment process, it was Woodrow Wilson who said that "nothing short of the grossest offenses against the plain law of the land will suffice to give them speed and effectiveness. Indignation so great as to overgrow party interest may secure a conviction; but nothing else can."

Common sense would be revolted if we engaged upon this process for petty reasons. Congress has a lot to do: appropriations, tax reform, health insurance, campaign finance reform, housing, environmental protection, energy sufficiency, mass transportation. Pettiness cannot be allowed to stand in the face of such overwhelming problems. So today we are not being petty. We are trying to be big because the task we have before us is a big one.

This morning, in a discussion of the evidence, we were told that the evidence which purports to support the allegations of misuse of the CIA by the President is thin. We are told that that evidence is insufficient. What that recital of the evidence this morning did not include is what the President did know on June 23, 1972. The President did know that it was Republican money, that it was money from the Committee for the Re-Election of the President, which was found in the possession of one of the burglars arrested on June 17.*

* The Watergate scandal hinged on how much President Nixon knew – and how much he covered up – about the break-in and wiretapping of the Democratic headquarters at the Watergate offices in Washington on June 17, 1972. One of the burglars was found with cash directly linked to Republican Party funds.

I. *We Know* Nature of Impeachment

    A. *Jr is* Chiefly designed for the President and his high ministers as a "bridle" on the Executive. (Hamilton, Federalist, No. 65 at 426)

    B. Designed as a method of national inquest into the conduct of public men. (Hamilton, Federalist No. 65 at 426)

    C. Framers confided to Congress the power, if need be, to remove the President, in order to strike a delicate balance between a President swollen with power and grown tyrannical; and preservation of the independence of the Executive. (Burger - 5) -

    D. A Narrowly channeled exception to the separation of powers. (Max Farrand, The Records of [the Federal Convention of 1787,] Chapters II & IV)

    E. Limited to "high crimes and misdemeanors" as opposed to the general term "maladministration." (Burger, 86 and 2 Farrand 550)

    F. To be used only for "great misdemeanors against the public." (Governor Johnston in the North Carolina Ratification Convention)

    G. ~~"The power of impeachment ought to be, like Goliath's sword, kept in the temple, and not used but on great occasions." (Lord Chancellor Somers in Parliament, 1691)~~

    H. "We do not trust out liberty to a particular branch: one branch is a check on the other" (George Nicholas in the Virginia Ratification Convention)

What the President did know on June 23 was the prior activities of E. Howard Hunt, which included his participation in the break-in of Daniel Ellsberg's psychiatrist, which included Howard Hunt's participation in the Dita Beard ITT affair, which included Howard Hunt's fabrication of cables designed to discredit the Kennedy administration.[†]

[†] E. Howard Hunt was the former CIA officer who led the break-in team; Daniel Ellsberg was the whistleblower behind the release of the Pentagon Papers; and the Dita Beard ITT affair refers to another scandal in which the Nixon administration dropped an anti-trust action in return for a cash donation to the Republican Party.

We were further cautioned today that perhaps these proceedings ought to be delayed because certainly there would be new evidence forthcoming from the President of the United States. There has not been even an obfuscated indication that this committee would receive any additional materials from the President. The committee subpoena is outstanding, and if the President wants to supply that material, the committee sits here.

The fact is that on yesterday, the American people waited with great anxiety for eight hours, not knowing whether their President would obey an order of the Supreme Court of the United States. At this point I would like to juxtapose a few of the impeachment criteria with some of the actions the President has engaged in.

Impeachment criteria: James Madison, from the Virginia ratification convention. "If the President be connected in any suspicious manner with any person and there be grounds to believe that he will shelter him, he may be impeached."

We have heard time and time again that the evidence reflects the payment to the defendants of money. The President had knowledge that these funds were being paid and that these were funds collected for the 1972 presidential campaign. We know that the President met with Mr. Henry Petersen twenty-seven times to discuss matters related to Watergate and immediately thereafter met with the very persons who were implicated in the information Mr. Petersen was receiving. The words are: "If the President be connected in any suspicious manner with any person and there be grounds to believe that he will shelter that person, he may be impeached."

Justice Story: "Impeachment is intended for occasional and extraordinary cases where a superior power acting for the whole people is put into operation to protect their rights and rescue their liberties from violations."

We know about the Huston plan. We know about the break-in of the psychiatrist's office. We know that there was absolute complete direction on September 3, when the President indicated that a surreptitious entry had been made in Dr. Fielding's office, after having met with Mr. Ehrlichman[‡] and Mr. Young. "Protect their rights." "Rescue their liberties from violation."

[‡] John Ehrlichman was Nixon's chief advisor on domestic affairs – he was also implicated in the Watergate scandal.

The Carolina ratification convention impeachment criteria: those are impeachable "who behave amiss or betray their public trust." Beginning shortly after the Watergate break-in and continuing to the present time, the President has engaged in a series of public statements and actions designed to thwart the lawful investigation by government prosecutors. Moreover, the President has made public announcements and assertions bearing on the Watergate case which the evidence will show he knew to be false.

These assertions, false assertions, impeachable, those who misbehave. Those who "behave amiss or betray the public trust." James Madison again at the Constitutional Convention: "A President is impeachable if he attempts to subvert the Constitution."

The Constitution charges the President with the task of taking care that the laws be faithfully executed, and yet the President has counseled his aides to commit perjury, willfully disregard the secrecy of grand jury proceedings, conceal surreptitious entry, attempt to compromise a federal judge while publicly displaying his cooperation with the processes of criminal justice.

"A President is impeachable if he attempts to subvert the Constitution." If the impeachment provision in the Constitution of the United States will not reach the offenses charged here, then perhaps that eighteenth-century Constitution should be abandoned to a twentieth-century paper shredder.

Has the President committed offenses and planned and directed and acquiesced in a course of conduct which the Constitution will not tolerate? That's the question. We know that. We know the question. We should now forthwith proceed to answer the question. It is reason, and not passion, which must guide our deliberations, guide our debate, and guide our decision.

# THE PERILS OF INDIFFERENCE

Elie Wiesel was born in Romania in 1928. At fifteen years of age, he and his three sisters, mother and father were taken to the Auschwitz concentration camp by the Nazis; by the time he escaped the Holocaust, Elie's parents and younger sister had been killed. After being liberated by American troops, he moved to Paris and became a journalist. By 1955 he had set up home in New York where he would become an award-winning novelist and, in 1986, recipient of the Nobel Peace Prize for his political activism. In 1999, to mark the turn of the new millennium, Wiesel was invited by President Bill Clinton and First Lady Hillary Rodham Clinton to speak at the White House, where he delivered an address titled "The Perils of Indifference: Lessons Learned from a Violent Century."

Mr. President, Mrs. Clinton, members of Congress, Ambassador Holbrooke, Excellencies, friends:

Fifty-four years ago to the day, a young Jewish boy from a small town in the Carpathian Mountains woke up, not far from Goethe's beloved Weimar, in a place of eternal infamy called Buchenwald. He was finally free, but there was no joy in his heart. He thought there never would be again.

Liberated a day earlier by American soldiers, he remembers their rage at what they saw. And even if he lives to be a very old man, he will always be grateful to them for that rage, and also for their compassion. Though he did not understand their language, their eyes told him what he needed to know – that they, too, would remember, and bear witness.

And now, I stand before you, Mr. President – Commander-in-Chief of the army that freed me, and tens of thousands of others – and I am filled with a profound and abiding gratitude to the American people.

Gratitude is a word that I cherish. Gratitude is what defines the humanity of the human being. And I am grateful to you, Hillary – or Mrs. Clinton – for what you said, and for what you are doing for children in the world, for the homeless, for the victims of injustice, the victims of destiny and society. And I thank all of you for being here.

We are on the threshold of a new century, a new millennium. What will the legacy of this vanishing century be? How will it be remembered in the new millennium? Surely it will be judged, and judged severely, in both moral and metaphysical terms. These failures have cast a dark shadow over humanity: two World Wars, countless civil wars, the senseless chain of assassinations – Gandhi, the Kennedys, Martin Luther King, Sadat, Rabin – bloodbaths in Cambodia and Nigeria, India and Pakistan, Ireland and Rwanda, Eritrea and Ethiopia, Sarajevo and Kosovo; the inhumanity in the gulag and the tragedy of Hiroshima. And, on a different level, of course, Auschwitz and Treblinka. So much violence, so much indifference.

What is indifference? Etymologically, the word means "no difference." A strange and unnatural state in which the lines blur between light and darkness, dusk and dawn, crime and punishment, cruelty and compassion, good and evil.

What are its causes and inescapable consequences? Is it a philosophy? Is there a philosophy of indifference conceivable? Can one possibly view indifference as a virtue? Is it necessary at times to practice it simply to keep one's sanity, live normally, enjoy a fine meal and a glass of wine, as the world around us experiences harrowing upheavals?

Of course, indifference can be tempting – more than that, seductive. It is so much easier to look away from victims. It is so much easier to avoid such rude interruptions to our work, our dreams, our hopes. It is, after all, awkward, troublesome, to be involved in another person's pain and despair. Yet, for the person who is indifferent, his or her neighbors are of no consequence. And, therefore, their lives are meaningless. Their hidden or even visible anguish is of no interest. Indifference reduces the other to an abstraction.

Over there, behind the black gates of Auschwitz, the most tragic of all prisoners were the "Muselmänner," as they were called. Wrapped in their torn blankets, they would sit or lie on the ground, staring vacantly into space, unaware of who or where they were, strangers to their surroundings. They no longer felt pain, hunger, thirst. They feared nothing. They felt nothing. They were dead and did not know it.

Rooted in our tradition, some of us felt that to be abandoned by humanity then was not the ultimate. We felt that to be abandoned by God was worse than to be punished by Him. Better an unjust God than an indifferent one. For us to be ignored by God was a harsher punishment than to be a victim of His anger. Man can live far from God – not outside God. God is wherever we are. Even in suffering? Even in suffering.

In a way, to be indifferent to that suffering is what makes the human being inhuman. Indifference, after all, is more dangerous than anger and hatred. Anger can at times be creative. One writes a great poem, a great symphony, one does something special for the sake of humanity because one is angry at the injustice that one witnesses. But indifference is never creative. Even hatred at times may elicit a response. You fight it. You denounce it. You disarm it. Indifference elicits no response. Indifference is not a response.

Indifference is not a beginning, it is an end. And, therefore, indifference is always the friend of the enemy, for it benefits the aggressor – never his victim, whose pain is magnified when he or she feels forgotten. The political prisoner in his cell, the hungry children, the homeless refugees – not to respond to their plight, not to relieve their solitude by offering them a spark of hope is to exile them from human memory. And in denying their humanity we betray our own.

Indifference, then, is not only a sin, it is a punishment. And this is one of the most important lessons of this outgoing century's wide-ranging experiments in good and evil.

In the place that I come from, society was composed of three simple categories: the killers, the victims, and the bystanders. During the darkest of times, inside the ghettoes and death camps – and I'm glad that Mrs. Clinton mentioned that we are now commemorating that event, that period, that we are now in the Days of Remembrance – but then, we felt abandoned, forgotten. All of us did.

And our only miserable consolation was that we believed that Auschwitz and Treblinka were closely guarded secrets; that the leaders of the free world did not know what was going on behind those black gates and barbed wire; that they had no knowledge of the war against the Jews that Hitler's armies and their accomplices waged as part of the war against the Allies.

→ Elie Wiesel, photographed by Sergey Bermeniev

If they knew, we thought, surely those leaders would have moved heaven and earth to intervene. They would have spoken out with great outrage and conviction. They would have bombed the railways leading to Birkenau, just the railways, just once.

And now we knew, we learned, we discovered that the Pentagon knew, the State Department knew. And the illustrious occupant of the White House then, who was a great leader – and I say it with some anguish and pain, because, today is exactly fifty-four years marking his death – Franklin Delano Roosevelt died on April the 12th, 1945, so he is very much present to me and to us.

No doubt, he was a great leader. He mobilized the American people and the world, going into battle, bringing hundreds and thousands of valiant and brave soldiers in America to fight fascism, to fight dictatorship, to fight Hitler. And so many of the young people fell in battle. And, nevertheless, his image in Jewish history – I must say it – his image in Jewish history is flawed.

The depressing tale of the St. Louis is a case in point. Sixty years ago, its human cargo – maybe 1,000 Jews – was turned back to Nazi Germany. And that happened after the Kristallnacht, after the first state-sponsored pogrom, with hundreds of Jewish shops destroyed, synagogues burned, thousands of people put in concentration camps. And that ship, which was already on the shores of the United States, was sent back.

I don't understand. Roosevelt was a good man, with a heart. He understood those who needed help. Why didn't he allow these refugees to disembark? A thousand people – in America, a great country, the greatest democracy, the most generous of all new nations in modern history. What happened? I don't understand. Why the indifference, on the highest level, to the suffering of the victims?

But then, there were human beings who were sensitive to our tragedy. Those non-Jews, those Christians, that we called the "Righteous Gentiles," whose selfless acts of heroism saved the honor of their faith. Why were they so few? Why was there a greater effort to save SS murderers after the war than to save their victims during the war?

Why did some of America's largest corporations continue to do business with Hitler's Germany until 1942? It has been suggested, and it was documented, that the Wehrmacht could not have conducted its invasion of France without oil obtained from American sources. How is one to explain their indifference?

And yet, my friends, good things have also happened in this traumatic century: the defeat of Nazism, the collapse of communism, the rebirth of Israel on its ancestral soil, the demise of apartheid, Israel's peace treaty with Egypt, the peace accord in Ireland. And let us remember the meeting, filled with drama and emotion, between Rabin and Arafat that you, Mr. President, convened in this very place. I was here and I will never forget it.

And then, of course, the joint decision of the United States and NATO to intervene in Kosovo and save those victims, those refugees, those who were uprooted by a man whom I believe that because of his crimes, should be charged with crimes against humanity. But this time, the world was not silent. This time, we do respond. This time, we intervene.

Does it mean that we have learned from the past? Does it mean that society has changed? Has the human being become less indifferent and more human? Have we really learned from our experiences? Are we less insensitive to the plight of victims of ethnic cleansing and other forms of injustices in places near and far? Is today's justified intervention in Kosovo, led by you, Mr. President, a lasting warning that never again will the deportation, the terrorization of children and their parents be allowed anywhere in the world? Will it discourage other dictators in other lands to do the same?

What about the children? Oh, we see them on television, we read about them in the papers, and we do so with a broken heart. Their fate is always the most tragic, inevitably. When adults wage war, children perish. We see their faces, their eyes. Do we hear their pleas? Do we feel their pain, their agony? Every minute one of them dies of disease, violence, famine. Some of them – so many of them – could be saved.

And so, once again, I think of the young Jewish boy from the Carpathian Mountains. He has accompanied the old man I have become throughout these years of quest and struggle. And together we walk towards the new millennium, carried by profound fear and extraordinary hope.

# THESE STATUES ARE NOT JUST STONE AND METAL

In April and May 2017, protests – many of them violent – erupted in New Orleans when four monuments were removed from the city at the behest of its mayor, Mitch Landrieu, in response to months of campaigning by black activists. The statues were of Confederate leaders Jefferson Davis, Robert E. Lee and P. G. T. Beauregard, and the Battle of Liberty Place monument, all of which were erected to commemorate white supremacy. Shortly after the final statue disappeared, Landrieu explained the decision in an impassioned speech that spoke not just to the local situation, but also to the tensions surfacing across the nation.

I thank you for coming today.

The soul of our beloved city is rooted in a history that has evolved over thousands of years; rooted in a diverse people who have been here together every step of the way – through good and through bad. It is a history that holds in its heart the stories of Native Americans – the Choctaw, the Houma, the Chitimacha. Hernando de Soto, Robert Cavelier, Sieur de la Salle, the Acadians, the Isleños, the enslaved people from Senegambia, Free People of Color, the Haitians, the Germans, both empires of France and Spain. The Italians, the Irish, the Cubans, the south and central Americans, the Vietnamese and so many more.

You see – New Orleans is truly a city of many nations, a melting pot, a bubbling caldron of many cultures. There is no other place quite like it in the world that so eloquently exemplifies the uniquely American motto: *e pluribus unum* – out of many we are one. But there are also other truths about our city that we must confront. New Orleans was one of America's largest slave markets: a port where hundreds of thousands of souls were bought, sold and shipped up the Mississippi River to lives of forced labor, of misery, of rape and of torture. America was a place where nearly 4,000 of our fellow citizens were lynched, 540 in Louisiana alone; where the courts enshrined "separate but equal;" where Freedom riders were beaten to a bloody pulp. So when people say to me that the monuments in question are history, well, what I just described to you is our history as well, and it is a searing truth.

And it immediately begs the questions, why there are no slave ship monuments, no prominent markers on public land to remember the lynchings or the slave blocks; nothing to remember this long chapter of our lives; of pain, of sacrifice, of shame . . . all of it happening on the soil of New Orleans? So for those self-appointed defenders of history and the monuments, they are eerily silent on what amounts to historical malfeasance, a lie by omission. There is a difference, you see, between remembrance of history and reverence of it.

For America and New Orleans, it has been a long, winding road, marked by tragedy and triumph. But we cannot be afraid of the truth. As President George

W. Bush said at the dedication ceremony for the National Museum of African American History and Culture, and I quote, "A great nation does not hide its history. It faces its flaws and it corrects them." So today I want to speak about why we chose to remove these four monuments to the Lost Cause of the Confederacy, but also how and why this process can move us towards healing and understanding each other. So, let's start with the facts.

The historic record is clear: the Robert E. Lee, Jefferson Davis, and P. G. T. Beauregard statues were not erected to just honor these men, but as part of the movement which became known as The Cult of the Lost Cause. This "cult" had one goal and one goal only – through monuments and through other means – to rewrite history to hide the truth, which is that the Confederacy was on the wrong side of humanity. First erected 166 years after the founding of our city and nineteen years after the Civil War, these monuments that we took down were meant to rebrand the history of our city and the ideals of the Confederacy. It is self-evident that these men did not fight for the United States of America, they fought against it. They may have been warriors, but in this cause they were not patriots. These statues are not just stone and metal. They are not just innocent remembrances of a benign history. These monuments celebrate a fictional, sanitized Confederacy; ignoring the death, ignoring the enslavement, ignoring the terror that it actually stood for.

After the Civil War, these monuments were a part of that terrorism as much as burning a cross on someone's lawn; they were erected purposefully to send a strong message to all who walked in their shadows about who was still in charge in this city. Should you have further doubt about the true goals of the Confederacy, in the very weeks before the war broke out, the Vice President of the Confederacy, Alexander Stephens, made it very clear that the Confederate cause was about maintaining slavery and white supremacy. In his now famous "cornerstone speech" he said that the Confederacy's "cornerstone rests upon the great truth, that the Negro is not equal to the white man; that slavery – subordination to a superior race – is his natural and normal condition. This, our new government," he said "is the first, in the history of the world, based upon this great physical, philosophical and moral truth."

Now, with these shocking words still ringing in your ears, I want to try to gently peel your hands from the grip on a false narrative of our history that I think weakens us, and make straight a wrong turn we made many years ago, so we can more closely connect with integrity to the founding principles of our nation and forge a clearer, straighter path toward a better city and toward a more perfect union.

Last year, President Barack Obama echoed these sentiments about the need to contextualize and remember all of our history. He recalled a piece of stone, a slave auction block engraved with a marker commemorating a single moment in 1830 when Andrew Jackson and Henry Clay stood and spoke from it. President

Obama said, "Consider what this artifact tells us about history . . . on a stone where day after day for years, men and women . . . bound and bought, sold and bid like cattle on a stone worn down by the tragedy of over a thousand bare feet. For a long time the only thing we considered important, the singular thing we once chose to commemorate as history with a plaque, were the unmemorable speeches of these two powerful men."

A piece of stone – one stone. Both stories history. One story told. One story forgotten or maybe even purposefully ignored. As clear as it is for me today . . . for a long time, even though I grew up in one of New Orleans' most diverse neighborhoods, even with my family's proud history of fighting for civil rights . . . I must have passed by these monuments a thousand times without giving them a second thought. So I am not judging anybody, I am not judging people. We all take our own journey on race.

I just hope people listen like I did when my dear friend Wynton Marsalis helped me see the truth. He asked me to think about all the people who have left New Orleans because of our exclusionary attitudes. Another friend asked me to consider these four monuments from the perspective of an African American mother or father trying to explain to their fifth-grade daughter why Robert E. Lee is sat atop of our city. Can you do it? Can you look into the eyes of this young girl and convince her that Robert E. Lee is there to encourage her? Do you think she feels inspired and hopeful by that story? Do these monuments help her see her future with limitless potential? Have you ever thought that if her potential is limited, yours and mine are too? We all know the answers to these very simple questions. When you look into this child's eyes is the moment when the searing truth comes into focus. This is the moment when we know what we must do. When we know what is right. We can't walk away from this truth.

Now I knew that taking down the monuments was going to be tough, but you elected me to do the right thing, not the easy thing and this is what that looks like. So relocating these monuments is not about taking something away from someone else. This is not about politics, this is not about blame, it's not about retaliation. This is not a naïve quest to solve all our problems at once.

This is, however, about showing the whole world that we as a city, that we as a people are able to acknowledge, to understand, to reconcile and, more importantly, choose a better future for ourselves making straight what has been crooked and making right what was wrong. Otherwise, we will continue to pay a price with discord, with division and, yes, with violence.

To literally put the Confederacy on a pedestal in our most prominent places in honor is an inaccurate recitation of our full past. It is an affront to our present, and it is a bad prescription for our future. History cannot be changed. It cannot be moved like a statue. What is done is done. The Civil War is over, the Confederacy lost and we are better for it. Surely we are far enough removed from this dark time to acknowledge that the cause of the Confederacy was wrong.

And in the second decade of the twenty-first century, asking African Americans – or anyone else for that matter – to drive by property that they own, occupied by reverential statues of men who fought to destroy the country and deny that person's humanity, seems perverse. It seems absurd. Centuries-old wounds are still raw because they never healed right in the first place. Here is the essential truth. We are better together than we are apart.

Indivisibility is our essence. Isn't this the gift that we, the people of New Orleans have given to the world? We radiate beauty and grace in our food, in our music, in our architecture, in our joy of life, in our celebration of death; in everything that we do. We gave the world this funky thing called jazz. It is the most uniquely American art form that has developed across the ages from different cultures. Think about second lines, think about Mardi Gras, think about muffalctta, think about the Saints, think about gumbo, think about red beans and rice. By God, just think.

All we hold dear is created by throwing everything in the pot; creating, producing something better; everything, everything a product of our historic diversity. We are proof that out of many we are one – and better for it! Out of many we are one – and we really do love it! And yet, we still seem to find so many excuses to not do the right thing. Again, remember President Bush's words: "A great nation does not hide its history. It faces its flaws and corrects them."

We forget, we deny how much we really depend on each other, how much we really need each other. We justify our silence and inaction by manufacturing noble causes that marinate in historical denial. We still find a way to say "wait, wait, wait," "not so fast," but like Dr. Martin Luther King Jr. said, "'Wait' has almost always meant never." We can't wait any longer. We need to change. And we need to change now.

No more waiting. This is not just about statues, this is about attitudes and it's about behavior as well. If we take down these statues and don't change to become a more open and inclusive society all of this would have been in vain. While some have driven by these statues every day and either revered their beauty or failed to see them at all, many of our neighbors and fellow Americans see them very, very clearly. Many are painfully aware of the long shadows their presence casts; not only literally but figuratively. And they clearly receive the message that the Confederacy and the Cult of the Lost Cause intended to deliver.

Earlier this week, as the Cult of the Lost Cause statue of P. G. T. Beauregard came down, world-renowned musician Terence Blanchard stood watching, his wife Robin and their two beautiful daughters at their side. Terence went to school on the edge of City Park named after one of America's greatest heroes and patriots, John F. Kennedy. But to get there he had to pass by this monument to a man who fought to deny him his humanity.

← A group of protestors gathers around the Robert E. Lee Monument in New Orleans prior to its removal, May 19, 2017, photographed by Bongo Najja Foluke

He said, "I've never looked at them as a source of pride . . . it's always made me feel as if they were put there by people who don't respect us. This is something I never thought I'd see in my lifetime. It's a sign that the world is changing." Yes, Terence, it is and it is long overdue. Now is the time to send a new message to the next generation of New Orleanians.

A message about the future, about the next 300 years and beyond; let us not miss this opportunity, New Orleans, and let us help the rest of America do the same. Because now is the time for choosing. Now is the time to actually make this city the city we should have always been, had we gotten it right the first time.

But this is a good place to stop for a moment and ask ourselves – at this point in our history – after [Hurricanes] Katrina, after Rita, after Ike, after Gustav, after the national recession, after the BP oil spill catastrophe and after the tornado – if presented with the opportunity to build monuments that told our story or to curate these particular spaces . . . would these be the monuments that we want the world to see? Is this really our story?

We have not erased history; we are becoming part of the city's history by righting the wrong image these monuments represent and crafting a better, more complete future for all of our children and for future generations. And unlike when these Confederate monuments were erected as symbols of white supremacy, we now have a chance to create not only new symbols, but to do it together, as one people. In our blessed land we come to the table of democracy as equals. We have to reaffirm our commitment to a future where each citizen is guaranteed the uniquely American gifts of life, liberty and the pursuit of happiness.

That is what really makes America great and today it is more important than ever to hold fast to these values and together say a self-evident truth that out of many we are one. That is why we reclaim these spaces for the United States of America. Because we are one nation, not two; indivisible with liberty and justice for all, not some. We all are part of one nation, and pledge allegiance to one flag, the flag of the United States of America. And here's the kicker. New Orleanians are in, all of the way. It is in this union, it is in this truth that real patriotism is rooted and flourishes. Instead of revering a four-year brief historical aberration that was called the Confederacy, we can celebrate all 300 years of our rich, diverse history as a place named New Orleans and set the tone for the next 300 years.

After decades of public debate, of anger, of anxiety, of anticipation, of humiliation and of frustration; after public hearings and approvals from three separate community boards and commissions; after two robust public hearings and a 6–1 vote by the duly elected City Council; after review by thirteen different federal and state judges, the full weight of the legislative, executive and judicial branches of government has been brought to bear and that is why these monuments are coming down in accordance with the law and will be removed.

So now is the time to come together. To heal and focus on our larger task. Not only building new symbols, but making this city a beautiful manifestation of what is possible and what we as a people can become.

Let us remember the once exiled, imprisoned and now universally loved Nelson Mandela and what he said after the fall of apartheid. "If the pain has often been unbearable and the revelations shocking to all of us, it is because they indeed bring us the beginnings of a common understanding of what happened and a steady restoration of this nation's humanity." So before we part let us again state clearly for all to hear.

The Confederacy was on the wrong side of history and humanity. It sought to tear apart our nation and subjugate our fellow Americans to slavery. This is a history we should never forget and one that we should never ever again put on a pedestal to be revered. As a community, we must recognize the significance of removing New Orleans's Confederate monuments. It is our acknowledgment that now is the time to take stock of, and then move past, a painful part of our history.

Anything less would render generations of courageous struggle and soul-searching a truly lost cause. Anything less would fall short of the immortal words of our greatest President, Abraham Lincoln, who with an open heart and clarity of purpose calls on us today across the ages to unite as one people when he said: "With malice toward none, with charity for all, with firmness in the right, as God gives us to see the right, let us strive on to finish the work we are in, to bind up the nation's wounds . . . to do all which may achieve and cherish – a just and lasting peace among ourselves and with all nations."

God bless you all. God bless New Orleans and God bless the United States of America.

# THE PLEASURE OF BOOKS

In April 1933, the German Student Union publicly announced plans for a nationwide series of book-burning events. Un-German, anti-Nazi literature would be set aflame in a bid to cleanse the country of such supposedly traitorous reading material. Indeed, those plans came to bear, and over the coming years many thousands of books were destroyed. Two days before the German population were hit with that initial announcement, the noted author and professor of English William Lyon Phelps gave a speech to the American public titled "The Pleasure of Books." It was broadcast on the radio to many millions.

The habit of reading is one of the greatest resources of mankind; and we enjoy reading books that belong to us much more than if they are borrowed. A borrowed book is like a guest in the house; it must be treated with punctiliousness, with a certain considerate formality. You must see that it sustains no damage; it must not suffer while under your roof. You cannot leave it carelessly, you cannot mark it, you cannot turn down the pages, you cannot use it familiarly. And then, some day, although this is seldom done, you really ought to return it.

But your own books belong to you; you treat them with that affectionate intimacy that annihilates formality. Books are for use, not for show; you should own no book that you are afraid to mark up, or afraid to place on the table, wide open and facedown. A good reason for marking favorite passages in books is that this practice enables you to remember more easily the significant sayings, to refer to them quickly, and then in later years, it is like visiting a forest where you once blazed a trail. You have the pleasure of going over the old ground, and recalling both the intellectual scenery and your own earlier self.

Everyone should begin collecting a private library in youth; the instinct of private property, which is fundamental in human beings, can here be cultivated with every advantage and no evils. One should have one's own bookshelves, which should not have doors, glass windows, or keys; they should be free and accessible to the hand as well as to the eye. The best of mural decorations is books; they are more varied in color and appearance than any wallpaper, they are more attractive in design, and they have the prime advantage of being separate personalities, so that if you sit alone in the room in the firelight, you are surrounded with intimate friends. The knowledge that they are there in plain view is both stimulating and refreshing. You do not have to read them all. Most of my indoor life is spent in a room containing 6,000 books; and I have a stock answer to the invariable question that comes from strangers. "Have you read all of these books?"

"Some of them twice." This reply is both true and unexpected.

There are of course no friends like living, breathing, corporeal men and women; my devotion to reading has never made me a recluse. How could it? Books are of the people, by the people, for the people. Literature is the immortal part of history; it is the best and most enduring part of personality. But book-friends have this advantage over living friends; you can enjoy the most truly aristocratic society in the world whenever you want it. The great dead are beyond our physical reach, and the great living are usually almost as inaccessible; as for our personal friends and acquaintances, we cannot always see them. Perchance they are asleep, or away on a journey. But in a private library, you can at any moment converse with Socrates or Shakespeare or Carlyle or Dumas or Dickens or Shaw or Barrie or Galsworthy. And there is no doubt that in these books you see these men at their best. They wrote for you. They "laid themselves out," they did their ultimate best to entertain you, to make a favorable impression. You are necessary to them as an audience is to an actor; only instead of seeing them masked, you look into their innermost heart of heart.

# THE DRIVE FOR FREEDOM

In May 2011, 32-year-old "accidental activist" Manal Al-Sharif spent a week in custody after uploading to the Internet footage of herself driving a car – an activity deemed unlawful in just one country: her home, Saudi Arabia. In fact, her actions were part of a larger campaign that she and some friends were coordinating in an effort to fight discrimination against women and force change.

The footage was viewed millions of times and as a result of its popularity other Saudi women followed suit. The next year, Al-Sharif was named by *Time* as one of the "100 Most Influential People." To this day, she continues to campaign for equal rights and in 2012 gave a powerful speech, in English, at the Oslo Freedom Forum in Norway.

Hello everyone, my name is Manal Al-Sharif and I'm from Saudi Arabia. I'd like to talk about two chapters in my life. I'll start with chapter one.

Chapter one in my life tells the story of my generation, and it starts with the year I was born in. It was 1979. In 1979 there was a siege of Mecca. Mecca is the holiest shrine for Muslims in the world. It was seized by Juhayman al-Otaybi, a militant, and some 400 men. The siege stayed for two weeks. The Saudi authorities had to use armed force, heavily armed force, to end the siege, and they had to behead Juhayman and his men publicly. After that event, the Saudi authorities were very anxious about the uprising of militants and extremists. Saudi Arabia at that time, in 1979, was newly formed, and was rapidly changing and adopting the civil new life. Those extremists, that was against their beliefs, so they wanted to stop this, so Saudi authorities had to abide by that. To prevent another uprising, they quickly moved to roll back the immoral liberties that had been tolerated in previous years.

Just like Juhayman, those extremists had long been upset with the gradual loosening of restrictions for women. In the weeks after the Mecca uprising, female announcers were removed from TV; pictures of women and printings were banned; employment of women was narrowed to two things, education and health care; music was banned; cinemas were closed. Separation between genders was strictly enforced, everywhere, from public places, government offices, banks, schools, even to our own houses. So each house in Saudi has two entrances: one for men and one for women. Petrodollars poured into these extremists' budgets. They used it to spread religious education and missionary organizations around the world, many of which preach hatred of the infidel, dedication to global jihad, and the rejection of anyone who does not share the same ideals. The Committee to Promote Virtue and Prevent Vice, or the religious police, was also given a free hand in society. They beheaded a monster, but enshrined his ideology of hate. Saudi authorities tried their best to make the story of Juhayman forgotten, so they removed all articles and records from magazines and newspapers, so people would forget about Juhayman.

I remember one day, it was Hajj time, and this is Kaaba, which is the holy shrine for Muslims. They lift the curtains up so you could see the walls. I was performing *tawaf* with my mother, where you have to walk in circles around the Kaaba. There was a hole in that wall, and Mom pointed to it and she said, "That's a hole from a bullet from the time of Juhayman." Juhayman was the name that brings terror to people of Mecca and Muslims around the world. For me that hole went beyond these walls, it went in time: it was like a hole that we fell in, and we kept going backwards in my country. So in the eighties and the years after, there was the Afghan war, and the Soviet Union. The new extremists were very powerful, promoting their ideas, and enforcing everyone to abide by their strict rules. Free leaflets, books, cassettes, calling for jihad in Afghanistan, and calling to dismiss any non-Muslim from the Arabian Peninsula, were given freely. I was one of the people who distributed these leaflets. A 22-year-old man was amongst those fighters. His name was Osama bin Laden. Those fighters at that time were our heroes.

* The Sahwa movement is an Islamic conservative faction that was at its peak in the mid-nineties.

In the Sahwa* time, those extremists, one of the main subjects they used to talk about was us women. For them a woman is always treated like the seductive fruit. This means if I leave the house and something bad happens, I'm responsible for that because men cannot control their instincts. So I was bound to stay home, according to their rules. For them I was *awrah*. *Awrah* is a sinful place of your body to show, or to disclose. For them my face was *awrah*, even my voice was *awrah*. My name was *awrah*. Women cannot be called by their name, so they are called "mother of [one of her sons]," or "wife of [the man's name]." There were no sports; there were no engineering schools for women. There was, of course, no driving. We didn't even have IDs with our pictures, except the passports when we leave the country. We were voiceless, we were faceless and we were nameless. We were just invisible.

Something happened at that time. In 1990, it was November 6th, and forty-seven courageous women emerged. They challenged the ban on women driving and they drove in Riyadh. These women were detained, banned from leaving the country, dismissed from their jobs. They stole their lives. I remember when I was a kid and we received the news. They told us, "Those women are really bad." A fatwa came from the Grand Mufti of Saudi Arabia, Sheikh Bin Baz, and he said women driving is banned in Islam. Based on that, an announcer came on TV and he said, "The Ministry of the Interior warns everyone in this country that women are not allowed to drive in the Kingdom of Saudi Arabia." Later on, we were not supposed to talk about women driving, whether in TV or in reports, or in magazines or newspapers. So another taboo was created. The first taboo was Juhayman and the second taboo was women driving.

Something also in the first chapter of my life happened. It was the bombing of Khobar Towers. They were bombed on June 25, 1996, and according to the Saudi government the attack was carried out by Saudi Islamic militants, including many veterans of the Afghan war. Nineteen U.S. Air Force personnel and one Saudi were killed and 372 people were injured that day. I remember my mother, when she saw this picture, she gasped. And she said, "Juhayman is back." I'm surprised to remember, at that time I was only seventeen, but I did not sympathize with the deaths. I was brainwashed, I was brought up, I was a project of a terrorist at that time.

The change in my life started happening in the year 2000. In the year 2000 the Internet was introduced to Saudi Arabia. That was the first time for me to go online. And I will explain why I am displaying this picture [of one of my paintings]. I was really extremist, so I used to cover from toe to head. They told us in school that it was sinful to draw portraits of animals or people, so I took all my paintings and I burned them. And I was burning inside and feeling this is so unfair. In the year 2000, when the Internet was introduced to Saudi Arabia, it was the first door for us – the young people, the youth – to the outside world, and I was very thirsty to learn about other cultures, about other religions. I started talking to people with different opinions to me, and questions started to raise in my head. I realized at that time how small the box I was in, when I stepped out of it. I started slowly losing my phobia of getting my pure beliefs polluted.

Let me tell you another story in my life. Do you remember the first time you listened to music? To be more specific, do you remember the first song you ever listened to? I remember. I was twenty-one years old. It was the first time in my life that I allowed myself to listen to music. I remember the song. It was "Show Me the Meaning of Being Lonely," by the Backstreet Boys. To help you understand, I used to burn my brother's music cassettes in the oven. Sorry, brother. I was that extreme. And then I listened to this song. They had been telling us music is Satan's flute, is a path to adultery. This song sounded so pure, so beautiful, so angelic – it can be anything but evil to me. And that day, I realized how lonely I was in the world I had isolated myself in.

A turning point in my life also was 9/11. And I think it was a turning point for so many people in my generation. When 9/11 happened, the extremists said it was God's punishment for America for what they had been doing to Muslims. I was confused which side to take. I watched the news that night, and I saw this picture. It was a video of a man throwing himself from one of these towers. He was escaping the fire. I remember that night I couldn't sleep. That picture of that man throwing himself was in my head, and it was ringing a bell. Something is wrong. There is no religion on earth that can accept such mercilessness, such cruelness. Al-Qaeda later announced their responsibility for these attacks. My heroes were nothing but bloody terrorists. And that was a turning point in my life. After 9/11, Saudi Arabia faced a sweep of terrorist attacks in our land. The very interesting thing? A few months after 9/11, they started, for the first time, issuing us IDs. Women. For the first time, they recognized us as citizens in our own country.

Now I will move to chapter two in my life, which I think everyone here has heard about: driving for freedom. Maybe there is a gap between chapter one and chapter two. In Saudi Arabia there is not much happening [at this time]. So maybe there is not much to tell you – what happened from chapter one to two. But chapter two. We were inspired by the Arab Spring, and we were led by personal struggles. We were a group of women, Saudi women, who started "Drive Your Own Life." And it was just a very simple campaign, using social media and calling women to drive on June 17th. One of the breakthrough things: I recorded a video explaining what is June 17th. And I recorded another video of me driving. I used my face, my voice and my real name. I was there to speak up for myself. I used to be ashamed of who I am, a woman. But not anymore. That video, when I posted it online, it got 700,000 views in one day. A day later, I was arrested and sent to jail. And there was this riot around the country, and people were divided into two parties. A party calling for my trial, even for flogging me in a public place. Facebook pages saying that men will hit women with their *igal*, part of a robe men wear on top of their head. And women replied back saying, "We will throw shoes at you if you hit us on June 17th." So it was just like a fight between the two.

But what I didn't know about until I was released from jail was all these people who were inspired by a very simple individual story, of something every one of us does every single day. It was something that inspired so many people around the world, and created a rally, that led to my release nine days later. When I left jail, lots of rumors, lots of harsh things happened in my life. That was the hardest thing: not facing what I did, but just facing the things I did not do. On June 17th, the day we called for women to drive, some 100 brave women drove despite all the streets that were packed with police cars, even religious police SUVs, in every corner. Some 100 women drove that day: none was arrested. We broke the women driving taboo.

* The Egyptian American journalist and author of *Headscarves and Hymens*.

I met Mona Eltahawy* in January [in Egypt]. She asked, "What's your secret?" And I told her, "Mona, they messed with the wrong woman." And she used that in her speech that night. And I say that what I feel is I measure the impact I make by how harsh the attacks are. The harsher the attacks were, the greater the impact was. That simple. We have started now a movement in Saudi Arabia. We call it the Saudi Women's Spring. My group is my right to dignity. And we believe in full citizenship for women, because the child cannot be free if his mother is not free. The husband cannot be free if his wife is not free. The parents are not free if their daughters are not free. The society is nothing if the women are nothing.

Freedom starts within. For me, here, I am free. But when I go back home to Saudi Arabia, the struggle has just begun. I don't know how long it will last, and I don't know when it will end. But for me, the struggle is not about driving a car. It is about being in the driver's seat of our destiny. It is to be free, not only to dream, but also to live. Thank you.

# WHEN ALL OTHER FRIENDS DESERT, HE REMAINS

George Graham Vest served as United States senator for Missouri from 1879 to 1903, having previously been a member of the Confederate Congress during the Civil War. However, it is for a speech he made many years earlier, while working as a lawyer, that Vest is widely remembered. This particular case concerned a dog named Old Drum, who had been unlawfully shot dead.

Old Drum's owner – Vest's client – believed the crime had been committed by a neighboring farmer. As the trial drew to a close, it came time for Vest to wrap up his argument: he did so by way of a speech so emotive that it not only convinced the jury of the farmer's guilt, but also resulted in a statue of Old Drum being erected outside the Johnson County Courthouse.

→ George Graham Vest, from the Brady-Handy photograph collection, Library of Congress

Gentlemen of the jury.

The best friend a man has in the world may turn against him and become his enemy. His son or daughter whom he has reared with loving care may prove ungrateful. Those who are nearest and dearest to us, those whom we trust with our happiness and our good name may become traitors to their faith. The money that a man has, he may lose. It flies away from him, perhaps when he needs it most. A man's reputation may be sacrificed in a moment of ill-considered action. The people who are prone to fall on their knees to do us honor when success is with us may be the first to throw the stone of malice when failure settles its cloud upon our heads.

The one absolutely unselfish friend that man can have in this selfish world, the one that never deserts him, the one that never proves ungrateful or treacherous, is his dog. Gentlemen of the jury, a man's dog stands by him in prosperity and in poverty, in health and in sickness. He will sleep on the cold ground, where the wintry winds blow and the snow drives fiercely, if only he can be near his master's side. He will kiss the hand that has no food to offer; he will lick the wounds and sores that come in an encounter with the roughness of the world. He guards the sleep of his pauper master as if he were a prince. When all other friends desert, he remains. When riches take wings, and reputation falls to pieces, he is as constant in his love as the sun in its journey through the heavens.

If fortune drives the master forth an outcast in the world, friendless and homeless, the faithful dog asks no higher privilege than that of accompanying him, to guard him against danger, to fight against his enemies. And when the last scene of all comes, and death takes his master in its embrace and his body is laid away in the cold ground, no matter if all other friends pursue their way, there by his graveside will the noble dog be found, his head between his paws and his eyes sad but open, in alert watchfulness, faithful and true even in death.

# DULUTH!

In 1871, a forty-year-old Democratic Congressman from Kentucky took to the floor of the House of Representatives with one aim: to oppose a proposed loan of federal lands to the St. Croix and Lake Superior Railroad. These lands were to be used for a new railroad that would begin in Houlton, Wisconsin, and end in the vicinity of Duluth, a small town that would soon become the butt of James Knott's sarcastic and lengthy attack. His speech brought the house down, as it did the bill; when he died, the *New York Times* labeled it "a classic." The residents of Duluth, one imagines, were not as impressed.

Mr. Speaker, if I could be actuated by any conceivable inducement to betray the sacred trust reposed in me by those to whose generous confidence I am indebted for the honor of a seat on this floor; if I could be influenced by any possible consideration to become instrumental in giving away, in violation of their known wishes, any portion of their interest in the public domain for the mere promotion of any railroad enterprise whatever, I should certainly feel a strong inclination to give this measure my most earnest and hearty support; for I am assured that its success would materially enhance the pecuniary prosperity of some of the most valued friends I have on earth – friends for whose accommodation I would be willing to make almost any sacrifice not involving my personal honor or my fidelity as the trustee of an express trust. And that fact of itself would be sufficient to countervail almost any objection I might entertain to the passage of this bill not inspired by an imperative and inexorable sense of public duty.

But, independent of the seductive influences of private friendship, to which I admit I am, perhaps, as susceptible as any of the gentlemen I see around me, the intrinsic merits of the measure itself are of such an extraordinary character as to commend it most strongly to the favorable consideration of every member of this House, myself not excepted, notwithstanding my constituents, in whose behalf alone I am acting here, would not be benefited by its passage one particle more than they would be by a project to cultivate an orange grove on the bleakest summit of Greenland's icy mountains. Now, sir, as to those great trunk lines of railway, spanning the continent from ocean to ocean, I confess my mind has never been fully made up. It is true they may afford some trifling advantages to local traffic, and they may even in time become the channels of a more extended commerce. Yet I have never been thoroughly satisfied either of the necessity or expediency of projects promising such meager results to the great body of our people. But with regard to the transcendent merits of the gigantic enterprise contemplated in this bill I never entertained the shadow of a doubt.

Years ago, when I first heard that there was somewhere in the vast *terra incognita*, somewhere in the bleak regions of the great Northwest, a stream of water known to the nomadic inhabitants of the neighborhood as the river St. Croix, I became satisfied that the construction of a railroad from that raging torrent to some point in the civilized world was essential to the happiness and prosperity of the American people, if not absolutely indispensable to the perpetuity of republican institutions on this continent. I felt instinctively that the boundless resources of that prolific region of sand and pine-shrubbery would never be fully developed without a railroad constructed and equipped at the expense of the Government, and perhaps not then. I had an abiding presentiment that, some day or other, the people of this whole country, irrespective of party affiliations, regardless of sectional prejudices, and "without distinction of race, color, or previous condition of servitude," would rise in their majesty and demand an outlet for the enormous agricultural productions of those vast and fertile pine-barrens, drained in the rainy season by the surging waters of the turbid St. Croix. [Knott reads out passages from an earlier debate on this bill.]

Now, sir, who, after listening to this emphatic and unequivocal testimony of these intelligent, competent, and able-bodied witnesses; who that is not as incredulous as St. Thomas himself, will doubt for a moment that the Goshen of America is to be found in the sandy valleys and upon the pine-clad hills of the St. Croix? Who will have the hardihood to rise in his seat on this floor and assert that, excepting the pine bushes, the entire region would not produce vegetation enough in ten years to fatten a grasshopper? Where is the patriot who is willing that his country shall incur the peril of remaining another day without the amplest railroad connection with such an inexhaustible mine of agricultural wealth?

Who will answer for the consequences of abandoning a great and warlike people, in possession of a country like that, to brood over the indifference and neglect of their government? How long would it be before they would take to studying the Declaration of Independence and hatching out the damnable heresy of secession? How long before the grim demon of civil discord would rear again his horrid head in our midst, "gnash loud his iron fangs and shake his crest of bristling bayonets?" (. . .)

Now, sir, I repeat I have been satisfied for years that if there was any portion of the inhabited globe absolutely in a suffering condition for the want of a railroad it was these teeming pine-barrens of the St. Croix. At what particular point on that noble stream such a road should be commenced I knew was immaterial, and so it seems to have been considered by the draftsman of this bill. It might be up at the spring or down at the foot log, or the water gate, or the fish dam, or anywhere along the bank, no matter where. But in what direction it should run, or where it should terminate, were always to my mind questions of the most painful perplexity. I could conceive of no place on "God's green earth" in such straitened circumstances for railroad facilities as to be likely to desire or willing to accept such a connection (. . .)

Hence, as I have said, sir, I was utterly at a loss to determine where the terminus of this great and indispensable road should be, until I accidentally overheard some gentleman the other day mention the name of "Duluth."

Duluth! The word fell upon my ear with peculiar and indescribable charm, like the gentle murmur of a low fountain stealing forth in the midst of roses, or the soft, sweet accents of an angel's whisper in the bright, joyous dream of sleeping innocence.

Duluth! 'Twas the name for which my soul had panted for years, as the hart panteth for the water-brooks. But where was Duluth? Never in all my limited reading had my vision been gladdened by seeing the celestial word in print. And I felt a profounder humiliation in my ignorance that its dulcet syllables had never before ravished my delighted ear. I was certain the draftsman of this bill had never heard of it, or it would have been designated as one of the termini of this road. I asked my friends about it, but they knew nothing of it. I rushed to the library and examined all the maps I could find. I discovered in one of them a delicate, hair-like line, diverging from the Mississippi near a place marked Prescott, which I supposed was intended to represent the river St. Croix, but I could nowhere find Duluth.

Nevertheless, I was confident it existed somewhere, and that its discovery would constitute the crowning glory of the present century, if not of all modern times. I knew it was bound to exist, in the very nature of things; that the symmetry and perfection of our planetary system would be incomplete without it; that the elements of material nature would long since have resolved themselves back into original chaos if there had been such a hiatus in creation as would have resulted from leaving out Duluth. In fact, sir, I was overwhelmed with the conviction that Duluth not only existed somewhere, but that, wherever it was, it was a great and glorious place. I was convinced that the greatest calamity that ever befell the benighted nations of the ancient world was in their having passed away without a knowledge of the actual existence of Duluth; that their fabled Atlantis, never seen save by the hallowed vision of inspired poesy, was, in fact, but another name for Duluth; that the golden orchard of the Hesperides was but a poetical synonym for the beer-gardens in the vicinity of Duluth. I was certain that Herodotus had died a miserable death because in all his travels and with all his geographical research he had never heard of Duluth. I knew that if the immortal spirit of Homer could look down from another heaven than that created by his own celestial genius upon the long lines of pilgrims from every nation of the earth to the gushing fountain of poesy opened by the touch of his magic wand, if he could be permitted to behold the vast assemblage of grand and glorious productions of the lyric art called into being by his own inspired strains, he would weep tears of bitter anguish that, instead of lavishing all the stores of his mighty genius upon the fall of Illion, it had not been his more blessed lot to crystallize in deathless song the rising glories of Duluth. Yet, sir, had it not been for this map, kindly furnished me by the Legislature of Minnesota, I might have gone down to my obscure and humble grave in an agony of despair because I could nowhere find Duluth. Had such been my melancholy fate, I have no doubt that with the last feeble pulsation of my breaking heart, with the last faint exhalation of my fleeting breath, I should have whispered, "Where is Duluth?"

But, thanks to the beneficence of that band of ministering angels who have their bright abodes in the far-off capital of Minnesota, just as the agony of my anxiety was about to culminate in the frenzy of despair, this blessed map was placed in my hands; and as I unfolded it a resplendent scene of ineffable glory opened before me, such as I imagine burst upon the enraptured vision of the wandering peri [fallen angel] through the opening gates of paradise. There, there for the first time, my enchanted eye rested upon the ravishing word "Duluth."

This map, sir, is intended, as it appears from its title, to illustrate the position of Duluth in the United States; but if gentlemen will examine it, I think they will concur with me in the opinion that it is far too modest in its pretensions. It not only illustrates the position of Duluth in the United States, but exhibits its relations with all created things. It even goes further than this. It lifts the shadowy veil of futurity and affords us a view of the golden prospects of Duluth far along the dim vista of ages yet to come.

If gentlemen will examine it, they will find Duluth not only in the center of the map, but represented in the center of a series of concentric circles one hundred miles apart, and some of them as much as four thousand miles in diameter, embracing alike in their tremendous sweep the fragrant savannas of the sunlit South and the eternal solitudes of snow that mantle the ice-bound North. How these circles were produced is perhaps one of those primordial mysteries that the most skilful paleologist will never be able to explain. But the fact is, sir, Duluth is pre-eminently a central place, for I am told by gentlemen who have been so reckless of their own personal safety as to venture away into those awful regions where Duluth is supposed to be, that it is so exactly in the center of the visible universe that the sky comes down at precisely the same distance all around it.

I find by reference to this map that Duluth is situated somewhere near the western end of Lake Superior, but as there is no dot or other mark indicating its exact location I am unable to say whether it is actually confined to any particular spot, or whether "it is just lying around there loose." I really cannot tell whether it is one of those ethereal creations of intellectual frostwork, more intangible than the rose-tinted clouds of a summer sunset; one of those airy exhalations of the speculator's brain, which I am told are ever flitting in the form of towns and

→ The position of Duluth in the United States, map by Morris H. Traubel, c.1878

MAP ILLUSTRATING THE POSITION OF

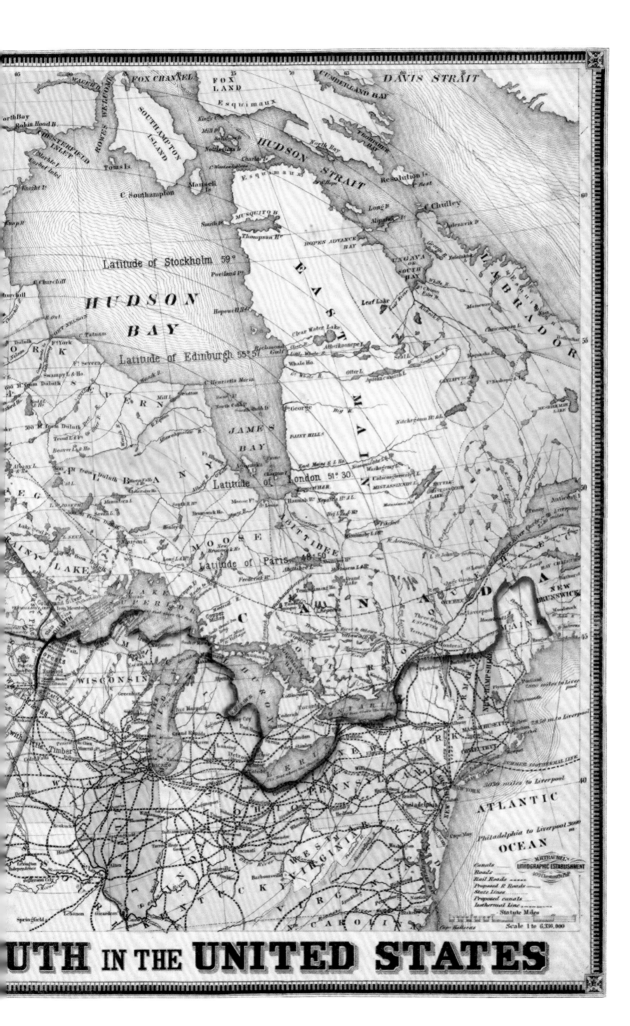

UTH IN THE UNITED STATES

cities along those lines of railroad, built with Government subsidies, luring the unwary settler as the mirage of the desert lures the famishing traveler on, and ever on, until it fades away in the darkening horizon, or whether it is a real, bona fide, substantial city, all "staked off," with the lots marked with their owners' names, like that proud commercial metropolis recently discovered on the desirable shores of San Domingo. But, however that may be, I am satisfied Duluth is there, or thereabout, for I see it stated here on this map that it is exactly thirty-nine hundred and ninety miles from Liverpool; though I have no doubt, for the sake of convenience, it will be moved back ten miles so as to make the distance an even four thousand.

Then, sir, there is the climate of Duluth, unquestionably the most salubrious and delightful to be found anywhere on the Lord's earth. Now, I have always been under the impression, as I presume other gentlemen have, that in the region around Lake Superior it was cold enough for at least nine months in the year to freeze the smoke-stack off a locomotive. But I see it represented on this map that Duluth is situated exactly halfway between the latitudes of Paris and Venice so that gentlemen who have inhaled the exhilarating airs of the one or basked in the golden sunlight of the other may see at a glance that Duluth must be a place of untold delights, a terrestrial paradise, fanned by the balmy zephyrs of an eternal spring, clothed in the gorgeous sheen of ever-blooming flowers, and vocal with the silvery melody of nature's choicest songsters. In fact, sir, since I have seen this map I have no doubt that Byron was vainly endeavoring to convey some faint conception of the delicious charms of Duluth when his poetic soul gushed forth in the rippling strains of that beautiful rhapsody:

> Know ye the land of the cedar and vine,
> Where the flowers ever blossom, the beams ever shine;
> Where the light wings of Zephyr, oppressed with perfume,
> Wax faint o'er the gardens of Gul in her bloom;
> Where the citron and olive are fairest of fruit,
> And the voice of the nightingale never is mute;
> Where the tints of the earth and the hues of the sky,
> In color though varied, in beauty may vie?*

* From *The Bride of Abydos* by Lord Byron (1788–1824).

As to the commercial resources of Duluth, sir, they are simply illimitable and inexhaustible, as is shown by this map. I see it stated here that there is a vast scope of territory, embracing an area of over two million square miles, rich in every element of material wealth and commercial prosperity, all tributary to Duluth. Look at it, sir [pointing to the map]. Here are inexhaustible mines of gold, immeasurable veins of silver, impenetrable depths of boundless forest, vast coal-measures, wide, extended plains of richest pasturage, all, all embraced in this vast territory, which must, in the very nature of things, empty the untold

← James Proctor Knott, from the Brady-Handy photograph collection, Library of Congress

treasures of its commerce into the lap of Duluth. Look at it, sir [pointing to the map]; do not you see from these broad, brown lines drawn around this immense territory that the enterprising inhabitants of Duluth intend some day to inclose it all in one vast corral, so that its commerce will be bound to go there whether it would or not? And here, sir [still pointing to the map], I find within a convenient distance the Piegan Indians, which, of all the many accessories to the glory of Duluth, I consider by far the most inestimable. For, sir, I have been told that when the smallpox breaks out among the women and children of that famous tribe, as it sometimes does, they afford the finest subjects in the world for the strategical experiments of any enterprising military hero who desires to improve himself in the noble art of war; especially for any valiant lieutenant general whose

> Trenchant blade, Toledo trusty,
> For want of fighting has grown rusty,
> And eats into itself for lack
> Of somebody to hew and hack.[†]

† From *Hubridas* by
Samuel Butler (1612–80).

(. . .) And here, sir, recurring to this map, I find in the immediate vicinity of the Piegans' "vast herds of buffalo" and "immense fields of rich wheat lands."

[THE SPEAKER: Is there objection to the gentleman from Kentucky continuing his remarks? . . .The Chair hears none. The gentleman will proceed.]

I was remarking, sir, upon these vast "wheat fields" represented on this map in the immediate neighborhood of the buffaloes and the Piegans, and was about to say that the idea of there being these immense wheat fields in the very heart of a wilderness, hundreds and hundreds of miles beyond the utmost verge of civilization, may appear to some gentlemen as rather incongruous, as rather too great a strain on the "blankets" of veracity. But to my mind there is no difficulty in the matter whatever. The phenomenon is very easily accounted for. It is evident, sir, that the Piegans sowed that wheat there and plowed it with buffalo bulls. Now, sir, this fortunate combination of buffaloes and Piegans, considering their relative position to each other and to Duluth, as they are arranged on this map, satisfies me that Duluth is destined to be the beef market of the world.

Here, you will observe, are the buffaloes, directly between the Piegans and Duluth and here, right on the road to Duluth, are the Creeks [another Native American tribe]. Now, sir, when the buffaloes are sufficiently fat from grazing on those immense wheat fields you see it will be the easiest thing in the world for the Piegans to drive them on down, stay all night with their friends, the Creeks, and go into Duluth in the morning. I think I see them now, sir, a vast herd of buffaloes, with their heads down, their eyes glaring, their nostrils dilated, their tongues out, and their tails curled over their backs, tearing along toward Duluth, with about a thousand Piegans on their grassbellied ponies, yelling at their heels! On they come! And as they sweep past the Creeks they join in the chase, and away they all go, yelling, bellowing, ripping, and tearing along, amid clouds of dust, until the last buffalo is safely penned in the stockyards of Duluth.

Sir, I might stand here for hours and hours and expatriate with rapture upon the gorgeous prospects of Duluth, as depicted upon this map. But human life is too short and time of this House far too valuable to allow me to linger longer upon the delightful theme. I think every gentleman on this floor is as well satisfied as I am that Duluth is destined to become the commercial metropolis of the universe, and that this road should be built at once. I am fully persuaded that no patriotic Representative of the American people, who has a proper appreciation of the associated glories of Duluth and the St. Croix, will hesitate a moment to say that every able-bodied female in the land between the ages of eighteen and forty-five who is in favor of woman's rights should be drafted and set to work upon this great work without delay. Nevertheless, sir, it grieves my very soul to be compelled to say that I cannot vote for the grant of lands provided for in this bill.

Ah! sir, you can have no conception of the poignancy of my anguish that I am deprived of that blessed privilege. There are two insuperable obstacles in the way. In the first place, my constituents, for whom I am acting here, have no more interest in this road than they have in the great question of culinary taste now perhaps agitating the public mind of Dominica, as to whether the illustrious commissioners who recently left this capital for the free and enlightened republic would be better fricasseed, boiled, or roasted, and in the second place those lands, which I am asked to give away, alas, are not mine to bestow! My relation to them is simply that of trustee to an express trust. And shall I ever betray that trust? Never, sir! Rather perish Duluth! Perish the paragon of cities! Rather let the freezing cyclones of the black Northwest bury it forever beneath the eddying sands of the raging St. Croix!

# IN EVENT OF MOON DISASTER

To  :  H. R. Haldeman

From:  Bill Safire                                    July 18, 1969.

------------------------------------------------------------

IN EVENT OF MOON DISASTER:

Fate has ordained that the men who went to the moon to explore in peace will stay on the moon to rest in peace.

These brave men, Neil Armstrong and Edwin Aldrin, know that there is no hope for their recovery.  But they also know that there is hope for mankind in their sacrifice.

These two men are laying down their lives in mankind's most noble goal:  the search for truth and understanding.

They will be mourned by their families and friends; they will be mourned by their nation; they will be mourned by the people of the world; they will be mourned by a Mother Earth that dared send two of her sons into the unknown.

In their exploration, they stirred the people of the world to feel as one; in their sacrifice, they bind more tightly the brotherhood of man.

In ancient days, men looked at stars and saw their heroes in the constellations.  In modern times, we do much the same, but our heroes are epic men of flesh and blood.

When *Los Angeles Times* reporter Jim Mann visited the U.S. National Archives on an unrelated research trip in the mid-1990s, he inadvertently uncovered and later published the text of a speech written twenty-five years earlier for then-President Richard Nixon. It was a haunting announcement that Nixon thankfully never had to deliver, and didn't even see. Titled "In Event of Moon Disaster" and sympathetically penned by presidential speechwriter William Safire, this eulogy of sorts was to be read to the general public should the Apollo 11 Lunar Module fail to leave the moon – and its passengers, Neil Armstrong and Buzz Aldrin, be marooned in the loneliest of places, hundreds of thousands of miles from home.

-2-

Others will follow, and surely find their way home. Man's search will not be denied. But these men were the first, and they will remain the foremost in our hearts.

For every human being who looks up at the moon in the nights to come will know that there is some corner of another world that is forever mankind.

PRIOR TO THE PRESIDENT'S STATEMENT:

The President should telephone each of the widows-to-be.

AFTER THE PRESIDENT'S STATEMENT, AT THE POINT WHEN NASA ENDS COMMUNICATIONS WITH THE MEN:

A clergyman should adopt the same procedure as a burial at sea, commending their souls to "the deepest of the deep," concluding with the Lord's Prayer.

# NORTH KOREA IS INDESCRIBABLE

In October 2014, 1,300 delegates from 196 countries traveled to Dublin to attend the One Young World Summit, an annual conference that aims to empower and connect like-minded young adults by discussing the world's burning issues. The theme of the 2014 gathering was "Peace and Conflict Resolution," with audiences addressed by the likes of Kofi Annan, Sir Bob Geldof and Mary Robinson; however, it was on the fourth and final day of proceedings that the most compelling and harrowing speech was delivered by Yeonmi Park, an understandably emotional young activist who in 2007 escaped North Korea with her family.

I have to do this because this is not me speaking. This is the people who want to tell the world what they want to say.

North Korea is an unimaginable country. There is only one channel on TV. There is no free Internet. We aren't to sing, say, wear or think what we want. North Korea is the only country in the world that executes people for making unauthorized international phone calls. North Koreans are being terrorized today. When I was growing up in North Korea, I never saw anything about love stories between men and women. No books, no songs, no press. No movies about love stories. There is no Romeo and Juliet. Every story was propaganda to brainwash us about the Kim dictators.

I was born in 1993 and I was abducted at birth, even before I knew the words "freedom" or "human rights." North Korea is so desperately seeking and dying for freedom at this moment.

When I was nine years old, I saw my friend's mother publicly executed. Her crime: watching a Hollywood movie. Expressing doubt about the cruelness of the regime can get three generations of a family imprisoned or executed.

When I was four years old, I was warned by my mother not to even whisper. The birds and mice couldn't hear me. I admit it: I thought the North Korean dictator could read my mind.

My father died in China after we escaped North Korea and I had to bury him at 3 a.m. in secret. I was fourteen years old. I couldn't even cry. I was afraid to be sent back to North Korea.

The day I escaped North Korea, I saw my mother raped. The rapist was a Chinese broker. He targeted me. I was thirteen years old. There is a saying in North Korea, "Women are weak, mothers are strong." My mother allowed herself to be raped in order to protect me. North Korean refugees, about 300,000, are vulnerable in China. Seventy percent of North Korean women and teenage girls are being victimized, sometimes sold for as little as $200.

We walked across the Gobi Desert following a compass. When this stopped working, we followed the stars to freedom. I felt only the stars were with us.

→ Yeonmi Park at the One Young World Summit, 2014

Mongolia was our freedom moment. Death or dignity. Armed with knives, we were prepared to kill ourselves if we were going to be sent back to North Korea. We wanted to live as humans.

People often ask me, "How can you help North Koreans?" There are many ways but I would like to mention three for now.

1. Educate yourself so that you can raise awareness about human crisis in North Korea.
2. Help and support North Korean refugees who are trying to escape to freedom.
3. Petition China to stop repatriation. We have to shine a light on the darkest place in the world.

It isn't just North Korean human rights, it's *our* rights that North Korean dictators have violated for seven decades. We need governments all around the world to put more pressure on China to stop repatriation. In particular, Chinese delegates of One Young World can play a part by speaking up.

North Korea is indescribable. No humans deserve to be oppressed just because of their birthplace. We need to focus less on the regime and more on the people who are being forgotten. One Young World, we are the ones who make them visible. Fellow delegates, please join me as you make this a global movement to free North Koreans.

When I was crossing the Gobi Desert, scared of dying, I thought nobody in this world cared. It seemed that only the stars were with me. But you have listened to my story. You have cared. Thank you very much.

# GIVE ME YOUR CHILDREN

Mordechai Chaim Rumkowksi was appointed as the "Eldest of the Jews" of the Łódź Ghetto in Poland, an urban slave camp created by the Nazis during World War II. The former Jewish businessman and director of a Jewish orphanage was expected to maintain order and productivity among the ghetto inmates, a job he was given after indicating that he would deliver Jewish labor on demand. In September 1942, Rumkowski was instructed by the ghetto's German overseer to hand over all children under the age of ten, along with the community's elderly and sick – 20,000 people in total – all of whom were to be deported to Chełmno and exterminated in mobile gas vans.

On the 4th of the month, he gave this harrowing speech to the ghetto's assembled inhabitants, producing widespread panic throughout the community.

The Łódź Ghetto continued to function until August 1944, by which time more than 200,000 Jews had passed through it, most of whom either died of starvation and exhaustion ("ghetto disease") or were deported to their untimely deaths. Rumkowski was one of the last to leave. Shortly after arriving at Auschwitz, he is rumored to have been beaten to death by former ghetto inmates in revenge for his abusive treatment of the Jews and his collaborative relationship with the Germans.

A grievous blow has struck the ghetto. They are asking us to give up the best we possess – the children and the elderly.

I was unworthy of having a child of my own, so I gave the best years of my life to children. I've lived and breathed with children. I never imagined I would be forced to deliver this sacrifice to the altar with my own hands. In my old age, I must stretch out my hands and beg: brothers and sisters, hand them over to me. Fathers and mothers, give me your children.

I had a suspicion something was going to befall us. I anticipated something and was always like a watchman, on guard to prevent it. But I was unsuccessful because I did not know what was threatening us. The taking of the sick from the hospitals caught me completely by surprise. And I give you the best proof there is of this: I had my own nearest and dearest among them and I could do nothing for them.

I thought that would be the end of it – that after that, they'd leave us in peace, the peace for which I long so much, for which I've always worked, which has been my goal. But something else, it turned out, was destined for us. Such is the fate of the Jews: always more suffering and always worse suffering, especially in times of war.

Yesterday afternoon, they gave me the order to send more than 20,000 Jews out of the ghetto, and if not – "We will do it!" So the question became, "Should we take it upon ourselves, do it ourselves, or leave it to others to do?" Well, we – that is, I and my closest associates – thought first not about "How many will perish?" but "How many is it possible to save?" And we reached the conclusion that, however hard it would be for us, we should take the implementation of this order into our own hands.

I must perform this difficult and bloody operation – I must cut off limbs in order to save the body itself. I must take children because, if not, others may be taken as well – God forbid.

I have no thought of consoling you today. Nor do I wish to calm you. I must lay bare your full anguish and pain. I come to you like a bandit, to take from you what you treasure most in your hearts. I have tried, using every possible means, to get the order revoked. I tried – when that proved to be impossible – to soften the order. Just yesterday, I ordered a list of children aged nine to ten. I wanted at least to save this one age-group: the nine- to ten-year-olds. But I was not granted this concession. On only one point did I succeed: in saving the ten-year-olds and up. Let this be a consolation to our profound grief.

There are, in the ghetto, many patients who can expect to live only a few days more, maybe a few weeks. I don't know if the idea is diabolical or not, but I must say it: "Give me the sick. In their place we can save the healthy."

I know how dear the sick are to any family, and particularly to Jews. However, when cruel demands are made, one has to weigh and measure: who shall, can and may be saved? And common sense dictates that the saved must be those who can be saved and those who have a chance of being rescued, not those who cannot be saved in any case . . .

We live in the ghetto, mind you. We live with so much restriction that we do not have enough even for the healthy, let alone for the sick. Each of us feeds the sick at the expense of our own health: we give our bread to the sick. We give them our meager ration of sugar, our little piece of meat. And what's the result? Not enough to cure the sick, and we ourselves become ill. Of course, such sacrifices are the most beautiful and noble. But there are times when one has to choose: sacrifice the sick, who haven't the slightest chance of recovery and who also may make others ill, or rescue the healthy.

I could not deliberate over this problem for long; I had to resolve it in favor of the healthy. In this spirit, I gave the appropriate instructions to the doctors, and they will be expected to deliver all incurable patients, so that the healthy, who want and are able to live, will be saved in their place. I understand you, mothers; I see your tears, all right. I also feel what you feel in your hearts, you fathers who will have to go to work in the morning after your children have been taken from you, when just yesterday you were playing with your dear little ones. All this I know and feel. Since four o'clock yesterday, when I first found out about the order, I have been utterly broken. I share your pain. I suffer because of your anguish, and I don't know how I'll survive this – where I'll find the strength to do so.

I must tell you a secret: they requested 24,000 victims, 3,000 a day for eight days. I succeeded in reducing the number to 20,000, but only on the condition that these be children under the age of ten. Children ten and older are safe. Since the children and the aged together equals only some 13,000 souls, the gap will have to be filled with the sick.

→ Mordechai Chaim Rumkowski, chairman of the Jewish Council, delivers a speech from his carriage, July 1940

SPEECHES OF NOTE

I can barely speak. I am exhausted; I only want to tell you what I am asking of you: help me carry out this action. I am trembling. I am afraid that others, God forbid, will do it themselves. A broken Jew stands before you. Do not envy me. This is the most difficult of all orders I have ever had to carry out at any time. I reach out to you with my broken, trembling hands and beg: give into my hands the victims. So that we can avoid having further victims, and a population of 100,000 Jews can be preserved. So they promised me: if we deliver our victims by ourselves, there will be peace.

[The crowd begins shouting, "We will not let the children go alone – we will all go."]

These are empty phrases. I don't have the strength to argue with you. If the authorities were to arrive, none of you would be shouting.

I understand what it means to tear off a part of the body. Yesterday, I begged on my knees, but it did not work. From small villages with Jewish populations of 7,000 to 8,000, barely 1,000 arrived here. So which is better? What do you want? That 80,000 to 90,000 Jews remain, or God forbid, that the whole population be annihilated?

You may judge as you please; my duty is to preserve the Jews who remain. I do not speak to hot-heads. I speak to your reason and conscience. I have done and will continue doing everything possible to keep arms from appearing in the streets and blood from being shed. The order could not be undone; it could only be reduced.

One needs the heart of a bandit to ask from you what I am asking. But put yourself in my place, think logically, and you'll reach the conclusion that I cannot proceed any other way. The part that can be saved is much larger than the part that must be given away.

# WHAT TO THE SLAVE IS THE FOURTH OF JULY?

Born into slavery in 1818, Frederick Douglass was twenty years of age and largely self-educated when he eventually managed to flee his final master. As a freeman, he truly flourished: before long, Douglass was touring the United States as a noted orator and leading abolitionist – his impact so great that he is now considered by many to be one of the most influential African Americans of the nineteenth century. In 1852, he was invited by the Rochester Ladies' Anti-Slavery Society to speak to a largely white audience of hundreds, on the subject of Independence Day. The searing speech he gave was both unexpected and unforgettable.

Mr. President, friends and fellow citizens:

He who could address this audience without a quailing sensation has stronger nerves than I have. I do not remember ever to have appeared as a speaker before any assembly more shrinkingly, nor with greater distrust of my ability, than I do this day. A feeling has crept over me quite unfavorable to the exercise of my limited powers of speech. The task before me is one which requires much previous thought and study for its proper performance. I know that apologies of this sort are generally considered flat and unmeaning. I trust, however, that mine will not be so considered. Should I seem at ease, my appearance would much misrepresent me. The little experience I have had in addressing public meetings, in country school houses, avails me nothing on the present occasion.

The papers and placards say that I am to deliver a Fourth of July Oration. This certainly sounds large, and out of the common way, for me. It is true that I have often had the privilege to speak in this beautiful Hall, and to address many who now honor me with their presence. But neither their familiar faces, nor the perfect gage I think I have of Corinthian Hall, seems to free me from embarrassment.

The fact is, ladies and gentlemen, the distance between this platform and the slave plantation, from which I escaped, is considerable – and the difficulties to be overcome in getting from the latter to the former are by no means slight. That I am here today is, to me, a matter of astonishment as well as of gratitude. You will not, therefore, be surprised, if in what I have to say I evince no elaborate preparation, nor grace my speech with any high-sounding exordium. With little experience and with less learning, I have been able to throw my thoughts hastily and imperfectly together; and trusting to your patient and generous indulgence I will proceed to lay them before you.

This, for the purpose of this celebration, is the Fourth of July. It is the birthday of your National Independence, and of your political freedom. This, to you, is what the Passover was to the emancipated people of God. It carries your minds back to the day, and to the act of your great deliverance; and to the signs, and to the wonders, associated with that act, and that day. This celebration also marks the beginning of another year of your national life; and reminds you that the Republic of America is now seventy-six years old. I am glad, fellow citizens, that your nation is so young. Seventy-six years, though a good old age for a man, is but a mere speck in the life of a nation. Three score years and ten is the allotted time for individual men; but nations number their years by thousands. According to this fact, you are, even now, only in the beginning of your national career, still lingering in the period of childhood. I repeat, I am glad this is so. There is hope in the thought, and hope is much needed, under the dark clouds which lower above the horizon. The eye of the reformer is met with angry flashes, portending disastrous times; but his heart may well beat lighter at the thought that America is young, and that she is still in the impressible stage of her existence. May he not hope that high lessons of wisdom, of justice and of truth, will yet give direction to her destiny? Were the nation older, the patriot's heart might be sadder, and the reformer's brow heavier. Its future might be shrouded in gloom, and the hope of its prophets go out in sorrow. There is consolation in the thought that America is young. Great streams are not easily turned from channels, worn deep in the course of ages. They may sometimes rise in quiet and stately majesty, and inundate the land, refreshing and fertilizing the earth with their mysterious properties. They may also rise in wrath and fury, and bear away, on their angry waves, the accumulated wealth of years of toil and hardship. They, however, gradually flow back to the same old channel, and flow on as serenely as ever. But, while the river may not be turned aside, it may dry up, and leave nothing behind but the withered branch, and the unsightly rock, to howl in the abyss-sweeping wind, the sad tale of departed glory. As with rivers so with nations.

Fellow citizens, I shall not presume to dwell at length on the associations that cluster about this day. The simple story of it is, that, seventy-six years ago, the people of this country were British subjects. The style and title of your "sovereign people" (in which you now glory) was not then born. You were under the British Crown. Your fathers esteemed the English Government as the home government; and England as the fatherland. This home government, you know, although a considerable distance from your home, did, in the exercise of its parental prerogatives, impose upon its colonial children such restraints, burdens and limitations, as, in its mature judgment, it deemed wise, right, and proper.

But your fathers, who had not adopted the fashionable idea of this day, of the infallibility of government, and the absolute character of its acts, presumed to differ from the home government in respect to the wisdom and the justice of some of those burdens and restraints. They went so far in their excitement as to pronounce the measures of government unjust, unreasonable, and oppressive, and altogether such as ought not to be quietly submitted to. I scarcely need say, fellow citizens, that my opinion of those measures fully accords with that of your fathers. Such a declaration of agreement on my part would not be worth much to anybody. It would certainly prove nothing as to what part I might have taken had I lived during the great controversy of 1776. To say now that America was right, and England wrong, is exceedingly easy. Everybody can say it; the dastard, not less than the noble brave, can flippantly discant on the tyranny of England towards the American Colonies. It is fashionable to do so; but there was a time when, to pronounce against England, and in favor of the cause of the colonies, tried men's souls. They who did so were accounted in their day plotters of mischief, agitators, and rebels, dangerous men. To side with the right against the wrong, with the weak against the strong, and with the oppressed against the oppressor! Here lies the merit, and the one which, of all others, seems unfashionable in our day. The cause of liberty may be stabbed by the men who glory in the deeds of your fathers. But, to proceed.

Feeling themselves harshly and unjustly treated by the home government, your fathers, like men of honesty, and men of spirit, earnestly sought redress. They petitioned and remonstrated; they did so in a decorous, respectful, and loyal manner. Their conduct was wholly unexceptionable. This, however, did not answer the purpose. They saw themselves treated with sovereign indifference, coldness, and scorn. Yet they persevered. They were not the men to look back.

As the sheet anchor takes a firmer hold, when the ship is tossed by the storm, so did the cause of your fathers grow stronger as it breasted the chilling blasts of kingly displeasure. The greatest and best of British statesmen admitted its justice, and the loftiest eloquence of the British Senate came to its support. But, with that blindness which seems to be the unvarying characteristic of tyrants, since Pharaoh and his hosts were drowned in the Red Sea, the British Government persisted in the exactions complained of.

The madness of this course, we believe, is admitted now, even by England; but we fear the lesson is wholly lost on our present rulers.

Oppression makes a wise man mad. Your fathers were wise men, and if they did not go mad, they became restive under this treatment. They felt themselves the victims of grievous wrongs, wholly incurable in their colonial capacity. With brave men there is always a remedy for oppression. Just here, the idea of a total separation of the colonies from the crown was born! It was a startling idea, much more so than we, at this distance of time, regard it. The timid and the prudent (as has been intimated) of that day were, of course, shocked and alarmed by it.

Such people lived then, had lived before, and will, probably, ever have a place on this planet; and their course, in respect to any great change (no matter how great the good to be attained, or the wrong to be redressed by it), may be

calculated with as much precision as can be the course of the stars. They hate all changes, but silver, gold, and copper change! Of this sort of change they are always strongly in favor.

These people were called Tories in the days of your fathers; and the appellation, probably, conveyed the same idea that is meant by a more modern, though a somewhat less euphonious term, which we often find in our papers, applied to some of our old politicians.

Their opposition to the then dangerous thought was earnest and powerful; but, amid all their terror and affrighted vociferations against it, the alarming and revolutionary idea moved on, and the country with it.

On the second of July, 1776, the old Continental Congress, to the dismay of the lovers of ease, and the worshippers of property, clothed that dreadful idea with all the authority of national sanction. They did so in the form of a resolution; and as we seldom hit upon resolutions, drawn up in our day, whose transparency is at all equal to this, it may refresh your minds and help my story if I read it.

Resolved, that these united colonies are, and of right, ought to be free and Independent States; that they are absolved from all allegiance to the British Crown; and that all political connection between them and the State of Great Britain is, and ought to be, dissolved.

Citizens, your fathers made good that resolution. They succeeded; and today you reap the fruits of their success. The freedom gained is yours; and you, therefore, may properly celebrate this anniversary. The Fourth of July is the first great fact in your nation's history – the very ringbolt in the chain of your yet undeveloped destiny.

Pride and patriotism, not less than gratitude, prompt you to celebrate and to hold it in perpetual remembrance. I have said that the Declaration of Independence is the ringbolt to the chain of your nation's destiny; so, indeed, I regard it. The principles contained in that instrument are saving principles. Stand by those principles, be true to them on all occasions, in all places, against all foes, and at whatever cost.

From the round top of your ship of state, dark and threatening clouds may be seen. Heavy billows, like mountains in the distance, disclose to the leeward huge forms of flinty rocks! That bolt drawn, that chain broken, and all is lost. Cling to this day – cling to it, and to its principles, with the grasp of a storm-tossed mariner to a spar at midnight.

The coming into being of a nation, in any circumstances, is an interesting event. But, besides general considerations, there were peculiar circumstances which make the advent of this republic an event of special attractiveness. The whole scene, as I look back to it, was simple, dignified, and sublime. The population of the country, at the time, stood at the insignificant number of three millions. The country was poor in the munitions of war. The population was weak and scattered, and the country a wilderness unsubdued. There were then no means of concert and combination, such as exist now. Neither steam nor lightning had then been reduced to order and discipline. From the Potomac to the Delaware was a journey of many days. Under these, and innumerable other disadvantages, your fathers declared for liberty and independence and triumphed.

Fellow citizens, I am not wanting in respect for the fathers of this republic. The signers of the Declaration of Independence were brave men. They were great men, too – great enough to give frame to a great age. It does not often happen to a nation to raise, at one time, such a number of truly great men. The point from which I am compelled to view them is not, certainly, the most favorable; and yet I cannot contemplate their great deeds with less than admiration. They were statesmen, patriots, and heroes, and for the good they did, and the principles they contended for, I will unite with you to honor their memory.

They loved their country better than their own private interests; and, though this is not the highest form of human excellence, all will concede that it is a rare virtue, and that when it is exhibited it ought to command respect. He who will, intelligently, lay down his life for his country is a man whom it is not in human nature to despise. Your fathers staked their lives, their fortunes, and their sacred honor, on the cause of their country. In their admiration of liberty, they lost sight of all other interests.

They were peace men; but they preferred revolution to peaceful submission to bondage. They were quiet men; but they did not shrink from agitating against oppression. They showed forbearance; but they knew its limits. They believed in order; but not in the order of tyranny. With them, nothing was "settled" that was not right. With them, justice, liberty, and humanity were "final"; not slavery and oppression. You may well cherish the memory of such men. They were great in their day and generation. Their solid manhood stands out the more as we contrast it with these degenerate times.

How circumspect, exact, and proportionate were all their movements! How unlike the politicians of an hour! Their statesmanship looked beyond the passing moment, and stretched away in strength into the distant future. They seized upon eternal principles, and set a glorious example in their defense. Mark them! Fully appreciating the hardships to be encountered, firmly believing in the right of their cause, honorably inviting the scrutiny of an on-looking world, reverently appealing to heaven to attest their sincerity, soundly comprehending the solemn responsibility they were about to assume, wisely measuring the terrible odds against them, your fathers, the fathers of this republic, did, most deliberately, under the inspiration of a glorious patriotism, and with a sublime faith in the great principles of justice and freedom, lay deep the corner-stone of the national super-structure, which has risen and still rises in grandeur around you.

Of this fundamental work, this day is the anniversary. Our eyes are met with demonstrations of joyous enthusiasm. Banners and pennants wave exultingly on the breeze. The din of business, too, is hushed. Even mammon seems to have quitted his grasp on this day. The ear-piercing fife and the stirring drum unite their accents with the ascending peal of a thousand church bells. Prayers are made, hymns are sung, and sermons are preached in honor of this day; while the quick martial tramp of a great and multitudinous nation, echoed back by all the hills, valleys, and mountains of a vast continent, bespeak the occasion, one of thrilling and universal interest – a nation's jubilee.

Friends and citizens, I need not enter further into the causes which led to this anniversary. Many of you understand them better than I do. You could instruct me in regard to them. That is a branch of knowledge in which you feel, perhaps, a much deeper interest than your speaker. The causes which led to the separation of the colonies from the British crown have never lacked for a tongue. They have all been taught in your common schools, narrated at your firesides, unfolded from your pulpits, and thundered from your legislative halls, and are as familiar to you as household words. They form the staple of your national poetry and eloquence.

I remember, also, that, as a people, Americans are remarkably familiar with all facts which make in their own favor. This is esteemed by some as a national trait – perhaps a national weakness. It is a fact, that whatever makes for the wealth or for the reputation of Americans – and can be had cheap! – will be found by Americans. I shall not be charged with slandering Americans if I say I think the American side of any question may be safely left in American hands.

I leave, therefore, the great deeds of your fathers to other gentlemen whose claim to have been regularly descended will be less likely to be disputed than mine!

My business, if I have any here today, is with the present. The accepted time with God and His cause is the ever-living now.

> Trust no future, however pleasant,
> Let the dead past bury its dead;
> Act, act in the living present,
> Heart within, and God overhead.

We have to do with the past only as we can make it useful to the present and to the future. To all inspiring motives, to noble deeds which can be gained from the past, we are welcome. But now is the time, the important time. Your fathers have lived, died, and have done their work, and have done much of it well. You live and must die, and you must do your work. You have no right to enjoy a child's share in the labor of your fathers, unless your children are to be blest by your labors. You have no right to wear out and waste the hard-earned fame of your fathers to cover your indolence. Sydney Smith tells us that men seldom eulogize the wisdom and virtues of their fathers, but to excuse some folly or wickedness of their own. This truth is not a doubtful one. There are illustrations of it near and remote, ancient and modern. It was fashionable, hundreds of years ago, for the children of Jacob to boast, we have "Abraham to our father," when they had long lost Abraham's faith and spirit. That people contented themselves under the shadow of Abraham's great name, while they repudiated the deeds which made his name great. Need I remind you that a similar thing is being done all over this country today? Need I tell you that the Jews are not the only people who built the tombs of the prophets, and garnished the sepulchers of the righteous? Washington could not die till he had broken the chains of his slaves. Yet his monument is built up by the price of human blood, and the traders in the bodies and souls of men shout, "We have Washington to our father." Alas that it should be so; yet it is.

> The evil that men do, lives after them,
> The good is oft interred with their bones.

Fellow citizens, pardon me, allow me to ask, why am I called upon to speak here today? What have I, or those I represent, to do with your national independence? Are the great principles of political freedom and of natural justice, embodied in that Declaration of Independence, extended to us? And am I, therefore, called upon to bring our humble offering to the national altar, and to confess the benefits and express devout gratitude for the blessings resulting from your independence to us?

Would to God, both for your sakes and ours, that an affirmative answer could be truthfully returned to these questions! Then would my task be light, and my burden easy and delightful. For who is there so cold, that a nation's sympathy could not warm him? Who so obdurate and dead to the claims of gratitude, that would not thankfully acknowledge such priceless benefits? Who so stolid and selfish, that would not give his voice to swell the hallelujahs of a nation's jubilee, when the chains of servitude had been torn from his limbs? I am not that man. In a case like that, the dumb might eloquently speak, and the "lame man leap as an hart."

But such is not the state of the case. I say it with a sad sense of the disparity between us. I am not included within the pale of this glorious anniversary! Your high independence only reveals the immeasurable distance between us. The blessings in which you, this day, rejoice are not enjoyed in common. The rich inheritance of justice, liberty, prosperity, and independence, bequeathed by your fathers, is shared by you, not by me. The sunlight that brought light and healing to you has brought stripes and death to me. This Fourth of July is yours, not mine. You may rejoice, I must mourn. To drag a man in fetters into the grand illuminated temple of liberty, and call upon him to join you in joyous anthems, were inhuman mockery and sacrilegious irony. Do you mean, citizens, to mock me, by asking me to speak today? If so, there is a parallel to your conduct. And let me warn you that it is dangerous to copy the example of a nation whose crimes, towering up to heaven, were thrown down by the breath of the Almighty, burying that nation in irrevocable ruin! I can today take up the plaintive lament of a peeled and woe-smitten people!

> By the rivers of Babylon, there we sat down. Yea! we wept when we remembered Zion. We hanged our harps upon the willows in the midst thereof. For there, they that carried us away captive, required of us a song; and they who wasted us required of us mirth, saying, Sing us one of the songs of Zion. How can we sing the Lord's song in a strange land? If I forget thee, O Jerusalem, let my right hand forget her cunning. If I do not remember thee, let my tongue cleave to the roof of my mouth.

Fellow citizens, above your national, tumultuous joy, I hear the mournful wail of millions whose chains, heavy and grievous yesterday, are, today, rendered more intolerable by the jubilee shouts that reach them. If I do forget, if I do not faithfully remember those bleeding children of sorrow this day, "may my right hand forget her cunning, and may my tongue cleave to the roof of my mouth!" To forget them, to pass lightly over their wrongs, and to chime in with the popular theme, would be treason most scandalous and shocking, and would make me a reproach before God and the world. My subject, then, fellow citizens, is American slavery. I shall see this day and its popular characteristics from the slave's point of view. Standing there identified with the American bondman, making his wrongs mine, I do not hesitate to declare, with all my soul, that the character and conduct of this nation never looked blacker to me than on this Fourth of July! Whether we turn to the declarations of the past, or to the professions of the present, the conduct of the nation seems equally hideous and revolting. America is false to the past, false to the present, and solemnly binds herself to be false to the future. Standing with God and the crushed and bleeding slave on this occasion, I will, in the name of humanity which is outraged, in the name of liberty which is fettered, in the name of the Constitution and the Bible which are disregarded and trampled upon, dare to call in question and to denounce, with all the emphasis I can command, everything that serves to perpetuate slavery – the great sin and shame of America! "I will not equivocate; I will not excuse"; I will use the severest language I can command; and yet not one word shall escape me that any man, whose judgment is not blinded by prejudice, or who is not at heart a slaveholder, shall not confess to be right and just.

But I fancy I hear some one of my audience say, "It is just in this circumstance that you and your brother abolitionists fail to make a favorable impression on the public mind. Would you argue more, and denounce less; would you persuade more, and rebuke less; your cause would be much more likely to succeed." But, I submit, where all is plain there is nothing to be argued. What point in the anti-slavery creed would you have me argue? On what branch of the subject do the people of this country need light? Must I undertake to prove that the slave is a man? That point is conceded already. Nobody doubts it. The slaveholders themselves acknowledge it in the enactment of laws for their government. They acknowledge it when they punish disobedience on the part of the slave. There are seventy-two crimes in the State of Virginia which, if committed by a black man (no matter how ignorant he be), subject him to the punishment of death; while only two of the same crimes will subject a white man to the like punishment. What is this but the acknowledgment that the slave is a moral, intellectual and responsible being? The manhood of the slave is conceded. It is admitted in the fact that Southern statute books are covered with enactments forbidding, under severe fines and penalties, the teaching of the slave to read or to write. When you can point to any such laws in reference to the beasts of the field, then I may consent to argue the manhood of the slave. When the dogs in your streets, when the fowls of the air, when the cattle on your hills, when the fish of the sea, and the reptiles that crawl, shall be unable to distinguish the slave from a brute, then will I argue with you that the slave is a man!

For the present, it is enough to affirm the equal manhood of the Negro race. Is it not astonishing that, while we are ploughing, planting, and reaping, using all kinds of mechanical tools, erecting houses, constructing bridges, building ships, working in metals of brass, iron, copper, silver, and gold; that, while we are reading, writing, and ciphering, acting as clerks, merchants, and secretaries, having among us lawyers, doctors, ministers, poets, authors, editors, orators, and teachers; that, while we are engaged in all manner of enterprises common to other men, digging gold in California, capturing the whale in the Pacific, feeding sheep and cattle on the hillside, living, moving, acting, thinking, planning, living in families as husbands, wives, and children, and, above all, confessing and worshipping the Christian's God, and looking hopefully for life and immortality beyond the grave, we are called upon to prove that we are men!

Would you have me argue that man is entitled to liberty? That he is the rightful owner of his own body? You have already declared it. Must I argue the wrongfulness of slavery? Is that a question for Republicans? Is it to be settled by the rules of logic and argumentation, as a matter beset with great difficulty, involving a doubtful application of the principle of justice, hard to be understood? How should I look today, in the presence of Americans, dividing and subdividing a discourse, to show that men have a natural right to freedom? Speaking of it relatively and positively, negatively and affirmatively. To do so, would be to make myself ridiculous, and to offer an insult to your understanding. There is not a man beneath the canopy of heaven that does not know that slavery is wrong for him.

What, am I to argue that it is wrong to make men brutes, to rob them of their liberty, to work them without wages, to keep them ignorant of their relations to their fellow men, to beat them with sticks, to flay their flesh with the lash, to load their limbs with irons, to hunt them with dogs, to sell them at auction, to sunder their families, to knock out their teeth, to burn their flesh, to starve them into obedience and submission to their masters? Must I argue that a system thus marked with blood, and stained with pollution, is wrong? No! I will not. I have better employment for my time and strength than such arguments would imply.

What, then, remains to be argued? Is it that slavery is not divine; that God did not establish it; that our doctors of divinity are mistaken? There is blasphemy in the thought. That which is inhuman cannot be divine! Who can reason on such a proposition? They that can, may; I cannot. The time for such argument is passed.

At a time like this, scorching irony, not convincing argument, is needed. O! had I the ability, and could reach the nation's ear, I would, today, pour out a fiery stream of biting ridicule, blasting reproach, withering sarcasm, and stern rebuke. For it is not light that is needed, but fire; it is not the gentle shower, but thunder. We need the storm, the whirlwind, and the earthquake. The feeling of the nation must be quickened; the conscience of the nation must be roused; the propriety of the nation must be startled; the hypocrisy of the nation must be exposed; and its crimes against God and man must be proclaimed and denounced.

What, to the American slave, is your Fourth of July? I answer: a day that reveals to him, more than all other days in the year, the gross injustice and cruelty to which he is the constant victim. To him, your celebration is a sham; your boasted liberty, an unholy license; your national greatness, swelling vanity; your sounds of rejoicing are empty and heartless; your denunciation of tyrants, brass-fronted impudence; your shouts of liberty and equality, hollow mockery; your prayers and hymns, your sermons and thanksgivings, with all your religious parade and solemnity, are, to him, mere bombast, fraud, deception, impiety and hypocrisy – a thin veil to cover up crimes which would disgrace a nation of savages. There is not a nation on the earth guilty of practices more shocking and bloody than are the people of the United States, at this very hour.

Go where you may, search where you will, roam through all the monarchies and despotisms of the Old World, travel through South America, search out every abuse, and when you have found the last, lay your facts by the side of the everyday practices of this nation, and you will say with me, that, for revolting barbarity and shameless hypocrisy, America reigns without a rival.

Take the American slave-trade, which we are told by the papers is especially prosperous just now. Ex-Senator Benton tells us that the price of men was never higher than now. He mentions the fact to show that slavery is in no danger. This trade is one of the peculiarities of American institutions. It is carried on in all the large towns and cities in one-half of this confederacy; and millions are pocketed every year by dealers in this horrid traffic. In several states this trade is a chief source of wealth. It is called (in contradistinction to the foreign slave-trade) "the internal slave-trade." It is, probably, called so, too, in order to divert from it the horror with which the foreign slave-trade is contemplated. That trade has long since been denounced by this government as piracy. It has been denounced with burning words from the high places of the nation as an execrable traffic. To arrest it, to put an end to it, this nation keeps a squadron, at immense cost, on the coast of Africa. Everywhere, in this country, it is safe to speak of this foreign slave-trade as a most inhuman traffic, opposed alike to the laws of God and of man. The duty to extirpate and destroy it is admitted even by our doctors of divinity. In order to put an end to it, some of these last have consented that their colored brethren (nominally free) should leave this country, and establish themselves on the western coast of Africa! It is, however, a notable fact that, while so much execration is poured out by Americans upon all those engaged in the foreign slave-trade, the men engaged in the slave-trade between the states pass without condemnation, and their business is deemed honorable.

Behold the practical operation of this internal slave-trade, the American slave-trade, sustained by American politics and American religion. Here you will see men and women reared like swine for the market. You know what is a swine-drover? I will show you a man-drover. They inhabit all our Southern States. They perambulate the country, and crowd the highways of the nation, with droves of human stock. You will see one of these human flesh jobbers, armed with pistol, whip, and bowie-knife, driving a company of a hundred men, women, and children, from the Potomac to the slave market at New Orleans. These wretched people are to be sold singly, or in lots, to suit purchasers. They are food for the cotton-field and the deadly sugar-mill. Mark the sad procession, as it moves wearily along, and the inhuman wretch who drives them. Hear his savage yells and his blood-curdling oaths, as he hurries on his affrighted captives! There, see the old man with locks thinned and gray. Cast one glance, if you please, upon that young mother, whose shoulders are bare to the scorching sun, her briny tears falling on the brow of the babe in her arms. See, too, that girl of thirteen, weeping, yes! weeping, as she thinks of the mother from whom she has been torn! The drove moves tardily. Heat and sorrow have nearly consumed their strength; suddenly you hear a quick snap, like the discharge of a rifle; the fetters clank, and the chain rattles simultaneously; your ears are saluted with a scream that seems to have torn its way to the center of your soul. The crack you heard was the sound of the slave-whip; the scream you heard was from the woman you saw with the babe. Her speed had faltered under the weight of her child and her chains! That gash on her shoulder tells her to move on. Follow this drove to New Orleans. Attend the auction; see men examined like horses; see the forms of women rudely and brutally exposed to the shocking gaze of American slave-buyers. See this drove sold and separated forever; and never forget the deep, sad sobs that arose from that scattered multitude. Tell me, citizens, where, under the sun, you can witness a spectacle more fiendish and shocking. Yet this is but a glance at the American slave-trade, as it exists, at this moment, in the ruling part of the United States.

I was born amid such sights and scenes. To me the American slave-trade is a terrible reality. When a child, my soul was often pierced with a sense of its horrors. I lived on Philpot Street, Fell's Point, Baltimore, and have watched from the wharves the slave ships in the Basin, anchored from the shore, with their cargoes of human flesh, waiting for favorable winds to waft them down the Chesapeake. There was, at that time, a grand slave mart kept at the head of Pratt Street, by Austin Woldfolk. His agents were sent into every town and county in Maryland, announcing their arrival, through the papers, and on flaming "hand-bills," headed "cash for Negroes." These men were generally well-dressed men, and very captivating in their manners; ever ready to drink, to treat, and to gamble. The fate of many a slave has depended upon the turn of a single card; and many a child has been snatched from the arms of its mother by bargains arranged in a state of brutal drunkenness.

The flesh-mongers gather up their victims by dozens, and drive them, chained, to the general depot at Baltimore. When a sufficient number has been collected here, a ship is chartered for the purpose of conveying the forlorn crew to Mobile, or to New Orleans. From the slave prison to the ship, they are usually driven in the darkness of night; for since the anti-slavery agitation, a certain caution is observed.

In the deep, still darkness of midnight, I have been often aroused by the dead, heavy footsteps, and the piteous cries of the chained gangs that passed our door. The anguish of my boyish heart was intense; and I was often consoled, when speaking to my mistress in the morning, to hear her say that the custom was very wicked; that she hated to hear the rattle of the chains and the heart-rending cries. I was glad to find one who sympathized with me in my horror.

Fellow citizens, this murderous traffic is, today, in active operation in this boasted republic. In the solitude of my spirit I see clouds of dust raised on the highways of the South; I see the bleeding footsteps; I hear the doleful wail of fettered humanity on the way to the slave-markets, where the victims are to be sold like horses, sheep, and swine, knocked off to the highest bidder. There I see the tenderest ties ruthlessly broken, to gratify the lust, caprice, and rapacity of the buyers and sellers of men. My soul sickens at the sight.

Is this the land your Fathers loved,
The freedom which they toiled to win?
Is this the earth whereon they moved?
Are these the graves they slumber in?

But a still more inhuman, disgraceful, and scandalous state of things remains to be presented. By an act of the American Congress, not yet two years old, slavery has been nationalized in its most horrible and revolting form. By that act, Mason and Dixon's line has been obliterated; New York has become as Virginia; and the power to hold, hunt and sell men, women and children, as slaves, remains no longer a mere state institution, but is now an institution of the whole United States. The power is coextensive with the star-spangled banner, and American Christianity. Where these go, may also go the merciless slave-hunter. Where these are, man is not sacred. He is a bird for the sportsman's gun. By that most foul and fiendish of all human decrees, the liberty and person of every man are put in peril. Your broad republican domain is hunting ground for men. Not for thieves and robbers, enemies of society, merely, but for men guilty of no crime. Your lawmakers have commanded all good citizens to engage in this hellish sport. Your President, your Secretary of State, your lords, nobles, and ecclesiastics enforce, as a duty you owe to your free and glorious country, and to your God, that you do this accursed thing. Not fewer than forty Americans have, within the past two years, been hunted down and, without a moment's warning, hurried away in chains, and consigned to slavery and excruciating torture. Some of these have had wives and children, dependent on them for bread; but of this, no account was made. The right of the hunter to his prey stands superior to the right of marriage, and to all rights in this republic, the rights of God included! For black men there is neither law nor justice, humanity nor religion. The Fugitive Slave Law* makes mercy to them a crime; and bribes the judge who tries them. An American judge gets ten dollars for every victim he consigns to slavery, and five, when he fails to do so. The oath of any two villains is sufficient, under this hell-black enactment, to send the most pious and exemplary black man into the remorseless jaws of slavery! His own testimony is nothing. He can bring no witnesses for himself. The minister of American justice is bound by the law to hear but one side; and that side is the side of the oppressor. Let this damning fact be perpetually told. Let it be thundered around the world that in tyrant-killing, king-hating, people-loving, democratic, Christian America the seats of justice are filled with judges who hold their offices under an open and palpable bribe, and are bound, in deciding the case of a man's liberty, to hear only his accusers!

In glaring violation of justice, in shameless disregard of the forms of administering law, in cunning arrangement to entrap the defenseless, and in diabolical intent, this Fugitive Slave Law stands alone in the annals of tyrannical

* The Fugitive Slave Law of 1850 was a notorious act that required all fugitive slaves to be returned to their masters on capture, even if they had escaped to the free states of the north. It denied the fugitive's right to a jury trial and required citizens to assist in the recovery of runaways, leading to its nickname of the "Bloodhound Law," after the dogs that were used to hunt down the slaves.

legislation. I doubt if there be another nation on the globe having the brass and the baseness to put such a law on the statute-book. If any man in this assembly thinks differently from me in this matter, and feels able to disprove my statements, I will gladly confront him at any suitable time and place he may select.

I take this law to be one of the grossest infringements of Christian liberty, and, if the churches and ministers of our country were not stupidly blind, or most wickedly indifferent, they, too, would so regard it.

At the very moment that they are thanking God for the enjoyment of civil and religious liberty, and for the right to worship God according to the dictates of their own consciences, they are utterly silent in respect to a law which robs religion of its chief significance and makes it utterly worthless to a world lying in wickedness. Did this law concern the "mint, anise and cummin"* – abridge the right to sing psalms, to partake of the sacrament, or to engage in any of the ceremonies of religion, it would be smitten by the thunder of a thousand pulpits. A general shout would go up from the church demanding repeal, repeal, instant repeal! And it would go hard with that politician who presumed to solicit the votes of the people without inscribing this motto on his banner. Further, if this demand were not complied with, another Scotland would be added to the history of religious liberty, and the stern old covenanters would be thrown into the shade. A John Knox would be seen at every church door and heard from every pulpit, and Fillmore would have no more quarter than was shown by Knox to the beautiful, but treacherous, Queen Mary of Scotland. The fact that the church of our country (with fractional exceptions) does not esteem "the Fugitive Slave Law" as a declaration of war against religious liberty implies that that church regards religion simply as a form of worship, an empty ceremony, and not a vital principle, requiring active benevolence, justice, love and good will towards man. It esteems sacrifice above mercy; psalm-singing above right doing; solemn meetings above practical righteousness. A worship that can be conducted by persons who refuse to give shelter to the houseless, to give bread to the hungry, clothing to the naked, and who enjoin obedience to a law forbidding these acts of mercy, is a curse, not a blessing to mankind. The Bible addresses all such persons as "scribes, pharisees, hypocrites, who pay tithe of mint, anise and cummin, and have omitted the weightier matters of the law, judgment, mercy and faith."

But the church of this country is not only indifferent to the wrongs of the slave, it actually takes sides with the oppressors. It has made itself the bulwark of American slavery, and the shield of American slave-hunters. Many of its most eloquent Divines, who stand as the very lights of the church, have shamelessly given the sanction of religion and the Bible to the whole slave system. They have taught that man may, properly, be a slave; that the relation of master and slave is ordained of God; that to send back an escaped bondman to his master is clearly

* A Biblical reference to tithes, from Matthew 23:23.

the duty of all the followers of the Lord Jesus Christ; and this horrible blasphemy is palmed off upon the world for Christianity.

For my part, I would say, welcome infidelity! welcome atheism! welcome anything! in preference to the gospel, as preached by those Divines! They convert the very name of religion into an engine of tyranny and barbarous cruelty, and serve to confirm more infidels, in this age, than all the infidel writings of Thomas Paine, Voltaire and Bolingbroke put together have done! These ministers make religion a cold and flinty-hearted thing, having neither principles of right action nor bowels of compassion. They strip the love of God of its beauty and leave the throne of religion a huge, horrible, repulsive form. It is a religion for oppressors, tyrants, man-stealers and thugs. It is not that "pure and undefiled religion" which is from above, and which is "first pure, then peaceable, easy to be entreated, full of mercy and good fruits, without partiality, and without hypocrisy." But a religion which favors the rich against the poor; which exalts the proud above the humble; which divides mankind into two classes, tyrants and slaves; which says to the man in chains, stay there; and to the oppressor, oppress on; it is a religion which may be professed and enjoyed by all the robbers and enslavers of mankind; it makes God a respecter of persons, denies his fatherhood of the race, and tramples in the dust the great truth of the brotherhood of man. All this we affirm to be true of the popular church, and the popular worship of our land and nation – a religion, a church, and a worship which, on the authority of inspired wisdom, we pronounce to be an abomination in the sight of God. In the language of Isaiah, the American church might be well addressed, "Bring no more vain oblations; incense is an abomination unto me: the new moons and Sabbaths, the calling of assemblies, I cannot away with; it is iniquity, even the solemn meeting. Your new moons and your appointed feasts my soul hateth. They are a trouble to me; I am weary to bear them; and when ye spread forth your hands I will hide mine eyes from you. Yea' when ye make many prayers, I will not hear. Your hands are full of blood; cease to do evil, learn to do well; seek judgment; relieve the oppressed; judge for the fatherless; plead for the widow."

The American church is guilty, when viewed in connection with what it is doing to uphold slavery; but it is superlatively guilty when viewed in its connection with its ability to abolish slavery.

The sin of which it is guilty is one of omission as well as of commission. Albert Barnes [the prominent American theologian and abolitionist] but uttered what the common sense of every man at all observant of the actual state of the case will receive as truth, when he declared that: "There is no power out of the church that could sustain slavery an hour, if it were not sustained in it."

Let the religious press, the pulpit, the Sunday School, the conference meeting, the great ecclesiastical, missionary, Bible and tract associations of the land array their immense powers against slavery, and slaveholding; and the whole system of crime and blood would be scattered to the winds, and that they do not do this involves them in the most awful responsibility of which the mind can conceive.

In prosecuting the anti-slavery enterprise, we have been asked to spare the church, to spare the ministry; but how, we ask, could such a thing be done? We are met on the threshold of our efforts for the redemption of the slave, by the church and ministry of the country, in battle arrayed against us; and we are compelled to fight or flee. From what quarter, I beg to know, has proceeded a fire so deadly upon our ranks, during the last two years, as from the Northern pulpit? As the champions of oppressors, the chosen men of American theology have appeared – men honored for their so-called piety, and their real learning. The Lords of Buffalo, the Springs of New York, the Lathrops of Auburn, the Coxes and Spencers of Brooklyn, the Gannets and Sharps of Boston, the Deweys of Washington, and other great religious lights of the land have, in utter denial of the authority of Him by whom they professed to be called to the ministry, deliberately taught us, against the example of the Hebrews, and against the remonstrance of the Apostles, that we ought to obey man's law before the law of God.

My spirit wearies of such blasphemy; and how such men can be supported, as the "standing types and representatives of Jesus Christ," is a mystery which I leave others to penetrate. In speaking of the American church, however, let it be distinctly understood that I mean the great mass of the religious organizations of our land. There are exceptions, and I thank God that there are. Noble men may be found, scattered all over these Northern States, of whom Henry Ward Beecher, of Brooklyn; Samuel J. May, of Syracuse; and my esteemed friend (Rev. R. R. Raymond) on the platform, are shining examples; and let me say further, that, upon these men lies the duty to inspire our ranks with high religious faith and zeal, and to cheer us on in the great mission of the slave's redemption from his chains.

One is struck with the difference between the attitude of the American church towards the anti-slavery movement, and that occupied by the churches in England towards a similar movement in that country. There, the church, true to its mission of ameliorating, elevating and improving the condition of mankind, came forward promptly, bound up the wounds of the West Indian slave, and restored him to his liberty. There, the question of emancipation was a high religious question. It was demanded in the name of humanity, and according to the law of the living God. The Sharps, the Clarksons, the Wilberforces, the Buxtons, the Burchells, and the Knibbs were alike famous for their piety and for their philanthropy. The anti-slavery movement there was not an anti-church movement, for the reason that the church took its full share in prosecuting that movement: and the anti-slavery movement in this country will cease to be an anti-church movement, when the church of this country shall assume a favorable instead of a hostile position towards that movement.

Americans! Your republican politics, not less than your republican religion, are flagrantly inconsistent. You boast of your love of liberty, your superior civilization, and your pure Christianity, while the whole political power of the nation (as embodied in the two great political parties) is solemnly pledged to support and perpetuate the enslavement of three millions of your countrymen. You hurl your anathemas at the crowned headed tyrants of Russia and Austria and pride yourselves on your Democratic institutions, while you yourselves consent to be the mere tools and bodyguards of the tyrants of Virginia and Carolina. You invite to your shores fugitives of oppression from abroad, honor them with banquets, greet them with ovations, cheer them, toast them, salute them, protect them and pour out your money to them like water; but the fugitives from oppression in your own land you advertise, hunt, arrest, shoot and kill. You glory in your refinement and your universal education; yet you maintain a system as barbarous and dreadful as ever stained the character of a nation – a system begun in avarice, supported in pride and perpetuated in cruelty. You shed tears over fallen Hungary, and make the sad story of her wrongs the theme of your poets, statesmen and orators, till your gallant sons are ready to fly to arms to vindicate her cause against the oppressor; but, in regard to the ten thousand wrongs of the American slave, you would enforce the strictest silence, and would hail him as an enemy of the nation who dares to make those wrongs the subject of public discourse! You are all on fire at the mention of liberty for France or for Ireland; but are as cold as an iceberg at the thought of liberty for the enslaved of America. You discourse eloquently on the dignity of labor; yet you sustain a system which, in its very essence, casts a stigma upon labor. You can bare your bosom to the storm of British artillery to throw off a three-penny tax on tea; and yet wring the last hard-earned farthing from the grasp of the black laborers of your country. You profess to believe "that, of one blood, God made all nations of men to dwell on the face of all the earth," and hath commanded all men, everywhere, to love one another; yet you notoriously hate (and glory in your hatred) all men whose skins are not colored like your own. You declare before the world, and are understood by the world to declare that you "hold these truths to be self-evident, that all men are created equal; and are endowed by their Creator with certain inalienable rights; and that among these are life, liberty, and the pursuit of happiness"; and yet you hold securely, in a bondage which, according to your own Thomas Jefferson, "is worse than ages of that which your fathers rose in rebellion to oppose," a seventh part of the inhabitants of your country.

Fellow citizens, I will not enlarge further on your national inconsistencies. The existence of slavery in this country brands your republicanism as a sham, your humanity as a base pretense, and your Christianity as a lie. It destroys your moral power abroad: it corrupts your politicians at home. It saps the foundation of religion; it makes your name a hissing and a bye-word to a mocking earth.

It is the antagonistic force in your government, the only thing that seriously disturbs and endangers your Union. It fetters your progress; it is the enemy of improvement; the deadly foe of education; it fosters pride; it breeds insolence; it promotes vice; it shelters crime; it is a curse to the earth that supports it; and yet you cling to it as if it were the sheet anchor of all your hopes. Oh! Be warned! Be warned! A horrible reptile is coiled up in your nation's bosom; the venomous creature is nursing at the tender breast of your youthful republic; for the love of God, tear away, and fling from you the hideous monster, and let the weight of twenty millions crush and destroy it forever!

But it is answered in reply to all this, that precisely what I have now denounced is, in fact, guaranteed and sanctioned by the Constitution of the United States; that the right to hold and to hunt slaves is a part of that Constitution framed by the illustrious fathers of this republic.

Then, I dare to affirm, notwithstanding all I have said before, your fathers stooped, basely stooped

> To palter with us in a double sense:
> And keep the word of promise to the ear,
> But break it to the heart.

And instead of being the honest men I have before declared them to be, they were the veriest impostors that ever practiced on mankind. This is the inevitable conclusion, and from it there is no escape; but I differ from those who charge this baseness on the framers of the Constitution of the United States. It is a slander upon their memory, at least, so I believe. There is not time now to argue the constitutional question at length; nor have I the ability to discuss it as it ought to be discussed. The subject has been handled with masterly power by Lysander Spooner, Esq., by William Goodell, by Samuel E. Sewall, Esq., and last, though not least, by Gerrit Smith, Esq. These gentlemen have, as I think, fully and clearly vindicated the Constitution from any design to support slavery for an hour.

Fellow citizens! There is no matter in respect to which the people of the North have allowed themselves to be so ruinously imposed upon as that of the pro-slavery character of the Constitution. In that instrument I hold there is neither warrant, license, nor sanction of the hateful thing; but interpreted, as it ought to be interpreted, the Constitution is a glorious liberty document. Read its preamble, consider its purposes. Is slavery among them? Is it at the gateway? Or is it in the temple? It is neither. While I do not intend to argue this question on the present occasion, let me ask, if it be not somewhat singular that, if the Constitution were intended to be, by its framers and adopters, a slaveholding instrument, why neither *slavery*, *slaveholding*, nor *slave* can anywhere be found in it. What would be thought of an instrument, drawn up, legally drawn up, for the purpose of entitling the city of Rochester to a tract of land, in which no mention of land was made? Now, there are certain rules of interpretation for the proper understanding of all legal instruments. These rules are well established. They are plain, common-sense rules, such as you and I, and all of us, can understand and apply, without having passed years in the study of law. I scout the idea that the question of the constitutionality or unconstitutionality of slavery is not a question for the people. I hold that every American citizen has a right to form an opinion of the Constitution, and to propagate that opinion, and to use all honorable means to make his opinion the prevailing one. Without this right, the liberty of an American citizen would be as insecure as that of a Frenchman. Ex-Vice-President Dallas tells us that the Constitution is an object to which no American mind can be too attentive, and no American heart too devoted. He further says, the Constitution, in its words, is plain and intelligible, and is meant for the home-bred, unsophisticated understandings of our fellow citizens. Senator Berrien tells us that the Constitution is the fundamental law, that which controls all others. The charter of our liberties, which every citizen has a personal interest in understanding thoroughly. The testimony of Senator Breese, Lewis Cass, and many others that might be named, who are everywhere esteemed as sound lawyers, so regard the Constitution. I take it, therefore, that it is not presumption in a private citizen to form an opinion of that instrument.

Now, take the Constitution according to its plain reading, and I defy the presentation of a single pro-slavery clause in it. On the other hand, it will be found to contain principles and purposes entirely hostile to the existence of slavery.

I have detained my audience entirely too long already. At some future period I will gladly avail myself of an opportunity to give this subject a full and fair discussion.

Allow me to say, in conclusion, notwithstanding the dark picture I have this day presented of the state of the nation, I do not despair of this country. There are forces in operation which must inevitably work the downfall of slavery.

"The arm of the Lord is not shortened," and the doom of slavery is certain. I, therefore, leave off where I began, with hope. While drawing encouragement from "the Declaration of Independence," the great principles it contains, and the genius of American Institutions, my spirit is also cheered by the obvious tendencies of the age. Nations do not now stand in the same relation to each other that they did ages ago. No nation can now shut itself up from the surrounding world and trot round in the same old path of its fathers without interference. The time was when such could be done. Long established customs of hurtful character could formerly fence themselves in, and do their evil work with social impunity. Knowledge was then confined and enjoyed by the privileged few, and the multitude walked on in mental darkness. But a change has now come over the affairs of mankind. Walled cities and empires have become unfashionable. The arm of commerce has borne away the gates of the strong city. Intelligence is penetrating the darkest corners of the globe. It makes its pathway over and under the sea, as well as on the earth. Wind, steam, and lightning are its chartered agents. Oceans no longer divide, but link nations together. From Boston to London is now a holiday excursion. Space is comparatively annihilated. Thoughts expressed on one side of the Atlantic are distinctly heard on the other.

The far off and almost fabulous Pacific rolls in grandeur at our feet. The Celestial Empire, the mystery of ages, is being solved. The fiat of the Almighty, "Let there be Light," has not yet spent its force. No abuse, no outrage, whether in taste, sport, or avarice, can now hide itself from the all-pervading light. The iron shoe and crippled foot of China must be seen in contrast with nature. Africa must rise and put on her yet unwoven garment. "Ethiopia shall stretch out her hand unto God." In the fervent aspirations of [reformer and abolitionist] William Lloyd Garrison, I say, and let every heart join in saying it:

> God speed the year of jubilee
> The wide world o'er!
> When from their galling chains set free,
> Th' oppress'd shall vilely bend the knee,
> And wear the yoke of tyranny
> Like brutes no more.
> That year will come, and freedom's reign.
> To man his plundered rights again
> Restore.
>
> God speed the day when human blood
> Shall cease to flow!
> In every clime be understood,
> The claims of human brotherhood,
> And each return for evil, good,
> Not blow for blow;
> That day will come all feuds to end,
> And change into a faithful friend
> Each foe.

# THIS AWFUL SLAUGHTER

Born in Mississippi in 1862, Ida B. Wells was a journalist and activist who spent much of her life tirelessly investigating and documenting the thousands of lynchings taking place at that time in the United States. In 1909, Wells co-founded what would become the National Association for the Advancement of Colored People, and in June of that year, at the association's first conference, she gave a speech about "this awful slaughter."

The lynching record for a quarter of a century merits the thoughtful study of the American people. It presents three salient facts: first, lynching is color-line murder. Second, crimes against women is the excuse, not the cause. Third, it is a national crime and requires a national remedy. Proof that lynching follows the color line is to be found in the statistics which have been kept for the past twenty-five years. During the few years preceding this period and while frontier law existed, the executions showed a majority of white victims. Later, however, as law courts and authorized judiciary extended into the far West, lynch law rapidly abated, and its white victims became few and far between. Just as the lynch-law regime came to a close in the West, a new mob movement started in the South.

This was wholly political, its purpose being to suppress the colored vote by intimidation and murder. Thousands of assassins banded together under the name of Ku Klux Klans, "Midnight Raiders," "Knights of the Golden Circle," et cetera, et cetera, spread a reign of terror, and by beating, shooting and killing colored people in a few years, the purpose was accomplished, and the black vote was suppressed. But mob murder continued. From 1882, in which year fifty-two were lynched, down to the present, lynching has been along the color line. Mob murder increased yearly until in 1892 more than 200 victims were lynched and statistics show that 3,284 men, women and children have been put to death in this quarter of a century. During the last ten years from 1899 to 1908 inclusive, the number lynched was 959. Of this number 102 were white, while the colored victims numbered 857. No other nation, civilized or savage, burns its criminals; only under that Stars and Stripes is the human holocaust possible. Twenty-eight human beings burned at the stake, one of them a woman and two of them children, is the awful indictment against American civilization – the gruesome tribute which the nation pays to the color line.

Why is mob murder permitted by a Christian nation? What is the cause of this awful slaughter? This question is answered almost daily – always the same shameless falsehood that "Negroes are lynched to protect womanhood." Standing before a Chautauqua assemblage, John Temple Graves, at once champion of lynching and apologist for lynchers, said: "The mob stands today

→ Ida B. Wells c.1893–4,
photographed by
Cihak and Zima

as the most potential bulwark between the women of the South and such a carnival of crime as would infuriate the world and precipitate the annihilation of the Negro race." This is the never-varying answer of lynchers and their apologists. All know that it is untrue. The cowardly lyncher revels in murder, then seeks to shield himself from public execration by claiming devotion to woman. But truth is mighty and the lynching record discloses the hypocrisy of the lyncher as well as his crime.

The Springfield, Illinois, mob rioted for two days, the militia of the entire state was called out, two men were lynched, hundreds of people driven from their homes, all because a white woman said a Negro assaulted her. A mad mob went to the jail, tried to lynch the victim of her charge and, not being able to find him, proceeded to pillage and burn the town and to lynch two innocent men. Later, after the police had found that the woman's charge was false, she published a retraction, the indictment was dismissed and the intended victim discharged. But the lynched victims were dead. Hundreds were homeless and Illinois was disgraced.

As a final and complete refutation of the charge that lynching is occasioned by crimes against women, a partial record of lynchings is cited. Two hundred and eighty-five persons were lynched for causes as follows: unknown cause, 92; no cause, 10; race prejudice, 49; miscegenation, 7; informing, 12; making threats, 11; keeping saloon, 3; practicing fraud, 5; practicing voodooism, 1; refusing evidence, 2; political causes, 5; disputing, 1; disobeying quarantine regulations, 2; slapping a child, 1; turning state's evidence, 3; protecting a Negro, 1; to prevent giving evidence, 1; knowledge of larceny, 1; writing letter to white woman, 1; asking white woman to marry; 1; jilting girl, 1; having smallpox, 1; concealing criminal, 2; threatening political exposure, 1; self-defense, 6; cruelty, 1; insulting language to woman, 5; quarreling with white man, 2; colonizing Negroes, 1; throwing stones, 1; quarreling, 1; gambling, 1.

Is there a remedy, or will the nation confess that it cannot protect its protectors at home as well as abroad? Various remedies have been suggested to abolish the lynching infamy, but year after year, the butchery of men, women and children continues in spite of plea and protest. Education is suggested as a preventive, but it is as grave a crime to murder an ignorant man as it is a scholar. True, few educated men have been lynched, but the hue and cry once started stops at no bounds, as was clearly shown by the lynchings in Atlanta, and in Springfield, Illinois.

Agitation, though helpful, will not alone stop the crime. Year after year statistics are published, meetings are held, resolutions are adopted and yet lynchings go on. Public sentiment does measurably decrease the sway of mob law, but the irresponsible bloodthirsty criminals who swept through the streets of Springfield, beating an inoffensive law-abiding citizen to death in one part of the town, and in another torturing and shooting to death a man who for threescore years had made a reputation for honesty, integrity and sobriety; had raised a family and had accumulated property; were not deterred from their heinous crimes by either education or agitation.

The only certain remedy is an appeal to law. Lawbreakers must be made to know that human life is sacred and that every citizen of this country is first a citizen of the United States and secondly a citizen of the state in which he belongs. This nation must assert itself and protect its federal citizenship at home as well as abroad. The strong arm of the government must reach across state lines whenever unbridled lawlessness defies state laws and must give to the individual under the Stars and Stripes the same measure of protection it gives to him when he travels in foreign lands.

Federal protection of American citizenship is the remedy for lynching. Foreigners are rarely lynched in America. If, by mistake, one is lynched, the national government quickly pays the damages. The recent agitation in California against the Japanese* compelled this nation to recognize that federal power must yet assert itself to protect the nation from the treason of sovereign

* In the early twentieth century, a rapid rise in Japanese immigration led to strong anti-Asian feelings in California, culminating in the city of San Francisco passing a law to segregate Japanese children within schools. President Roosevelt negotiated a "Gentlemen's Agreement" with Japan in 1907 to try to calm the situation.

states. Thousands of American citizens have been put to death and no President has yet raised his hand in effective protest, but a simple insult to a native of Japan was quite sufficient to stir the government at Washington to prevent the threatened wrong. If the government has power to protect a foreigner from insult, certainly it has power to save a citizen's life.

The practical remedy has been more than once suggested in Congress. Senator Gallinger, of New Hampshire, in a resolution introduced in Congress called for an investigation "with the view of ascertaining whether there is a remedy for lynching which Congress may apply." The Senate Committee has under consideration a bill drawn by A. E. Pillsbury, formerly Attorney General of Massachusetts, providing for federal prosecution of lynchers in cases where the state fails to protect citizens or foreigners. Both of these resolutions indicate that the attention of the nation has been called to this phase of the lynching question.

As a final word, it would be a beginning in the right direction if this conference can see its way clear to establish a bureau for the investigation and publication of the details of every lynching, so that the public could know that an influential body of citizens has made it a duty to give the widest publicity to the facts in each case; that it will make an effort to secure expressions of opinion all over the country against lynching for the sake of the country's fair name; and lastly, but by no means least, to try to influence the daily papers of the country to refuse to become accessory to mobs either before or after the fact.

Several of the greatest riots and most brutal burnt offerings of the mobs have been suggested and incited by the daily papers of the offending community. If the newspaper which suggests lynching in its accounts of an alleged crime could be held legally as well as morally responsible for reporting that "threats of lynching were heard"; or, "it is feared that if the guilty one is caught, he will be lynched"; or, "there were cries of 'lynch him,' and the only reason the threat was not carried out was because no leader appeared," a long step toward a remedy will have been taken.

In a multitude of counsel there is wisdom. Upon the grave question presented by the slaughter of innocent men, women and children there should be an honest, courageous conference of patriotic, law-abiding citizens anxious to punish crime promptly, impartially and by due process of law, also to make life, liberty and property secure against mob rule.

Time was when lynching appeared to be sectional, but now it is national – a blight upon our nation, mocking our laws and disgracing our Christianity. "With malice toward none but with charity for all" let us undertake the work of making the "law of the land" effective and supreme upon every foot of American soil – a shield to the innocent; and to the guilty, punishment swift and sure.

STATEMENT BY SENATOR ROBERT F. KENNEDY ON THE

DEATH OF THE REVEREND MARTIN LUTHER KING

RALLY IN INDIANAPOLIS, INDIANA - April 4, 1968


I have bad news for you, for all of our fellow citizens, and people who love peace all over the world, and that is that Martin Luther King was shot and killed tonight.

Martin Luther King dedicated his life to love and to justice for his fellow human beings, and he died because of that effort.

In this difficult day, in this difficult time for the United States, it is perhaps well to ask what kind of a nation we are and what direction we want to move in. For those of you who are black -- considering the evidence there evidently is that there were white people who were responsible -- you can be filled with bitterness, with hatred, and a desire for revenge. We can move in that direction as a country, in great polarization -- black people amongst black, white people amongst white, filled with hatred toward one another.

Or we can make an effort, as Martin Luther King did, to understand and to comprehend, and to replace that violence, that stain of bloodshed that has spread across our land, with an effort to understand with compassion and love.

For those of you who are black and are tempted to be filled with hatred and distrust at the injustice of such an act, against all white people, I can only say that I feel in my own heart the same kind of feeling. I had a member of my family killed, but he was killed by a white man. But we have to make an effort in the United States, we have to make an effort to understand, to go beyond these rather difficult times.

My favorite poet was Aeschylus. He wrote: "In our sleep, pain which cannot forget falls drop by drop upon the heart until, in our own despair, against our will, comes wisdom through the awful grace of God."

What we need in the United States is not division; what we need in the United States is not hatred; what we need in the United States is not violence or lawlessness, but love and wisdom, and compassion toward one another, and a feeling of justice towards those who still suffer within our country, whether they be white or they be black.

So I shall ask you tonight to return home, to say a prayer for the family of Martin Luther King, that's true, but more importantly to say a prayer for our own country, which all of us love -- a prayer for understanding and that compassion of which I spoke.

We can do well in this country. We will have difficult times. We've had difficult times in the past. We will have difficult times in the future. It is not the end of violence; it is not the end of lawlessness; it is not the end of disorder.

But the vast majority of white people and the vast majority of black people in this country want to live together, want to improve the quality of our life, and want justice for all human beings who abide in our land.

Let us dedicate ourselves to what the Greeks wrote so many years ago: to tame the savageness of man and to make gentle the life of this world.

Let us dedicate ourselves to that, and say a prayer for our country and for our people.

# WE CAN DO WELL IN THIS COUNTRY

Much of the world began to mourn in unison on April 4, 1968, as news circulated that Nobel Peace Prize–winning civil rights leader Martin Luther King Jr. had been shot dead at a motel in Memphis. Shortly after, as Senator Robert F. Kennedy boarded a flight to Indianapolis, Indiana, to attend a campaign rally, word reached him of the shooting. Hours later, when he reached his destination, he learned of King's death. It was then that he delivered this extemporaneous speech, with great skill and compassion, to a mainly black crowd. It was also the first time he spoke of the death of his brother, John F. Kennedy, five years previously.

Tragically, two months after he gave this speech, Robert F. Kennedy was also assassinated.

Ladies and gentlemen: I'm only going to talk to you just for a minute or so this evening, because I have some very sad news for all of you – could you lower those signs, please? – I have some very sad news for all of you, and, I think, sad news for all of our fellow citizens, and people who love peace all over the world; and that is that Martin Luther King was shot and was killed tonight in Memphis, Tennessee.

Martin Luther King dedicated his life to love and to justice between fellow human beings. He died in the cause of that effort. In this difficult day, in this difficult time for the United States, it's perhaps well to ask what kind of a nation we are and what direction we want to move in. For those of you who are black – considering the evidence evidently is that there were white people who were responsible – you can be filled with bitterness, and with hatred, and a desire for revenge.

We can move in that direction as a country, in greater polarization – black people amongst blacks, and white amongst whites, filled with hatred toward one another. Or we can make an effort, as Martin Luther King did, to understand, and to comprehend, and replace that violence, that stain of bloodshed that has spread across our land, with an effort to understand, compassion and love.

For those of you who are black and are tempted to be filled with hatred and mistrust of the injustice of such an act, against all white people, I would only say that I can also feel in my own heart the same kind of feeling. I had a member of my family killed, but he was killed by a white man. But we have to make an effort in the United States, we have to make an effort to understand, to get beyond, or go beyond these rather difficult times.

My favorite poem, my favorite poet, was Aeschylus. And he once wrote:

← The edited version of Kennedy's extemporaneous speech, released on the same day as an official statement

Even in our sleep, pain which cannot forget
falls drop by drop upon the heart,
until, in our own despair,

against our will,
comes wisdom
through the awful grace of God.

What we need in the United States is not division; what we need in the United States is not hatred; what we need in the United States is not violence and lawlessness, but is love and wisdom, and compassion toward one another, and a feeling of justice toward those who still suffer within our country, whether they be white or whether they be black.

So I ask you tonight to return home, to say a prayer for the family of Martin Luther King – yeah, it's true – but more importantly to say a prayer for our own country, which all of us love – a prayer for understanding and that compassion of which I spoke.

We can do well in this country. We will have difficult times. We've had difficult times in the past. And we will have difficult times in the future. It is not the end of violence; it is not the end of lawlessness; and it's not the end of disorder.

But the vast majority of white people and the vast majority of black people in this country want to live together, want to improve the quality of our life, and want justice for all human beings that abide in our land.

→ Robert F. Kennedy announcing the death of Martin Luther King Jr. on April 4, 1968

Let us dedicate ourselves to what the Greeks wrote so many years ago: to tame the savageness of man and make gentle the life of this world. Let us dedicate ourselves to that, and say a prayer for our country and for our people.

Thank you very much.

# WE WANT PEACE AND LOVE

Born in Nebraska in 1822, Red Cloud grew up to become an important and powerful figure in the Oglala Lakota, a Sioux tribe that he led for forty-one years through sporadic periods of conflict. In 1870, with relations strained between his tribe and the American government, Red Cloud and twenty other Oglalas paid a visit to Washington to speak with President Ulysses S. Grant, on what became known as Red Cloud's Peace Crusade. Days after leaving the White House, they reached New York, and it was there that Red Cloud addressed an audience with a speech reported by the *New York Times* the next day:

"No one who listened to Red Cloud's remarkable speech yesterday can doubt that he is a man of very great talents. He has spent his life fighting the battles of his people, and one day he is transplanted to Cooper Institute, and asked to put on a clean shirt, a new waistcoat, a high crowned hat, and then make a speech. His earnest manner, his impassioned gestures, the eloquence of his hands, and the magnetism, which he evidently exercises over his audience, produced a vast effect on the dense throng which listened to him yesterday. 'You have children, and so have we. We want to rear our children well, and ask you to help us in doing so.' It seems to us that this is not an unreasonable request even though it does come from a 'savage.'"

My brothers and my friends who are before me today: God Almighty has made us all, and He is here to hear what I have to say to you today. The Great Spirit made us both. He gave us lands and He gave you lands. You came here and we received you as brothers. When the Almighty made you, He made you all white and clothed you. When He made us He made us with red skins and poor. When you first came we were very many and you were few. Now you are many and we are few.

You do not know who appears before you to speak. He is a representative of the original American race, the first people of this continent. We are good, and not bad. The reports which you get about us are all on one side. You hear of us only as murderers and thieves. We are not so. If we had more lands to give to you we would give them, but we have no more. We are driven into a very little island, and we want you, our dear friends, to help us with the government of the United States.

The Great Spirit made us poor and ignorant. He made you rich and wise and skillful in things which we knew nothing about. The good Father made you to eat tame game and us to eat wild game. Ask anyone who has gone through to California. They will tell you we have treated them well. You have children. We, too, have children, and we wish to bring them up well. We ask you to help us do it.

At the mouth of Horse Creek, in 1852, the Great Father made a treaty with us. We agreed to let him pass through our territory unharmed for fifty-five years. We kept our word. We committed no murders, no depredations, until the troops came there. When the troops were sent there trouble and disturbance arose.

← Chief Red Cloud, photographed by Joseph A. Kern

Since that time there have been various goods sent from time to time to us, but only once did they reach us, and soon the Great Father took away the only good man he had sent us, Colonel Fitzpatrick. The Great Father said we must go to farming and some of our men went to farming near Fort Laramie, and were treated very badly indeed.

We came to Washington to see our Great Father that peace might be continued. The Great Father that made us both wishes peace to be kept; we want to keep peace. Will you help us? In 1868 men came out and brought papers. We could not read them, and they did not tell us truly what was in them. We thought the treaty was to remove the forts, and that we should then cease from fighting. But they wanted to send us traders on the Missouri. We did not want to go on the Missouri, but wanted traders where we were. When I reached Washington the Great Father explained to me what the treaty was, and showed me that interpreters had deceived me.

All I want is right and justice. I have tried to get from the Great Father what is right and just. I have not altogether succeeded. I want you to help me to get what is right and just. I represent the whole Sioux nation, and they will be bound by what I say. I am no Spotted Tail, to say one thing one day and be bought for a pin the next. Look at me, I am poor and naked, but I am the Chief of the nation. We do not want riches, but we want to train our children right. Riches would do us no good. We could not take them with us to the other world. We do not want riches; we want peace and love.

The riches that we have in this world, Secretary Cox said truly, we cannot take with us to the next world. Then I wish to know why Commissioners are sent out to us who do nothing but rob us and get the riches of this world away from us! I was brought up among the traders, and those who came out there in the early times treated me well and I had a good time with them. They taught us to wear clothes and to use tobacco and ammunition. But, by and by, the Great Father sent out a different kind of men; men who cheated and drank whisky; men who were so bad that the Great Father could not keep them at home and so sent them out there.

I have sent a great many words to the Great Father but they never reached him. They were drowned on the way, and I was afraid the words I spoke lately to the Great Father would not reach you, so I came to speak to you myself; and now I am going away to my home.

I want to have men sent out to my people whom we know and can trust. I am glad I have come here. You belong in the East and I belong in the West, and I am glad I have come here and that we could understand one another. I am very much obliged to you for listening to me. I go home this afternoon. I hope you will think of what I have said to you. I bid you all an affectionate farewell.

# WE JUST DON'T KNOW

By the time of her death in 2012, Wisława Szymborska – born in the Polish town of Kórnik in 1923 – had won most of the awards available to a modern-day poet, and with good reason. Her many collections of intelligent, historical, humor-tinged poetry were acclaimed by critics and readers alike over the course of her life. In 1996, she won arguably her highest accolade, the Nobel Prize in Literature, and was invited to deliver a speech in response. The irresistible combination of Szymborska's self-effacing nature and unremitting honesty resulted in a Nobel acceptance speech like no other.

They say the first sentence in any speech is always the hardest. Well, that one's behind me, anyway. But I have a feeling that the sentences to come – the third, the sixth, the tenth, and so on, up to the final line – will be just as hard, since I'm supposed to talk about poetry. I've said very little on the subject, next to nothing, in fact. And whenever I have said anything, I've always had the sneaking suspicion that I'm not very good at it. This is why my lecture will be rather short. All imperfection is easier to tolerate if served up in small doses.

Contemporary poets are skeptical and suspicious even, or perhaps especially, about themselves. They publicly confess to being poets only reluctantly, as if they were a little ashamed of it. But in our clamorous times it's much easier to acknowledge your faults, at least if they're attractively packaged, than to recognize your own merits, since these are hidden deeper and you never quite believe in them yourself. . . . When filling in questionnaires or chatting with strangers, that is, when they can't avoid revealing their profession, poets prefer to use the general term "writer" or replace "poet" with the name of whatever job they do in addition to writing. Bureaucrats and bus passengers respond with a touch of incredulity and alarm when they find out that they're dealing with a poet. I suppose philosophers may meet with a similar reaction. Still, they're in a better position, since as often as not they can embellish their calling with some kind of scholarly title. Professor of philosophy – now that sounds much more respectable.

But there are no professors of poetry. This would mean, after all, that poetry is an occupation requiring specialized study, regular examinations, theoretical articles with bibliographies and footnotes attached, and finally, ceremoniously conferred diplomas. And this would mean, in turn, that it's not enough to cover pages with even the most exquisite poems in order to become a poet. The crucial element is some slip of paper bearing an official stamp. Let us recall that the pride of Russian poetry, the future Nobel Laureate Joseph Brodsky, was once sentenced to internal exile precisely on such grounds. They called him "a parasite," because he lacked official certification granting him the right to be a poet. . . .

Several years ago, I had the honor and pleasure of meeting Brodsky in person. And I noticed that, of all the poets I've known, he was the only one who enjoyed calling himself a poet. He pronounced the word without inhibitions.

Just the opposite – he spoke it with defiant freedom. It seems to me that this must have been because he recalled the brutal humiliations he had experienced in his youth.

In more fortunate countries, where human dignity isn't assaulted so readily, poets yearn, of course, to be published, read and understood, but they do little, if anything, to set themselves above the common herd and the daily grind. And yet it wasn't so long ago, in this century's first decades, that poets strove to shock us with their extravagant dress and eccentric behavior. But all this was merely for the sake of public display. The moment always came when poets had to close the doors behind them, strip off their mantles, fripperies and other poetic paraphernalia, and confront – silently, patiently awaiting their own selves – the still white sheet of paper. For this is finally what really counts.

It's not accidental that film biographies of great scientists and artists are produced in droves. The more ambitious directors seek to reproduce convincingly the creative process that led to important scientific discoveries or the emergence of a masterpiece. And one can depict certain kinds of scientific labor with some success. Laboratories, sundry instruments, elaborate machinery brought to life: such scenes may hold the audience's interest for a while. And those moments of uncertainty – will the experiment, conducted for the thousandth time with some tiny modification, finally yield the desired result? – can be quite dramatic. Films about painters can be spectacular, as they go about re-creating every stage of a famous painting's evolution, from the first penciled line to the final brush-stroke. Music swells in films about composers: the first bars of the melody that rings in the musician's ears finally emerge as a mature work in symphonic form. Of course this is all quite naive and doesn't explain the strange mental state popularly known as inspiration, but at least there's something to look at and listen to.

But poets are the worst. Their work is hopelessly unphotogenic. Someone sits at a table or lies on a sofa while staring motionless at a wall or ceiling. Once in a while this person writes down seven lines only to cross out one of them fifteen minutes later, and then another hour passes, during which nothing happens. . . . Who could stand to watch this kind of thing?

I've mentioned inspiration. Contemporary poets answer evasively when asked what it is, and if it actually exists. It's not that they've never known the blessing of this inner impulse. It's just not easy to explain something to someone else that you don't understand yourself.

When I'm asked about this on occasion, I hedge the question too. But my answer is this: inspiration is not the exclusive privilege of poets or artists generally. There is, has been and will always be a certain group of people whom

→ Wisława
Szymborska,
photographed by
Joanna Helander

inspiration visits. It's made up of all those who've consciously chosen their calling and do their job with love and imagination. It may include doctors, teachers, gardeners – and I could list a hundred more professions. Their work becomes one continuous adventure as long as they manage to keep discovering new challenges in it. Difficulties and setbacks never quell their curiosity. A swarm of new questions emerges from every problem they solve. Whatever inspiration is, it's born from a continuous "I don't know."

There aren't many such people. Most of the earth's inhabitants work to get by. They work because they have to. They didn't pick this or that kind of job out of passion; the circumstances of their lives did the choosing for them. Loveless work, boring work, work valued only because others haven't got even that much, however loveless and boring – this is one of the harshest human miseries. And there's no sign that coming centuries will produce any changes for the better as far as this goes.

And so, though I may deny poets their monopoly on inspiration, I still place them in a select group of Fortune's darlings.

At this point, though, certain doubts may arise in my audience. All sorts of torturers, dictators, fanatics and demagogues struggling for power by way of a few loudly shouted slogans also enjoy their jobs, and they too perform their duties with inventive fervor. Well, yes, but they "know." They know, and whatever they know is enough for them once and for all. They don't want to find out about anything else, since that might diminish their arguments' force. And any knowledge that doesn't lead to new questions quickly dies out: it fails to maintain the temperature required for sustaining life. In the most extreme cases, cases well known from ancient and modern history, it even poses a lethal threat to society.

This is why I value that little phrase "I don't know" so highly. It's small, but it flies on mighty wings. It expands our lives to include the spaces within us as well as those outer expanses in which our tiny Earth hangs suspended. If Isaac Newton had never said to himself "I don't know," the apples in his little orchard might have dropped to the ground like hailstones and at best he would have stooped to pick them up and gobble them with gusto. Had my compatriot Marie Skłodowska Curie never said to herself "I don't know," she probably would have wound up teaching chemistry at some private high school for young ladies from good families, and would have ended her days performing this otherwise perfectly respectable job. But she kept on saying "I don't know," and these words led her, not just once but twice, to Stockholm, where restless, questing spirits are occasionally rewarded with the Nobel Prize.

Poets, if they're genuine, must also keep repeating "I don't know." Each poem marks an effort to answer this statement, but as soon as the final full stop hits the page, the poet begins to hesitate, starts to realize that this particular answer was pure makeshift that's absolutely inadequate to boot. So the poets keep on trying, and sooner or later the consecutive results of their self-dissatisfaction are clipped together with a giant paperclip by literary historians and called their "oeuvre. . . ."

I sometimes dream of situations that can't possibly come true. I audaciously imagine, for example, that I get a chance to chat with Ecclesiastes, the author of that moving lament on the vanity of all human endeavors. I would bow very deeply before him, because he is, after all, one of the greatest poets, for me at least. That done, I would grab his hand. "'There's nothing new under the sun': that's what you wrote, Ecclesiastes. But you yourself were born new under the sun. And the poem you created is also new under the sun, since no one wrote it down before you. And all your readers are also new under the sun, since those who lived before you couldn't read your poem. And that cypress that you're sitting under hasn't been growing since the dawn of time. It came into being by way of another cypress similar to yours, but not exactly the same. And Ecclesiastes, I'd also like to ask you what new thing under the sun you're planning to work on now? A further supplement to the thoughts you've already expressed? Or maybe you're tempted to contradict some of them now? In your earlier work you mentioned joy – so what if it's fleeting? So maybe your new-under-the-sun poem will be about joy? Have you taken notes yet, do you have drafts? I doubt you'll say, 'I've written everything down, I've got nothing left to add.' There's no poet in the world who can say this, least of all a great poet like yourself."

The world – whatever we might think when terrified by its vastness and our own impotence, or embittered by its indifference to individual suffering, of people, animals, and perhaps even plants, for why are we so sure that plants feel no pain; whatever we might think of its expanses pierced by the rays of stars surrounded by planets we've just begun to discover, planets already dead? still dead? we just don't know; whatever we might think of this measureless theater to which we've got reserved tickets, but tickets whose lifespan is laughably short, bounded as it is by two arbitrary dates; whatever else we might think of this world – it is astonishing.

But "astonishing" is an epithet concealing a logical trap. We're astonished, after all, by things that deviate from some well-known and universally acknowledged norm, from an obviousness we've grown accustomed to. Now the point is, there is no such obvious world. Our astonishment exists per se and isn't based on comparison with something else.

Granted, in daily speech, where we don't stop to consider every word, we all use phrases like "the ordinary world," "ordinary life," "the ordinary course of events. . . . " But in the language of poetry, where every word is weighed, nothing is usual or normal. Not a single stone and not a single cloud above it. Not a single day and not a single night after it. And above all, not a single existence, not anyone's existence in this world.

It looks like poets will always have their work cut out for them.

# THESE, TOO, BELONG TO US

The New York World's Fair of 1939–40 remains one of the largest ever held, visited by a staggering 44 million people. In 1940, not long after World War II had begun, the fair's organizers attempted to pay homage to the diversity of the U.S. population by erecting a "Wall of Fame," on which was inscribed the names and professions of hundreds of the nation's most notable "immigrants, Negroes and American Indians." At the Wall of Fame's inauguration, Albert Einstein gave the following little-known speech.

It is a fine and high-minded idea, also in the best sense a proud one, to erect at the World's Fair a wall of fame to immigrants and Negroes of distinction.

The significance of the gesture is this. It says: these, too, belong to us, and we are glad and grateful to acknowledge the debt that the community owes them. And focusing on these particular contributors, Negroes and immigrants, shows that the community feels a special need to show regard and affection for those who are often regarded as step-children of the nation – for why else this combination?

If, then, I am to speak on the occasion, it can only be to say something on behalf of these step-children. As for the immigrants, they are the only ones to whom it can be accounted a merit to be Americans. For they have had to take trouble for their citizenship, whereas it has cost the majority nothing at all to be born in the land of civic freedom.

As for the Negroes, the country has still a heavy debt to discharge for all the troubles and disabilities it has laid on the Negro's shoulders, for all that his fellow-citizens have done and to some extent still are doing to him. To the Negro and his wonderful songs and choirs, we are indebted for the finest contribution in the realm of art which America has so far given to the world. And this great gift we owe, not to those whose names are engraved on this "Wall of Fame," but to the children of the people, blossoming namelessly as the lilies of the field. In a way, the same is true of the immigrants. They have contributed in their way to the flowering of the community, and their individual striving and suffering have remained unknown.

One more thing I would say with regard to immigration generally: there exists on the subject a fatal miscomprehension. Unemployment is not decreased by restricting immigration. For unemployment depends on faulty distribution of work among those capable of work. Immigration increases consumption as much as it does demand on labor. Immigration strengthens not only the internal economy of a sparsely populated country, but also its defensive power.

→ Albert Einstein delivering a speech in Washington, DC, in May 1940

The Wall of Fame arose out of a high-minded ideal; it is calculated to stimulate just and magnanimous thoughts and feelings. May it work to that effect.

Ich danke Ihnen für die freundliche Aufforderung. Leider kann ich derselben nicht persönlich Folge leisten, weil ich bis Mitte September in Saranac Lake sein werde. Für den Fall aber, dass Sie von einer message Gebrauch machen wollen, sende ich Ihnen eine solche.

– – – –

Es zeugt von einer edlen und grossherzigen, aber auch im besten Sinne selbstbewussten Auffassung, wenn auf der Worlds fair Eingewanderten und Negern von Verdienst ein besonderes Merkzeichen errichtet wird.

Dies will sagen: Auch diese gehören zu uns, und wir erkennen es gerne und dankbar an, was die Gemeinschaft ihnen verdankt. Da Zusammenstellung Eingewanderte und Neger zeigt, dass man das Bedürfnis fühlt, auch denen Liebe und Achtung zu zeigen, die gewissermassen als Stiefkinder der Nation empfunden werden. denn was sonst könnte man als das Gemeinsame dieser beiden Kategorien ansehen?

Wenn ich also nun bei dieser Gelegenheit etwas sagen soll, so kann es nur etwas zugunsten dieser Stiefkinder sein. Was zunächst die Eingewanderten anlangt, so sind sie ja die einzigen, die es sich zum Verdienst anrechnen dürfen, Amerikaner zu sein. Denn diese Menschen haben sich um ihre Bürgerschaft redlich bemühen müssen, während alle übrigen es gar keine Mühe gekostet hat, im Lande bürgerlicher Freiheit par excellence geboren zu werden. Was aber die Neger anlangt so hat ihnen das Land eine schwere Schuld abzutilgen für alle Plage und Benachteiligung, die sie von ihren Mitbürgern erlitten haben und in gewissem Ausmasse immer noch erledeln.

Den Negern verdanken wir in ihren wunderbaren Liedern und Chören den schönsten künstlerischen Beitrag, den Amerika bisher der Welt geschenkt hat. Dies wunderbare Geschenk verdanken wir aber nicht jenen, deren Namen auf dem „Wall of Fame" verzeichnet sind, sondern Kindern des Volkes, die namenlos blühten wie die Lilien des Feldes.

Bei den Eingewanderten verhält es sich in gewissem Sinne ähnlich. Sie alle haben zur Blüte der Gemeinschaft in ihrer Art beigetragen, unbewusst in ihrem individuellen Streben und Leiden.

Bei dem Gedanken an die Eingewanderten wird man an die Frage der Einwanderung überhaupt erinnert. Auf diesem Gebiete herrscht leider ein verhängnisvolles Vorurteil. Durch Beschränkung der Einwanderung vermindert man nicht die Arbeitslosigkeit. Letztere beruht ausschliesslich auf einer ungünstigen Verteilung der Arbeit unter die Arbeitsfähigen. Einwanderung vermehrt aber ebenso den Bedarf an Wirken wie das Angebot an Arbeitskraft. Einwanderung stärkt nicht nur den Wirtschafts-Körper eines schwach bevölkerten Landes sondern auch seine Verteidigungskraft nach aussen.

Der Wall of Fame ist aus grossherziger Gesinnung erwachsen und geeignet, grosszügiges und gerechtes Denken und Fühlen hervorzurufen. Möge er in diesem Sinne wirken.

# POLITICS UNSETTLES MEN

On January 28, 1914, Winnipeg's Walker Theatre became the setting for a mock parliamentary debate. It was arranged by the Political Equality League of Manitoba, a Canadian organization that regularly and with some success fought for women's suffrage. This particular event had been provoked by a recent speech from the mouth of the then-Premier of Manitoba, Sir Rodmond Roblin, that saw him question women's right to vote. It was a speech that was subsequently turned on its head that evening at the theatre by activist and writer Nellie McClung, who reframed Roblin's stance to highlight its absurdity. It was a roaring success: in fact, McClung's satirical speech went down so well that it was repeated on numerous occasions.

Gentlemen of the delegation, it gives me great pleasure to welcome you here today. We like delegations, and although this is the first time you have asked us for the vote, we hope it will not be the last. Come any time and ask for anything you like. We wish to congratulate you, too, on the quiet and ladylike way in which you have come into our presence; and we assure you that if the working men in England had fought for their franchise in such a pleasing and dignified way, the results would have been entirely different. If they had used these peaceful means and no other, they might still be enjoying the distinction and privilege of waiting on members of Parliament.

But I cannot do what you ask me to do, for the facts are all against you. Manhood suffrage has not been a success in the unhappy countries where it has been tried. They either do not vote at all, or else they vote too much, and the best men shrink away from the polls as from a pestilence.

Manhood suffrage would plunge our fair province into a perfect debauchery of extravagance, a perfect nightmare of expense. Think of the increased size of the voters list – we have trouble enough with it now. Of course, with the customary hot-headedness of reformers, you never thought of that, oh, no, just like a man, you never thought of the expense.

I tell you frankly, I won't do it, for I have always loved and reverenced men. Yet though I love them, I know their frailties. If once they are let vote, they become addicted to it, and even if the polls are only open once every four years, I tell you, I know men, they are creatures of habit, and they'll hang around the polls all the rest of the time.

Man was made for something higher and holier than voting. Men were made to support families and homes which are the bulwark of the nation. What is home without a father? What is home without a bank account? The man who pays the grocer rules the world. In this agricultural province, man's place is the farm. Shall I call men away from the useful plough and the necessary harrow to talk loud on street corners about things which do not concern them? Shall I cheat the farm by turning honest ploughmen into dishonest and scheming

→ Nellie McClung in 1914, photographed by Cyril Jessop

politicians? I tell you no, for I was born on the farm and I am not ashamed to say so – the farm, the farm, the dear, old farm – we'll never mortgage the farm.

In the United States of America, when men vote, there is one divorce for every marriage, for politics unsettle men, and that leads to unsettled bills and broken furniture, and broken vows. When you ask me for the vote, you are asking me to break up peaceful and happy homes and wreck innocent lives, and I tell you again, frankly, I will not do it. I am an old-fashioned woman; I believe in the sanctity of marriage. Politics unsettles men, and enters every department of life, with its blighting influence. It even confuses our vital statistics. They tell me that where men vote, when the election is very close, men have been known to come back and vote years after they were dead. Now, do you think I am going to let the hallowed calm of our cemeteries be invaded by the raucous voice of politics?

I know I am a factor in the affairs of this province. If it were not for this fatal modesty which on more than one occasion has almost blighted my career, I would say that I know I have written my name large across the province, so large indeed we had to move the boundaries to get it all in, and my most earnest wish for this bright land of promise is that I may long be spared to guide its destiny among the nations of the earth. I know there is no one but me who can guide the ship of state. I actually tremble when I think what might happen to these leaderless lambs. But I must not dwell on such an overwhelming calamity, but go forward in the strong hope that I may long be spared to be the proud standard-bearer of the grand old flag of this grand old party, which has gone down many times to disgrace but, thank God, never defeat.

# LET FREEDOM REIGN

Nelson Mandela spent twenty-seven years of his life imprisoned in his home country of South Africa as a result of his anti-apartheid activities and attempts to overthrow the government. Eighteen of those long years were spent on Robben Island in a cell measuring 8 feet by 7 feet. In 1994, four years after his widely celebrated release, Mandela made history by becoming South Africa's first black president. It was the country's first multiracial, democratic election, and one which heralded the fall of the apartheid he had fought for so long. On the day he was sworn in, with a billion people watching the ceremony all over the globe, Mandela gave this speech.

Your Majesties, Your Royal Highnesses, distinguished guests, comrades and friends,

Today, all us do, by our presence here, and by our celebrations in other parts of our country and the world, confer glory and hope to newborn liberty.

Out of the experience of an extraordinary human disaster that lasted too long must be born a society of which all humanity will be proud.

Our daily deeds as ordinary South Africans must produce an actual South African reality that will reinforce humanity's belief in justice, strengthen its confidence in the nobility of the human soul and sustain all our hopes for a glorious life for all.

All this we owe both to ourselves and to the peoples of the world who are so well represented here today.

To my compatriots, I have no hesitation in saying that each one of us is as intimately attached to the soil of this beautiful country as are the famous jacaranda trees of Pretoria and the mimosa trees of the bushveld.

Each time one of us touches the soil of this land, we feel a sense of personal renewal. The national mood changes as the seasons change.

We arc moved by a sense of joy and exhilaration when the grass turns green and the flowers bloom.

That spiritual and physical oneness we all share with this common homeland explains the depth of the pain we all carried in our hearts as we saw our country tear itself apart in terrible conflict, and as we saw it spurned, outlawed and isolated by the peoples of the world, precisely because it had become the universal base of the pernicious ideology and practice of racism and racial oppression.

We, the people of South Africa, feel fulfilled that humanity has taken us back into its bosom, that we, who were outlaws not so long ago, have today been given the rare privilege to be host to the nations of the world on our own soil.

We thank all our distinguished international guests for having come to take possession with the people of our country what is, after all, a common victory for justice, for peace, for human dignity.

We trust that you will continue to stand by us as we tackle the challenges of building peace, prosperity, non-sexism, non-racialism and democracy.

We deeply appreciate the role that the masses of our people and their political mass – democratic, religious, women, youth, business, traditional – and other leaders have played to bring about this conclusion. Not least amongst them is my Second Deputy President, the Honourable F. W. de Klerk.

We would also like to pay tribute to our security forces, in all their ranks, for the distinguished role they have played in securing our first democratic elections and the transition to democracy, from bloodthirsty forces which still refuse to see the light.

The time for the healing of the wounds has come.

The moment to bridge the chasms that divide us has come.

The time to build is upon us.

We have, at last, achieved our political emancipation. We pledge ourselves to liberate all our people from the continuing bondage of poverty, deprivation, suffering, gender and other discrimination.

We succeeded to take our last steps to freedom in conditions of relative peace. We commit ourselves to the construction of a complete, just and lasting peace.

We have triumphed in the effort to implant hope in the breasts of the millions of our people. We enter into a covenant that we shall build the society in which all South Africans, both black and white, will be able to walk tall, without any fear in their hearts, assured of their inalienable right to human dignity – a rainbow nation at peace with itself and the world.

As a token of its commitment to the renewal of our country, the new Interim Government of National Unity will, as a matter of urgency, address the issue of amnesty for various categories of our people who are currently serving terms of imprisonment.

We dedicate this day to all the heroes and heroines in this country and the rest of the world who sacrificed in many ways and surrendered their lives so that we could be free.

Their dreams have become reality. Freedom is their reward.

We are both humbled and elevated by the honour and privilege that you, the people of South Africa, have bestowed on us, as the first President of a united, democratic, non-racial and non-sexist South Africa, to lead our country out of the valley of darkness.

We understand it still that there is no easy road to freedom.

We know it well that none of us acting alone can achieve success.

← South African President Nelson Mandela taking the oath on May 10, 1994, photographed by Walter Dhladhla

We must therefore act together as a united people, for national reconciliation, for nation building, for the birth of a new world.

Let there be justice for all.

Let there be peace for all.

Let there be work, bread, water and salt for all.

Let each know that for each the body, the mind and the soul have been freed to fulfil themselves.

Never, never and never again shall it be that this beautiful land will again experience the oppression of one by another and suffer the indignity of being the skunk of the world.

The sun shall never set on so glorious a human achievement.

Let freedom reign. God bless Africa. I thank you.

# WIRES AND LIGHTS IN A BOX

Half a century after his death, Edward R. Murrow remains a giant in the world of broadcast journalism. During his distinguished career at television network CBS, he expertly and without condescension informed audiences throughout and beyond World War II. In 1958, at an event being held in his honor – an event attended by the executives of many networks – Murrow took the opportunity to deliver the following speech; a now-legendary, impassioned plea for those assembled to recognize and fulfill their responsibilities as educators of the masses.

This just might do nobody any good. At the end of this discourse a few people may accuse this reporter of fouling his own comfortable nest, and your organization may be accused of having given hospitality to heretical and even dangerous thoughts. But I am persuaded that the elaborate structure of networks, advertising agencies and sponsors will not be shaken or altered. It is my desire, if not my duty, to try to talk to you journeymen with some candor about what is happening to radio and television in this generous and capacious land. I have no technical advice or counsel to offer those of you who labor in this vineyard – the one that produces words and pictures. You will, I am sure, forgive me for not telling you that the instruments with which you work are miraculous, that your responsibility is unprecedented or that your aspirations are frequently frustrated. It is not necessary to remind you of the fact that your voice, amplified to the degree where it reaches from one end of the country to the other, does not confer upon you greater wisdom than when your voice reached only from one end of the bar to the other. All of these things you know.

You should also know at the outset that, in the manner of witnesses before Congressional committees, I appear here voluntarily – by invitation – that I am an employee of the Columbia Broadcasting System, that I am neither an officer nor any longer a director of that corporation and that these remarks are strictly of a "do-it-yourself" nature. If what I have to say is responsible, then I alone am responsible for the saying of it. Seeking neither approbation from my employers, nor new sponsors, nor acclaim from the critics of radio and television, I cannot very well be disappointed. Believing that potentially the commercial system of broadcasting as practiced in this country is the best and freest yet devised, I have decided to express my concern about what I believe to be happening to radio and television. These instruments have been good to me beyond my due. There exists in my mind no reasonable grounds for any kind of personal complaint. I have no feud, either with my employers, any sponsors, or with the professional critics of radio and television. But I am seized with an abiding fear regarding what these two instruments are doing to our society, our culture and our heritage.

Our history will be what we make it. And if there are any historians about fifty or a hundred years from now, and there should be preserved the kinescopes for one week of all three networks, they will there find recorded in black-and-white, or perhaps in color, evidence of decadence, escapism and insulation from the realities of the world in which we live. I invite your attention to the television schedules of all networks between the hours of 8 and 11 p.m., Eastern Time. Here you will find only fleeting and spasmodic reference to the fact that this nation is in mortal danger. There are, it is true, occasional informative programs presented in that intellectual ghetto on Sunday afternoons. But during the daily peak viewing periods, television in the main insulates us from the realities of the world in which we live. If this state of affairs continues, we may alter an advertising slogan to read: LOOK NOW, AND PAY LATER.

For surely we shall pay for using this most powerful instrument of communication to insulate the citizenry from the hard and demanding realities which must indeed be faced if we are to survive. And I mean the word "survive," quite literally. If there were to be a competition in indifference, or perhaps in insulation from reality, then Nero and his fiddle, Chamberlain and his umbrella, could not find a place on an early afternoon sustaining show. If Hollywood were to run out of Indians, the program schedules would be mangled beyond all recognition. Then perhaps, some young and courageous soul with a small budget might do a documentary telling what, in fact, we have done – and are still doing – to the Indians in this country. But that would be unpleasant. And we must at all costs shield the sensitive citizen from anything that is unpleasant.

I am entirely persuaded that the American public is more reasonable, restrained and more mature than most of our industry's program planners believe. Their fear of controversy is not warranted by the evidence. I have reason to know, as do many of you, that when the evidence on a controversial subject is fairly and calmly presented, the public recognizes it for what it is – an effort to illuminate rather than to agitate.

Several years ago, when we undertook to do a program on Egypt and Israel, well-meaning, experienced and intelligent friends in the business said, "This you cannot do. This time you will be handed your head. It is an emotion-packed controversy, and there is no room for reason in it." We did the program. Zionists, anti-Zionists, the friends of the Middle East, Egyptian and Israeli officials said, I must confess with a faint tone of surprise, "It was a fair account. The information was there. We have no complaints."

Our experience was similar with two half-hour programs dealing with cigarette smoking and lung cancer. Both the medical profession and the tobacco industry cooperated, but in a rather wary fashion. But at the end of the day they were both reasonably content. The subject of radioactive fallout and the banning of nuclear tests was, and is, highly controversial. But according to what little evidence there is, viewers were prepared to listen to both sides with reason and restraint. This is not said to claim any special or unusual competence in the presentation of controversial subjects, but rather to indicate that timidity in these areas is not warranted by the evidence.

Recently, network spokesmen have been disposed to complain that the professional critics of television in print have been rather beastly. There have been ill-disguised hints that somehow competition for the advertising dollar has caused the critics in print to gang up on television and radio. This reporter has no desire to defend the critics. They have space in which to do that on their own behalf. But it remains a fact that the newspapers and magazines are the only instruments of mass communication which remain free from sustained and regular critical comment. I would suggest that if the network spokesmen are so anguished about what appears in print, then let them come forth and engage in a little sustained and regular comment regarding newspapers and magazines. It is an ancient and sad fact that most people in network television, and radio, have an exaggerated regard for what appears in print. And there have been cases where executives have refused to make even private comment on a program for which they are responsible until they had read the reviews in print. This is hardly an exhibition of confidence in their own judgment.

The oldest excuse of the networks for their timidity is their youth. Their spokesmen say, "We are young. We have not developed the traditions nor acquired the experience of the older media." If they but knew it, they are building those traditions and creating those precedents every day. Each time they yield to a voice from Washington or any political pressure, each time they eliminate something that might offend some section of the community, they are creating their own body of precedent and tradition, and it will continue to pursue them. They are, in fact, not content to be half safe.

Nowhere is this better illustrated than by the fact that the chairman of the Federal Communications Commission publicly prods broadcasters to engage in their legal right to editorialize. Of course, to undertake an editorial policy – overt, clearly labeled, and obviously unsponsored – requires a station or a network to be responsible. Most stations today probably do not have the manpower to assume this responsibility, but the manpower could be recruited. Editorials, of course, would not be profitable. If they had a cutting edge, they might even offend. It is much easier, much less troublesome, to use this money-making machine of television and radio merely as a conduit through which to channel anything that will be paid for that is not libelous, obscene or defamatory. In that way one has the illusion of power without responsibility.

So far as radio – that most satisfying, ancient but rewarding instrument – is concerned, the diagnosis of the difficulties is not too difficult. And obviously I speak only of news and information. In order to progress, it need only go backward. Back to the time when singing commercials were not allowed on news reports, when there was no middle commercial in a fifteen-minute news report, when radio was rather proud, and alert, and fast. I recently asked a network official, "Why this great rash of five-minute news reports (including three commercials) on weekends?" And he replied, "Because that seems to be the only thing we can sell."

Well, in this kind of complex and confusing world, you can't tell very much about the "why" of the news in a broadcast where only three minutes is available for news. The only man who could do that was Elmer Davis,[*] and his kind aren't around anymore. If radio news is to be regarded as a commodity, only acceptable when saleable, and only when packaged to fit the advertising appropriate of a sponsor, then I don't care what you call it – I say it isn't news.

My memory – and I have not yet reached the point where my memories fascinate me – but my memory also goes back to the time when the fear of a slight reduction in business did not result in an immediate cutback in bodies in the news and public affairs department, at a time when network profits had just reached an all-time high. We would all agree, I think, that whether on a station or a network, the stapling machine is a very poor substitute for a newsroom typewriter, and somebody to beat it properly.

One of the minor tragedies of television news and information is that the networks will not even defend their vital interests. When my employer, CBS, through a combination of enterprise and good luck, did an interview with Nikita Khrushchev, the President uttered a few ill-chosen, uninformed words on the subject, and the network thereupon practically apologised. This produced something of a rarity: many newspapers defended the CBS right to produce the program and commended it for its initiative. The other networks remained silent.

Likewise, when John Foster Dulles,[†] by personal decree, banned American journalists from going to Communist China, and subsequently offered seven contradictory explanations, for his fiat the networks entered only a mild protest. Then they apparently forgot the unpleasantness. Can it be that this national industry is content to serve the public interest only with the trickle of news that comes out of Hong Kong, to leave its viewers in ignorance of the cataclysmic changes that are occurring in a nation of 600 million people? I have no illusions about the difficulties of reporting from a dictatorship, but our British and French allies have been better served – in their public interest – with some very useful information from their reporters in Communist China.

One of the basic troubles with radio and television news is that both instruments have grown up as an incompatible combination of show business, advertising and news. Each of the three is a rather bizarre and, at times, demanding profession. And when you get all three under one roof, the dust never settles. The top management of the networks, with a few notable exceptions, has been trained in advertising, research, sales or show business. But by the nature of the corporate structure, they also make the final and crucial

[*] Legendary American news reporter and director of the United States Office of War Information during World War II.

[†] The then-secretary of state under President Eisenhower.

decisions having to do with news and public affairs. Frequently they have neither the time nor the competence to do this. It is, after all, not easy for the same small group of men to decide whether to buy a new station for millions of dollars, build a new building, alter the rate card, buy a new Western, sell a soap opera, decide what defensive line to take in connection with the latest Congressional inquiry, how much money to spend on promoting a new program, what additions or deletions should be made in the existing covey or clutch of vice-presidents, and at the same time – frequently on the same long day – to give mature, thoughtful consideration to the manifold problems that confront those who are charged with the responsibility for news and public affairs.

Sometimes there is a clash between the public interest and the corporate interest. A telephone call or a letter from a proper quarter in Washington is treated rather more seriously than a communication from an irate but not politically potent viewer. It is tempting enough to give away a little air time for frequently irresponsible and unwarranted utterances in an effort to temper the wind of political criticism. But this could well be the subject of a separate and even lengthier and drearier dissertation.

Upon occasion, economics and editorial judgment are in conflict. And there is no law which says that dollars will be defeated by duty. Not so long ago the President of the United States delivered a television address to the nation. He was discoursing on the possibility or the probability of war between this nation and the Soviet Union and Communist China. It would seem to have been a reasonably compelling subject, with a degree of urgency attached. Two networks, CBS and NBC, delayed that broadcast for an hour and fifteen minutes. If this decision was dictated by anything other than financial reasons, the networks didn't deign to explain those reasons. That hour-and-fifteen-minute delay, by the way, is a little more than twice the time required for an ICBM‡ to travel from the Soviet Union to major targets in the United States. It is difficult to believe that this decision was made by men who love, respect and understand news.

‡ An intercontinental ballistic missile, designed for the delivery of nuclear weapons.

I have been dealing largely with the deficit side of the ledger, and the items could be expanded. But I have said, and I believe, that potentially we have in this country a free enterprise system of radio and television which is superior to any other. But to achieve its promise, it must be both free and enterprising. There is no suggestion here that networks or individual stations should operate as philanthropies. But I can find nothing in the Bill of Rights or in the Communications Act which says that they must increase their net profits each year, lest the republic collapse. I do not suggest that news and information should be subsidized by foundations or private subscriptions. I am aware that the networks have expended, and are expending, very considerable sums of money on public affairs programs from which they cannot receive any financial reward. I have had the privilege at CBS of presiding over a considerable number of such programs. And I am able to stand here and say, that I have never had a program turned down by my superiors just because of the money it would cost.

But we all know that you cannot reach the potential maximum audience in marginal time with a sustaining program. This is so because so many stations on the network – any network – will decline to carry it. Every licensee who applies for a grant to operate in the public interest, convenience and necessity makes certain promises as to what he will do in terms of program content. Many recipients of licenses have, in blunt language, just plain welshed on those promises. The money-making machine somehow blunts their memories. The only remedy for this is closer inspection and punitive action by the FCC. But in the view of many, this would come perilously close to supervision of program content by a federal agency.

So it seems that we cannot rely on philanthropic support or foundation subsidies. We cannot follow the sustaining route. The networks cannot pay all the freight. And the FCC cannot, will not, or should not discipline those who abuse the facilities that belong to the public. What, then, is the answer? Do we merely stay in our comfortable nests, concluding that the obligation of these instruments has been discharged when we work at the job of informing the public for a minimum of time? Or do we believe that the preservation of the republic is a seven-day-a-week job, demanding more awareness, better skills and more perseverance than we have yet contemplated?

I am frightened by the imbalance, the constant striving to reach the largest possible audience for everything; by the absence of a sustained study of the state of the nation. [Journalist] Heywood Broun once said, "No body politic is healthy until it begins to itch." I would like television to produce some itching pills rather than this endless outpouring of tranquilizers. It can be done. Maybe it won't be, but it could. But let us not shoot the wrong piano player. Do not be deluded into believing that the titular heads of the networks control what appears on their networks. They all have better taste. All are responsible to stockholders, and in my experience all are honorable men. But they must schedule what they can sell in the public market.

And this brings us to the nub of the question. In one sense it rather revolves around the phrase heard frequently along Madison Avenue: "The Corporate Image." I am not precisely sure what this phrase means, but I would imagine that it reflects a desire on the part of the corporations who pay the advertising bills to have a public image, or believe that they are not merely bodies with no souls, panting in pursuit of elusive dollars. They would like us to believe that they can distinguish between the public good and the private or corporate gain. So the question is this: are the big corporations who pay the freight for radio and television programs to use that time exclusively for the sale of goods and services? Is it in their own interest and that of the stockholders so to do? The sponsor of an hour's television program is not buying merely the six minutes devoted to his commercial message. He is determining, within broad limits, the sum total of the impact of the entire hour. If he always, invariably, reaches for the largest possible audience, then this process of insulation, of escape from reality, will continue to be massively financed, and its apologists will continue to make winsome speeches about giving the public what it wants, or letting the public decide.

I refuse to believe that the presidents and chairmen of the boards of these big corporations want their corporate image to consist exclusively of a solemn voice in an echo chamber, or a pretty girl opening the door of a refrigerator, or a horse that talks. They want something better, and on occasion some of them have demonstrated it. But most of the men whose legal and moral responsibility it is to spend the stockholders' money for advertising are, in fact, removed from the realities of the mass media by five, six, or a dozen contraceptive layers of vice-presidents, public relations counsel and advertising agencies. Their business is to sell goods, and the competition is pretty tough.

But this nation is now in competition with malignant forces of evil who are using every instrument at their command to empty the minds of their subjects and fill those minds with slogans, determination and faith in the future. If we go on as we are, we are protecting the mind of the American public from any real contact with the menacing world that squeezes in upon us. We are engaged in a great experiment to discover whether a free public opinion can devise and direct methods of managing the affairs of the nation. We may fail. But in terms of information, we are handicapping ourselves needlessly.

Let us have a little competition not only in selling soap, cigarettes and automobiles, but in informing a troubled, apprehensive but receptive public. Why should not each of the twenty or thirty big corporations – and they dominate radio and television – decide that they will give up one or two of their regularly scheduled programs each year, turn the time over to the networks and say in effect: "This is a tiny tithe, just a little bit of our profits. On this particular night we aren't going to try to sell cigarettes or automobiles; this is merely a gesture to indicate our belief in the importance of ideas." The networks should, and I think they would, pay for the cost of producing the program. The advertiser, the sponsor, would get name credit but would have nothing to do with the content of the program. Would this blemish the corporate image? Would the stockholders rise up and object? I think not. For if the premise upon which our pluralistic society rests – which as I understand it is that if the people are given sufficient undiluted information, they will then somehow, even after long, sober second thoughts, reach the right conclusion – if that premise is wrong, then not only the corporate image but the corporations and the rest of us are done for.

There used to be an old phrase in this country, employed when someone talked too much. I am grateful to all of you for not having employed it earlier. The phrase was: "Go hire a hall." Under this proposal, the sponsor would have hired the hall; he has bought the time. The local station operator, no matter how indifferent, is going to carry the program– he has to – he's getting paid for it. Then it's up to the networks to fill the hall. I am not here talking about editorializing but about straightaway exposition as direct, unadorned and impartial as fallible human beings can make it. Just once in a while let us exalt the importance of ideas and information. Let us dream to the extent of saying that on a given Sunday night the time normally occupied by [variety show host] Ed Sullivan is given over to a clinical survey of the state of American education, and a week or two later the time normally used by [talk show host] Steve Allen is devoted to a thoroughgoing study of American policy in the Middle East. Would the corporate image of their respective sponsors be damaged? Would the stockholders rise up and complain? Would anything happen other than that a few million people would have received a little illumination on subjects that may well determine the future of this country, and therefore also the future of the corporations? This method would also provide real competition between the networks as to which could outdo the others in the palatable presentation of information. It would provide an outlet for the young men of skill, and there are many, even of dedication, who would like to do something other than devise methods of insulating while selling.

There may be other and simpler methods of utilizing these instruments of radio and television in the interest of a free society. But I know of none that could be so easily accomplished inside the framework of the existing commercial system. I don't know how you would measure the success or failure of a given program. And it would be very hard to prove the magnitude of the benefit accruing to the corporation which gave up one night of a variety or quiz show in order that the network might marshal its skills to do a thoroughgoing job on the present status of NATO, or plans for controlling nuclear tests. But I would reckon that the president, and indeed the stockholders of the corporation who sponsored such a venture, would feel just a little bit better about both the corporation and the country.

It may be that this present system, with no modifications and no experiments, can survive. Perhaps the money-making machine has some kind of built-in perpetual motion, but I do not think so. To a very considerable extent, the media of mass communications in a given country reflects the political, economic and social climate in which it grows and flourishes. That is the reason our system differs from the British and the French, and also from the Russian and the Chinese. We are currently wealthy, fat, comfortable and complacent. We have currently a built-in allergy to unpleasant or disturbing information. And our mass media reflect this. But unless we get up off our fat surpluses and recognize that television in the main is being used to distract, delude, amuse and insulate us, then television and those who finance it, those who look at it and those who work at it, may see a totally different picture too late.

EDWARD R. MURROW:   RADIO AND TELEVISION NEWS DIRECTORS CONVENTION
CHICAGO,  OCTOBER 15, 1958.


This just might do nobody any good.  At the end of this discourse a few
people may accuse this reporter of fouling his own comfortable nest;  and your
organization may be accused of having given hospitality to heretical and even
dangerous thoughts.

But the elaborate structure of networks, advertising agencies and sponsors
will not be shaken or altered.  It is my desire if not my duty to try to talk to
you journeymen with some candor about what is happening to radio and television in
this generous and capacious land.

I have no technical advice or counsel to offer those of you who labor in
this vineyard that produces words and pictures.  You will forgive me for not
telling you that the instruments with which you work are miraculous; that your
responsibility is unprecedented; or that your aspirations are frequently
frustrated.  It is not necessary to remind you of the fact that your voice is
amplified to the degree where it reaches from one end of the country to the other
does not confer upon you greater wisdom or understanding than you possessed when
your voice reached only from one end of the bar to the other.  All of these things
you know.

You should also know at the outset that, in the manner of witnesses before
Congressional Committees, I appear here voluntarily - by invitation - that I am
an employee of the Columbia Broadcasting System - that I am neither an officer
nor a director of that Corporation - and that these remarks are of a "do-it-
yourself" nature.  If what I have to say is responsible, then I alone am responsible for the saying of it.  Seeking neither approbation from my employers, nor
new sponsors, nor acclaim from the critics of radio and television, I cannot well
be disappointed.  Believing that potentially the commercial system of broadcasting as practised in this country is the best and freest yet devised, I have
decided to express my concern about what I believe to be happening to radio and

I do not advocate that we turn television into a 27-inch wailing wall, where longhairs constantly moan about the state of our culture and our defense. But I would just like to see it reflect occasionally the hard, unyielding realities of the world in which we live. I would like to see it done inside the existing framework, and I would like to see the doing of it redound to the credit of those who finance and program it. Measure the results by Nielsen, Trendex or Silex – it doesn't matter. The main thing is to try. The responsibility can be easily placed, in spite of all the mouthings about giving the public what it wants. It rests on big business, and on big television, and it rests on the top. Responsibility is not something that can be assigned or delegated. And it promises its own reward: both good business and good television.

Perhaps no one will do anything about it. I have ventured to outline it against a background of criticism that may have been too harsh only because I could think of nothing better. Someone once said – and I think it was [writer and political activist] Max Eastman – that "that publisher serves his advertiser best who best serves his readers." I cannot believe that radio and television, or the corporations that finance the programs, are serving well or truly their viewers or their listeners, or themselves.

I began by saying that our history will be what we make it. If we go on as we are, then history will take its revenge, and retribution will not limp in catching up with us.

We are to a large extent an imitative society. If one or two or three corporations would undertake to devote just a small fraction of their advertising appropriation along the lines that I have suggested, the procedure might well grow by contagion; the economic burden would be bearable, and there might ensue a most exciting adventure – exposure to ideas and the bringing of reality into the homes of the nation.

To those who say people wouldn't look; they wouldn't be interested; they're too complacent, indifferent and insulated, I can only reply: there is, in one reporter's opinion, considerable evidence against that contention. But even if they are right, what have they got to lose? Because if they are right, and this instrument is good for nothing but to entertain, amuse and insulate, then the tube is flickering now and we will soon see that the whole struggle is lost.

This instrument can teach, it can illuminate; yes, and even it can inspire. But it can do so only to the extent that humans are determined to use it to those ends. Otherwise, it's nothing but wires and lights in a box. There is a great and perhaps decisive battle to be fought against ignorance, intolerance and indifference. This weapon of television could be useful.

Stonewall Jackson,§ who is generally believed to have known something about weapons, is reported to have said, "When war comes, you must draw the sword and throw away the scabbard." The trouble with television is that it is rusting in the scabbard during a battle for survival. Thank you for your patience.

# WHAT ADULTS CAN LEARN FROM KIDS

Adora Svitak has achieved more during her childhood than most could hope to achieve in their entire lifetime. Born in 1997, she began writing fiction at the age of four and by the age of seven was typing hundreds of thousands of words each year on her laptop. Aged eleven, she became a published novelist, and not for the last time. She was also an accomplished public speaker before reaching her teenage years, and addressed crowds around the world. In 2010, at the TED Talks conference, she gave her most high-profile speech to date. It has since been watched 5 million times online.

Now, I want to start with a question: when was the last time you were called childish? For kids like me, being called childish can be a frequent occurrence. Every time we make irrational demands, exhibit irresponsible behavior or display any other signs of being normal American citizens, we are called childish. Which really bothers me. After all, take a look at these events: imperialism and colonization, world wars, George W. Bush. Ask yourself, who's responsible? Adults.

Now, what have kids done? Well, Anne Frank touched millions with her powerful account of the Holocaust, Ruby Bridges helped to end segregation in the United States, and, most recently, Charlie Simpson helped to raise about $160,000 for Haiti on his little bike. So, as you can see evidenced by such examples, age has absolutely nothing to do with it. The traits the word "childish" addresses are seen so often in adults that we should abolish this age-discriminatory word when it comes to criticizing behavior associated with irresponsibility and irrational thinking.

Then again, who's to say that certain types of irrational thinking aren't exactly what the world needs? Maybe you've had grand plans before but stopped yourself, thinking, "That's impossible," or, "That costs too much," or, "That won't benefit me." For better or worse, we kids aren't hampered as much when it comes to thinking about reasons why not to do things. Kids can be full of inspiring aspirations and hopeful thinking. Like my wish that no one went hungry or that everything were a free kind of utopia. How many of you still dream like that and believe in the possibilities? Sometimes a knowledge of history and the past failures of utopian ideals can be a burden because you know that if everything were free, then the food stocks would become depleted and scarce and lead to chaos. On the other hand, we kids still dream about perfection. And that's a good thing because in order to make anything a reality, you have to dream about it first.

→ Adora Svitak,
November 5, 2014,
photographed by
Diarmuid Greene

In many ways, our audacity to imagine helps push the boundaries of possibility. For instance, the Museum of Glass in Tacoma, Washington, my

home state, has a program called Kids Design Glass, and kids draw their own ideas for glass art. Now, the resident artist said they got some of their best ideas through the program because kids don't think about the limitations of how hard it can be to blow glass into certain shapes; they just think of good ideas. Now, when you think of glass, you might think of colorful Chihuly designs or maybe Italian vases, but kids challenge glass artists to go beyond that into the realm of broken-hearted snakes and bacon boys, who you can see has meat vision.

Now, our inherent wisdom doesn't have to be insider's knowledge. Kids already do a lot of learning from adults, and we have a lot to share. I think that adults should start learning from kids. Now, I do most of my speaking in front of an education crowd, teachers and students, and I like this analogy: it shouldn't just be a teacher at the head of the classroom telling students, "Do this, do that." The students should teach their teachers. Learning between grown-ups and kids should be reciprocal. The reality, unfortunately, is a little different, and it has a lot to do with trust, or a lack of it.

Now, if you don't trust someone, you place restrictions on them, right? If I doubt my older sister's ability to pay back the 10 percent interest I established on her last loan, I'm going to withhold her ability to get more money from me until she pays it back. True story, by the way. Now, adults seem to have a prevalently restrictive attitude towards kids from every "don't do that, don't do this" in the school handbook to restrictions on school Internet use. As history points out, regimes become oppressive when they're fearful about keeping control. And although adults may not be quite at the level of totalitarian regimes, kids have no or very little say in making the rules, when really the attitude should be reciprocal, meaning that the adult population should learn and take into account the wishes of the younger population.

Now, what's even worse than restriction is that adults often underestimate kids' abilities. We love challenges, but when expectations are low, trust me, we will sink to them. My own parents had anything but low expectations for me and my sister. OK, so they didn't tell us to become doctors or lawyers or anything like that, but my dad did read to us about Aristotle and pioneer germ fighters when lots of other kids were hearing "The Wheels on the Bus Go Round and Round." Well, we heard that one too, but "Pioneer Germ Fighters" totally rules.

I loved to write from the age of four, and when I was six my mom bought me my own laptop equipped with Microsoft Word. Thank you Bill Gates and thank you Ma. I wrote over 300 short stories on that little laptop, and I wanted to get published. Instead of just scoffing at this heresy that a kid wanted to get published or saying wait until you're older, my parents were really supportive. Many publishers were not quite so encouraging, one large children's publisher ironically saying that they didn't work with children – children's publisher not working with children? I don't know, you're kind of alienating a large client there. Now, one publisher, Action Publishing, was willing to take that leap and trust me and to listen to what I had to say. They published my first book, *Flying Fingers*, and from there on, it's gone to speaking at hundreds of schools, keynoting to thousands of educators and finally, today, speaking to you.

I appreciate your attention today, because to show that you truly care, you listen. But there's a problem with this rosy picture of kids being so much better than adults. Kids grow up and become adults just like you. Or just like you? Really? The goal is not to turn kids into your kind of adult, but rather better adults than you have been, which may be a little challenging considering you guys' credentials. But the way progress happens is because new generations and new eras grow and develop and become better than the previous ones. It's the reason we're not in the Dark Ages anymore. No matter your position or place in life, it is imperative to create opportunities for children so that we can grow up to blow you away.

Adults and fellow TEDsters, you need to listen and learn from kids and trust us and expect more from us. You must lend an ear today, because we are the leaders of tomorrow, which means we're going to be taking care of you when you're old and senile. No, just kidding. No, really, we are going to be the next generation, the ones who will bring this world forward. And in case you don't think that this really has meaning for you, remember that cloning is possible, and that involves going through childhood again, in which case you'll want to be heard just like my generation. Now, the world needs opportunities for new leaders and new ideas. Kids need opportunities to lead and succeed. Are you ready to make the match? Because the world's problems shouldn't be the human family's heirloom.

Thank you.

# DEFY THE GODS

When Salman Rushdie walked out on stage at Bard College in May 1996, he did so not just to accept an honorary degree and address 247 students soon to graduate, but also to thank the college for offering him a safe haven. The previous decade, his life had been threatened by Ayatollah Khomeini's fatwa ordering Muslims to kill Rushdie following publication of his novel, *The Satanic Verses*.

Members of the Class of 1996, I see in the newspaper that Southampton University on Long Island got Kermit the Frog to give the Commencement address this year. You, unfortunately, have to make do with me. The only Muppet connection I can boast is that my former editor at Alfred Knopf was also the editor of that important self-help text, *Miss Piggy's Guide to Life*. I once asked him how it had been to work with such a major star and he replied, reverentially, 'Salman: the pig was divine.'

In England, where I went to college, we don't do things quite this way on graduation day, so I've been doing a little research into Commencement and its traditions. The first American friend I asked told me that in her graduation year – not at this college, I hasten to add – she and her fellow-students were so incensed at the choice of Commencement speaker – whom I suppose I should not name – oh, all right then, it was [Republican diplomat] Jeane Kirkpatrick – that they boycotted the ceremony and staged a sit-in in one of the college buildings instead. It is a considerable relief, therefore, to note that you are all here.

As for myself, I graduated from Cambridge University in 1968 – the great year of student protest – and I have to tell you that I almost didn't make it. This story has nothing to do with politics or demonstrations; it is, rather, the improbable and cautionary tale of a thick brown gravy-and-onion sauce. It begins a few nights before my graduation day, when some anonymous wit chose to redecorate my room, in my absence, by hurling a bucketful of the aforesaid gravy-and-onions all over the walls and furniture, to say nothing of my record player and my clothes. With that ancient tradition of fairness and justice upon which the colleges of Cambridge pride themselves, my college instantly held me solely responsible for the mess, ignored all my representations to the contrary, and informed me that unless I paid for the damage before the ceremony, I would not be permitted to graduate. It was the first, but, alas, not the last occasion on which I would find myself wrongly accused of muckspreading. I paid up, I have to report, and was therefore declared eligible to receive my degree; in a defiant spirit, possibly influenced by my recent gravy experience, I went to the ceremony wearing brown shoes, and was promptly plucked out of the parade of my gowned and properly black-shod contemporaries, and ordered back to my quarters to change.

I am not sure why people in brown shoes were deemed to be dressed improperly, but once again I was facing a judgment against which there could be no appeal. Once again, I gave in, sprinted off to change my shoes, got back to the parade in the nick of time; and at length, after these vicissitudes, when my turn came, I was required to hold a university officer by his little finger, and to follow him slowly up to where the Vice-Chancellor sat upon a mighty throne. As instructed, I knelt at his feet, held up my hands, palms together, in a gesture of supplication, and begged in Latin for the degree, for which, I could not help thinking, I had worked extremely hard for three years, supported by my family at considerable expense. I recall being advised to hold my hands way up above my head, in case the elderly Vice-Chancellor, leaning forward to clutch at them, should topple off his great chair and land on top of me. I did as I was advised; the elderly gentleman did not topple; and, also in Latin, he finally admitted me to the degree of Bachelor of Arts. Looking back at that day, I am a little appalled by my passivity, hard though it is to see what else I could have done. I could have not paid up, not changed my shoes, not knelt to supplicate for my BA. I preferred to surrender, and get the degree. I have grown more stubborn since.

I have come to the conclusion, which I now offer you, that I was wrong to compromise; wrong to make an accommodation with injustice, no matter how persuasive the reasons. Injustice, today, still conjures up, in my mind, the memory of gravy. Injustice, for me, is a brown, lumpy, congealing fluid, and it smells pungently, tearfully, of onions. Unfairness is the feeling of running back to your room, flat out, at the last minute, to change your outlawed brown shoes. It is the business of being forced to beg, on your knees, in a dead language, for what is rightfully yours.

This, then, is what I learned on my own graduation day; this is the message I have derived from the parables of the Unknown Gravy-Bomber, the Vetoed Footwear, and the Unsteady Vice-Chancellor upon his Throne, and which I pass on to you today: first, if, as you go through life, people should some day accuse you of what one might call aggravated gravy abuse – and they will, they will – and if in fact you are innocent of abusing gravy, do not take the rap. Second: those who would reject you because you are wearing the wrong shoes are not worth being accepted by. And third: kneel before no man. Stand up for your rights.

I like to think that Cambridge University, where I was so happy for three marvellous years, and from which I gained so much – I hope your years at Bard have been as happy, and that you feel you have gained as much – that Cambridge University, with its finely developed British sense of irony, intended me to learn precisely these valuable lessons from the events of that strange graduation day.

Members of the Class of 1996, we are here to celebrate with you one of the great days of your lives. We participate today in the rite of passage by which you are released from this life of preparation into that life for which you are now as prepared as anyone ever is. As you stand at the gate of the future, I should like to share with you a piece of information about the extraordinary institution you are leaving, which will explain the reason why it is such a particular pleasure for me to be with you today. In 1989, within weeks of the threat made against me by the mullahs of Iran, I was approached by the President of Bard, through my literary agent, and asked if I would consider accepting a place on the faculty of this college. More than a place; I was assured that I could find, here in Annandale, among the Bard community, many friends, and a safe haven in which I could live and work. Alas, I was not able, in those difficult days, to take up this courageous offer, but I have never forgotten that at a moment when red-alert signals were flashing all over the world, and all sorts of people and institutions were running scared, Bard College did the opposite – that it moved towards me, in intellectual solidarity and human concern, and made, not lofty speeches, but a concrete offer of help. I hope you will all feel proud that Bard, quietly, without fanfares, made such a principled gesture at such a time.

I am certainly extremely proud to be a recipient of Bard's honorary degree, and to have been accorded the exceptional privilege of addressing you today. Hubris, according to the Greeks, was the sin of defying the gods, and could, if you were really unlucky, unleash against you the terrifying, avenging figure of the goddess Nemesis, who carried in one hand an apple-bough and, in the other, the Wheel of Fortune, which would one day circle round to the inevitable moment of vengeance. As I have been, in my time, accused not only of gravy abuse and wearing brown shoes but of hubris, too, and since I have come to believe that such defiance is an inevitable and essential aspect of what we call freedom, I thought I might commend it to you. For in the years to come you will find yourselves up against gods of all sorts, big and little gods, corporate and incorporeal gods, all of them demanding to be worshipped and obeyed – the myriad deities of money and power, of convention and custom, that will seek to limit and control your thoughts and lives.

Defy them; that's my advice to you. Thumb your noses; cock your snooks. For, as the myths tell us, it is by defying the gods that human beings have best expressed their humanity. The Greeks tell many stories of quarrels between us and the gods. Arachne, the great artist of the loom, sets her skills of weaving and embroidery against those of the goddess of wisdom herself, Minerva or Pallas Athene; and impudently chooses to weave versions of only those scenes which reveal the mistakes and weaknesses of the gods – the rape of Europa, Leda and the Swan. For this – for the irreverence, not for her lesser skill – for what we would now call art, and chutzpah – the goddess changes her mortal rival into a spider. Queen Niobe of Thebes tells her people not to worship

Latona, the mother of Diana and Apollo, saying, 'What folly is this! – To prefer beings whom you never saw to those who stand before your eyes!' For this sentiment, which today we would call humanism, the gods murder her children and husband, and she metamorphoses into a rock, petrified with grief, from which there trickles an unending river of tears. Prometheus the Titan steals fire from the gods and gives it to mankind. For this – for what we would now call the desire for progress, for improved scientific and technological capabilities – he is bound to a rock while a great bird gnaws eternally at his liver, which regenerates as it is consumed.

The interesting point is that the gods do not come out of these stories at all well. If Arachne is overly proud when she seeks to compete with a goddess, it is only an artist's pride, joined to the gutsiness of youth; whereas Minerva, who could afford to be gracious, is merely vindictive. The story increases Arachne's shadow, as they say, and diminishes Minerva's. It is Arachne who gains, from the tale, a measure of immortality. And the cruelty of the gods to the family of Niobe proves her point. Who could prefer the rule of such cruel gods to self-rule, the rule of men and women by men and women, however flawed that may be? Once again, the gods are weakened by their show of strength, while the human beings grow stronger, even though – even as – they are destroyed. And tormented Prometheus, of course, Prometheus with his gift of fire, is the greatest hero of all.

It is men and women who have made the world, and they have made it in spite of their gods. The message of the myths is not the one the gods would have us learn – that we should behave ourselves and know our place – but its exact opposite. It is that we must be guided by our natures. Our worst natures can, it's true, be arrogant, venal, corrupt or selfish; but in our best selves, we – that is, you – can and will be joyous, adventurous, cheeky, creative, inquisitive, demanding, competitive, loving and defiant.

Do not bow your heads. Do not know your place. Defy the gods. You will be astonished how many of them turn out to have feet of clay. Be guided, if possible, by your better natures. Great good luck and many congratulations to you all.

# GENTLEMEN OF THE JURY, IT CANNOT BE

On May 16, 1851, the French political journal *L'Evenement* published a detailed and highly critical report on the mishandled execution of one Claude Montcharmont, who had struggled to such an extent on approaching the guillotine that his executioner was forced to reschedule the beheading. The journalist behind the article, Charles Hugo, was soon arrested for disrespecting the law. At his trial the next month, a speech was delivered to the jury by his father, the esteemed novelist Victor Hugo, who had spent much of his life campaigning for the abolition of capital punishment. Victor Hugo's passionate defense fell on deaf ears. Charles was imprisoned for six months.

Gentlemen of the jury, if there is a culprit here, it is not my son, it is myself. It is I. I, who for these twenty-five years have opposed capital punishment, have contended for the inviolability of human life, have committed this crime for which my son is now arraigned. Here, I denounce myself, Mr. Advocate General. I have committed it under all aggravated circumstances, deliberately, repeatedly, tenaciously. Yes, this old and absurd "lex talionis" [an eye for an eye] – this law of blood for blood – I have combated all my life; all my life, gentlemen of the jury. And while I have breath, I will continue to combat it, by all my efforts as a writer, by all my words and all my votes as a legislator. I declare it before the crucifix; before that victim of the penalty of death, who sees and hears us; before that gibbet, to which, two thousand years ago, for the eternal instruction of the generations, the human law nailed the divine.

In all that my son has written on the subject of capital punishment – and for writing and publishing that for which he is now before you on trial – in all that he has written, he has merely proclaimed the sentiments with which, from his infancy, I have inspired him. Gentlemen jurors, the right to criticize a law and to criticize it severely, especially a penal law, is placed beside the duty of amelioration, like the torch beside the work under the artisan's hand. The right of the journalist is as sacred, as necessary, as imprescriptible, as the right of the legislator.

What are the circumstances? A man, a convict, a sentenced wretch, is dragged on a certain morning to one of our public squares. There he finds the scaffold. He shudders, he struggles, he refuses to die. He is young yet – only twenty-nine. Ah! I know what you will say: "He is a murderer!" But hear me. Two officers seize him. His hands, his feet, are tied. He throws off the two officers. A frightful struggle ensues. His feet, bound as they are, become entangled in the ladder. He uses the scaffold against the scaffold! The struggle is prolonged. Horror seizes on the crowd. The officers – sweat and shame on their brows; pale, panting, terrified, despairing; despairing with I know not what horrible despair; shrinking under that public reprobation which ought to

have visited the penalty and spared the passive instrument, the executioner – the officers strive savagely. The victim clings to the scaffold and shrieks for pardon. His clothes are torn, his shoulders bloody. Still he resists.

At length, after three-quarters of an hour of this monstrous effort, of this spectacle without a name, of this agony – agony for all, be it understood; agony for the assembled spectators as well as for the condemned man – after this age of anguish, gentlemen of the jury, they take back the poor wretch to his prison. The people breathe again. The people, naturally merciful, hope that the man will be spared. But no. The guillotine, though vanquished, remains standing. There it frowns all day, in the midst of a sickened population. And at night, the officers, reinforced, drag forth the wretch again, so bound that he is but an inert weight. They drag him forth, haggard, bloody, weeping, pleading, howling for life, calling upon God, calling upon his father and mother. For like a very child had this man become in the prospect of death. They drag him forth to execution. He is hoisted onto the scaffold, and his head falls. And then through every conscience runs a shudder. Never had legal murder appeared with an aspect so indecent, so abominable. All feel jointly implicated in the deed. It is at this moment that from a young man's breast escapes a cry, wrung from his very heart. A cry of pity and anguish. A cry of horror. A cry of humanity. And this cry you would punish. And, in the face of the appalling facts which I have narrated, you would say to the guillotine, "Thou art right!" And to pity, saintly pity, "Thou art wrong!"

← Victor Hugo in 1876, photographed by Étienne Carjat

Gentlemen of the jury, it cannot be. Gentlemen, I have finished.

# BE BOLD

Susan Sontag had many strings to her bow. At various points she was a successful and prolific writer of numerous novels, works of nonfiction, short stories, essays, plays and even films, which she also directed. For some time she taught philosophy to university students, as well as being a committed human rights activist throughout her life and winning close to a dozen awards and honors. All of which made Sontag the perfect person to give a wise commencement speech – in fact, the only one she would ever deliver – to the outgoing students of Wellesley College in 1983.

This is my first commencement, and I think it's a wonderful college to be having it. I liked hearing a woman chaplain give an invocation; I admire your distinguished and extraordinary president; and I agree heartily with the content of the two speeches, especially their upfront feminist sentiments, just delivered by two graduating seniors. . . .

Graduation is one of the few genuine rites of passage left in our society. You are, individually and collectively, passing symbolically from one place to another, from an old to a new status. And, like all such rites, it is both retrospective and prospective. You are graduating (or being graduated) from college, which is the end of something. But the ceremony we are participating in is called commencement.

That necessarily seasonal, minor literary form called the "commencement address" also faces in two directions. It usually starts with an analysis of the society or the era – appropriately pessimistic. It generally concludes with a heavy dose of exhortation, in which the young graduates, after having been suitably alarmed, are nevertheless urged to be of good cheer as they go forth into the arena of struggle that is your life, and this world.

As a writer, therefore fascinated by genres, as well as an American, and therefore prone to sermonizing, I shall respect the tradition. The times we live in are indeed alarming. It is a time of the most appalling escalation of violence – violence to the environment, both "nature" and "culture"; violence to all living beings. A time in which an ideology of exterminism, institutionalized in the nuclear arms race, has gained increasing credence – threatening life itself. It is also a time of a vertiginous drop in cultural standards, of virulent anti-intellectualism, and of triumphant mediocrity – a mediocrity that characterizes the educational system that you have just passed through, or has passed you through (for all the efforts and goodwill of many of your teachers). Trivializing standards, using as their justification the ideal of democracy, have made the very idea of a serious humanist education virtually unintelligible to most people. A vast system of mental lobotomization has been put into operation that sets

→ Susan Sontag, 2000, photographed by Rossano B. Maniscalchi

the standards to which all accede. (I am speaking, of course, of American television.)

A singularly foolish and incompetent president sets the tone for an extraordinary regression in public ideals, strengthening apathy and a sense of hopelessness before the self-destructive course of foreign policy and the arms race. The best critical impulses in our society – such as that which has given rise to feminist consciousness – are under vicious attack. An increasing propaganda for conformism in morals and in art instructs us that originality and individuality will always be defeated, and simply do not pay. There is a strengthening of the power of censors within and without. The constraints which govern us in this society have little in common with the grim normalcy of totalitarian societies. Our society does not censor as totalitarian societies do; on the contrary, our society promises liberty, self-fulfillment, and self-expression. But many features of our so-called culture have as their goal and result the reduction of our mental life, or our mental operation; and this is precisely, I would argue, what censorship is about. Censorship does not exist in order to keep secrets. The secrets that censors target, such as sex, are usually open secrets. Censorship is a formal principle. It has no predetermined subject. It exists in order to promote and defend power against the challenge of individuality. It exists in order to maintain optimism, to suppress pessimism; that is to give pessimism – which often means truthfulness – a bad conscience.

Of course, the grim assessments of our era – such as I have just outlined – can themselves become a species of conformity. But only if we have too simple a sense of our lives. Whenever we speak, we tend to make matters sound simpler than they are, and than we know they are.

I have said that this rite of passage – commencement – is one that faces in two directions. Your old status and your new status. The past and the present. The present and the future. But I would urge that it is not just a description of today's exercises but a model for how you should try to live. As if you were always graduating, ending and, simultaneously, always beginning. And your sense of the world, and of the large amount of life before you, also should face in two directions. It is true that the macro-news – the news about the world – is bad.

It is also true that your news may not be bad; indeed, that you have a duty not to let it be as bad for you. Perhaps the main point of knowing a rule is to be an exception to it.

If your liberal arts education has meant anything, it has given you some notions of a critical opposition to the way things are (and are generally defined – for example, for you as women). This attitude of opposition is not justified as a strategy, as a means to an end, a way of changing the world. It is, rather, the best way of being in the world.

As individuals we are never outside of some system which bestows significance. But we can become aware that our lives consist, both really and potentially, of many systems. That we always have choices, options – and that it is a failure of imagination (or fantasy) not to perceive this. The large system of significance in which we live is called "culture." In that sense, no one is without a culture. But in a stricter sense, culture is not a given but an achievement, that we have to work at all our lives. Far from being given, culture is something we have to strive to protect against all incursions. Culture is the opposite of provinciality – the provinciality of the intellect, and the provinciality of the heart. (Far from being merely national, or local, it is properly international.) The highest culture is self-critical and makes us suspicious and critical of state power.

The liberal arts education you have received is not a luxury, as some of you may think, but a necessity – and more. For there is an intrinsic connection between a liberal arts education, by which I mean an education in the traditions and methods of "high" culture, and the very existence of liberty. Liberty means the right to diversity, to difference; the right to difficulty. It is the study of history and philosophy – it's the love of arts, in all the non-linear complexity of their traditions – that teaches us that.

Perhaps the most useful suggestion I can make on the day when most of you are ceasing to be students is that you go on being students – for the rest of your lives. Don't move to a mental slum.

If you go on being students, if you do not consider you have graduated and that your schooling is done, perhaps you can at least save yourselves and thereby make a space for others, in which they too can resist the pressures to conformity, the public drone and the inner and outer censors – such as those who tell you that you belong to a "post-feminist generation."

There are other counsels that might be useful. But if I had to restrict myself to just one, I would want to praise the virtue of obstinacy. (This is something anyone who is a writer knows a good deal about: for without obstinacy, or stubbornness, or tenacity, or pigheadedness, nothing gets written.) For whatever you want to do, if it has any quality or distinction or creativity – or, as women, if it defies sexual stereotypes – you can be sure that most people and many institutions will be devoted to encouraging you not to do it. If you want to do creative work – if you want, even though women, to lead unservile lives – there will be many obstacles. And you will have many excuses. These do not mitigate the failure. "Whatever prevents you from doing your work," a writer once observed, "has become your work."

All counsels of courage usually contain, at the end, a counsel of prudence. In Spenser's *The Faerie Queene, Book III*, there is a place called the Castle of Busyrane, on whose outer gate is written BE BOLD, and on the second gate, BE BOLD, BE BOLD, and on the inner iron door, BE NOT TOO BOLD.

This is not the advice I am giving. I would urge you to be as imprudent as you dare. BE BOLD, BE BOLD, BE BOLD. Keep on reading. (Poetry. And novels from 1700 to 1940.) Lay off the television. And remember when you hear yourself saying one day that you don't have time any more to read – or listen to music, or look at paintings, or go to the movies, or do whatever feeds your head now – then you're getting old. That means they got to you, after all.

I wish you Love. Courage. And Fantasy.

# WHEN TO TAKE MY NAME OFF THE DOOR

At the end of 1967, having spent thirty-two years creating and nurturing some of the best-known advertising campaigns and brand icons in history – Tony the Tiger, the Jolly Green Giant, and the Marlboro Man to name just three – advertising executive Leo Burnett stepped down as chairman of his hugely influential Chicago agency, Leo Burnett Company, Inc. On the day of his retirement, Burnett performed one of his last acts as chairman when he delivered an inspiring speech to his assembled employees, titled "When to Take My Name Off the Door." Its sentiments still echo around the company's offices to this day.

This agency means everything in the world to me. Especially its philosophy and its character. And so does its future. Not just next year and the year after that but ten, twenty, even fifty years from now. Especially if my name is still connected with it. Because of this connection, I got a little wound up recently and decided that the only way I could really bring home to you the things I want to say was by saying them from the heart. And under this title: When to take my name off the door.

Somewhere along the line, after I am finally off the premises, you – or your successors – may want to take my name off the premises, too. You may want to call yourselves "Twain, Rogers, Sawyer, and Finn, Inc." or "Ajax Advertising" or something. That will certainly be OK with me, if it's good for you. But let me tell you when I might demand that you take my name off the door. . . .

That will be the day when you spend more time trying to make money and less time making advertising. Our kind of advertising.

When you forget that the sheer fun of ad-making and the lift you get out of it, the creative climate of the place, should be as important as money to the very special breed of writers and artists and business professionals who compose this company of ours, and make it tick.

When you lose that restless feeling that nothing you do is ever quite good enough. When you lose your itch to do the job well for its own sake – regardless of the client, or the money, or the effort it takes.

When you lose your passion for thoroughness; your hatred of loose ends.

When you stop reaching for the manner, the overtones, the marriage of words and pictures that produces the fresh, the memorable, and the believable effect. When you stop rededicating yourselves every day to the idea that better advertising is what the Leo Burnett Company is all about.

When you are no longer what Thoreau called "a corporation with a conscience," which means to me a corporation of conscientious men and women. When you begin to compromise your integrity, which has always been the heart's blood, the very guts of this agency.

When you stoop to convenient expediency and rationalize yourselves into acts of opportunism, for the sake of a fast buck.

When you show the slightest sign of crudeness, inappropriateness, or smart-aleckness, and lose that subtle sense of the fitness of things.

When your main interest becomes a matter of size just to be big, rather than good, hard, wonderful work.

When your outlook narrows down to the number of windows, from zero to five, in the walls of your office.

When you lose your humility and become big-shot weisenheimers, a little too big for your boots.

When the apples come down to being just apples for eating, or for polishing – no longer a part of our tone, our personality.*

When you disapprove of something, and start tearing the hell out of the man who did it rather than the work itself.

When you stop building on strong and vital ideas, and start a routine production line. When you start believing that, in the interest of efficiency, a creative spirit and the urge to create can be delegated and administered, and forget that they can only be nurtured, stimulated, and inspired.

When you start giving lip service to this being a creative agency and stop really being one.

Finally, when you lose your respect for the lonely man – the man at his typewriter, or his drawing board, or behind his camera, or just scribbling notes with one of our big black pencils, or working all night on a media plan. When you forget that the lonely man – and thank God for him – has made the agency we now have, possible. When you forget he's the man who, because he is reaching harder, sometimes actually gets hold of, for a moment, one of those hot, unreachable stars.

That, boys and girls, is when I shall insist you take my name off the door.

And by golly, it will be taken off the door. Even if I have to materialize long enough some night to rub it out myself, on every one of your floors.

And before I dematerialize again, I will paint out that star-reaching symbol too. And burn all the stationery. Perhaps tear up a few ads in passing. And throw every goddamned apple down the elevator shafts. You just won't know the place, the next morning. You'll have to find another name.

But right now dear Leo Burnett Company Inc., dear Leo Burnett Company of Canada Ltd., dear Leo Burnett Company Ltd. of London, and dear D. P. Brother and Company and incorporated division of Leo Burnett Company incorporated, keep right on with what you're doing but more of it. More of it. I'm very proud of you and wish you a Merry Christmas and a big New Year, personally, unincorporated and unlimited.

← American advertising executive Leo Burnett, Chicago, IL, August 8, 1960

# LET US BE THAT SIGNPOST

Mhairi Black was just twenty years old and the youngest Member of Parliament since 1667 when, in 2015, as newly elected MP for Paisley and Renfrewshire South in Scotland, she gave this rousing "maiden speech" in the House of Commons. With the confidence of a politician many years her senior, Black took no prisoners as she sternly lambasted the Conservative government's treatment of the country's poorest, and used this most newsworthy of opportunities to highlight their increasing and unsustainable dependency on food banks. Within hours, thanks to a combination of her eloquence, age, and the extraordinary speed at which news now travels our ever-connected globe, Black's speech had been seen by millions of people.

Firstly, in my maiden speech I want to pay tribute to my predecessor Douglas Alexander. He served the constituency for many years. After all, I was only three when he was elected. But it is because of that fact that I want to thank him for all he did for the constituency and I especially want to take a moment to commend him for the dignified way that he handled himself on what must have been a very difficult election night. He did himself proud, and he did his party proud, and I wish him the best for the future.

Now, when I discovered that it was of tradition to speak about the history of your constituency in a maiden speech, I decided to do some research, despite the fact I've lived there all my life. And as one of the tail-end doing the maiden speech of my colleagues in the SNP* I've noticed that my colleagues quite often mention Rabbie Burns a lot and they all try to form this intrinsic connection between him and their own constituency and own him for themselves. I, however, feel no need to do this, for during my research I discovered a fact which trumps them all. William Wallace was born in my constituency.

* Scottish National Party

Now, my constituency has a fascinating history far beyond the Hollywood film and the historical name. From the mills of Paisley, to the industries of Johnstone, right out to the weavers in Kilbarchan, it's got a wonderful population with a cracking sense of humour and much to offer both the tourists and to those who reside there. But the truth is that within my constituency it's not all fantastic. We've watched our town centres deteriorate. We've watched our communities decline. Our unemployment level is higher than that of the UK average. One in five children in my constituency go to bed hungry at night. Paisley job centre has the third highest number of sanctions in the whole of Scotland.

Now, before I was elected I volunteered for a charitable organisation and there was a gentleman who I grew very fond of. He was one of these guys who has been battered by life in every way imaginable. You name it, he's been through it. And he used to come in to get food from this charity, and it was the only food that he had access to and it was the only meal he would get. And I sat with him and he told me about his fear of going to the job centre. He said, 'I've heard the stories, Mhairi, they try and trick you out, they'll tell you you're a liar. I'm not a liar, Mhairi, I'm not.' And I told him, 'It's OK, calm down. Go, be honest, it'll be fine.'

I then didn't see him for about two or three weeks. I did get very worried, and when he finally did come back in I said to him, 'How did you get on?'

And without saying a word he burst into tears. That grown man standing in front of a twenty-year-old crying his eyes out, because what had happened to him was the money that he would normally use to pay for his travel to come to the charity to get his food – he decided that in order to afford to get to the job centre he would save that money. Because of this, he didn't eat for five days, he didn't drink. When he was on the bus on the way to the job centre he fainted due to exhaustion and dehydration. He was fifteen minutes late for the job centre and he was sanctioned for thirteen weeks.

Now, when the chancellor spoke in his budget about fixing the roof while the sun is shining, I would have to ask: on who is the sun shining? When he spoke about benefits not supporting certain kinds of lifestyles, is that the kind of lifestyle that he was talking about?

If we go back even further when the Minister for Employment was asked to consider if there was a correlation between the number of sanctions and the rise in food bank use, she stated, and I quote, 'Food banks play an important role in local welfare provision.' Renfrewshire has the third highest use of food bank use and food bank use is going up and up. Food banks are not part of the welfare state; they are a symbol that the welfare state is failing.

Now, the Government quite rightly pays for me through taxpayers' money to be able to live in London whilst I serve my constituents. My housing is subsidised by the taxpayer. Now, the chancellor in his budget said it is not fair that families earning over £40,000 in London should have their rents paid for by other working people. But it is OK so long as you're an MP? In this budget the chancellor also abolished any housing benefit for anyone below the age of twenty-one. So we are now in the ridiculous situation whereby because I am an MP, not only am I the youngest, but I am now also the only twenty-year-old in the whole of the UK that the chancellor is prepared to help with housing. We now have one of the most uncaring, uncompromising and out of touch governments that the UK has seen since Thatcher.

It is here that I must now turn to those who I share a bench with. Now I have been in this chamber for ten weeks, and I have very deliberately stayed quiet and have listened intently to everything that has been said. I have heard multiple speeches from Labour benches standing to talk about the worrying rise of nationalism in Scotland, when in actual fact all these speeches have served to do is to demonstrate how deep the lack of understanding about Scotland is within the Labour party.

I, like so many SNP members, come from a traditional socialist Labour family and I have never been quiet in my assertion that I feel it is the Labour party that left me, not the other way about. The SNP did not triumph on a wave of nationalism; in fact nationalism has nothing to do with what's happened in Scotland. We triumphed on a wave of hope: hope that there was something different, something better to the Thatcherite neo-liberal policies that are produced from this chamber. Hope that representatives genuinely could give a voice to those who don't have one.

I don't mention this in order to pour salt into wounds which I am sure are very open and very sore for many members on these benches, both politically and personally. Colleagues, possibly friends, lost their seats. I mention it in order to hold a mirror to the face of a party that seems to have forgotten the very people they're supposed to represent, the very things they're supposed to fight for.

After hearing the Labour leader's intentions to support the changes of tax credits that the chancellor has put forward, I must make this plea through the words of one of your own and a personal hero of mine. Tony Benn once said that in politics there are weathercocks and signposts. Weathercocks will spin in whatever direction the wind of public opinion may blow them, no matter what principle they have, to compromise. And then there are signposts, signposts which stand true, and tall, and principled. And they point in a direction and they say this is the way to a better society and it is my job to convince you why. Tony Benn was right when he said the only people worth remembering in politics are signposts.

Now, yes, we will have political differences; yes, in other parliaments we may be opposing parties, but within this chamber we are not. No matter how much I may wish it, the SNP is not the sole opposition to this Government, but nor is the Labour party. It is together with all the parties on these benches that we must form an opposition, and in order to be effective we must oppose not abstain. So I reach out a genuine hand of friendship which I can only hope will be taken. Let us come together, let us be that opposition, let us be that signpost of a better society. Ultimately people are needing a voice, people are needing help. Let's give them it.

# I BELIEVE IN THE HUMAN RACE

Few sportspeople in history have made as deep an impact as Jackie Robinson, a man of immense talent who in 1947, against all odds, became the first black person to play Major League Baseball – an achievement which made waves not just in the sport of baseball, but also in the civil rights movement. But his work continued long after the end of his wildly successful baseball career, at which point Robinson remained in the public eye as he campaigned against, among other things, racial segregation.

In 1952, mid-career, Robinson eloquently described his journey in a speech that was broadcast as part of NPR's "This I Believe" series.

At the beginning of the World Series of 1947, I experienced a completely new emotion, when the National Anthem was played. This time, I thought, it was being played for me, as much as for anyone else. This is organized Major League Baseball, and I am standing here with all the others; and everything that takes place includes me.

About a year later, I went to Atlanta, Georgia, to play in an exhibition game. On the field, for the first time in Atlanta, there were Negroes and whites. Other Negroes, besides me. And I thought: what I have always believed has come to be.

And what is it that I have always believed? First, that imperfections are human. But that wherever human beings were given room to breathe and time to think, those imperfections would disappear, no matter how slowly. I do not believe that we have found or even approached perfection. That is not necessarily in the scheme of human events. Handicaps, stumbling blocks, prejudices – all of these are imperfect. Yet, they have to be reckoned with because they are in the scheme of human events.

Whatever obstacles I found made me fight all the harder. But it would have been impossible for me to fight at all, except that I was sustained by the personal and deep-rooted belief that my fight had a chance. It had a chance because it took place in a free society. Not once was I forced to face and fight an immovable object. Not once was the situation so cast-iron rigid that I had no chance at all. Free minds and human hearts were at work all around me; and so there was a probability of improvement. I look at my children now, and know that I must still prepare them to meet obstacles and prejudices.

But I can tell them, too, that they will never face some of these prejudices because other people have gone before them. And to myself I can say that, because progress is unalterable, many of today's dogmas will have vanished by the time they grow into adults. I can say to my children: there is a chance for you. No guarantee, but a chance.

And this chance has come to be, because there is nothing static with free people. There is no Middle Ages logic so strong that it can stop the human tide from flowing forward. I do not believe that every person, in every walk of life, can succeed in spite of any handicap. That would be perfection. But I do believe – and with every fiber in me – that what I was able to attain came to be because we put behind us (no matter how slowly) the dogmas of the past: to discover the truth of today; and perhaps find the greatness of tomorrow.

I believe in the human race.

I believe in the warm heart.

I believe in man's integrity.

I believe in the goodness of a free society.

And I believe that the society can remain good only as long as we are willing to fight for it – and to fight against whatever imperfections may exist.

My fight was against the barriers that kept Negroes out of baseball. This was the area where I found imperfection, and where I was best able to fight. And I fought because I knew it was not doomed to be a losing fight. It couldn't be a losing fight – not when it took place in a free society.

And in the largest sense, I believe that what I did was done for me, and that it was my faith in God that sustained me in my fight. And that what was done for me must and will be done for others.

→ An early draft of Jackie Robinson's speech

## THIS I BELIEVE ... JACK ROBINSON

I cannot ever put aside the feeling ... the belief ... that what has happened to me is based upon a fundamental implied in every document upon which our form of government is based. A free society has room for motion ... and when the hearts and minds of a free society are given space to breathe and think ... then that society will always seek and find improvement.

I do not believe that we have found perfection...I DO believe that what I as an individual do ... that what every member of our society does ... can help us attain perfection. Handicaps, stumbling blocks, prejudices ... all of these are imperfect. Obstacks If there were obstacles in MY path ... they made me fight all the harder. But my fight took place in a free society ... and that meant that I never once was forced to face an imovable object ... that never once was dogma so implacable that Ihad no chance at all. Free minds were at work...because our society is free .... and that which once was wrong, gave way to a further step toward improvment.

Each time I look at my children, I can say to them... whatever the obstacle...there's a chance for you. A chance for you to do whatever you want ... to become whatever you want to become ... and this chance exists so long as our free society exists. Here, there is nothing static ... no medieval logic that can prevent any of us from taking a forward step.

To say that every person, in every walk of life, will find success fulfillment....this I do NOT believe. But I believe with every fiber in me that what I have attained ... I attained because slowly,all of Us in this society of ours...slowly we put behind us the dogmas of the past and fight for and find the fresh, exhilarating air of

...discover the greater truth of today...and seek the greatness of tomorrow.

I believe in the human race....I believe in the warm heart... I believe in the goodness to be found in every free society. And I believe that under the American Flag, goodness, and righteousness cannot long be stifled. That injustice will wither....and that what I did was done TO me....and FOR me.  That ours IS a free society... and whax the hearts and minds of a free society are given space to
       that
breathe and think...and that when this happens, what was done for me must always be done for others.

# YOU HAVE TO GIVE THEM HOPE

The indefatigable Harvey Milk became the first openly gay elected official in the history of U.S. politics when he was elected to the San Francisco Board of Supervisors in 1977 after his fourth attempt. It was as a result of his tireless campaigning that Milk developed his best-known address, originally conceived as a stump speech in June 1977 with which to enthuse potential voters; by the time this 1978 iteration was delivered, Milk was elected and his speech perfected. Eight months later, Harvey Milk was assassinated.

My name is Harvey Milk, and I'm here to recruit you.

I've been saving this one for years. It's a political joke. I can't help it. I've got to tell it. I've never been able to talk to this many political people before, so if I tell you nothing else, you may be able to go home laughing a bit.

This ocean liner was going across the ocean, and it sank. And there was one little piece of wood floating. And three people swam to it. And they realized only one person could hold on to it. So they had a little debate about which was the person.

It so happened that the three people were the Pope, the President and Mayor Daley. The Pope said he was the titular head of one of the greatest religions of the world, and he was spiritual adviser to many, many millions. And he went on and pontificated. And they thought it was a good argument.

Then the President said he was the leader of the largest and most powerful nation of the world. What takes place in this country affects the whole world. And they thought that was a good argument.

And Mayor Daley said he was the mayor of the backbone of the United States. And what took place in Chicago affected the world. And what took place in the Archdiocese of Chicago affected Catholicism. And they thought that was a good argument.

So they did it the democratic way and voted. And Daley won seven to two.

About six months ago, Anita Bryant, in her speaking to God, said that the drought in California was because of the gay people. On November 9, the day after I got elected, it started to rain. On the day I got sworn in, we walked to City Hall. And it was kind of nice. And as soon as I said the words "I do," it started to rain again. It's been raining since then. And the people of San Francisco figure the only way to stop it is to do a recall petition. That's the local joke.

So much for that. Why are we here? Why are gay people here? And what's happening? What's happening to me is the antithesis of what you read about in the papers and what you hear about on the radio. You hear about and read about this movement to the right, that we must band together and fight back this movement to the right. And I'm here to go ahead and say that what you hear and read is what they want you to think.

Because it's not happening. The major media in this country has talked about the movement to the right, so the legislators think that there is indeed a movement to the right and that the Congress and the legislators and the City Council will start to move to the right the way the major media want them. So they keep on talking about this move to the right.

So let's look at 1977, and see if there was indeed a movement to the right. In 1977, gay people had their rights taken away from them in Miami. But you must remember that in the week before Miami and the week after that, the word "homosexual" or "gay" appeared in every single newspaper in this nation in articles both pro and con. And every radio station and every TV station and every household, for the first time in the history of the world, everybody was talking about it, good or bad.

Unless you have dialogue, unless you open the walls of dialogue, you can never reach to change people's opinion. In those two weeks, more good and bad, but more about the word "homosexual" and "gay" was written than probably in the history of mankind. Once you have dialogue starting, you know you can break down prejudice.

In 1977, we saw a dialogue start. In 1977, we saw a gay person elected in San Francisco. In 1977, we saw the state of Mississippi decriminalize marijuana. In 1977, we saw the convention of conventions in Houston. And I want to know where the movement to the right was happening.

What that is, is a record of what happened last year. What we must do is make sure that 1978 continues the movement that is really happening and that the media don't want you to know about. That is the movement to the left. It is up to CDC to put the pressures on Sacramento–not just to bring flowers to Sacramento–but to break down the walls and the barriers so the movement to the left continues and progress continues in the nation.

We have before us coming up several issues we must speak out on. Probably the most important issue outside the Briggs[*] – which we will come to – but we do know what will take place this June. We know that there's an issue on the ballot called Jarvis-Gann.[†] We hear the taxpayers talk about it on both sides. But what you don't hear is that it's probably the most racist issue on the ballot in a long time.

In the city and the county of San Francisco, if it passes and we indeed have to lay off people, who will they be? The last in, not the first in, and who are the last in but the minorities? Jarvis-Gann is a racist issue. We must address that issue. We must not talk away from it. We must not allow them to talk about the money it's going to save, because look at who's going to save the money and look at who's going to get hurt.

We also have another issue that we have started in some of the north counties. And I hope in some of the south counties it continues. In San

[*] The Briggs Initiative – or California Proposition 6 – was a drive led by conservative legislator John Briggs to ban gay and lesbian people from working in California's public schools.

[†] Howard Jarvis and Paul Gann were the strongest advocates of California Proposition 13, a controversial initiative seeking to limit property taxation, which would also reduce local government revenue.

Francisco elections we're asking – at least we hope to ask – that the U.S. government put pressure on the closing of the South African consulate. That must happen.

There is a major difference between an embassy in Washington, which is a diplomatic bureau, and a consulate in major cities. A consulate is there for one reason only, to promote business, economic gains, tourism, investment. And every time you have a business going to South Africa, you're promoting a regime that's offensive.

In the city of San Francisco, if every one of 51 percent of that city were to go to South Africa, they would be treated as second-class citizens. That is an offense to the people of San Francisco. And I hope all my colleagues up there will take every step we can to close down that consulate and hope that people in other parts of the state follow us in that lead.

The battles must be started someplace. And CDC is a great place to start the battles.‡ I know we are pressed for time, so I'm going to cover just one more little point. That is, to understand why it's important that gay people run for office, and that gay people get elected. I know there are many people in this room who are gay who are running for a central committee. And I encourage you.

There's a major reason why. If my non-gay friends and supporters in this room understand it, they'll probably understand why I've run so often before I finally made it. You see right now, there's a controversy going on in this convention about the gay governor. Is he speaking out enough? Is he strong enough for gay rights? And there is controversy. And for us to say that there is not would be foolish. Some people are satisfied. And some people are not.

You see there is a major difference – and it remains a vital difference – between a friend and a gay person, a friend in office and a gay person in office. Gay people have been slandered nationwide. We've been tarred and we've been brushed with the picture of pornography. In Dade County, we were accused of child molestation. It is not enough anymore just to have friends represent us, no matter how good that friend may be.

The black community made up its mind to that a long time ago. The myths against blacks can only be dispelled by electing black leaders so the black community could be judged by its leaders and not by the myths or the black criminals. The Spanish community must not be judged by Latin criminals or myths. The Asian community must not be judged by Asian criminals or myths. The Italian community must not be judged by the Mafia or myths.

And the time has come when the gay community must not be judged for our criminals and our myths. Like every other group, we must be judged by our leaders and by those who are themselves gay, those who are visible. For invisible, we remain in limbo. A myth. A person with no parents, no brothers, no sisters, no friends who are straight, no important positions in employment.

‡ This address was given at the gay caucus of the California Democratic Council.

← Harvey Milk addressing the crowd at the 1978 San Francisco Gay Freedom Day Parade

A tenth of the nation's supposedly composed of stereotypes and would-be seducers of children. And no offense meant to those stereotypes, but today the black community is not judged by its friends but by its black legislators and leaders. And we must give people the chance to judge us by our leaders and legislators.

A gay person in office can set a tone, can command respect, not only from the larger community, but from the young people in our own community who need both examples and hope. The first gay people we elect must be strong. They must not be content to sit in the back of the bus. They must not be content to accept pabulum. They must be above wheeling and dealing. They must be, for the good of all of us, independent, unbought.

The anger and the frustrations that some of us feel is because we are misunderstood. And friends can't feel that anger and frustration. They can sense it in us, but they can't feel it. Because a friend has never gone through what is known as "coming out." I will never forget what it was like coming out and having nobody to look up toward.

I remember the lack of hope, and our friends can't fulfill it. I can't forget the looks on faces of people who have lost hope, be they gay, be they seniors, be they blacks looking for an almost impossible job, be they Latins trying to explain their problems and aspirations in a tongue that's foreign to them. I personally will never forget that people are more important than buildings.

I use the word "I" because I am proud. I stand here tonight in front of my gay sisters, brothers and friends, because I'm proud of you. I think it's time that we have many legislators who are gay and proud of that fact and do not have to remain in the closet. I think a gay person, upfront, will not walk away from a responsibility and be afraid of being tossed out of office.

§ In 1977, Anita Bryant ran a campaign to repeal a local ordinance in Dade County, Florida, which prohibited discrimination on the basis of sexual orientation.

After Dade County,§ I walked among the angry and frustrated night after night. And I looked at their faces. And in San Francisco, three days before Gay Pride Day, a person was killed just because he was gay. And that night I walked among the sad and the frustrated at City Hall in San Francisco, and later that night, as they lit candles on Castro Street and stood in silence, reaching out for some symbolic thing that would give them hope. These were strong people whose faces I knew from the shop, the streets, meetings, and people who I never saw before but I knew. They were strong, but even they needed hope.

And the young gay people in the Altoona, Pennsylvanias, and the Richmond, Minnesotas, who are coming out and hear Anita Bryant on television and her story. The only thing they have to look forward to is hope. And you have to give them hope. Hope for a better world, hope for a better tomorrow, hope for a better place to come to if the pressures at home are too great. Hope that all will be all right. Without hope, not only are the gays, but the blacks, the seniors, the handicapped, the "us-es." The "us-es" will give up.

And if you help elect the Central Committee and other offices, more gay people – that gives a green light to all who feel disenfranchised, a green light to move forward. It means hope to a nation that has given up, because if a gay person makes it, the doors are open to everyone. So if there's a message I have to give, it is that I found one overriding thing about my personal election. It's the fact that if a gay person can be elected, it's a green light. And you and you and you – you have to give people hope. Thank you very much.

# THE MORALITY OF BIRTH CONTROL

In October 1916, New York–born women's rights activist Margaret Sanger opened the first family-planning clinic in the United States. Just days later she was arrested for the crime of handing out contraceptives. This would not be her last brush with the law. At New York's Town Hall on November 13, 1921, shortly before she was to give a speech to attendees of the first American Birth Control Conference – which she had organized – Sanger was again arrested amidst a police raid of the venue. Five days later, never one to admit defeat, she simply delivered her speech in a different space, voicing her support of both birth control and the then fashionable – though now highly controversial – practice of eugenics. Her popularity soared. In 1942, the American Birth Control League was renamed Planned Parenthood.

The meeting tonight is a postponement of one which was to have taken place at the Town Hall last Sunday evening. It was to be a culmination of a three-day conference, two of which were held at the Hotel Plaza, in discussing the birth control subject in its various and manifold aspects.

The one issue upon which there seems to be most uncertainty and disagreement exists in the moral side of the subject of birth control. It seemed only natural for us to call together scientists, educators, members of the medical profession and the theologians of all denominations to ask their opinion upon this uncertain and important phase of the controversy. Letters were sent to the most eminent men and women in the world. We asked in this letter, the following questions:

1. Is overpopulation a menace to the peace of the world?
2. Would the legal dissemination of scientific birth control information through the medium of clinics by the medical profession be the most logical method of checking the problem of overpopulation?
3. Would knowledge of birth control change the moral attitude of men and women toward the marriage bond or lower the moral standards of the youth of the country?
4. Do you believe that knowledge which enables parents to limit the families will make for human happiness, and raise the moral, social and intellectual standards of population?

We sent such a letter not only to those who, we thought, might agree with us, but we sent it also to our known opponents. Most of these people answered. Everyone who answered did so with sincerity and courtesy, with the exception of one group whose reply to this important question as demonstrated at the Town Hall last Sunday evening was a disgrace to liberty-loving people, and to all traditions we hold dear in the United States. I believed that the discussion of the moral issue was one which did not solely belong to theologians and to scientists, but belonged to the people. And because I believed that the people of this country may and can discuss this subject with dignity and with intelligence I desired to bring them together, and to discuss it in the open.

When one speaks of morals, one refers to human conduct. This implies action of many kinds, which in turn depends upon the mind and the brain. So that in speaking of morals one must remember that there is a direct connection between morality and brain development. Conduct is said to be action in pursuit of ends, and if this is so, then we must hold that irresponsibility and recklessness in our action is immoral, while responsibility and forethought put into action for the benefit of the individual and the race becomes in the highest sense the finest kind of morality.

We know that every advance that woman has made in the last half century has been made with opposition, all of which has been based upon the grounds of immorality. When women fought for higher education, it was said that this would cause her to become immoral and she would lose her place in the sanctity of the home. When women asked for the franchise it was said that this would lower her standard of morals, that it was not fit that she should meet with and mix with the members of the opposite sex, but we notice that there was no objection to her meeting with the same members of the opposite sex when she went to church.

The church has ever opposed the progress of woman on the ground that her freedom would lead to immorality. We ask the church to have more confidence in women. We ask the opponents of this movement to reverse the methods of the church, which aims to keep women moral by keeping them in fear and in ignorance, and to inculcate into them a higher and truer morality based upon knowledge. And ours is the morality of knowledge. If we cannot trust woman with the knowledge of her own body, then I claim that two thousand years of Christian teaching has proved to be a failure.

We stand on the principle that birth control should be available to every adult man and woman. We believe that every adult man and woman should be taught the responsibility and the right use of knowledge. We claim that woman should have the right over her own body and to say if she shall or if she shall not be a mother, as she sees fit. We further claim that the first right of a child is to be desired. While the second right is that it should be conceived in love, and the third, that it should have a heritage of sound health.

Upon these principles the birth control movement in America stands. When it comes to discussing the methods of birth control, that is far more difficult. There are laws in this country which forbid the imparting of practical information to the mothers of the land. We claim that every mother in this country, either sick or well, has the right to the best, the safest, the most scientific information. This information should be disseminated directly to

← The Sanger Clinic,
46 Amboy Street, Brooklyn,
1916 – the first birth control
clinic in the United States

the mothers through clinics by members of the medical profession, registered nurses and registered midwives.

Our first step is to have the backing of the medical profession so that our laws may be changed, so that motherhood may be the function of dignity and choice, rather than one of ignorance and chance. Conscious control of offspring is now becoming the ideal and the custom in all civilized countries. Those who oppose it claim that however desirable it may be on economic or social grounds, it may be abused and the morals of the youth of the country may be lowered. Such people should be reminded that there are two points to be considered. First, that such control is the inevitable advance in civilization. Every civilization involves an increasing forethought for others, even for those yet unborn. The reckless abandonment of the impulse of the moment and the careless regard for the consequences is not morality. The selfish gratification of temporary desire at the expense of suffering to lives that will come may seem very beautiful to some, but it is not our conception of civilization, nor is it our concept of morality.

In the second place, it is not only inevitable, but it is right to control the size of the family for by this control and adjustment we can raise the level and the standards of the human race. While Nature's way of reducing her numbers is controlled by disease, famine and war, primitive man has achieved the same results by infanticide, exposure of infants, the abandonment of children, and by abortion. But such ways of controlling population are no longer possible for us. We have attained high standards of life, and along the lines of science must we conduct such control. We must begin farther back and control the beginnings of life. We must control conception. This is a better method, it is a more civilized method, for it involves not only greater forethought for others, but finally a higher sanction for the value of life itself.

Society is divided into three groups. Those intelligent and wealthy members of the upper classes who have obtained knowledge of birth control and exercise it in regulating the size of their families. They have already benefited by this knowledge, and are today considered the most respectable and moral members of the community. They have only children when they desire, and all society points to them as types that should perpetuate their kind.

The second group is equally intelligent and responsible. They desire to control the size of their families, but are unable to obtain knowledge or to put such available knowledge into practice.

The third are those irresponsible and reckless ones having little regard for the consequence of their acts, or whose religious scruples prevent their exercising control over their numbers. Many of this group are diseased, feeble-minded, and are of the pauper element dependent entirely upon the normal and fit members of society for their support. There is no doubt in the minds of all thinking people that the procreation of this group should be stopped. For if they are not able to support and care for themselves, they should certainly not be allowed to bring offspring into this world for others to look after. We do not believe that filling the earth with misery, poverty and disease is moral. And it is our desire and intention to carry on our crusade until the perpetuation of such conditions has ceased.

We desire to stop at its source the disease, poverty and feeble-mindedness and insanity which exist today, for these lower the standards of civilization and make for race deterioration. We know that the masses of people are growing wiser and are using their own minds to decide their individual conduct. The more people of this kind we have, the less immorality shall exist. For the more responsible people grow, the higher do they and shall they attain real morality.

UNITED NATIONS CONFERENCE ON
ENVIRONMENT AND DEVELOPMENT

Rio de Janeiro 3–14 June 1992

# WE ARE ALL IN THIS TOGETHER

Born in Vancouver in 1979, Severn Cullis-Suzuki was just nine years of age when she co-founded the Environmental Children's Organization in an effort to spread the word among young people on the many environmental issues facing the world. Her most impressive achievement came in 1992 when she and a handful of fellow young activists raised enough money to travel to Brazil to attend the United Nations Earth Summit – a global conference attended by representatives from 172 countries. The delegates surely could not have imagined that the most profound speech of the event would come from a twelve-year-old girl intent on protecting the planet for the sake of her generation.

Hello, I'm Severn Suzuki speaking for ECO – the Environmental Children's Organization.

We are a group of twelve- and thirteen-year-olds trying to make a difference: Vanessa Suttie, Morgan Geisler, Michelle Quigg and me. We've raised all the money to come here ourselves, to come 5,000 miles to tell you adults you must change your ways. Coming up here today, I have no hidden agenda. I am fighting for my future.

Losing my future is not like losing an election or a few points on the stock market. I am here to speak for all generations to come.

I am here to speak on behalf of the starving children around the world whose cries go unheard.

I am here to speak for the countless animals dying across this planet because they have nowhere left to go.

I am afraid to go out in the sun now because of the holes in the ozone. I am afraid to breathe the air because I don't know what chemicals are in it.

I used to go fishing in Vancouver, my home, with my dad, until just a few years ago we found the fish full of cancers. And now we hear of animals and plants going extinct every day – vanishing forever.

In my life, I have dreamt of seeing the great herds of wild animals, jungles and rainforests full of birds and butterflies, but now I wonder if they will even exist for my children to see.

Did you have to worry about these little things when you were my age?

All this is happening before our eyes and yet we act as if we have all the time we want and all the solutions. I'm only a child and I don't have all the solutions, but I want you to realise, neither do you!

You don't know how to fix the holes in our ozone layer.

You don't know how to bring salmon back up a dead stream.

You don't know how to bring back an animal now extinct.

And you can't bring back the forests that once grew where there is now desert.

← The United Nations Earth Summit in Rio de Janeiro, Brazil, June 2, 1992

If you don't know how to fix it, please stop breaking it!

Here, you may be delegates of your governments, business people, organisers, reporters or politicians – but really you are mothers and fathers, sisters and brothers, aunts and uncles – and all of you are someone's child.

I'm only a child yet I know we are all part of a family, 5 billion strong, in fact, 30 million species strong, and borders and governments will never change that.

I'm only a child yet I know we are all in this together and should act as one single world towards one single goal.

In my anger, I am not blind, and in my fear, I am not afraid of telling the world how I feel.

In my country, we make so much waste, we buy and throw away, buy and throw away, and yet northern countries will not share with the needy. Even when we have more than enough, we are afraid to share, we are afraid to let go of some of our wealth.

In Canada, we live the privileged life, with plenty of food, water and shelter – we have watches, bicycles, computers and television sets – the list could go on for two days.

Two days ago here in Brazil, we were shocked when we spent some time with some children living on the streets. This is what one child told us: 'I wish I was rich and if I were, I would give all the street children food, clothes, medicine, shelter and love and affection.'

If a child on the street who has nothing is willing to share, why are we who have everything still so greedy?

I can't stop thinking that these are children my own age, that it makes a tremendous difference where you are born, that I could be one of those children living in the favelas of Rio; I could be a child starving in Somalia; a victim of war in the Middle East or a beggar in India.

I'm only a child yet I know if all the money spent on war was spent on ending poverty and finding environmental answers and finding treaties, what a wonderful place this earth would be!

At school, even in kindergarten, you teach us how to behave in the world. You teach us:

Not to fight with others,

To work things out,

To respect others,

To clean up our mess,

Not to hurt other creatures,

To share – not be greedy.

Then why do you go out and do the things you tell us not to do?

Do not forget why you're attending these conferences, who you're doing this for – we are your own children. You are deciding what kind of world we are growing up in. Parents should be able to comfort their children by saying 'everything's going to be all right', 'we're doing the best we can' and 'it's not the end of the world'.

But I don't think you can say that to us any more. Are we even on your list of priorities? My dad always says, 'You are what you do, not what you say.'

Well, what you do makes me cry at night. You grown-ups say you love us. But I challenge you, please make your actions reflect your words. Thank you.

# BE YE NOT AFRAID

It was on August 19, 2013, that gay marriage finally became legal in New Zealand, two months after the Marriage (Definition of Marriage) Amendment Bill was passed in the New Zealand House of Representatives and a long twelve years after the Netherlands became the first nation to allow two people of the same sex to marry. Sadly, even in 2013, not everyone supported such a development and on that momentous day in April, having recently been contacted by various opponents of the bill, Member of Parliament Maurice Williamson gave a speech that was soon watched and applauded by millions online.

Sir, I want to first of all congratulate Louisa Wall for this bill, and I want to say, sir, that the good news about the years in this parliament is you learn to deflect all of the dreadful sort of fire and brimstone accusations that are going to happen, sir.

I've had a reverend in my local electorate call the Gay Onslaught will start the day after this bill is passed. Sir, we're really struggling to know what the Gay Onslaught will look like. We don't know if it will come down the Pakuranga Highway as a series of troops, or whether it will be a gas that flows in over the electorate and blocks us all in.

I also, sir, had a Catholic priest tell me that I was supporting an unnatural act. I found that quite interesting coming from someone who has taken an oath of celibacy for his whole life. Celibacy – OK, we'll go with celibacy. I haven't done it, so I don't know what it's about.

I also had a letter telling me I would burn in the fires of Hell for eternity, and that was a bad mistake, because I've got a degree in physics. I used the thermodynamic laws of physics. I put in my body weight and my humidity and so on. I assumed the furnace to be at 5,000 degrees, and I will last for just on 2.1 seconds. It's hardly eternity – what do you think?

And some more disgusting claims about what adoption would be. Well, sir, I've got three fantastic adopted kids. I know how good adoption is and I found some of it just disgraceful. I found some of the bullying tactics really evil. And, sir, I gave up being scared of bullies when I was at primary school.

However, a huge amount of the opposition was from moderates; from people who were concerned, who were seriously worried what this might do to the fabric of our society. I respect their concern. I respect their worry. They were worried about what it may do to their families and so on.

Let me repeat to them now, sir. All we are doing with this bill is allowing two people who love each other to have that love recognised by way of marriage. That is all we are doing. We are not declaring nuclear war on a foreign state; we are not bringing a virus in that could wipe out our agriculture sector forever.

We are allowing two people who love each other to have that recognised, and I can't see what's wrong with that for love nor money, sir. I just cannot. I cannot understand why someone would be opposed. I understand why people don't like what it is that others do – that's fine, we're all in that category.

But I give a promise to those people who are opposed to this bill, right now. I give you a watertight guaranteed promise: the sun will still rise tomorrow. Your teenage daughter will still argue back with you as if she knows everything. Your mortgage will not grow. You will not have skin diseases or rashes or toads in your bed, sir. The world will just carry on.

So don't make this into a big deal – this is fantastic for the people it affects, but for the rest of us, life will go on. And finally can I say, sir, one of the messages I had was that this bill was the cause of our drought. This bill was the cause of our drought!

Well, if any of you follow my Twitter account, you will see that in the Pakuranga electorate this morning it was pouring with rain – we had the most enormous big gay rainbow across my electorate. It has to be a sign, sir. It has to be a sign; if you're a believer, it's certainly a sign.

And can I finish for all those who are concerned about this with a quote from the Bible. It's Deuteronomy – I thought Deuteronomy was a cat out of *Cats*, but never mind – it's Deuteronomy, Chapter 1, Verse 29 . . .

'Be ye not afraid.'

# SPEECH CANNOT CONTAIN OUR LOVE

Born in 1833, Robert G. Ingersoll began practicing law at the age of twenty-four and by 1866, having just served in the Civil War, he was appointed Attorney General of Illinois. But it is for his countless memorable speeches that he is widely remembered, some of which lasted for hours. In Washington one June afternoon of 1879, a particularly powerful example was given by Ingersoll: a eulogy, delivered at the funeral of his dear brother, Ebon C. Ingersoll. Such was its beauty, it was printed in the *New York Tribune* the following day.

My friends, I am going to do that which the dead oft promised he would do for me.

The loved and loving brother, husband, father, friend, died where manhood's morning almost touches noon, and while the shadows still were falling toward the west.

He had not passed on life's highway the stone that marks the highest point, but, being weary for a moment, lay down by the wayside, and, using his burden for a pillow, fell into that dreamless sleep that kisses down his eyelids still. While yet in love with life and raptured with the world, he passed to silence and pathetic dust.

Yet, after all, it may be best, just in the happiest, sunniest hour of all the voyage, while eager winds are kissing every sail, to dash against the unseen rock, and in an instant hear the billows roar above a sunken ship. For, whether in mid-sea or 'mong the breakers of the farther shore, a wreck at last must mark the end of each and all. And every life, no matter if its every hour is rich with love and every moment jeweled with a joy, will, at its close, become a tragedy as sad and deep and dark as can be woven of the warp and woof of mystery and death.

This brave and tender man in every storm of life was oak and rock, but in the sunshine he was vine and flower. He was the friend of all heroic souls. He climbed the heights and left all superstitions far below, while on his forehead fell the golden dawning of the grander day.

He loved the beautiful, and was with color, form, and music touched to tears. He sided with the weak, and with a willing hand gave alms; with loyal heart and with purest hands he faithfully discharged all public trusts.

He was a worshiper of liberty, a friend of the oppressed. A thousand times I have heard him quote these words: "For justice all place a temple, and all seasons, summer." He believed that happiness was the only good, reason the only torch, justice the only worship, humanity the only religion, and love the only priest. He added to the sum of human joy; and were everyone to whom he did some loving service to bring a blossom to his grave, he would sleep tonight beneath a wilderness of flowers.

Life is a narrow vale between the cold and barren peaks of two eternities. We strive in vain to look beyond the heights. We cry aloud, and the only answer is the echo of our wailing cry. From the voiceless lips of the unreplying dead there comes no word; but in the night of death hope sees a star, and listening love can hear the rustle of a wing.

He who sleeps here, when dying, mistaking the approach of death for the return of health, whispered with his last breath: "I am better now." Let us believe, in spite of doubts and dogmas, and tears and fears, that these dear words are true of all the countless dead.

And now to you who have been chosen, from among the many men he loved, to do the last sad office for the dead, we give his sacred dust. Speech cannot contain our love.

There was, there is, no greater, stronger, manlier man.

# LOOK AT THE VIEW

In 1999, Pulitzer Prize–winning columnist and author Anna Quindlen was asked to deliver a commencement speech to the graduating students of Villanova University in Pennsylvania – an invitation she was honored to accept. Some time later, with her speech already drafted, Quindlen faced a wall of resistance from a group of students whose politics were at such odds with hers –

Quindlen is a longtime supporter of women's reproductive rights – that they didn't want her to speak. And so she didn't. Instead, Quindlen sent a copy of the speech to an interested student, who then circulated her words to all and sundry. Online ovations followed, as did a best-selling book based on the commencement address that never was.

It's a great honor for me to be the third member of my family to receive an honorary doctorate from this great university. It's an honor to follow my great-uncle Jim, who was a gifted physician, and my uncle Jack, who is a remarkable businessman. Both of them could have told you something important about their professions, about medicine or commerce.

I have no specialized field of interest or expertise, which puts me at a disadvantage, talking to you today. I'm a novelist. My work is human nature. Real life is all I know. Don't ever confuse the two, your life and your work. The second is only part of the first.

Don't ever forget what a friend once wrote Senator Paul Tsongas when the senator decided not to run for reelection because he'd been diagnosed with cancer: "No man ever said on his deathbed, 'I wish I had spent more time in the office.'" Don't ever forget the words my father sent me on a postcard last year: "If you win the rat race, you're still a rat." Or what John Lennon wrote before he was gunned down in the driveway of the Dakota: "Life is what happens while you are busy making other plans."

You walk out of here this afternoon with only one thing that no one else has. There will be hundreds of people out there with your same degree; there will be thousands of people doing what you want to do for a living. But you will be the only person alive who has sole custody of your life. Your particular life. Your entire life. Not just your life at a desk, or your life on a bus, or in a car, or at the computer. Not just the life of your minds, but the life of your heart. Not just your bank account, but your soul.

People don't talk about the soul very much anymore. It's so much easier to write a résumé than to craft a spirit. But a résumé is a cold comfort on a winter night, or when you're sad, or broke, or lonely, or when you've gotten back the test results and they're not so good.

Here is my résumé: I am a good mother to three children. I have tried never to let my profession stand in the way of being a good parent. I no longer consider myself the center of the universe. I show up. I listen, I try to laugh.

→ Anna Quindlen, 1990s, photographed by Frank Capri

I am a good friend to my husband. I have tried to make marriage vows mean what they say. I show up. I listen. I try to laugh. I am a good friend to my friends, and they to me. Without them, there would be nothing to say to you today, because I would be a cardboard cutout. But I call them on the phone, and I meet them for lunch. I show up. I listen. I try to laugh.

I would be rotten, or at best mediocre at my job, if those other things were not true. You cannot be really first rate at your work if your work is all you are.

So here is what I wanted to tell you today:

Get a life. A real life, not a manic pursuit of the next promotion, the bigger paycheck, the larger house. Do you think you'd care so very much about those things if you blew an aneurysm one afternoon, or found a lump in your breast? Get a life in which you notice the smell of saltwater pushing itself on a breeze over Seaside Heights, a life in which you stop and watch how a red-tailed hawk circles over the water gap or the way a baby scowls with concentration when she tries to pick up a Cheerio with her thumb and first finger.

Get a life in which you are not alone. Find people you love, and who love you. And remember that love is not leisure, it is work. Each time you look at your diploma, remember that you are still a student, still learning how to best treasure your connection to others. Pick up the phone. Send an e-mail. Write a letter. Kiss your mom. Hug your dad. Get a life in which you are generous.

Look around at the azaleas in the suburban neighborhood where you grew up; look at a full moon hanging silver in a black, black sky on a cold night.

And realize that life is the best thing ever, and that you have no business taking it for granted. Care so deeply about its goodness that you want to spread it around. Once in a while take money you would have spent on beers and give it to charity. Work in a soup kitchen. Be a big brother or sister.

All of you want to do well. But if you do not do good, too, then doing well will never be enough. It is so easy to waste our lives: our days, our hours, our minutes. It is so easy to take for granted the color of the azaleas, the sheen of the limestone on Fifth Avenue, the color of our kid's eyes, the way the melody in a symphony rises and falls and disappears and rises again. It is so easy to exist instead of live. I learned to live many years ago.

Something really, really bad happened to me, something that changed my life in ways that, if I had my druthers, it would never have been changed at all. And what I learned from it is what, today, seems to be the hardest lesson of all. I learned to love the journey, not the destination. I learned that it is not a dress rehearsal, and that today is the only guarantee you get. I learned to look at all the good in the world and to try to give some of it back because I believed in it completely and utterly. And I tried to do that, in part, by telling others what I had learned. By telling them this:

Consider the lilies of the field. Look at the fuzz on a baby's ear. Read in the backyard with the sun on your face. Learn to be happy. And think of life as a terminal illness because if you do you will live it with joy and passion, as it ought to be lived.

Well, you can learn all those things, out there, if you get a life, a full life, a professional life, yes, but another life, too, a life of love and laughs and a connection to other human beings. Just keep your eyes and ears open. Here you could learn in the classroom. There the classroom is everywhere. The exam comes at the very end. No man ever said on his deathbed, "I wish I had spent more time at the office." I found one of my best teachers on the boardwalk at Coney Island maybe fifteen years ago. It was December, and I was doing a story about how the homeless survive in the winter months.

He and I sat on the edge of the wooden supports, dangling our feet over the side, and he told me about his schedule: panhandling the boulevard when the summer crowds were gone, sleeping in a church when the temperature went below freezing, hiding from the police amidst the Tilt-a-Whirl and the Cyclone and some of the other seasonal rides. But he told me that most of the time he stayed on the boardwalk, facing the water, just the way we were sitting now, even when it got cold and he had to wear his newspapers after he read them.

And I asked him why. Why didn't he go to one of the shelters? Why didn't he check himself into the hospital for detox? And he just stared out at the ocean and said, "Look at the view, young lady. Look at the view."

And every day, in some little way, I try to do what he said. I try to look at the view. And that's the last thing I have to tell you today, words of wisdom from a man with not a dime in his pocket, no place to go, nowhere to be. Look at the view. You'll never be disappointed.

# COURAGE

Despite having produced dozens of successful novels and plays during his long and illustrious career, J. M. Barrie is to most people simply the creator of Peter Pan, a character so woven into the fabric of youth that to imagine one's early years without him seems impossible.

In 1922, as the world was still recovering from the losses of the First World War, Barrie unveiled another talent when he delivered his inaugural rectorial address to the students of St. Andrews University in Fife, Scotland, on the subject of courage.

You have had many rectors here in St Andrews who will continue in bloom long after the lowly ones, such as I am, are dead and rotten and forgotten. They are the roses in December; you remember someone said that God gave us memory so that we might have roses in December. But I do not envy the great ones. In my experience – and you may find in the end it is yours also – the people I have cared for most and who have seemed most worth caring for – my December roses – have been very simple folk. Yet I wish that for this hour I could swell into someone of importance, so as to do you credit. I suppose you had a melting for me because I was hewn out of one of your own quarries, walked similar academic groves, and have trudged the road on which you will soon set forth. I would that I could put into your hands a staff for that somewhat bloody march, for though there is much about myself that I conceal from other people, to help you I would expose every cranny of my mind.

But, alas, when the hour strikes for the rector to answer to his call he is unable to become the undergraduate he used to be, and so the only door into you is closed. We, your elders, are much more interested in you than you are in us. We are not really important to you. I have utterly forgotten the address of the rector of my time, and even who he was, but I recall vividly climbing up a statue to tie his colours round its neck and being hurled therefrom with contumely. We remember the important things. I cannot provide you with that staff for your journey; but perhaps I can tell you a little about it, how to use it and lose it and find it again, and cling to it more than ever. You shall cut it – so it is ordained – every one of you for himself, and its name is Courage. You must excuse me if I talk a good deal about courage to you today. There is nothing else much worth speaking about to undergraduates or graduates or white-haired men and women. It is the lovely virtue – the rib of Himself that God sent down to His children.

My special difficulty is that though you have had literary rectors here before, they were the big guns, the historians, the philosophers; you have had none, I think, who followed my more humble branch, which may be described as playing hide and seek with angels. My puppets seem more real to me than myself, and I could get on much more swingingly if I made one of them deliver this address. It is M'Connachie who has brought me to this pass. M'Connachie, I should explain, as I have undertaken to open the innermost doors, is the name I give to the unruly half of myself: the writing half. We are complement and supplement. I am the half that is dour and practical and canny, he is the fanciful half; my desire is to be the family solicitor, standing firm on my hearthrug among the harsh realities of the office furniture; while he prefers to fly around on one wing. I should not mind him doing that, but he drags me with him. I have sworn that M'Connachie shall not interfere with this address today; but there is no telling. I might have done things worthwhile if it had not been for M'Connachie, and my first piece of advice to you at any rate shall be sound: don't copy me. A good subject for a rectorial address would be the mess the rector himself has made of life. I merely cast this forth as a suggestion, and leave the working of it out to my successor. I do not think it has been used yet.

My own theme is Courage, as you should use it in the great fight that seems to me to be coming between youth and their betters; by youth, meaning, of course, you, and by your betters us. I want you to take up this position: that youth have for too long left exclusively in our hands the decisions in national matters that are more vital to them than to us. Things about the next war, for instance, and why the last one ever had a beginning. I use the word 'fight' because it must, I think, begin with a challenge; but the aim is the reverse of antagonism, it is partnership. I want you to hold that the time has arrived for youth to demand that partnership, and to demand it courageously. That to gain courage is what you came to St Andrews for. With some alarums and excursions into college life. That is what I propose, but, of course, the issue lies with M'Connachie.

Your betters had no share in the immediate cause of the war; we know what nation has that blot to wipe out; but for fifty years or so we heeded not the rumblings of the distant drum, I do not mean by lack of military preparations; and when war did come we told youth, who had to get us out of it, tall tales of what it really is and of the clover beds to which it leads.

We were not meaning to deceive, most of us were as honourable and as ignorant as the youth themselves; but that does not acquit us of failings such as stupidity and jealousy, the two black spots in human nature which, more than love of money, are at the root of all evil. If you prefer to leave things as they are we shall probably fail you again. Do not be too sure that we have learned our lesson, and are not at this very moment doddering down some brimstone path.

I am far from implying that even worse things than war may not come to a State. There are circumstances in which nothing can so well become a land, as I think this land proved when the late war did break out and there was but one thing to do. There is a form of anaemia that is more rotting than even an unjust war. The end will indeed have come to our courage and to us when we are afraid in dire mischance to refer the final appeal to the arbitrament of arms. I suppose all the lusty of our race, alive and dead, join hands on that.

> And he is dead who will not fight;
> And who dies fighting has increase.

But if you must be in the struggle, the more reason you should know why, before it begins, and have a say in the decision whether it is to begin. The youth who went to the war had no such knowledge, no such say; I am sure the survivors, of whom there must be a number here today, want you to be wiser than they were, and are certainly determined to be wiser next time themselves. If you are to get that partnership, which, once gained, is to be for mutual benefit, it will be, I should say, by banding yourselves with these men, not defiantly but firmly, not for selfish ends but for your country's good. In the meantime they have one bulwark; they have a general who is befriending them as I think never, after the fighting was over, has a general befriended his men before. Perhaps the seemly thing would be for us, their betters, to elect one of these young survivors of the carnage to be our rector. He ought now to know a few things about war that are worth our hearing. If his theme were the rector's favourite, diligence, I should be afraid of his advising a great many of us to be diligent in sitting still and doing no more harm.

Of course he would put it more suavely than that, though it is not, I think, by gentleness that you will get your rights; we are dogged ones at sticking to what we have got, and so will you be at our age. But avoid calling us ugly names; we may be stubborn and we may be blunderers, but we love you more than aught else in the world, and once you have won your partnership we shall all be welcoming you. I urge you not to use ugly names about anyone. In the war it was not the fighting men who were distinguished for abuse; as has been well said, 'Hell hath no fury like a non-combatant.' Never ascribe to an opponent motives meaner than your own. There may be students here today who have decided this session to go in for immortality, and would like to know of an easy way of accomplishing it. That is a way, but not so easy as you think. Go through life without ever ascribing to your opponents' motives meaner than your own. Nothing so lowers the moral currency; give it up, and be great.

Another sure way to fame is to know what you mean. It is a solemn thought that almost no one – if he is truly eminent – knows what he means. Look at the great ones of the earth, the politicians. We do not discuss what they say, but what they may have meant when they said it. In 1922 we are all wondering, and so are they, what they meant in 1914 and afterwards. They are publishing books trying to find out; the men of action as well as the men of words. There are exceptions. It is not that our statesmen are 'sugared mouths with minds therefrae'; many of them are the best men we have got, upright and anxious, nothing cheaper than to miscall them. The explanation seems just to be that it is so difficult to know what you mean, especially when you have become a swell. No longer apparently can you deal in 'russet yeas and honest kersey noes'; gone for ever is simplicity, which is as beautiful as the divine plain face of Lamb's Miss Kelly.* Doubts breed suspicions, a dangerous air. Without suspicion there might have been no war. When you are called to Downing Street to discuss what you want of your betters with the Prime Minister he won't be suspicious, not as far as you can see; but remember the atmosphere of generations you are in, and when he passes you the toast-rack say to yourselves, if you would be in the mode, 'Now, I wonder what he means by that.'

Even without striking out in the way I suggest, you are already disturbing your betters considerably. I sometimes talk this over with M'Connachie, with whom, as you may guess, circumstances compel me to pass a good deal of my time. In our talks we agree that we, your betters, constantly find you forgetting that we are your betters. Your answer is that the war and other happenings have shown you that age is not necessarily another name for sapience; that our avoidance of frankness in life and in the arts is often, but not so often as you think, a cowardly way of shirking unpalatable truths, and that you have taken us off our pedestals because we look more natural on the ground. You who are at the rash age even accuse your elders, sometimes not without justification, of being more rash than yourselves. 'If Youth but only knew,' we used to teach you to sing; but now, just because Youth has been to the war, it wants to change the next line into 'If Age had only to do.'

In so far as this attitude of yours is merely passive, sullen, negative, as it mainly is, despairing of our capacity and anticipating a future of gloom, it is no game for man or woman. It is certainly the opposite of that for which I plead. Do not stand aloof, despising, disbelieving, but come in and help – insist on coming in and helping. After all, we have shown a good deal of courage; and your part is to add a greater courage to it. There are glorious years lying ahead of you if you choose to make them glorious. God's in His Heaven still. So forward, brave hearts. To what adventures I cannot tell, but I know that your God is watching to see whether you are adventurous. I know that the great partnership is only a first step, but I do not know what are to be the next and the next. The partnership is but a tool; what are you to do with it? Very little, I warn you, if you are merely thinking of yourselves; much if what is at the marrow of your thoughts is a future that even you can scarcely hope to see.

Learn as a beginning how world-shaking situations arise and how they may be countered. Doubt all your betters who would deny you that right of partnership. Begin by doubting all such in high places – except, of course, your professors. But doubt all other professors – yet not conceitedly, as some do, with their noses in the air; avoid all such physical risks. If it necessitates your pushing some of us out of our places, still push; you will find it needs some shoving. But the things courage can do! The things that even incompetence can do if it works with singleness of purpose. The war has done at least one big thing: it has taken spring out of the year. And, this accomplished, our leading people are amazed to find that the other seasons are not conducting themselves as usual. The spring of the year lies buried in the fields of France and elsewhere. By the time the next eruption comes it may be you who are responsible for it and your sons who are in the lava. All, perhaps, because this year you let things slide.

We are a nice and kindly people, but it is already evident that we are stealing back into the old grooves, seeking cushions for our old bones, rather than attempting to build up a fairer future. That is what we mean when we say that the country is settling down. Make haste, or you will become like us, with only the thing we proudly call experience to add to your stock, a poor exchange for the generous feelings that time will take away. We have no intention of giving you your share. Look around and see how much share Youth has now that the war is over. You got a handsome share while it lasted.

I expect we shall beat you; unless your fortitude be doubly girded by a desire to send a message of cheer to your brothers who fell, the only message, I believe, for which they crave; they are not worrying about their Aunt Jane. They want to know if you have learned wisely from what befell them; if you have, they will be braced in the feeling that they did not die in vain. Some of them think they did. They will not take our word for it that they did not. You are their living image; they know you could not lie to them, but they distrust our flattery and our cunning faces. To us they have passed away; but are you who stepped into their heritage only yesterday, whose books are scarcely cold to their hands, you who still hear their cries being blown across the links – are you already relegating them to the shades? The gaps they have left in this university are among the most honourable of her wounds. But we are not here to acclaim them. Where they are now, 'hero' is, I think, a very little word. They call to you to find out in time the truth about this great game, which your elders play for stakes and Youth plays for its life.

I do not know whether you are grown a little tired of that word 'hero', but I am sure the heroes are. That is the subject of one of our unfinished plays; M'Connachie is the one who writes the plays. If any one of you here proposes to be a playwright you can take this for your own and finish it. The scene is a school, schoolmasters present, but if you like you could make it a university, professors present. They are discussing an illuminated scroll about a student fallen in the war, which they have kindly presented to his parents; and unexpectedly the parents enter. They are an old pair, backbent, they have been stalwarts in their day but have now gone small; they are poor, but not so poor that they could not send their boy to college. They are in black, not such a rusty black either, and you may be sure she is the one who knows what to do with his hat. Their faces are gnarled, I suppose – but I do not need to describe that pair to Scottish students. They have come to thank the Senatus for their lovely scroll and to ask them to tear it up. At first they had been enamoured to read of what a scholar their son was, how noble and adored by all. But soon a fog settled over them, for this grand person was not the boy they knew. He had many a fault well known to them; he was not always so noble; as a scholar he did no more than scrape through; and he sometimes made his father rage and his mother grieve. They had liked to talk such memories as these together, and smile over them, as if they were bits of him he had left lying about the house. So thank you kindly, and would you please give them back their boy by tearing up the scroll? I see nothing else for our dramatist to do. I think he should ask an alumna of St Andrews to play the old lady [indicating Miss Ellen Terry[†]]. The loveliest of all young actresses, the dearest of all old ones; it seems only yesterday that all the men of imagination proposed to their beloveds in some such frenzied words as these, 'As I can't get Miss Terry, may I have you?'

† Dame Ellen Terry (1847–1928) was the leading Shakespearean actress of her day.

This play might become historical as the opening of your propaganda in the proposed campaign. How to make a practical advance? The League of Nations is a very fine thing, but it cannot save you, because it will be run by us. Beware your betters bringing presents. What is wanted is something run by yourselves. You have more in common with the Youth of other lands than Youth and Age can ever have with each other; even the hostile countries sent out many a son very like ours, from the same sort of homes, the same sort of universities, who had as little to do as our youth had with the origin of the great adventure. Can we doubt that many of these on both sides who have gone over and were once opponents are now friends? You ought to have a League of Youth of all countries as your beginning, ready to say to all governments, 'We will fight each other but only when we are sure of the necessity.' Are you equal to your job, you young men? If not, I call upon the red-gowned women to lead the way. I sound to myself as if I were advocating a rebellion, though I am really asking for a larger friendship. Perhaps I may be arrested on leaving the hall. In such a cause I should think that I had at last proved myself worthy to be your rector.

You will have to work harder than ever, but possibly not so much at the same things; more at modern languages certainly if you are to discuss that League of Youth with the students of other nations when they come over to St Andrews for the conference. I am far from taking a side against the classics. I should as soon argue against your having tops to your heads; that way lie the best tops. Science, too, has at last come to its own in St Andrews. It is the surest means of teaching you how to know what you mean when you say. So you will have to work harder. Izaak Walton quotes the saying that doubtless the Almighty could have created a finer fruit than the strawberry, but that doubtless also He never did. Doubtless also He could have provided us with better fun than hard work, but I don't know what it is. To be born poor is probably the next best thing. The greatest glory that has ever come to me was to be swallowed up in London, not knowing a soul, with no means of subsistence, and the fun of working till the stars went out. To have known anyone would have spoilt it. I did not even quite know the language. I rang for my boots, and they thought I said a glass of water, so I drank the water and worked on. There was no food in the cupboard, so I did not need to waste time in eating. The pangs and agonies when no proof came. How courteously tolerant was I of the postman without a proof for us; how M'Connachie, on the other hand, wanted to punch his head. The magic days when our article appeared in an evening paper. The promptitude with which I counted the lines to see how much we should get for it. Then M'Connachie's superb air of dropping it into the gutter. Oh, to be a freelance of journalism again – that darling jade! Those were days. Too good to last. Let us be grave. Here comes a rector.

But now, on reflection, a dreadful sinking assails me, that this was not really work. The artistic callings – you remember how Stevenson thumped them – are merely doing what you are clamorous to be at; it is not real work unless you would rather be doing something else. My so-called labours were just M'Connachie running away with me again. Still, I have sometimes worked; for instance, I feel that I am working at this moment. And the big guns are in the same plight as the little ones. Carlyle, the king of all rectors, has always been accepted as the arch-apostle of toil, and has registered his many woes. But it will not do. Despite sickness, poortith [poverty], want and all, he was grinding all his life at the one job he revelled in. An extraordinarily happy man, though there is no direct proof that he thought so.

There must be many men in other callings besides the arts lauded as hard workers who are merely out for enjoyment. Our chancellor [indicating Lord Haig‡]? If our chancellor has always a passion to be a soldier, we must reconsider him as a worker. Even our principal? How about the light that burns in our principal's room after decent people have gone to bed? If we could climb up and look in – I should like to do something of that kind for the last time – should we find him engaged in honest toil, or guiltily engrossed in chemistry?

You will all fall into one of those two callings, the joyous or the uncongenial; and one wishes you into the first, though our sympathy, our esteem, must go rather to the less fortunate, the braver ones who 'turn their necessity to glorious gain' after they have put away their dreams. To the others will go the easy prizes of life, success, which has become a somewhat odious onion nowadays, chiefly because we so often give the name to the wrong thing. When you reach the evening of your days you will, I think, see – with, I hope, becoming cheerfulness – that we are all failures, at least all the best of us. The greatest Scotsman that ever lived wrote himself down a failure:

> The poor inhabitant below
> Was quick to learn and wise to know

‡ Field Marshal Douglas Haig, 1st Earl Haig was chancellor of St. Andrews from 1922 to 1928; before that he was J. M. Barrie's predecessor as rector. Haig would become famous for leading the British Expeditionary Force on the Western Front during the First World War, with the country suffering over two million casualties under his command.

→ J. M. Barrie, 1902, photographed by George Charles Beresford

And keenly felt the friendly glow
And softer flame.
But thoughtless follies laid him low,
And stained his name.

Perhaps the saddest lines in poetry, written by a man who could make things new for the gods themselves.

If you want to avoid being like Burns there are several possible ways. Thus you might copy us, as we shine forth in our published memoirs, practically without a flaw. No one so obscure nowadays but that he can have a book about him. Happy the land that can produce such subjects for the pen.

But do not put your photograph at all ages into your autobiography. That may bring you to the ground. 'My Life; and what I have done with it'; that is the sort of title, but it is the photographs that give away what you have done with it. Grim things, those portraits; if you could read the language of them you would often find it unnecessary to read the book. The face itself, of course, is still more tell-tale, for it is the record of all one's past life. There the man stands in the dock, page by page; we ought to be able to see each chapter of him melting into the next like the figures in the cinematograph. Even the youngest of you has got through some chapters already. When you go home for the next vacation someone is sure to say, 'John has changed a little; I don't quite see in what way, but he has changed.' You remember they said that last vacation. Perhaps it means that you look less like your father. Think that out. I could say some nice things of your betters if I chose.

In youth you tend to look rather frequently into a mirror, not at all necessarily from vanity. You say to yourself, 'What an interesting face; I wonder what he is to be up to?' Your elders do not look into the mirror so often. We know what he has been up to. As yet there is unfortunately no science of reading other people's faces; I think a chair for this should be founded in St Andrews.

The new professor will need to be a sublime philosopher, and for obvious reasons he ought to wear spectacles before his senior class. It will be a gloriously optimistic chair, for he can tell his students the glowing truth, that what their faces are to be like presently depends mainly on themselves. Mainly, not altogether:

I am the master of my fate,
I am the captain of my soul.

I found the other day an old letter from Henley that told me of the circumstances in which he wrote that poem.[§] 'I was a patient,' he writes, 'in the old infirmary of Edinburgh. I had heard vaguely of [Joseph] Lister, and went there as a sort of forlorn hope on the chance of saving my foot. The great

§ 'Invictus' by Ernest Henley.

surgeon received me, as he did and does everybody, with the greatest kindness, and for twenty months I lay in one or other ward of the old place under his care. It was a desperate business, but he saved my foot, and here I am.' There he was, ladies and gentlemen, and what he was doing during that 'desperate business' was singing that he was master of his fate.

If you want an example of courage try Henley. Or Stevenson. I could tell you some stories about these two, but they would not be dull enough for a rectorial address. For courage, again, take Meredith, whose laugh was 'as broad as a thousand beeves at pasture'. Take, as I think, the greatest figure literature has still left us, to be added today to the roll of St Andrews' alumni, though it must be in absence. The pomp and circumstance of war will pass, and all others now alive may fade from the scene, but I think the quiet figure of Hardy will live on.

I seem to be taking all my examples from the calling I was lately pretending to despise. I should like to read you some passages of a letter from a man of another calling, which I think will hearten you. I have the little filmy sheets here. I thought you might like to see the actual letter; it has been a long journey; it has been to the South Pole. It is a letter to me from Captain Scott of the Antarctic, and was written in the tent you know of, where it was found long afterwards with his body and those of some other very gallant gentlemen, his comrades. The writing is in pencil, still quite clear, though toward the end some of the words trail away as into the great silence that was waiting for them. It begins:

'We are pegging out in a very comfortless spot. Hoping this letter may be found and sent to you, I write you a word of farewell. I want you to think well of me and my end.' (After some private instructions too intimate to read, he goes on): 'Goodbye – I am not at all afraid of the end, but sad to miss many a simple pleasure which I had planned for the future in our long marches . . . We are in a desperate state – feet frozen, etc, no fuel, and a long way from food, but it would do your heart good to be in our tent, to hear our songs and our cheery conversation . . .' Later – (it is here that the words become difficult) – 'We are very near the end . . . We did intend to finish ourselves when things proved like this, but we have decided to die naturally without.'

I think it may uplift you all to stand for a moment by that tent and listen, as he says, to their songs and cheery conversation. When I think of Scott I remember the strange Alpine story of the youth who fell down a glacier and was lost, and of how a scientific companion, one of several who accompanied him, all young, computed that the body would again appear at a certain date and place many years afterwards. When that time came round some of the survivors returned to the glacier to see if the prediction would be fulfilled; all old men now; and the body reappeared as young as on the day he left them. So Scott and his comrades emerge out of the white immensities always young.

How comely a thing is affliction borne cheerfully, which is not beyond the reach of the humblest of us. What is beauty? It is these hard-bitten men singing courage to you from their tent; it is the waves of their island home crooning of their deeds to you who are to follow them. Sometimes beauty boils over and then spirits are abroad. Ages may pass as we look or listen, for time is annihilated. There is a very old legend told to me by [Fridtjof] Nansen the explorer – I like well to be in the company of explorers – the legend of a monk who had wandered into the fields and a lark began to sing. He had never heard a lark before, and he stood there entranced until the bird and its song had become part of the heavens. Then he went back to the monastery and found there a doorkeeper whom he did not know and who did not know him. Other monks came, and they were all strangers to him. He told them he was Father Anselm, but that was no help. Finally they looked through the books of the monastery, and these revealed that there had been a Father Anselm there a hundred or more years before. Time had been blotted out while he listened to the lark.

That, I suppose, was a case of beauty boiling over, or a soul boiling over; perhaps the same thing. Then spirits walk.

They must sometimes walk St Andrews. I do not mean the ghosts of queens or prelates, but one that keeps step, as soft as snow, with some poor student. He sometimes catches sight of it. That is why his fellows can never quite touch him, their best beloved; he half knows something of which they know nothing – the secret that is hidden in the face of the Mona Lisa. As I see him, life is so beautiful to him that its proportions are monstrous. Perhaps his childhood may have been overfull of gladness; they don't like that. If the seekers were kind he is the one for whom the flags of his college would fly one day. But the seeker I am thinking of is unfriendly, and so our student is 'the lad that will never be told'. He often gaily forgets, and thinks he has slain his foe by daring him, like him who, dreading water, was always the first to leap into it. One can see him serene, astride a Scotch cliff, singing to the sun the farewell thanks of a boy:

> Throned on a cliff serene Man saw the sun
> hold a red torch above the farthest seas,
> and the fierce island pinnacles put on
> in his defence their sombre panoplies;
> Foremost the white mists eddied, trailed and spun
> like seekers, emulous to clasp his knees,
> till all the beauty of the scene seemed one,
> led by the secret whispers of the breeze.
>
> The sun's torch suddenly flashed upon his face
> and died; and he sat content in subject night
> and dreamed of an old dead foe that had sought and found him;
> a beast stirred boldly in his resting-place;

And the cold came; Man rose to his master-height,
shivered, and turned away; but the mists were round him.

If there is any of you here so rare that the seekers have taken an ill-will to
him, as to the boy who wrote those lines, I ask you to be careful. Henley says in
that poem we were speaking of:

Under the bludgeonings of Chance
My head is bloody but unbowed.

A fine mouthful, but perhaps 'My head is bloody and bowed' is better.

Let us get back to that tent with its songs and cheery conversation. Courage.
I do not think it is to be got by your becoming solemn-sides before your time.
You must have been warned against letting the golden hours slip by. Yes, but
some of them are golden only because we let them slip. Diligence – ambition;
noble words, but only if 'touched to fine issues'. Prizes may be dross, learning
lumber, unless they bring you into the arena with increased understanding.
Hanker not too much after worldly prosperity – that corpulent cigar; if you
became a millionaire you would probably go swimming around for more like a
diseased goldfish. Look to it that what you are doing is not merely toddling to
a competency. Perhaps that must be your fate, but fight it and then, though you
fail, you may still be among the elect of whom we have spoken. Many a brave
man has had to come to it at last. But there are the complacent toddlers from
the start. Favour them not, ladies, especially now that every one of you carries
a possible maréchal's baton under her gown. 'Happy', it has been said by a
distinguished man, 'is he who can leave college with an unreproaching
conscience and an unsullied heart.' I don't know; he sounds to me like a sloppy,
watery sort of fellow; happy, perhaps, but if there be red blood in him
impossible. Be not disheartened by ideals of perfection which can be achieved
only by those who run away. Nature, that 'thrifty goddess', never gave you 'the
smallest scruple of her excellence' for that. Whatever bludgeonings may be
gathering for you, I think one feels more poignantly at your age than ever again in
life. You have not our December roses to help you; but you have June coming,
whose roses do not wonder, as do ours even while they give us their fragrance –
wondering most when they give us most – that we should linger on an empty
scene. It may indeed be monstrous but possibly courageous.

Courage is the thing. All goes if courage goes. What says our glorious
Johnson of courage: 'Unless a man has that virtue he has no security for
preserving any other.' We should thank our Creator three times daily for courage
instead of for our bread, which, if we work, is surely the one thing we have a
right to claim of Him. This courage is a proof of our immortality, greater even
than gardens 'when the eve is cool'. Pray for it. 'Who rises from prayer a better

man, his prayer is answered.' Be not merely courageous, but light-hearted and gay. There is an officer who was the first of our army to land at Gallipoli. He was dropped overboard to light decoys on the shore, so as to deceive the Turks as to where the landing was to be. He pushed a raft containing these in front of him. It was a frosty night, and he was naked and painted black. Firing from the ships was going on all around. It was a two-hours' swim in pitch darkness. He did it, crawled through the scrub to listen to the talk of the enemy, who were so near that he could have shaken hands with them, lit his decoys and swam back. He seems to look on this as a gay affair. He is a V.C. now, and you would not think to look at him that he could ever have presented such a disreputable appearance. Would you [indicating Colonel Freyberg[**]]?

Those men of whom I have been speaking as the kind to fill the fife could all be light-hearted on occasion. I remember Scott by Highland streams trying to rouse me by maintaining that haggis is boiled bagpipes; Henley in dispute as to whether, say, Turgenieff or Tolstoi could hang the other on his watch-chain; he sometimes clenched the argument by casting his crutch at you; Stevenson responded in the same gay spirit by giving that crutch to John Silver; you remember with what adequate results. You must cultivate this light-heartedness if you are to hang your betters on your watch-chains. Dr Johnson – let us have him again – does not seem to have discovered in his travels that the Scots are a light-hearted nation. Boswell took him to task for saying that the death of Garrick had eclipsed the gaiety of nations. 'Well, sir,' Johnson said, 'there may be occasions when it is permissible to,' etc. But Boswell would not let go. 'I cannot see, sir, how it could in any case have eclipsed the gaiety of nations, as England was the only nation before whom he had ever played.' Johnson was really stymied, but you would never have known it. 'Well, sir,' he said, holing out, 'I understand that Garrick once played in Scotland, and if Scotland has any gaiety to eclipse, which, sir, I deny . . .'

Prove Johnson wrong for once at the Students' Union and in your other societies. I much regret that there was no Students' Union at Edinburgh in my time. I hope you are fairly noisy and that members are sometimes let out. Do you keep to the old topics? King Charles's head; and Bacon wrote Shakespeare, or if he did not he missed the opportunity of his life. Don't forget to speak scornfully of the Victorian age; there will be time for meekness when you try to better it. Very soon you will be Victorian or that sort of thing yourselves; next session probably, when the freshmen come up. Afterwards, if you go in for my sort of calling, don't begin by thinking you are the last word in art; quite possibly you are not; steady yourself by remembering that there were great men before William K. Smith. Make merry while you may. Yet light-heartedness is not for ever and a day. At its best it is the gay companion of innocence; and when innocence goes – as it must go – they soon trip off together, looking for something younger. But courage comes all the way:

[**] Lieutenant General Bernard Freyberg, 1st Baron Freyberg (1889–1963) was nicknamed "the Salamander of the British Empire" by Winston Churchill for his skill at surviving hostile situations.

Fight on, my men, says Sir Andrew Barton,
I am hurt, but I am not slaine;
I'll lie me down and bleed a-while,
And then I'll rise and fight againe.

Another piece of advice; almost my last. For reasons you may guess I must give this in a low voice. Beware of M'Connachie. When I look in a mirror now it is his face I see. I speak with his voice. I once had a voice of my own, but nowadays I hear it from far away only, a melancholy, lonely, lost little pipe. I wanted to be an explorer, but he willed otherwise. You will all have your M'Connachies luring you off the high road. Unless you are constantly on the watch, you will find that he has slowly pushed you out of yourself and taken your place. He has rather done for me. I think in his youth he must somehow have guessed the future and been fleggit [frightened] by it, flichtered from the nest like a bird, and so our eggs were left, cold. He has clung to me, less from mischief than for companionship; I half like him and his penny whistle; with all his faults he is as Scotch as peat; he whispered to me just now that you elected him, not me, as your rector.

A final passing thought. Were an old student given an hour in which to revisit the St Andrews of his day, would he spend more than half of it at lectures? He is more likely to be heard clattering up bare stairs in search of old companions. But if you could choose your hour from all the 500 years of this seat of learning, wandering at your will from one age to another, how would you spend it? A fascinating theme; so many notable shades at once astir that St Leonard's and St Mary's grow murky with them. Hamilton, Melville, Sharpe, Chalmers, down to Herkless, that distinguished principal, ripe scholar and warm friend, the loss of whom I deeply deplore with you. I think if that hour were mine, and though at St Andrews he was but a passer-by, I would give a handsome part of it to a walk with Doctor Johnson. I should like to have the time of day passed to me in twelve languages by the Admirable Crichton. A wave of the hand to Andrew Lang; and then for the archery butts with the gay Montrose, all a-ruffled and ringed, and in the gallant St Andrews student manner, continued as I understand to this present day, scattering largess as he rides along,

But where is now the courtly troupe
That once went riding by?
I miss the curls of Canteloupe,
The laugh of Lady Di.

We have still left time for a visit to a house in South Street, hard by St Leonard's. I do not mean the house you mean. I am a Knox man. But little will that avail, for M'Connachie is a Queen Mary man. So, after all, it is at her door we chap, a last futile effort to bring that woman to heel. One more house of call, a student's room, also in South Street. I have chosen my student, you see, and I have chosen well; him that sang:

> Life has not since been wholly vain,
> And now I bear
> Of wisdom plucked from joy and pain
> Some slender share.
>
> But howsoever rich the store,
> I'd lay it down
> To feel upon my back once more
> The old red gown.

Well, we have at last come to an end. Some of you may remember when I began this address; we are all older now. I thank you for your patience. This is my first and last public appearance, and I never could or would have made it except to a gathering of Scottish students. If I have concealed my emotions in addressing you it is only the thrawn national way that deceives everybody except Scotsmen. I have not been as dull as I could have wished to be; but looking at your glowing faces, cheerfulness and hope would keep breaking through. Despite the imperfections of your betters we leave you a great inheritance, for which others will one day call you to account. You come of a race of men the very wind of whose name has swept to the ultimate seas. Remember:

> Heaven doth with us as we with torches do,
> Not light them for themselves . . .

Mighty are the universities of Scotland, and they will prevail. But even in your highest exultations never forget that they are not four, but five. The greatest of them is the poor, proud homes you come out of, which said so long ago: 'There shall be education in this land.' She, not St Andrews, is the oldest university in Scotland, and all the others are her whelps.

In bidding you goodbye, my last words must be of the lovely virtue. Courage, my children and 'greet the unseen with a cheer'. 'Fight on, my men,' said Sir Andrew Barton. Fight on – you – for the old red gown till the whistle blows.

# THIS IS MY SWAN SONG

Had you peered through the window of Delmonico's restaurant in New York City on December 5, 1905, you may have caught sight of Samuel Clemens, otherwise known as Mark Twain, mere days past his seventieth birthday, giving a speech to an audience of 170 well-heeled literati, all of whom had been invited to this celebratory dinner by Colonel George Harvey, editor of the *North American Review*. Before Twain rose to address a room that also boasted a forty-piece orchestra for the evening, his friend and fellow writer William Dean Howells introduced the great man.

WILLIAM DEAN HOWELLS:

These cheers, Mr. President, and ladies and gentlemen, are more terrifying to me than the dead silence of which I would gladly be a part. Since you have thought me fit, I could not wish a greater pleasure than that which you have proffered to me. I have written something prefatory to the toast I shall propose, and I wish before reading it to offer you what I believe ought to be a biographical explanation.

Mr. Clemens has always had the effect on me of throwing me into a poetic ecstasy. I know it is very uncommon. Most people speak of him in prose, and I dare say there will be a deal of prosing about him tonight; but for myself, I am obliged to resort to meter whenever I think of him. I fancy there is some strong undercurrent of poetry in the man which drags me down and sweeps me along with him.

I remember three years ago, when he was a comparative youth of sixty-seven, I was called upon to respond to some sort of toast, and I instantly fell into rhyme. I don't know that I shall quite be able to scramble out of it tonight. At that time I praised him in what I ventured to call a double-barreled sonnet; it was a sonnet of twenty-eight lines instead of fourteen. Tonight, as he has the Psalmist's age limit, I thought perhaps a psalm would be more fitting; the psalm of David, if we could not get anything better. But I found myself quite helpless when it came to the matter of preparation, and I fell back on the Shakespearean sonnet. I found myself, however, obliged to write a Shakespearean sonnet of extraordinary length. Shakespeare wrote sonnets of fourteen lines, mine is of twenty-eight. But you will find Shakespeare again has been improved upon since he died. Mr. Bernard Shaw now writes plays twice as good as Shakespeare – and I write sonnets twice as long as Shakespeare. I don't know that I need delay you longer from the pleasure before you, but such as my sonnet is I will read it. This is a sonnet to Mark Twain.

A traveler from the Old World just escaped
    Our customs with his life, had found his way
To a place up-town, where a Colossus shaped
    Itself, sky-scraper high, against the day.
A vast smile, dawning from its mighty lips,
    Like sunshine on its visage seemed to brood;
One eye winked in perpetual eclipse,
    In the other a huge tear of pity stood.
Wisdom in chunks about its temples shone;
    Its measureless bulk grotesque, exultant, rose;
And while Titanic puissance clothed it on,
    Patience with foreigners was in its pose.
So that, "What art thou?" the emboldened traveler spoke,
And it replies, "I am the American joke.

"I am the joke that laughs the proud to scorn;
    I mock at cruelty, I banish care,
I cheer the lowly, chipper the forlorn,
    I bid the oppressor and hypocrite beware.
I tell the tale that makes men cry for joy;
    I bring the laugh that has no hate in it;
In the heart of age I wake the undying boy;
    My big stick blossoms with a thornless wit,
The lame dance with delight in me, my mirth
    Reaches the deaf untrumpeted; the blind
My point can see. I jolly the whole earth,
    But most I love to jolly my own kind,
Joke of a people great, gay, bold, and free,
I type their master-mood. Mark Twain made me."

Now, ladies and gentlemen, and Colonel Harvey, I will try not to be greedy on your behalf in wishing the health of our honored and, in view of his great age, our revered guest. I will not say, "Oh King, live forever," but "Oh King, live as long as you like!"

MARK TWAIN:

Well, if I made that joke, it is the best one I ever made, and it is in the prettiest language, too. I never can get quite to that height. But I appreciate that joke, and I shall remember it – and I shall use it when occasion requires.

    I have had a great many birthdays in my time. I remember the first one very well, and I always think of it with indignation; everything was so crude, unaesthetic, primeval. Nothing like this at all. No proper appreciative preparation made; nothing really ready. Now, for a person born with high and delicate instincts – why, even the cradle wasn't whitewashed – nothing ready at all. I hadn't any hair, I hadn't any teeth, I hadn't any clothes, I had to go to my first banquet just like that. Well, everybody came swarming in. It was the merest little bit of a village – hardly that, just a little hamlet, in the backwoods of Missouri, where nothing ever happened, and the people were all interested, and they all came; they looked me over to see if there was anything fresh in my line. Why, nothing ever happened in that village – I – why, I was the only thing that had really happened there for months and months and months; and although I say it myself that shouldn't, I came the nearest to being a real event that had happened in that village in more than two years.

Well, those people came, they came with that curiosity which is so provincial, with that frankness which also is so provincial, and they examined me all around and gave their opinion. Nobody asked them, and I shouldn't have minded if anybody had paid me a compliment, but nobody did. Their opinions were all just green with prejudice, and I feel those opinions to this day. Well, I stood that as long as – well, you know I was born courteous, and I stood it to the limit. I stood it an hour, and then the worm turned. I was the worm; it was my turn to turn, and I turned. I knew very well the strength of my position; I knew that I was the only spotlessly pure and innocent person in that whole town, and I came out and said so. And they could not say a word. It was so true. They blushed; they were embarrassed. Well, that was the first after-dinner speech I ever made. I think it was after dinner.

It's a long stretch between that first birthday speech and this one. That was my cradle-song, and this is my swan-song, I suppose. I am used to swan-songs; I have sung them several times. This is my seventieth birthday, and I wonder if you all rise to the size of that proposition, realizing all the significance of that phrase, seventieth birthday.

The seventieth birthday! It is the time of life when you arrive at a new and awful dignity; when you may throw aside the decent reserves which have oppressed you for a generation and stand unafraid and unabashed upon your seven-terraced summit and look down and teach – unrebuked. You can tell the world how you got there. It is what they all do. You shall never get tired of telling by what delicate arts and deep moralities you climbed up to that great place. You will explain the process and dwell on the particulars with senile rapture. I have been anxious to explain my own system this long time, and now at last I have the right.

I have achieved my seventy years in the usual way: by sticking strictly to a scheme of life which would kill anybody else. It sounds like an exaggeration, but that is really the common rule for attaining to old age. When we examine the program of any of these garrulous old people we always find that the habits which have preserved them would have decayed us; that the way of life which enabled them to live upon the property of their heirs so long, as [celebrated lawyer and diplomat] Mr. Choate says, would have put us out of commission ahead of time. I will offer here, as a sound maxim, this: that we can't reach old age by another man's road.

I will now teach, offering my way of life to whomsoever desires to commit suicide by the scheme which has enabled me to beat the doctor and the hangman for seventy years. Some of the details may sound untrue, but they are not. I am not here to deceive; I am here to teach.

We have no permanent habits until we are forty. Then they begin to harden, presently they petrify, then business begins. Since forty I have been regular about going to bed and getting up – and that is one of the main things. I have made it a rule to go to bed when there wasn't anybody left to sit up with; and I have made it a rule to get up when I had to. This has resulted in an unswerving regularity of irregularity. It has saved me sound, but it would injure another person.

In the matter of diet – which is another main thing – I have been persistently strict in sticking to the things which didn't agree with me until one or the other of us got the best of it. Until lately I got the best of it myself. But last spring I stopped frolicking with mincepie after midnight; up to then I had always believed it wasn't loaded. For thirty years I have taken coffee and bread at eight in the morning, and no bite nor sup until seven-thirty in the evening. Eleven hours. That is all right for me, and is wholesome, because I have never had a headache in my life, but headachy people would not reach seventy comfortably by that road, and they would be foolish to try it. And I wish to urge upon you this – which I think is wisdom – that if you find you can't make seventy by any but an uncomfortable road, don't you go. When they take off the Pullman and retire you to the rancid smoker, put on your things, count your checks, and get out at the first way station where there's a cemetery.

I have made it a rule never to smoke more than one cigar at a time. I have no other restriction as regards smoking. I do not know just when I began to smoke, I only know that it was in my father's lifetime, and that I was discreet. He passed from this life early in 1847, when I was a shade past eleven; ever since then I have smoked publicly. As an example to others, and not that I care for moderation myself, it has always been my rule never to smoke when asleep, and never to refrain when awake. It is a good rule. I mean, for me; but some of you know quite well that it wouldn't answer for everybody that's trying to get to be seventy.

I smoke in bed until I have to go to sleep; I wake up in the night, sometimes once, sometimes twice, sometimes three times, and I never waste any of these opportunities to smoke. This habit is so old and dear and precious to me that I would feel as you, sir, would feel if you should lose the only moral you've

SPEECHES OF NOTE

got – meaning the chairman – if you've got one: I am making no charges. I will grant, here, that I have stopped smoking now and then, for a few months at a time, but it was not on principle, it was only to show off; it was to pulverize those critics who said I was a slave to my habits and couldn't break my bonds.

Today it is all of sixty years since I began to smoke the limit. I have never bought cigars with life-belts around them. I early found that those were too expensive for me. I have always bought cheap cigars – reasonably cheap, at any rate. Sixty years ago they cost me four dollars a barrel, but my taste has improved, latterly, and I pay seven now. Six or seven. Seven, I think. Yes, it's seven. But that includes the barrel. I often have smoking parties at my house; but the people that come have always just taken the pledge. I wonder why that is?

As for drinking, I have no rule about that. When the others drink I like to help, otherwise I remain dry, by habit and preference. This dryness does not hurt me, but it could easily hurt you, because you are different. You let it alone.

Since I was seven years old I have seldom taken a dose of medicine, and have still seldomer needed one. But up to seven I lived exclusively on allopathic medicines. Not that I needed them, for I don't think I did; it was for economy; my father took a drug store for a debt, and it made cod-liver oil cheaper than the other breakfast foods. We had nine barrels of it, and it lasted me seven years. Then I was weaned. The rest of the family had to get along with rhubarb and ipecac and such things, because I was the pet. I was the first Standard Oil Trust. I had it all. By the time the drug store was exhausted my health was established, and there has never been much the matter with me since. But you know very well it would be foolish for the average child to start for seventy on that basis. It happened to be just the thing for me, but that was merely an accident; it couldn't happen again in a century.

I have never taken any exercise, except sleeping and resting, and I never intend to take any. Exercise is loathsome. And it cannot be any benefit when you are tired; and I was always tired. But let another person try my way, and see where he will come out.

I desire now to repeat and emphasize that maxim: we can't reach old age by another man's road. My habits protect my life, but they would assassinate you.

I have lived a severely moral life. But it would be a mistake for other people to try that, or for me to recommend it. Very few would succeed: you have to have a perfectly colossal stock of morals; and you can't get them on a margin; you have to have the whole thing, and put them in your box. Morals are an acquirement – like music, like a foreign language, like piety, poker, paralysis – no man is born with them. I wasn't myself, I started poor. I hadn't a single moral. There is hardly a man in this house that is poorer than I was then. Yes, I started like that – the world before me, not a moral in the slot. Not even an insurance moral. I can remember the first one I ever got. I can remember the landscape, the weather, the – I can remember how everything looked. It was an old moral, an old second-hand moral, all out of repair, and didn't fit, anyway. But if you are careful with a thing like that, and keep it in a dry place, and save it for processions, and Chautauquas, and World's Fairs, and so on, and disinfect it now and then, and give it a fresh coat of whitewash once in a while, you will be surprised to see how well she will last and how long she will keep sweet, or at least inoffensive. When I got that moldy old moral, she had stopped growing, because she hadn't any exercise; but I worked her hard, I worked her Sundays and all. Under this cultivation she waxed in might and stature beyond belief, and served me well and was my pride and joy for sixty-three years; then she got to associating with insurance presidents, and lost flesh and character, and was a sorrow to look at and no longer competent for business. She was a great loss to me. Yet not all loss. I sold her – ah, pathetic skeleton, as she was – I sold her to Leopold, the pirate King of Belgium; he sold her to our Metropolitan Museum, and it was very glad to get her, for without a rag on, she stands 57 feet long and 16 feet high, and they think she's a brontosaur. Well, she looks it. They believe it will take nineteen geological periods to breed her match.

Morals are of inestimable value, for every man is born crammed with sin microbes, and the only thing that can extirpate these sin microbes is morals. Now you take a sterilized Christian – I mean, you take the sterilized Christian, for there's only one. Dear sir, I wish you wouldn't look at me like that.

Threescore years and ten!

It is the Scriptural statute of limitations. After that, you owe no active duties; for you the strenuous life is over. You are a time-expired man, to use Kipling's military phrase: you have served your term, well or less well, and you are mustered out. You are become an honorary member of the republic, you are emancipated, compulsions are not for you, nor any bugle-call but "lights out." You pay the time-worn duty bills if you choose, or decline if you prefer – and without prejudice – for they are not legally collectable.

The previous-engagement plea, which in forty years has cost you so many twinges, you can lay aside forever, on this side of the grave you will never need it again. If you shrink at thought of night, and winter, and the late home-coming from the banquet and the lights and the laughter through the deserted streets – a desolation which would not remind you now, as for a generation it did, that your friends are sleeping, and you must creep in a-tiptoe and not disturb them, but would only remind you that you need not tiptoe, you can never disturb them more – if you shrink at thought of these things, you need only reply, "Your invitation honors me, and pleases me because you still keep me in your remembrance, but I am seventy; seventy, and would nestle in the chimney-corner, and smoke my pipe, and read my book, and take my rest, wishing you well in all affection, and that when you in your return shall arrive at pier No. 70 you may step aboard your waiting ship with a reconciled spirit, and lay your course toward the sinking sun with a contented heart."

WHO **QUEEN ELIZABETH II** | WHERE **NEVER DELIVERED** | WHEN **WRITTEN 1983**

# THIS SOLEMN AND AWFUL DUTY

SECRET

THIS DOCUMENT IS THE PROPERTY OF HER BRITANNIC MAJESTY'S GOVERNMENT

MISC 93(83) 31 COPY NO

4 March 1983

CABINET

WINTEX-CIMEX(83) COMMITTEE

EXERCISE EXERCISE EXERCISE

Text of a Message to the Nation broadcast by
Her Majesty The Queen at Noon on Friday 4 March 1983

***********

When I spoke to you less than three months ago we were all enjoying the warmth and fellowship of a family Christmas. Our thoughts were concentrated on the strong links that bind each generation to the ones that came before and those that will follow. The horrors of war could not have seemed more remote as my family and I shared our Christmas joy with the growing family of the Commonwealth.

Now this madness of war is once more spreading through the world and our brave country must again prepare itself to survive against great odds.

I have never forgotten the sorrow and pride I felt as my sister and I huddled around the nursery wireless set listening to my father's inspiring words on that fateful day in 1939. Not for a single moment did I imagine that this solemn and awful duty would one day fall to me.

We all know that the dangers facing us today are greater by far than at any time in our long history. The enemy is not the soldier with his rifle nor even the airman prowling the skies above our cities and towns but the deadly power of abused technology.

But whatever terrors lie in wait for us all the qualities that have helped to keep our freedom intact twice already during this sad century will once more be our strength.

1

SECRET

Relations between the West and the USSR plummeted to stomach-churning depths in 1983. The deterioration began in March, with President Ronald Reagan labeling the Soviet Union an "evil empire" in a speech; he then, from a separate podium that same month, aggravated Moscow by proposing a ballistic missile defense system dubbed "Star Wars" by the media. Further problems arose in September, with Korean Air Lines Flight 007 being shot down by a Soviet fighter plane. The icing on this grimmest of cakes came in November, courtesy of Able Archer 83, a NATO military exercise in which a nuclear escalation was simulated to test the resources and preparedness of Western forces, but which the USSR incorrectly believed to be a cover for a genuine attack.

In Britain, a similar exercise took place that saw officials also imagining World War III. This was the speech they wrote for the Queen.

My husband and I share with families up and down the land the fear we feel for sons and daughters, husbands and brothers who have left our side to serve their country. My beloved son Andrew is at this moment in action with his unit and we pray continually for his safety and for the safety of all servicemen and women at home and overseas.

It is this close bond of family life that must be our greatest defence against the unknown. If families remain united and resolute, giving shelter to those living alone and unprotected, our country's will to survive cannot be broken.

My message to you therefore is simple. Help those who cannot help themselves, give comfort to the lonely and the homeless and let your family become the focus of hope and life to those who need it.

As we strive together to fight off the new evil let us pray for our country and men of goodwill wherever they may be.

God Bless you all.

**************

EXERCISE                    EXERCISE                    EXERCISE

2

# I AM AN AFRICAN

In 1996, two years after a momentous shift that saw Nelson Mandela become the first post-apartheid president of South Africa, the country adopted a revised, non-discriminatory constitution on which to build a new future.

On May 8 of that year, to mark the occasion, an iconic speech was delivered on behalf of the African National Congress by Mandela's future successor and then-deputy, Thabo Mbeki.

Chairperson, Esteemed President of the democratic Republic, Honourable Members of the Constitutional Assembly, our distinguished domestic and foreign guests, friends:

On an occasion such as this, we should, perhaps, start from the beginning.

So, let me begin.

I am an African.

I owe my being to the hills and the valleys, the mountains and the glades, the rivers, the deserts, the trees, the flowers, the seas and the ever-changing seasons that define the face of our native land.

My body has frozen in our frosts and in our latter-day snows. It has thawed in the warmth of our sunshine and melted in the heat of the midday sun. The crack and the rumble of the summer thunders, lashed by startling lightning, have been a cause both of trembling and of hope.

The fragrances of nature have been as pleasant to us as the sight of the wild blooms of the citizens of the veld.

The dramatic shapes of the Drakensberg, the soil-coloured waters of the Lekoa, iGqili noThukela, and the sands of the Kgalagadi, have all been panels of the set on the natural stage on which we act out the foolish deeds of the theatre of the day.

At times, and in fear, I have wondered whether I should concede equal citizenship of our country to the leopard and the lion, the elephant and the springbok, the hyena, the black mamba and the pestilential mosquito.

A human presence among all of these, a feature on the face of our native land thus defined, I know that none dare challenge me when I say – I am an African!

I owe my being to the Khoi and the San whose desolate souls haunt the great expanses of the beautiful Cape – they who fell victim to the most merciless genocide our native land has ever seen, they who were the first to lose their lives in the struggle to defend our freedom and independence and they who, as a people, perished in the result.

Today, as a country, we keep an inaudible and audible silence about these ancestors of the generations that live, fearful to admit the horror of a former deed, seeking to obliterate from our memories a cruel occurrence which, in its remembering, should teach us not and never to be inhuman again.

I am formed of the migrants who left Europe to find a new home on our native land. Whatever their own actions, they remain still part of me.

In my veins courses the blood of the Malay slaves who came from the East. Their proud dignity informs my bearing, their culture a part of my essence. The stripes they bore on their bodies from the lash of the slave master are a reminder embossed on my consciousness of what should not be done.

I am the grandchild of the warrior men and women that Hintsa and Sekhukhune led, the patriots that Cetshwayo and Mphephu took to battle, the soldiers Moshoeshoe and Ngungunyane taught never to dishonour the cause of freedom.

My mind and my knowledge of myself is formed by the victories that are the jewels in our African crown, the victories we earned from Isandhlwana to Khartoum, as Ethiopians, as the Ashanti of Ghana, as the Berbers of the desert.

I am the grandchild who lays flowers on the Boer graves at St Helena, the Bahamas and the Vrouemonument, who sees in the mind's eye and suffers the suffering of a simple peasant folk: death, concentration camps, destroyed homesteads, a dream in ruins.

I am the child of Nongqawuse. I am he who made it possible to trade in the world markets in diamonds, in gold, in the same food for which our stomachs yearn.

I come of those who were transported from India and China, whose being resided in the fact, solely, that they were able to provide physical labour, who taught me that we could both be at home and be foreign, who taught me that human existence itself demanded that freedom was a necessary condition for that human existence.

Being part of all of these people, and in the knowledge that none dares contest that assertion, I shall claim that I am an African.

I have seen our country torn asunder as these, all of whom are my people, engaged one another in a titanic battle, the one to redress a wrong that had been caused by one to another and the other, to defend the indefensible.

I have seen what happens when one person has superiority of force over another, when the stronger appropriate to themselves the prerogative even to annul the injunction that God created all men and women in His image.

I know what it signifies when race and colour are used to determine who is human and who, sub-human.

I have seen the destruction of all sense of self-esteem, the consequent striving to be what one is not, simply to acquire some of the benefits which those who had imposed themselves as masters had ensured that they enjoy.

I have experience of the situation in which race and colour is used to enrich some and impoverish the rest.

I have seen the corruption of minds and souls as a result of the pursuit of an ignoble effort to perpetrate a veritable crime against humanity.

I have seen concrete expression of the denial of the dignity of a human being emanating from the conscious, systemic and systematic oppressive and repressive activities of other human beings.

There the victims parade with no mask to hide the brutish reality – the beggars, the prostitutes, the street children, those who seek solace in substance abuse, those who have to steal to assuage hunger, those who have to lose their sanity because to be sane is to invite pain.

Perhaps the worst among these, who are my people, are those who have learnt to kill for a wage. To these the extent of death is directly proportional to their personal welfare.

And so, like pawns in the service of demented souls, they kill in furtherance of the political violence in KwaZulu-Natal. They murder the innocent in the taxi wars.

They kill slowly or quickly in order to make profits from the illegal trade in narcotics. They are available for hire when husband wants to murder wife and wife, husband.

Among us prowl the products of our immoral and amoral past – killers who have no sense of the worth of human life, rapists who have absolute disdain for the women of our country, animals who would seek to benefit from the vulnerability of the children, the disabled, and the old, the rapacious who brook no obstacle in their quest for self-enrichment.

All this I know and know to be true because I am an African!

Because of that, I am also able to state this fundamental truth that I am born of a people who are heroes and heroines.

I am born of a people who would not tolerate oppression.

I am of a nation that would not allow that fear of death, of torture, of imprisonment, of exile or persecution should result in the perpetuation of injustice.

The great masses who are our mother and father will not permit that the behaviour of the few results in the description of our country and people as barbaric.

Patient because history is on their side, these masses do not despair because today the weather is bad. Nor do they turn triumphalist when, tomorrow, the sun shines.

Whatever the circumstances they have lived through and because of that experience, they are determined to define for themselves who they are and who they should be.

← Thabo Mbeki in Johannesburg, South Africa, 1993

We are assembled here today to mark their victory in acquiring and exercising their right to formulate their own definition of what it means to be African.

The Constitution whose adoption we celebrate constitutes an unequivocal statement that we refuse to accept that our African-ness shall be defined by our race, our colour, our gender or our historical origins.

It is a firm assertion made by ourselves that South Africa belongs to all who live in it, black and white.

It gives concrete expression to the sentiment we share as Africans, and will defend to the death, that the people shall govern.

It recognises the fact that the dignity of the individual is both an objective which society must pursue, and is a goal which cannot be separated from the material well-being of that individual.

It seeks to create the situation in which all our people shall be free from fear, including the fear of the oppression of one national group by another, the fear of the disempowerment of one social echelon by another, the fear of the use of state power to deny anybody their fundamental human rights and the fear of tyranny.

It aims to open the doors so that those who were disadvantaged can assume their place in society as equals with their fellow human beings without regards to colour, to race, to gender, to age or to geographic dispersal.

It provides the opportunity to enable each one and all to state their views, to promote them, to strive for their implementation in the process of governance without fear that a contrary view will be met with repression.

It creates a law-governed society which shall be inimical to arbitrary rule.

It enables the resolution of conflicts by peaceful means rather than resort to force.

It rejoices in the diversity of our people and creates the space for all of us voluntarily to define ourselves as one people.

As an African, this is an achievement of which I am proud, proud without reservation and proud without any feeling of conceit.

Our sense of elevation at this moment also derives from the fact that this magnificent product is the unique creation of African hands and African minds.

But it also constitutes a tribute to our loss of vanity that we could, despite the temptation to treat ourselves as an exceptional fragment of humanity, draw on the accumulated experience and wisdom of all humankind, to define for ourselves what we want to be.

Together with the best in the world, we too are prone to pettiness, to petulance, selfishness and shortsightedness.

But it seems to have happened that we looked at ourselves and said the time had come that we make a superhuman effort to be other than human, to respond to the call to create for ourselves a glorious future, to remind ourselves of the Latin saying: Gloria est consequenda – glory must be sought after.

Today it feels good to be an African.

It feels good that I can stand here as a South African and as a foot soldier of a titanic African army, the African National Congress, to say to all the parties represented here, to the millions who made an input into the processes we are concluding, to our outstanding compatriots who have presided over the birth of our founding document, to the negotiators who pitted their wits one against the other, to the unseen stars who shone unseen as the management and administration of the Constitutional Assembly, the advisers, the experts and the publicists, to the mass communication media, to our friends across the globe – congratulations and well done!

I am an African.

I am born of the peoples of the continent of Africa.

The pain of the violent conflict that the peoples of Liberia, and of Somalia, of the Sudan, of Burundi and Algeria is a pain I also bear.

The dismal shame of poverty, suffering and human degradation of my continent is a blight that we share.

The blight on our happiness that derives from this and from our drift to the periphery of the ordering of human affairs leaves us in a persistent shadow of despair.

This is a savage road to which nobody should be condemned. The evolution of humanity says that Africa reaffirms that she is continuing her rise from the ashes.

Whatever the setbacks of the moment, nothing can stop us now! Whatever the difficulties, Africa shall be at peace!

Thank you very much.

# ALIENATION

Had you opened the *New York Times* to page 39 on June 20, 1972, you would have been greeted by the text of what they called "the greatest speech since President Lincoln's Gettysburg Address." In fact, these words had been written and delivered two months earlier by a forty-year-old Scotsman named Jimmy Reid, a trade union activist and newly appointed rector of the University of Glasgow whose rallying cries in 1971 had inspired thousands of workers at the local shipyards to refuse the mass layoffs imposed on them by the government. By the time Reid gave this celebrated address to the students of Glasgow University, in which he implored them to "avoid the rat race," the yards had been given a second chance.

Alienation is the precise and correctly applied word for describing the major social problem in Britain today. People feel alienated by society. In some intellectual circles it is treated almost as a new phenomenon. It has, however, been with us for years. What I believe is true is that today it is more widespread, more pervasive than ever before. Let me right at the outset define what I mean by alienation. It is the cry of men who feel themselves the victims of blind economic forces beyond their control. It's the frustration of ordinary people excluded from the processes of decision-making. The feeling of despair and hopelessness that pervades people who feel with justification that they have no real say in shaping or determining their own destinies.

Many may not have rationalised it. May not even understand, may not be able to articulate it. But they feel it. It therefore conditions and colours their social attitudes. Alienation expresses itself in different ways in different people. It is to be found in what our courts often describe as the criminal antisocial behaviour of a section of the community. It is expressed by those young people who want to opt out of society, by drop-outs, the so-called maladjusted, those who seek to escape permanently from the reality of society through intoxicants and narcotics. Of course, it would be wrong to say it was the sole reason for these things. But it is a much greater factor in all of them than is generally recognised.

Society and its prevailing sense of values leads to another form of alienation. It alienates some from humanity. It partially dehumanises some people, makes them insensitive, ruthless in their handling of fellow human beings, self-centred and grasping. The irony is, they are often considered normal and well-adjusted. It is my sincere contention that anyone who can be totally adjusted to our society is in greater need of psychiatric analysis and treatment than anyone else. They remind me of the character in the novel *Catch*-22, the father of Major Major. He was a farmer in the American Midwest. He hated suggestions for things like medi-care, social services, unemployment benefits or civil rights. He was, however, an enthusiast for the agricultural

→ James Reid's speech was so popular that it was published as a twelve-page pamphlet by the University of Glasgow – this was its cover

# ALIENATION

## James Reid

Rectorial
Address
1972

# UNIVERSITY OF GLASGOW

policies that paid farmers for not bringing their fields under cultivation. From the money he got for not growing alfalfa he bought more land in order not to grow alfalfa. He became rich. Pilgrims came from all over the state to sit at his feet and learn how to be a successful non-grower of alfalfa. His philosophy was simple. The poor didn't work hard enough and so they were poor. He believed that the good Lord gave him two strong hands to grab as much as he could for himself. He is a comic figure. But think – have you not met his like here in Britain? Here in Scotland? I have.

It is easy and tempting to hate such people. However, it is wrong. They are as much products of society, and of a consequence of that society, human alienation, as the poor drop-out. They are losers. They have lost the essential elements of our common humanity. Man is a social being. Real fulfilment for any person lies in service to his fellow men and women. The big challenge to our civilisation is not Oz, a magazine I haven't seen, let alone read. Nor is it permissiveness, although I agree our society is too permissive. Any society which, for example, permits over one million people to be unemployed is far too permissive for my liking. Nor is it moral laxity in the narrow sense that this word is generally employed – although in a sense here we come nearer to the problem. It does involve morality, ethics, and our concept of human values. The challenge we face is that of rooting out anything and everything that distorts and devalues human relations.

Let me give two examples from contemporary experience to illustrate the point.

Recently on television I saw an advert. The scene is a banquet. A gentleman is on his feet proposing a toast. His speech is full of phrases like 'this full-bodied specimen'. Sitting beside him is a young, buxom woman. The image she projects is not pompous but foolish. She is visibly preening herself, believing that she is the object of the bloke's eulogy. Then he concludes – 'and now I give . . .', then a brand name of what used to be described as Empire sherry. Then the laughter. Derisive and cruel laughter. The real point, of course, is this. In this charade, the viewers were obviously expected to identify not with the victim but with her tormentors.

The other illustration is the widespread, implicit acceptance of the concept and term 'the rat race'. The picture it conjures up is one where we are scurrying around scrambling for position, trampling on others, back-stabbing, all in pursuit of personal success. Even genuinely intended, friendly advice can sometimes take the form of someone saying to you, 'Listen, you look after number one.' Or as they say in London, 'Bang the bell, Jack, I'm on the bus.'

To the students [of Glasgow University] I address this appeal. Reject these attitudes. Reject the values and false morality that underlie these attitudes. A rat race is for rats. We're not rats. We're human beings. Reject the insidious pressures in society that would blunt your critical faculties to all that is happening around you, that would caution silence in the face of injustice lest you jeopardise your chances of promotion and self-advancement. This is how it starts, and before you know where you are, you're a fully paid-up member of the rat-pack. The price is too high. It entails the loss of your dignity and human spirit. Or as Christ put it, 'What doth it profit a man if he gain the whole world and suffer the loss of his soul?'

Profit is the sole criterion used by the establishment to evaluate economic activity. From the rat race to lame ducks. The vocabulary in vogue is a give-away. It's more reminiscent of a human menagerie than human society. The power structures that have inevitably emerged from this approach threaten and undermine our hard-won democratic rights. The whole process is towards the centralisation and concentration of power in fewer and fewer hands. The facts are there for all who want to see. Giant monopoly companies and consortia dominate almost every branch of our economy. The men who wield effective control within these giants exercise a power over their fellow men which is frightening and is a negation of democracy.

Government by the people for the people becomes meaningless unless it includes major economic decision-making by the people for the people. This is not simply an economic matter. In essence it is an ethical and moral question, for whoever takes the important economic decisions in society ipso facto determines the social priorities of that society.

From the Olympian heights of an executive suite, in an atmosphere where your success is judged by the extent to which you can maximise profits, the overwhelming tendency must be to see people as units of production, as indices in your accountants' books. To appreciate fully the inhumanity of this situation, you have to see the hurt and despair in the eyes of a man suddenly told he is redundant, without provision made for suitable alternative employment, with the prospect in the west of Scotland, if he is in his late forties or fifties, of spending the rest of his life in the Labour Exchange. Someone, somewhere has decided he is unwanted, unneeded, and is to be thrown on the industrial scrap heap. From the very depth of my being, I challenge the right of any man or any group of men, in business or in government, to tell a fellow human being that he or she is expendable.

The concentration of power in the economic field is matched by the centralisation of decision-making in the political institutions of society. The power of Parliament has undoubtedly been eroded over past decades, with more and more authority being invested in the Executive. The power of local authorities has been and is being systematically undermined. The only justification I can see for local government is as a counter-balance to the centralised character of national government.

Local government is to be restructured. What an opportunity, one would think, for decentralising as much power as possible back to the local communities. Instead, the proposals are for centralising local government. It's once again a blueprint for bureaucracy, not democracy. If these proposals are implemented, in a few years when asked 'Where do you come from?' I can reply: 'The Western Region.' It even sounds like a hospital board.

It stretches from Oban to Girvan and eastwards to include most of the Glasgow conurbation. As in other matters, I must ask the politicians who favour these proposals – where and how in your calculations did you quantify the value of a community? Of community life? Of a sense of belonging? Of the feeling of identification? These are rhetorical questions. I know the answer. Such human considerations do not feature in their thought processes.

Everything that is proposed from the establishment seems almost calculated to minimise the role of the people, to miniaturise man. I can understand how attractive this prospect must be to those at the top. Those of us who refuse to be pawns in their power game can be picked up by their bureaucratic tweezers and dropped in a filing cabinet under 'M' for malcontent or maladjusted. When you think of some of the high flats around us, it can hardly be an accident that they are as near as one could get to an architectural representation of a filing cabinet.

If modern technology requires greater and larger productive units, let's make our wealth-producing resources and potential subject to public control and to social accountability. Let's gear our society to social need, not personal greed. Given such creative re-orientation of society, there is no doubt in my mind that in a few years we could eradicate in our country the scourge of poverty, the underprivileged, slums and insecurity.

Even this is not enough. To measure social progress purely by material advance is not enough. Our aim must be the enrichment of the whole quality of life. It requires a social and cultural, or if you wish, a spiritual transformation of our country. A necessary part of this must be the restructuring of the institutions of government and, where necessary, the evolution of additional structures so as to involve the people in the decision-making processes of our society. The so-called experts will tell you that this would be cumbersome or marginally inefficient. I am prepared to sacrifice a margin of efficiency for the value of the people's participation. Anyway, in the longer term, I reject this argument.

To unleash the latent potential of our people requires that we give them responsibility. The untapped resources of the North Sea are as nothing compared to the untapped resources of our people. I am convinced that the great mass of our people go through life without even a glimmer of what they could have contributed to their fellow human beings. This is a personal tragedy. It's a social crime. The flowering of each individual's personality and talents is the pre-condition for everyone's development.

In this context education has a vital role to play. If automation and technology is accompanied as it must be with full employment, then the leisure time available to man will be enormously increased. If that is so, then our whole concept of education must change. The whole object must be to equip and educate people for life, not solely for work or a profession. The creative use of leisure, in communion with and in service to our fellow human beings, can and must become an important element in self fulfilment.

Universities must be in the forefront of development, must meet social needs and not lag behind them. It is my earnest desire that this great University of Glasgow should be in the vanguard, initiating changes and setting the example for others to follow. Part of our educational process must be the involvement of all sections of the university on the governing bodies. The case for student representation is unanswerable. It is inevitable.

My conclusion is to re-affirm what I hope and certainly intend to be the spirit permeating this address. It's an affirmation of faith in humanity. All that is good in man's heritage involves recognition of our common humanity, an unashamed acknowledgement that man is good by nature. Burns expressed it in a poem that technically was not his best, yet captured the spirit. In 'Why should we idly waste our prime . . .':

> The golden age, we'll then revive, each man shall be a brother,
> In harmony we all shall live and till the earth together,
> In virtue trained, enlightened youth shall move each fellow creature,
> And time shall surely prove the truth that man is good by nature.

It's my belief that all the factors to make a practical reality of such a world are maturing now. I would like to think that our generation took mankind some way along the road towards this goal. It's a goal worth fighting for.

# REMEMBER THE TRAGEDY OF WAR

On June 8, 1972, a napalm bomb was dropped from a South Vietnamese plane onto Tràng Bàng, a village thought to have been a VietCong stronghold. The explosion caused many to flee, including the family of Kim Phuc Phan Thi, a nine-year-old girl whose attempted escape, with her burnt clothes ripped from her flesh, was photographed by Nick Ut and published internationally. It instantly became an iconic, harrowing snapshot of the Vietnam War. Luckily, despite extensive injuries, Kim survived, and on Veterans Day in 1996 she gave a short, emotional speech at the Vietnam Veterans Memorial.

Dear friends:

I am very happy to be with you today. I thank you for giving me the opportunity to talk and meet with you on this Veterans Day.

As you know I am the little girl who was running to escape from the napalm fire. I do not want to talk about the war because I cannot change history.

I only want you to remember the tragedy of war in order to do things to stop fighting and killing around the world.

I have suffered a lot from both physical and emotional pain. Sometimes I thought I could not live, but God saved me and gave me faith and hope.

Even if I could talk face to face with the pilot who dropped the bombs, I would tell him we cannot change history but we should try to do good things for the present and for the future to promote peace.

I did not think that I could marry nor have any children because of my burns, but now I have a wonderful husband and lovely son and a happy family.

Dear friends, I just dream one day people all over the world can live in real peace: no fighting and no hostility. We should work together to build peace and happiness for all people in all nations.

Thank you so much for letting me be a part of this important day.

# THERE IS AN ALTERNATIVE TO WAR

On March 20, 2003, a U.S.-led coalition of military forces began a "shock and awe" bombing campaign that would kickstart an invasion of Iraq. According to a radio address by the incumbent president, George W. Bush, the purpose was to disarm the country of "weapons of mass destruction, to end Saddam Hussein's support for terrorism, and to free the Iraqi people." The war lasted for more than eight years and no such weapons were ever found. Some estimates suggest that more than 1.2 million people became casualties of this conflict, though the true figure will never be known. A month before the invasion began, on February 14, the French Secretary of Foreign Affairs, Dominique de Villepin, delivered a speech at the UN Security Council in which he opposed the use of such military force, and proposed that similar results could be achieved by diplomatic means. Sadly, his calls for a peaceful resolution fell on deaf ears.

* Hans Blix and Mohamed ElBaradei led the team of UN weapons inspectors in Iraq. Their report stated that they had as yet found no evidence of weapons of mass destruction.

Mr. President, Mr. Secretary-General, distinguished ministers, distinguished ambassadors, I would like to thank Mr. Blix and Mr. ElBaradei* for the information they have given us on the continuing inspections in Iraq. I would like to reiterate to them France's confidence and complete support in their work.

You know the value that France has placed on the unity of the Security Council from the outset of the Iraq crisis. This unity rests on two fundamental elements at this time. We are pursuing together the objective of effectively disarming Iraq. We have an obligation to achieve results. Let us not cast doubt on our common commitment to this goal. We shoulder collectively this onerous responsibility, which must leave no room for ulterior motives or assumptions.

Let us be clear. Not one of us feels the least indulgence towards Saddam Hussein and the Iraqi regime. In unanimously adopting Resolution 1441,† we collectively expressed our agreement with the two-stage approach proposed by France: disarmament through inspections and, should this strategy fail, consideration by the Security Council of all the options, including the recourse to force. It was clearly in the event inspections failed and only in that event that a second resolution could be justified.

† United Nations Security Council Resolution 1441 demanded that Iraq should disarm fully and readmit weapons inspectors or "face serious consequences."

The question today is simple. Do we believe in good conscience that disarmament via inspections is now leading us to a dead end, or do we believe that the possibilities regarding inspections presented in 1441 have still not been fully explored?

In response to this question, France believes two things. First, the option of inspections has not been taken to the end. It can provide an effective response to the imperative of disarming Iraq.

Secondly, the use of force would be so fraught with risk for people, for the region and for international stability that it should only be envisioned as a last resort.

So what have we just learned from the reports by Mr. Blix and Mr. ElBaradei? We have just learned that the inspections are purchasing results. Of course, each of us wants more, and we will continue together to put pressure on Baghdad to obtain more. But the inspections are purchasing results. At earlier reports to the Security Council on January 27, the executive chairman of UNMOVIC [the United Nations Monitoring, Verification and Inspection Commission] and the director-general of the IAEA [International Atomic Energy Agency] identified in detail areas in which progress was expected. Significant gains have now been made on several of these fronts.

In the chemical and biological areas, the Iraqis have provided the inspectors with new documentation. They have also announced they are reestablishing two commissions of inquiry, led by former officials of weapons programs in accordance with Mr. Blix's requests.

In the ballistic area, the information provided by Iraq has enabled the inspectors to make progress. We now know exactly the real capabilities of the Al-Samoud missile. The unauthorized programs must now be dismantled in accordance with Mr. Blix's conclusions.

In the nuclear domain, useful information has been given to the IAEA on the most important points discussed by Mr. ElBaradei on January 27: the acquisition of magnets that could be used to enrich uranium and the list of contacts between Iraq and the country likely to have provided it with uranium.

And so here we are at the heart of the logic of Resolution 1441, which must ensure effective inspections through precisely identifying banned programs and then eliminating them. We all realize that success in the inspections presupposes that we get full and complete cooperation from Iraq. France has consistently demanded this.

Real progress is emerging. Iraq has agreed to aerial reconnaissance over its territory; it has allowed Iraqi scientists to be questioned by inspectors without witnesses; a bill barring all activities linked to weapons of mass destruction programs is being adopted, which is in accordance with the long-standing request from the inspectors; and Iraq is providing a detailed list of experts who witnessed the destruction of military programs in 1991.

France, naturally, expects these commitments to be durably verified as facts. Beyond that, we must maintain strong pressure on Iraq so that it goes further in its cooperation. Progress like this strengthens us in our conviction that inspections can be effective. But we must not shut our eyes to the amount of work that still remains. Questions still have to be cleared up, verifications made, and installations and equipment probably still have to be destroyed. To do this, we must give the inspections every chance of succeeding.

I made some proposals to the council on February 5, and since then, we detailed them in a working document addressed to Mr. Blix and Mr. ElBaradei, which was distributed to council members. What is the spirit of those

FRANCE

proposals? They are practical and concrete proposals that can be implemented quickly. They are designed to enhance the efficiency of inspection operations. They fall within the framework of Resolution 1441, and consequently, they do not require a new resolution by this council. They come to support the efforts of Mr. Blix and Mr. ElBaradei, who are, naturally, the best place to tell us which ones they wish to ensure maximum effectiveness in their work. In their reports, they have already made useful and operational comments.

France has already announced it has additional resources available to Mr. Blix and Mr. ElBaradei, beginning with our Mirage IV reconnaissance aircraft.

Oh, yes, I hear criticism. There are those who think that inspections, in their very essence, cannot be effective at all. But let me recall that that was the very foundation of Resolution 1441, and that inspections are producing results. One may judge them inadequate, but the results are there.

Then there are those who believe that continuing the inspection process is a kind of delaying tactic to prevent or avert military intervention. That naturally raises a question of how much time is allowed Iraq. And this brings us to the heart of the matter. What is at stake is our credibility and our sense of responsibility. Let us have the courage to see things as they are. There are two options. The option of war might seem a priori to be the swiftest, but let us not forget that having won the war, peace has to be built. Let us not delude ourselves. This will be long and difficult because it will be necessary to preserve Iraq's unity and to restore stability in a lasting way in a country and a region harshly affected by the intrusion of force.

Faced with that prospective, there is an alternative – inspections – which allow us to move forward day by day with the effective and peaceful disarmament of Iraq. In the end, is that choice not the most sure and most rapid?

No one today can claim that the path of war will be shorter than the path of inspections. No one can claim that it would lead to a safer, more just, more stable world, for war is always the sanction of failure. Would this be our sole recourse in the face of the many challenges at this time?

So let us give the United Nations inspectors the time they need for their mission to succeed, but also let us all be vigilant and ask Mr. Blix and Mr. ElBaradei to report regularly to the council.

France, for its part, would propose another meeting on March 14 at the ministerial level to assess the situation. We would then be able to judge the progress made and what remains to be done.

Given this context, the use of force is not justified at this time. There is an alternative to war: disarming Iraq via inspections. Moreover, premature recourse to the military option would be fraught with risks. The authority of our action is based today on the unity of the international community. Premature military intervention will bring this unity into question, and that would detract

← French Foreign Minister Dominique de Villepin delivers a speech at the UN headquarters, February 14, 2003

from its legitimacy and in the long run, its effectiveness. Such intervention could have incalculable consequences for the stability of this scarred and fragile region. It would compound the sense of injustice, increase tension and risk paving the way to other conflicts.

We all share the same priority: fighting terrorism mercilessly. This fight requires total determination. Since the tragedy of September 11, this has been one of the highest priorities facing our peoples. France has been struck hard by this terrible scourge several times, and it is wholly mobilized in this fight which involves all of us, which we must pursue together. That was the sense of the Security Council meeting held on January 20 and France's initiative.

Ten days ago, the U.S. Secretary of State, Mr. Powell, reported alleged links between al-Qaeda and the Baghdad regime. Given the present state of our research and intelligence in liaison with our allies, nothing allows us to establish such links. But we must assess the impact that disputed military action would have on this level. Would such intervention today not be liable to exacerbate divisions between societies, cultures, peoples; divisions that nurture terrorism?

All along, France has been saying we do not exclude the possibility that force may have to be used one day. If the inspectors' reports concluded it was impossible to continue inspections, the council would then have to take a decision and its members would have to meet all of their responsibilities.

In such an eventuality, I just want to recall now the questions I stressed at our last debate on February 4, which we must answer.

To what extent do the nature and extent of the threat justify immediate recourse to force?

How do we ensure that the considerable risks of such intervention can actually be kept under control?

In any case, in such an eventuality, it is the unity of the international community that would ensure and guarantee its effectiveness. It is the United Nations that, whatever happens, will still tomorrow be at the center of the peace to be built.

To those who are anguished, wondering when and how we are going to cede to war, I would like to say that nothing at any time in this council will be done in haste, in misunderstanding, out of suspicion or out of fear.

In this temple of the United Nations, we are the guardians of an ideal, the guardians of a conscience. The onerous responsibility and immense honor we have must lead us to give priority to disarmament through peace.

This message comes to you today from an old country, France, from a continent, Europe, that has known war, occupation, barbarity. It is an old country that does not forget and is very aware of all it owes to freedom fighters who came from America and elsewhere.

And yet France has always stood upright in the face of history before mankind. Faithful to its values, it wants resolutely to act together with all members of the international community. France believes in our ability to build together a better world.

Thank you, Mr. President.

# WE ARE ALL BOUND UP TOGETHER

It was largely thanks to the influence of Frances Harper's uncle, a civil rights activist who brought her up from the age of three, that his multitalented niece grew up to become an abolitionist and prominent member of the American Anti-Slavery Society. But she was also a published poet, a novelist, a teacher, and a skilled orator. In May 1866, at the National Women's Rights Convention in New York City, the latter of those skills was clear for all to hear when she addressed the audience on the subject of equal rights.

I feel I am something of a novice upon this platform. Born of a race whose inheritance has been outrage and wrong, most of my life had been spent in battling against those wrongs. But I did not feel as keenly as others, that I had these rights, in common with other women, which are now demanded. About two years ago, I stood within the shadows of my home. A great sorrow had fallen upon my life. My husband had died suddenly, leaving me a widow, with four children, one my own, and the others stepchildren. I tried to keep my children together. But my husband died in debt; and before he had been in his grave three months, the administrator had swept the very milk-crocks and wash tubs from my hands. I was a farmer's wife and made butter for the Columbus market; but what could I do, when they had swept all away? They left me one thing – and that was a looking glass! Had I died instead of my husband, how different would have been the result! By this time he would have had another wife, it is likely; and no administrator would have gone into his house, broken up his home, and sold his bed, and taken away his means of support.

I took my children in my arms, and went out to seek my living. While I was gone, a neighbor to whom I had once lent five dollars went before a magistrate and swore that he believed I was a non-resident, and laid an attachment on my very bed. And I went back to Ohio with my orphan children in my arms, without a single feather bed in this wide world, that was not in the custody of the law. I say, then, that justice is not fulfilled so long as woman is unequal before the law.

We are all bound up together in one great bundle of humanity, and society cannot trample on the weakest and feeblest of its members without receiving the curse in its own soul. You tried that in the case of the Negro. You pressed him down for two centuries; and in so doing you crippled the moral strength and paralyzed the spiritual energies of the white men of the country. When the hands of the black were fettered, white men were deprived of the liberty of speech and the freedom of the press. Society cannot afford to neglect the enlightenment of any class of its members. At the South, the legislation of the country was in behalf of the rich slaveholders, while the poor white man was neglected. What is the consequence today? From that very class of neglected

→ Frances Harper, photographer unknown

poor white men comes the man who stands today, with his hand upon the helm of the nation. He fails to catch the watchword of the hour, and throws himself, the incarnation of meanness, across the pathway of the nation. My objection to Andrew Johnson[*] is not that he has been a poor white man; my objection is that he keeps "poor whits" all the way through. That is the trouble with him.

This grand and glorious revolution which has commenced will fail to reach its climax of success, until throughout the length and breadth of the American Republic, the nation shall be so color-blind, as to know no man by the color of his skin or the curl of his hair. It will then have no privileged class, trampling upon and outraging the unprivileged classes, but will be then one great privileged nation, whose privilege will be to produce the loftiest manhood and womanhood that humanity can attain.

I do not believe that giving the woman the ballot is immediately going to cure all the ills of life. I do not believe that white women are dew-drops just exhaled from the skies. I think that like men they may be divided into three classes, the good, the bad, and the indifferent. The good would vote according to their convictions and principles; the bad, as dictated by prejudice or malice; and the indifferent will vote on the strongest side of the question, with the winning party.

You white women speak here of rights. I speak of wrongs. I, as a colored woman, have had in this country an education which has made me feel as if I were in the situation of Ishmael, my hand against every man, and every man's hand against me. Let me go tomorrow morning and take my seat in one of your street cars – I do not know that they will do it in New York, but they will in Philadelphia – and the conductor will put up his hand and stop the car rather than let me ride.

Going from Washington to Baltimore this spring, they put me in the smoking car. Aye, in the capital of the nation, where the black man consecrated himself to the nation's defense, faithful when the white man was faithless, they put me in the smoking car! They did it once; but the next time they tried it, they failed; for I would not go in. I felt the fight in me; but I don't want to have to fight all the time. Today I am puzzled where to make my home. I would like to make it in Philadelphia, near my own friends and relations. But if I want to ride in the streets of Philadelphia, they send me to ride on the platform with the driver. Have women nothing to do with this? Not long since, a colored woman took her seat in an Eleventh Street car in Philadelphia, and the conductor stopped the car, and told the rest of the passengers to get out, and left the car with her in it alone, when they took it back to the station. One day I took my seat in a car, and the conductor came to me and told me to take another seat. I just screamed "murder." The man said if I was black I ought to behave myself. I knew that if he was white he was not behaving himself. Are there not wrongs to be righted?

* Andrew Johnson (1808–75) was a Democrat and Southern Unionist from a poverty-stricken background, who became president after Lincoln was assassinated in 1865. He opposed giving citizenship to former slaves and is widely seen as being one of the worst presidents in U.S. history.

† In March 1857, the U.S. Supreme Court ruled that a slave, Dred Scott, who had moved with his master to a free state, was not entitled to his freedom after his master had died, and that African Americans were not and could never be citizens of the United States. The decision was one of the factors that pushed the country closer to civil war.

‡ This refers to Harriet Tubman (1822–1913), the famous abolitionist, spy for the U.S. Army and key conductor in the Underground Railroad, a network of safe houses that formed a route for slaves to escape to freedom.

In advocating the cause of the colored man, since the Dred Scott decision,† I have sometimes said I thought the nation had touched bottom. But let me tell you there is a depth of infamy lower than that. It is when the nation, standing upon the threshold of a great peril, reached out its hands to a feebler race, and asked that race to help it, and when the peril was over, said, "You are good enough for soldiers, but not good enough for citizens. . . ."

We have a woman in our country who has received the name of "Moses,"‡ not by lying about it, but by acting it out – a woman who has gone down into the Egypt of slavery and brought out hundreds of our people into liberty. The last time I saw that woman, her hands were swollen. That woman who had led one of Montgomery's most successful expeditions, who was brave enough and secretive enough to act as a scout for the American army, had her hands all swollen from a conflict with a brutal conductor, who undertook to eject her from her place. That woman, whose courage and bravery won a recognition from our army and from every black man in the land, is excluded from every thoroughfare of travel. Talk of giving women the ballot-box? Go on. It is a normal school, and the white women of this country need it. While there exists this brutal element in society which tramples upon the feeble and treads down the weak, I tell you that if there is any class of people who need to be lifted out of their airy nothings and selfishness, it is the white women of America.

# EVIL

Russian poet Iosif Aleksandrovich Brodsky, later known as Joseph Brodsky, was born in Leningrad in 1940 to Jewish parents. In 1972, as a result of his heritage and the fact that his poetry had been deemed "anti-Soviet" by the Russian authorities, he was given no option but to leave the country of his birth and move to the United States, where he would flourish. In 1984, a few years before winning the Nobel Prize and then becoming

United States Poet Laureate, Brodsky was invited to give the commencement speech at Williams College in Massachusetts. He accepted, and used the occasion to not just warn the outgoing students that they would at some point be confronted with evil, but also to explain why "turning the other cheek" was not always the best response.

Ladies and gentlemen of the class of 1984:

No matter how daring or cautious you may choose to be, in the course of your life you are bound to come into direct physical contact with what's known as Evil. I mean here not a property of the gothic novel but, to say the least, a palpable social reality that you in no way can control. No amount of good nature or cunning calculations will prevent this encounter. In fact, the more calculating, the more cautious you are, the greater is the likelihood of this rendezvous, the harder its impact. Such is the structure of life that what we regard as Evil is capable of a fairly ubiquitous presence if only because it tends to appear in the guise of good. You never see it crossing your threshold announcing itself: "Hi, I'm Evil!" That, of course, indicates its secondary nature, but the comfort one may derive from this observation gets dulled by its frequency.

A prudent thing to do, therefore, would be to subject your notions of good to the closest possible scrutiny, to go, so to speak, through your entire wardrobe checking which of your clothes may fit a stranger. That, of course, may turn into a full-time occupation, and well it should. You'll be surprised how many things you considered your own and good can easily fit, without much adjustment, your enemy. You may even start to wonder whether he is not your mirror image, for the most interesting thing about Evil is that it is wholly human. To put it mildly, nothing can be turned and worn inside out with greater ease than one's notion of social justice, public conscience, a better future, etc. One of the surest signs of danger here is the number of those who share your views, not so much because unanimity has a knack of degenerating into uniformity as because of the probability – implicit in great numbers – that noble sentiment is being faked.

By the same token, the surest defense against Evil is extreme individualism, originality of thinking, whimsicality, even – if you will – eccentricity. That is, something that can't be feigned, faked, imitated; something even a seasoned impostor couldn't be happy with. Something, in other words, that can't be shared, like your own skin – not even by a minority. Evil is a sucker for solidity. It always goes for big numbers, for confident granite, for ideological purity, for drilled armies and balanced sheets. Its proclivity for such things has to do presumably with its innate insecurity, but this realization, again, is of small comfort when Evil triumphs.

Which it does: in so many parts of the world and inside ourselves. Given its volume and intensity, given, especially, the fatigue of those who oppose it, Evil today may be regarded not as an ethical category but as a physical phenomenon no longer measured in particles but mapped geographically. Therefore the reason I am talking to you about all this has nothing to do with your being young, fresh, and facing a clean slate. No, the slate is dark with dirt and it's hard to believe in either your ability or your will to clean it. The purpose of my talk is simply to suggest to you a mode of resistance which may come in handy to you one day; a mode that may help you to emerge from the encounter with Evil perhaps less soiled if not necessarily more triumphant than your precursors. What I have in mind, of course, is the famous business of turning the other cheek.

I assume that one way or another you have heard about the interpretations of this verse from the Sermon on the Mount by Leo Tolstoy, Mahatma Gandhi, Martin Luther King, and many others. In other words, I assume that you are familiar with the concept of nonviolent, or passive, resistance, whose main principle is returning good for evil, that is, not responding in kind. The fact that the world today is what it is suggests, to say the least, that this concept is far from being cherished universally. The reasons for its unpopularity are twofold. First, what is required for this concept to be put into effect is a margin of democracy. This is precisely what 86 percent of the globe lacks. Second, the common sense that tells a victim that his only gain in turning the other cheek and not responding in kind yields, at best, a moral victory, i.e., quite immaterial. The natural reluctance to expose yet another part of your body to a blow is justified by a suspicion that this sort of conduct only agitates and enhances Evil; that moral victory can be mistaken by the adversary for his impunity.

There are other, graver reasons to be suspicious. If the first blow hasn't knocked all the wits out of the victim's head, he may realize that turning the other cheek amounts to manipulation of the offender's sense of guilt, not to speak of his karma. The moral victory itself may not be so moral after all, not only because suffering often has a narcissistic aspect to it, but also because it renders the victim superior, that is, better than his enemy. Yet no matter how evil your enemy is, the crucial thing is that he is human; and although incapable of loving another like ourselves, we nonetheless know that evil takes root when one man starts to think that he is better than another. (This is why you've been hit on your right cheek in the first place.) At best, therefore, what one can get

from turning the other cheek to one's enemy is the satisfaction of alerting the latter to the futility of his action. "Look," the other cheek says, "what you are hitting is just flesh. It's not me. You can't crush my soul." The trouble, of course, with this kind of attitude is that the enemy may just accept the challenge.

Twenty years ago the following scene took place in one of the numerous prison yards of northern Russia. At seven o'clock in the morning the door of a cell was flung open and on its threshold stood a prison guard who addressed its inmates: "Citizens! The collective of this prison's guards challenges you, the inmates, to socialist competition in cutting the lumber amassed in our yard." In those parts there is no central heating, and the local police, in a manner of speaking, tax all the nearby lumber companies for one tenth of their produce. By the time I am describing, the prison yard looked like a veritable lumber yard: the piles were two to three stories high, dwarfing the one-storied quadrangle of the prison itself. The need for cutting was evident, although socialist competitions of this sort had happened before. "And what if I refuse to take part in this?" inquired one of the inmates. "Well, in that case no meals for you," replied the guard.

Then axes were issued to inmates, and the cutting started. Both prisoners and guards worked in earnest, and by noon all of them, especially the always underfed prisoners, were exhausted. A break was announced and people sat down to eat: except the fellow who asked the question. He kept swinging his axe. Both prisoners and guards exchanged jokes about him, something about Jews being normally regarded as smart people whereas this man . . . and so forth. After the break they resumed the work, although in a somewhat more flagging manner. By four o'clock the guards quit, since for them it was the end of their shift; a bit later the inmates stopped too. The man's axe still kept swinging. Several times he was urged to stop, by both parties, but he paid no attention. It seemed as though he had acquired a certain rhythm he was unwilling to break; or was it a rhythm that possessed him?

To the others, he looked like an automaton. By five o'clock, by six o'clock, the axe was still going up and down. Both guards and inmates were now watching him keenly, and the sardonic expression on their faces gradually gave way first to one of bewilderment and then to one of terror. By seven-thirty the man stopped, staggered into his cell, and fell asleep. For the rest of his stay in that prison, no call for socialist competition between guards and inmates was issued again, although the wood kept piling up.

I suppose the fellow could do this – twelve hours of straight cutting – because at the time he was quite young. In fact, he was then twenty-four. Only a little older than you are. However, I think there could have been another reason for his behavior that day. It's quite possible that the young man – precisely because he was young – remembered the text of the Sermon on the Mount better than Tolstoy and Gandhi did. Because the Son of Man was in the habit of

← Joseph Brodsky, 1992

speaking in triads, the young man could have recalled that the relevant verse doesn't stop at "but whosoever shall smite thee on thy right cheek, turn to him the other also" but continues without either period or comma:

> And if any man will sue thee at the law, and take away thy coat, let him have thy cloak also. And whosoever shall compel thee to go a mile, go with him twain.

Quoted in full, these verses have in fact very little to do with nonviolent or passive resistance, with the principles of not responding in kind and returning good for evil. The meaning of these lines is anything but passive for it suggests that evil can be made absurd through excess; it suggests rendering evil absurd through dwarfing its demands with the volume of your compliance, which devalues the harm. This sort of thing puts a victim into a very active position, into the position of a mental aggressor. The victory that is possible here is not a moral but an existential one. The other cheek here sets in motion not the enemy's sense of guilt (which he is perfectly capable of quelling) but exposes his senses and faculties to the meaninglessness of the whole enterprise: the way every form of mass production does.

Let me remind you that we are not talking here about a situation involving a fair fight. We are talking about situations where one finds oneself in a hopelessly inferior position from the very outset, where one has no chance of fighting back, where the odds are overwhelmingly against one. In other words, we are talking about the very dark hours in one's life, when one's sense of moral superiority over the enemy offers no solace, when this enemy is too far gone to be shamed or made nostalgic for abandoned scruples, when one has at one's disposal only one's face, coat, cloak, and a pair of feet that are still capable of walking a mile or two.

In this situation there is very little room for tactical maneuver. So turning the other cheek should be your conscious, cold, deliberate decision. Your chances of winning, however dismal they are, all depend on whether or not you know what you are doing. Thrusting forward your face with the cheek toward the enemy, you should know that this is just the beginning of your ordeal as well as that of the verse – and you should be able to see yourself through the entire sequence, through all three verses from the Sermon on the Mount. Otherwise, a line taken out of context will leave you crippled.

To base ethics on a faultily quoted verse is to invite doom, or else to end up becoming a mental bourgeois enjoying the ultimate comfort: that of his convictions. In either case (of which the latter with its membership in well-intentioned movements and nonprofit organizations is the least palatable) it results in yielding ground to Evil, in delaying the comprehension of its weaknesses. For Evil, may I remind you, is only human.

Ethics based on this faultily quoted verse have changed nothing in post-Gandhi India, save the color of its administration. From a hungry man's point of view, though, it's all the same who makes him hungry. I submit that he may even prefer a white man to be responsible for his sorry state if only because this way social evil may appear to come from elsewhere and may perhaps be less efficient than the suffering at the hand of his own kind. With an alien in charge, there is still room for hope, for fantasy.

Similarly in post-Tolstoy Russia, ethics based on this misquoted verse undermined a great deal of the nation's resolve in confronting the police state. What has followed is known all too well: six decades of turning the other cheek transformed the face of the nation into one big bruise, so that the state today, weary of its violence, simply spits at that face. As well as at the face of the world. In other words, if you want to secularize Christianity, if you want to translate Christ's teachings into political terms, you need something more than modern political mumbo-jumbo: you need to have the original – in your mind at least if it hasn't found room in your heart. Since He was less a good man than divine spirit, it's fatal to harp on His goodness at the expense of His metaphysics.

I must admit that I feel somewhat uneasy talking about these things: because turning or not turning that other cheek is, after all, an extremely intimate affair. The encounter always occurs on a one-to-one basis. It's always your skin, your coat and cloak, and it is your limbs that will have to do the walking. To advise, let alone to urge, anyone about the use of these properties is, if not entirely wrong, indecent. All I aspire to do here is to erase from your minds a cliché that harmed so many and yielded so little. I also would like to instill in you the idea that as long as you have your skin, coat, cloak and limbs, you are not yet defeated, whatever the odds are.

There is, however, a greater reason for one to feel uneasy about discussing these matters in public; and it's not only your own natural reluctance to regard your young selves as potential victims. No, it's rather mere sobriety, which makes one anticipate among you potential villains as well, and it is a bad strategy to divulge the secrets of resistance in front of the potential enemy. What perhaps relieves one from a charge of treason or, worse still, of projecting the tactical status quo into the future, is the hope that the victim will always be more inventive, more original in his thinking, more enterprising than the villain. Hence the chance that the victim may triumph.

# IN CASE OF FAILURE

On June 6, 1944, five long years into World War II, more than 150,000 Allied troops descended on the beaches of Normandy, France, in a long, meticulously planned and ultimately successful effort to liberate mainland Europe from the grip of Nazi Germany. The evening prior, General Dwight D. Eisenhower prepared for the possibility of failure by writing a speech – a succinct and illuminating four sentences in which he takes full responsibility for the operation's shortcomings. This sheet of notepaper, mistakenly dated July 5, then remained in Eisenhower's wallet for a month, its words forever unspoken.

Eisenhower later remarked to an aide that similar speeches were prepared before every military operation during World War II. This is the only one he kept.

→ Eisenhower tucked this draft into his wallet, where it remained, undelivered

Our landings in the Cherbourg-Havre area have failed to gain a satisfactory foothold and I have withdrawn the troops. My decision to attack at this time and place was based upon the best information available. The troops, the air and the Navy did all that bravery and devotion to duty could do. If any blame or fault attaches to the attempt it is mine alone.

Our landings in the
Cherbourg — Havre area
have failed to gain a
satisfactory foothold and
~~I have withdrawn~~
the troops. ~~have been~~
~~withdrawn.~~) ~~This particular~~
~~operation~~ My decision to
attack at this time and place
was based upon the best
information available. ——
The troops, the air and the
Navy did all that ~~devotion~~
Bravery and devotion to duty
could do. If any blame
or fault attaches to the attempt
it is mine alone.

——————     July 5

# ITS NAME IS FREEDOM

In 2014, at the 65th National Book Awards in New York, the long and illustrious career of science fiction and fantasy novelist Ursula K. Le Guin was celebrated. She was awarded the Medal for Distinguished Contribution to American Letters for her "exceptional impact on this country's literary heritage." Introduced by fellow author Neil Gaiman as a "giant of literature," Le Guin took to the stage to remind all assembled of the importance of their work.

To the givers of this beautiful reward, my thanks, from the heart. My family, my agents, my editors, know that my being here is their doing as well as my own, and that the beautiful reward is theirs as much as mine. And I rejoice in accepting it for, and sharing it with, all the writers who've been excluded from literature for so long – my fellow authors of fantasy and science fiction, writers of the imagination, who for fifty years have watched the beautiful rewards go to the so-called realists.

Hard times are coming, when we'll be wanting the voices of writers who can see alternatives to how we live now, can see through our fear-stricken society and its obsessive technologies to other ways of being, and even imagine real grounds for hope. We'll need writers who can remember freedom – poets, visionaries – realists of a larger reality.

Right now, we need writers who know the difference between production of a market commodity and the practice of an art. Developing written material to suit sales strategies in order to maximize corporate profit and advertising revenue is not the same thing as responsible book publishing or authorship.

Yet I see sales departments given control over editorial. I see my own publishers, in a silly panic of ignorance and greed, charging public libraries for an e-book six or seven times more than they charge customers. We just saw a profiteer try to punish a publisher for disobedience, and writers threatened by corporate fatwa. And I see a lot of us, the producers, who write the books and make the books, accepting this – letting commodity profiteers sell us like deodorant, and tell us what to publish, what to write.

Books aren't just commodities; the profit motive is often in conflict with the aims of art. We live in capitalism, its power seems inescapable – but then, so did the divine right of kings. Any human power can be resisted and changed by human beings. Resistance and change often begin in art. Very often in our art, the art of words.

I've had a long career as a writer, and a good one, in good company. Here at the end of it, I don't want to watch American literature get sold down the river. We who live by writing and publishing want and should demand our fair share of the proceeds; but the name of our beautiful reward isn't profit. Its name is freedom.

→ Ursula K. Le Guin, 1989, photographed by Dana Gluckstein

# HE IS CHALLENGING THE AXIOMS OF SCIENCE

In October 1930, the Joint British Committee for the Promotion of the Physical and Economic Welfare of Eastern Jewry organized a fundraising dinner at London's Savoy Hotel – an event which raised around $610,000 for the cause. A thousand people attended, many of whom were highly respected in their fields, and speakers that evening included such luminaries as author H. G. Wells, Astronomer Royal Frank Watson Dyson, and playwright George Bernard Shaw. On Shaw's shoulders fell quite a task: to introduce and toast the guest of honor, Albert Einstein, who had just arrived in the country.

GEORGE BERNARD SHAW:

My lords, ladies and gentlemen, when my friend Mr Wallrock asked me to undertake this duty I could not help wondering whether he really grasped the magnitude of the honour he was conferring upon me or the impossibility of my discharging it adequately. But there are some magnitudes which are so great that they have to be expressed by the symbol zero, and I was able to say, 'Well, I can do it as well as anybody else.' I will do my best.

Here in London we are still a great centre. I do not suppose that we shall be a great centre long – all that will presently be transferred to the United States – but for the moment I am speaking in a capital where the reception of great men is a very common event. We have a string of great statesmen, great financiers, great diplomatists, great generals – even occasionally an author – and we make speeches and we toast them, and we make pictures as we talk. In London things are fixed ahead, and we know where we have to be. But still the event is not a very striking one. In truth in London great men are six a penny, and they are a very mixed lot, and when we drink to their health and make a speech, we have to be guilty of scandalous suppression and disgraceful hypocrisy. There is always a great deal to conceal. If you take the typical great man of our historic epoch, and suppose that I had to rise here tonight to propose the toast of Napoleon – well, undoubtedly I could say many very flattering things about Napoleon. But the one thing which I should not be able to say about him would be perhaps the most important thing, and that was, that it would perhaps have been better for the human race if he had never been born.

Well, tonight at least, perhaps it will be for the only time in our lives, we have no suppressions to make, no hypocrisy to be guilty of. I have said that great men are a mixed lot, but there are orders of great men. There are great men who are great men amongst small men, but there are also great men who are great amongst great men, and that is the sort of great man whom you have amongst you here tonight. Napoleon, and other great men of his type, they were makers of empire, but there is an order of men who get beyond that. They are not makers of empire, but they are makers of universes. And when they have made those universes, their hands are unstained by the blood of any human being on Earth. They are very rare. I go back 2,500 years, and how many of them can I count in that period? I can count them on the fingers of my two hands: Pythagoras, Ptolemy, Aristotle, Copernicus, Kepler, Galileo, Newton, Einstein. And I still have two fingers left vacant.

Since the death of Newton, 300 years have passed, nine generations of men. And those nine generations of men have not enjoyed the privilege which we are enjoying here tonight of standing face to face with one of those eight great men, and looking forward to the privilege of hearing his voice. And another 300 years may very well pass before another generation will enjoy that privilege. And I must – even amongst those eight men, I must even make a distinction. I have called them makers of universes, but some of them were only repairers of universes. Only three of them made universes. Ptolemy made a universe which lasted 1,400 years. Newton also made a universe, which has lasted 300 years. Einstein has made a universe, and I can't tell you how long that will last.

These great men, they have been the leaders of one side of a great movement of humanity which has two sides. We call the one side, Religion; and we call the other, Science. Now, religion is always right. Religion solves every problem, and thereby abolishes problems from the universe because, when you have solved a problem, the problem no longer exists. Religion gives us certainty, stability, peace. It gives us absolutes, which we so long for. It protects us against that progress which we all dread, almost more than anything else. Science is the very opposite of that. Science is always wrong. And science never solves a problem without raising ten more problems to confront us. All these great men – what have they been doing? Ptolemy, as I say, created a universe. Copernicus proved that Ptolemy was wrong. Kepler proved that Copernicus was wrong. Galileo proved that Aristotle was wrong. And now you are expecting me to say that Newton proved that they were all wrong. But, you forget, when science reached Newton, science came up against that incalculable, that illogical, that hopelessly inconsequent and extraordinary natural phenomenon, an Englishman. That had never happened to it before. As an Englishman, Newton was able to combine mental power so extraordinary that if I were speaking fifty years ago, as I am old enough to have done, I should have said that his was the greatest mind that any man had ever been endowed with. And he contrived to combine the exercise of that wonderful mind with credulity, with superstition, with delusion which would not have imposed on a moderately intelligent rabbit. As an Englishman also, he knew his people, he knew his language, he knew his own soul. And knowing that language, he knew that an honest thing was a square thing; an honest bargain was a square

deal; an honest man was a square man, who acted on the square. That is to say, the universe that he created had above everything to be a rectilinear universe.

Now, see the dilemma in which this placed Newton. He knew his universe; he knew that it consisted of heavenly bodies all in motion; and he also knew that the one thing that you cannot do to any body in motion whatsoever is to make it move in a straight line. You may fire it out of a cannon with the strongest charge that you can put into it. You may have the cannon contrived to have, as they say, the flattest trajectory that a cannon can have. It is no use. The projectile will not go in a straight line. If you take a poor man – the poorer the better – if you blindfold that man, and if you say, 'I will give you £1,000 if you, blindfolded, will walk 1,000 yards in a straight line,' he will do his best for the sake of the thousand pounds to walk in a straight line, but he will walk in an elliptical orbit and come back to exactly the same place. Now, what was Newton to do? How was he to make the universe English?

Well, mere facts will never daunt an Englishman. They never have stopped one yet, and they did not stop Newton. Newton invented – invented, mind you; some people would say discovered, I advisedly say he invented – a force, which would make the straight line, take the straight lines of his universe and bend them. And that was the force of gravitation. And when he had invented this force, he had created a universe which was wonderful and consistent in itself, and which was thoroughly British. And when applying his wonderful genius, when he had completed the book of that universe, what sort of book was it? It was a book which told you the stations of all the heavenly bodies. It showed their distances apart, it showed the rate at which they were travelling, it showed – gave you the exact hour – at which they would arrive at such and such a point to make an eclipse or at which they would strike this earth and knock it into bits, as Sirius is going to do some day. In other words, it was not a magical marvellous thing like a Bible. It was a matter-of-fact British thing like a *Bradshaw!*[*] For 300 years, we believed in that *Bradshaw* and in that Newtonian universe, as I suppose no system has ever been believed in before. The more civilised, the more educated we were, the more firmly would we believe in it. I believed in it. I was brought up to believe in it.

Then, an amazing thing happened. A young professor got up in the middle of Europe. And, without betraying any consciousness of saying anything extraordinary, he addressed himself to our astronomers. And he said, 'Excuse me, gentlemen, but if you will attentively observe the next eclipse of the sun, you will find out what is wrong with the perihelion of Mercury.' And all Europe staggered. It said, 'Something wrong? Something wrong in the Newtonian universe? How can that be?' And, 'Listen,' we said, 'this man is a blasphemer! Burn him alive! Confute him! Madman!' But the astronomers only looked rather foolish. And, they said, 'Oh, let us wait for the eclipse.' But we said, 'No, this is not a question of the eclipse. This man has said that there is something wrong with the perihelion of Mercury. Do you mean to say that there is something wrong with the perihelion of Mercury?' And then they said, 'Oh yes, we knew it all along.' They said, 'Newton knew it.'

'Well,' we said then, 'why didn't you tell us so before?' Our faith began to shake, and we said, 'If this young man, when the eclipse comes, gets away with it, then the next thing that he will be doing, he will be questioning the existence of gravitation!' And the young professor smiled. And he said, 'No, I – uh – I mean no harm to gravitation. Gravitation is a very useful hypothesis. And, after all, it gives you fairly close results, fairly close results. But, personally and for my part, I can do without it.' And we said, 'What do you mean, do without it? What about that apple?' The young professor said, he said, 'What happened to that apple is really a very curious and interesting question. You see, Newton did not know what happened to the apple. The only real authority on the subject of what happened to the apple was the apple itself!

'Now apples are very intelligent. If you watch apples carefully, you will learn that they behave much more sensibly than men often do, but unfortunately we do not know their language, and,' the professor said, 'what Newton ought to have done would be to see something fall that could tell the story afterwards, could explain itself. He should have reflected that not only apples fall, but men fall. And,' he said, 'I, instead of sitting about in orchards and watching apples fall, what did I do? I frequented cities in quarters where building operations were going on. I knew as a man of science that it was statistically certain that, sooner or later, I should see a man fall off a scaffolding. And I did. And I went to that man – in hospital – and, after condoling with him in the usual fashion, saying how sorry I was for his accident, and how he was, I came to business. I said, "When you came off that scaffolding, did the earth attract you?" The man said, "Certainly not! Gar nicht! On the contrary, the earth repelled me with such violence that here I am in hospital with most of my bones broken!"' And the professor could only say, 'Well, my friend, you have been lucky enough to escape without breaking your own back, but you have broken Newton's back.' That was very clear. And, we turned round and we said, 'Well! This is all very well, but what about the straight line? If there is no gravitation, why do not the heavenly bodies travel in a straight line right out of the universe?' The professor said, 'Why should they? That is not the way the world is made. The world is not a British rectilinear world. It is a curvilinear world. And the heavenly bodies go in curves because that is the natural way for them to go.' And, at that word, the whole Newtonian universe crumbled up and vanished and was succeeded by the Einsteinian universe. Now, I am sorry to have to say it, you know. You must remember that our distinguished visitor could not say that himself. It would not be nice for him to say it. It would not be courteous. But I, standing here in England, I feel that we had better confess it just this once and have done with it and acknowledge it. Well! I was greatly impressed when I heard these things, because I said, 'Here is a wonderful man.'

This man is not merely challenging statements of fact made by scientific men or other men. Any man can challenge a statement of fact. The Flat Earth man, lecturing in Hyde Park, he is challenging statements of fact. Our friends at Scotland Yard, not far from here, spend their lives questioning statements of fact. But this man is not challenging the facts of science: he is challenging the axioms of science. And, what is more, not only is he challenging the axioms of science, but the axioms of science have surrendered to his challenge. And then came in my special and particular point of view. I said, 'These are not results worked out by a mathematician, the results of equations marked out on paper. These are the intuitions of an artist. And I as an artist claim kinship with that great discoverer.' I claim to be a man of science in the same sense that he is a man of science. I have reminded myself that Leonardo da Vinci the artist, born twenty-one years before Copernicus, wrote down in his notebook, not as the result of elaborate calculation but as a perfectly simple and plain and obvious matter of fact, 'The Earth is a moon of the sun.' And later on, came the English artist William Hogarth, a contemporary of Newton – their lives overlapped by thirty years – and when Newton said, 'The line of nature is a straight line,' William Hogarth said, 'The line of nature is a curve.' He anticipated our guest. But he was not mathematician enough to work out the entire consequences. And so, I flatter myself that I too am an artist.

I think my speech will be understood by our guest here tonight. Now, I must come to my peroration. I have spoken enough. Within the last month or so, there has come to me, and come to many of you, our visitor's profession of faith, his creed. And that has interested me very much because I must confess to you that there is not a single creed of an established church on Earth at present that I can subscribe to. But to our visitor's creed I can subscribe to every single item. I rejoice at the new universe to which he has introduced us. I rejoice in the fact that he has destroyed all the old sermons, all the old absolutes, all the old cut-and-dried conceptions even of time and space, which were so discouraging because they seemed all so solid that you never could get any further. I want to get further always. I want more and more problems. And our visitor has raised endless and wonderful problems, and has begun solving them.

Well, in that confession, there is one passage which must touch us all, and that is the eloquent and moving passage in which he has said to us that he had to confess that one of the needs of his nature is a certain solitude. We may well understand that a man with faculties so much greater than ours must feel lonely amongst us occasionally. This is a very distinguished assembly, but it is not an assembly composed exclusively of Einsteins. And that he should feel a certain solitude is inevitable. But I have to apologise to him, for thrusting all this noisy publicity upon his solitude. But he has come to meet you, and he has come to invite our intrusion for the sake of the poorest of the poor in this world, of whom you've heard something from previous speakers.

Well, I will ask him therefore to forgive the intrusion and to remember this: that in our humble little way, we all have our little solitudes. My friend Mr Wells has spoken to us sometimes of the secret places of the heart. There are also the lonely places of the mind. And our minds are so small that instead of, like our visitor, having a spacious solitude, in which you can seek the solutions of problems, in which you can contemplate things greater and happier and more wonderful than mankind, we are too often in our little solitudes; we are like children crying in the dark, and wanting to get out of it. Nevertheless, our little solitude gives us something of a key to his solitude. And from our little solitude to his great and august solitude, we want to send this evening our admiration, our good wishes, and our prayers.

Now, my lords and ladies and gentlemen, are you ready for the toast? I now give you: health and length of days to the greatest of our contemporaries: Einstein.

ALBERT EINSTEIN:

You, Mr. Shaw, have succeeded in gaining the love and the joyful admiration of mankind by a path which for others has led to martyrdom. You have not only preached to mankind morality but even dared to mock at what to others appeared unapproachable. What you have done can be done only by the born artist. From your box of tricks you have taken countless puppets, which, while resembling men, are not of flesh and bone but consist entirely of spirit, wit and grace. And yet, in a way even more than ourselves, they resemble men and women and make us forget almost that they are not the creations of nature but only the creations of Bernard Shaw. You make these gracious puppets dance in a little world guarded by the graces who allow no resentment to enter in.

Whoever has glanced into this little world sees the world of our reality in a new light. He sees your puppets blending into real people so that the latter suddenly look quite different from before. By thus holding the mirror before us, you have been able as no other contemporary to effect in us a liberation and to take from us something of the heaviness of life. For this we are all grateful to you and also to fate – that with all our earthly ailments has also been granted to us a physician and liberator of the soul. I personally thank you for the unforgettable words which you have addressed to my mythical namesake who has made my life so burdensome; who in spite of his awkwardness and respectable dimensions is after all a very harmless fellow.

But to you, however, I say that the being and fate of our people depend less upon external factors than that we remain true to our moral traditions which have carried us through the centuries in spite of the heavy storms which broke in upon us. In the service of life, sacrifice becomes a grace.

# THE WORK WAS ONE OF PURE SCIENCE

French Polish scientist Marie Curie broke ground on numerous occasions during a career dedicated to the research of radioactivity, most notably as the first person to be awarded the Nobel Prize twice. In May 1921, she traveled to the United States to raise money for new research, to visit President Warren Harding at the White House and to deliver a speech at Vassar College in which she described her painstaking discovery of the element radium twenty-five years earlier.

I could tell you many things about radium and radioactivity and it would take a long time. But as we cannot do that, I shall only give you a short account of my early work about radium. Radium is no more a baby, it is more than twenty years old, but the conditions of the discovery were somewhat peculiar and so it is always of interest to remember them and to explain them.

We must go back to the year 1897. Professor Curie and I worked at that time in the laboratory of the school of Physics and Chemistry where Professor Curie held his lectures. I was engaged in some work on uranium rays, which had been discovered two years before by Professor Becquerel. I shall tell you how these uranium rays may be detected. If you take a photographic plate and wrap it in black paper and then on this plate, protected from ordinary light, put some uranium salt and leave it a day, and the next day the plate is developed, you notice on the plate a black spot at the place where the uranium salt was. This spot has been made by special rays which are given out by the uranium and are able to make an impression on the plate in the same way as ordinary light. You can also test those rays in another way, by placing them on an electroscope. You know what an electroscope is.* If you charge it, you can keep it charged several hours and more, unless uranium salts are placed near to it. But if this is the case the electroscope loses its charge and the gold or aluminum leaf falls gradually in a progressive way. The speed with which the leaf moves may be used as a measure of the intensity of the rays; the greater the speed, the greater the intensity.

* A scientific instrument for detecting the presence of an electric charge or of ionizing radiation, usually consisting of a pair of thin gold leaves suspended from an electrical conductor.

I spent some time in studying the way of making good measurements of the uranium rays, and then I wanted to know if there were other elements giving out rays of the same kind. So I took up a work about all known elements and their compounds and found that uranium compounds are active, and also all thorium compounds, but other elements were not found active, nor were their compounds. As for the uranium and thorium compounds, I found that they were active in proportion to their uranium or thorium content. The more uranium or thorium, the greater the activity, the activity being an atomic property of the elements uranium and thorium.

→ Marie Curie with President Warren G. Harding on May 20, 1921, six days after she delivered her speech

Then I took up measurements of minerals and I found that several of those which contain uranium or thorium or both were active. But then the activity was not what I could expect, it was greater than for uranium or thorium compounds, like the oxides which are almost entirely composed of these elements. Then I thought that there should be in the minerals some unknown element having a much greater radioactivity than uranium or thorium. And I wanted to find and to separate that element and I settled to that work with Professor Curie. We thought it would be done in several weeks or months, but it was not so. It took many years of hard work to finish that task. There was not one new element, there were several of them. But the most important is radium, which could be separated in a pure state.

All the tests for the separation were done by the method of electrical measurements with some kind of electroscope. We just had to make chemical separations and to examine all products obtained with respect to their activity. The product which retained the radioactivity was considered as that one which had kept the new element; and, as the radioactivity was more strong in some products, we knew that we had succeeded in concentrating the new element. The radioactivity was used in the same way as a spectroscopical test.[†]

† In chemistry, spectroscopy is used to detect very small amounts of an element and depends upon the measurement of the wavelength and the intensity of electromagnetic radiation.

The difficulty was that there is not much radium in a mineral: this we did not know at the beginning. But we now know that there is not even one part of radium in a million parts of good ore. And too, to get a small quantity of pure radium salt, one is obliged to work up a huge quantity of ore. And that was very hard in a laboratory.

We had not even a good laboratory at that time. We worked in a hangar where there were no improvements, no good chemical arrangements. We had no help, no money. And because of that the work could not go on as it would have done under better conditions. I did myself the numerous crystallizations which were wanted to get the radium salt separated from the barium salt, with which it is obtained out of the ore. And in 1902 I finally succeeded in getting pure radium chloride and determining the atomic weight of the new element radium, which is 226, while that of barium is only 137.

Later I could also separate the metal radium, but that was a very difficult work, and – as it is not necessary for the use of radium to have it in this state – it is not generally prepared that way.

Now, the special interest of radium is in the intensity of its rays, which is several million times greater than the uranium rays. And the effects of the rays make the radium so important. If we take a practical point of view, then the most important property of the rays is the production of physiological effects on the cells of the human organism. These effects may be used for the cure of several diseases. Good results have been obtained in many cases. What is considered particularly important is the treatment of cancer. The medical utilization of radium makes it necessary to get that element in sufficient quantities. And so a factory of radium was started to begin with in France and later in America, where a big quantity of ore named carnotite is available. America does produce many grams of radium every year, but the price is still very high because the quantity of radium contained in the ore is so small. The radium is more than a hundred thousand times dearer than gold.

But we must not forget that when radium was discovered no one knew that it would prove useful in hospitals. The work was one of pure science. And this is a proof that scientific work must not be considered from the point of view of the direct usefulness of it. It must be done for itself, for the beauty of science, and then there is always the chance that a scientific discovery may become, like the radium, a benefit for humanity.

But science is not rich, it does not dispose of important means, it does not generally meet recognition before the material usefulness of it has been proved. The factories produce many grams of radium every year, but the laboratories have very small quantities. It is the same for my laboratory and I am very grateful to the American women who wish me to have more of radium and give me the opportunity of doing more work with it.

The scientific history of radium is beautiful. The properties of the rays have been studied very closely. We know that particles are expelled from radium with a very great velocity near to that of the light. We know that the atoms of radium are destroyed by expulsion of these particles, some of which are atoms of helium. And in that way it has been proved that the radioactive elements are constantly disintegrating and that they produce at the end ordinary elements, principally helium and lead. That is, as you see, a theory of transformation of atoms which are not stable, as was believed before, but may undergo spontaneous changes.

Radium is not alone in having these properties. Many having other radioelements‡ are known already – the polonium, the mesothorium, the radiothorium, the actinium. We know also radioactive gases, named emanations. There is a great variety of substances and effects in radioactivity. There is always a vast field left to experimentation and I hope that we may have some beautiful progress in the following years. It is my earnest desire that some of you should carry on this scientific work and keep for your ambition the determination to make a permanent contribution to science.

‡ Any element that is naturally radioactive.

# ACKNOWLEDGMENTS

I am not very good at making books and it is no exaggeration to say that you are only holding *Speeches of Note* in your hands thanks to the patience, assistance and hard work of a number of people who are not me, all of whom deserve thanks and rapturous applause. First and foremost, Karina, who against all odds has not only remained my wife during the stressful production of four "Of Note" books, but who also worked on this particular title as permissions editor, a role of unimaginable complexity and horror. I simply could not have finished this book without her, for those reasons and more.

Thanks, also, to the following lovely people: my excellent publisher at Hutchinson, Sarah Rigby, who is a saint deserving of a medal of some sort, and everyone else at Penguin Random House, including Najma Finlay, Celeste Ward-Best, Jocasta Hamilton, Phil Brown, Lauren Wakefield and Isabelle Everington; the designers and typesetters of these beautiful pages, Will Webb and Lindsay Nash; my agent, Caroline Michel, and her entire team at Peters Fraser & Dunlop; Dan Kieran, John Mitchinson and everyone else at the magnificent Unbound; Jamie Byng for his energy and support; the superhuman archivists of this world; everyone who has told me of their favourite speech during the past few years of research; and my friends and family. Special mention must go to the supremely talented Matthew Richardson, whose illustrations bring a number of these speeches to life in ways I couldn't have imagined, and to Helen Osborne at Heart Agency for her help and patience.

And last but not least, enormous thanks to all of the speechwriters featured in this book and to their estates, and to everyone who initially pledged for this book when it was first announced on Unbound.co.uk. Without you, *Speeches of Note* would simply not exist.

Shaun Usher

# INDEX

SPEECHES OF NOTE

# PERMISSION CREDITS